RIoT Control

RIoT Control
Understanding and Managing Risks and the Internet of Things

Tyson Macaulay

AMSTERDAM • BOSTON • HEIDELBERG • LONDON
NEW YORK • OXFORD • PARIS • SAN DIEGO
SAN FRANCISCO • SINGAPORE • SYDNEY • TOKYO

Morgan Kaufmann is an imprint of Elsevier

British Library Cataloguing-in-Publication Data
A catalogue record for this book is available from the British Library

Library of Congress Cataloging-in-Publication Data
A catalog record for this book is available from the Library of Congress

ISBN: 978-0-12-419971-2

For Information on all Morgan Kaufmann publications
visit our website at https://www.elsevier.com

  Working together
to grow libraries in
developing countries

www.elsevier.com • www.bookaid.org

Publisher: Todd Green
Acquisition Editor: Todd Green
Editorial Project Manager: Lindsay Lawrence
Production Project Manager: Priya Kumaraguruparan
Designer: Alan Studholme

Typeset by MPS Limited, Chennai, India

Contents

Comments From Reviewers

I owe a debt to my reviewers. Not only have they offered comments to me about drafts of this book but also provided me critical insights at different points in the research and writing.

Tyson

R. Samani
Vice President and Chief Technology Officer, EMEA, Intel Security

The world is exciting, isn't it? I mean, consider the integration of technology within every room of our homes, from traditional computers and mobile devices to connected doorbells and alarm systems. As we jump feet first into dependency with such a brave new world, a question about trust still remains unanswered. Indeed, if we check the relevant Twitter timelines to trace the vulnerabilities within these "smart" environments, news about baby monitors being hacked and disruption to electricity supplies suggests that any provision of security into this new world is sorely lacking.

I believe the term *security* is fundamentally flawed for two reasons. First, privacy is not suitably addressed. Consider the number of devices growing within every aspect of our lives, collecting information every time we go online or indeed make a slice of toast. Second, the question is not about security and privacy, but rather the broader realm of trust. Trust is critical. I mean, would you take a journey in a car knowing that vulnerabilities exist, allowing someone to take control?

It is, therefore, encouraging to see Tyson produce this book. Having worked with Tyson for a number of years, I am confident that this will be technically accurate, but perhaps more important, I am hopeful that its contents are adopted into the devices that we will all depend upon.

D. McMahon
Chief Strategist, ADGA

In the next few years, the largest mobile device that you will own will be your car. Analogously, the next-generation ships and aircraft of our nation's military will be billion-dollar mobile weaponized computing devices and data centers; assimilated into the IoT and operating in the cloud.

Cyberspace is a complex, hyperconnected, nonlinear, and nondeterministic system; the behavior of which parallels weather models, biological ecosystems, and neuroscience. In fact, the power of the Internet has exceeded the power of the human brain. Nowadays, our world is principally described by data, and subject to global influence at the speed-of-light. The IoT will expand a domain previously inhabited by humans to one that is shared with machines.

Cyberspace has undergone dramatic global disruptive changes in the past few years, particularly in highly contested areas of the network. There is a change of sea-state globally—a perfect storm—the repercussions of which have begun to undermine the legitimacy of government, the projection of military force, and viability of business in the global market. There has been a profound shift of power and control of the Internet from west to east. Similarly, global Internet demographics are migrating toward the digital natives of emerging states.

The balance between privacy of the individual and security is in fast flux. Metadata have been around since the telegraph, and some are just engaging with privacy implications today. Now, machine-to-machine (M2M) communication of the IoT is at our doorstep. Operating in a global, hypercompetitive market requires fundamentally reframing strategies that enhance one's cybersecurity posture while safeguarding privacy.

We are entering a period of instability, rapid convergence, and risk within a complex system where social media provides a frictionless state between the human terrain, the network, and the IoT, evolving to the Internet of Everything (IoE). In IoE, a thought communicated by disruptive technology has enabled the open empowerment of global commons and precipitated the collapse of nations. The Quantum Internet is next, and will provide orders of magnitude more speed and processing to the machines, and the ability to sense our world and humans at far greater degrees of fidelity and acuity.

Open media, big data, ubiquitous mobile communications, and the IoT are at the center of identity, security, defense, and privacy issues facing us today. Yet, in many countries around the world, open access to the Internet is balkanized, blocked, censored, shaped, controlled, and denied.

Traditional security, policy, standards, and doctrine are largely driven only by the threat that we perceive clearly within our field of view, and the most obvious tangible impacts felt to the business. The picture is also distorted by our own constrained competitive capabilities, organizational boundaries, sparse fiscal investments, and legal constraints onto an adversary that shares none of these restrictions.

The adversary is sophisticated, dispersed, and highly adaptive. Criminal enterprises, hacktivists, and terrorists have already demonstrated levels of sophistication equal to or greater than most nation-states, owing to commercialization of technology, superior freedom to manoeuver, and the asymmetric nature of cyberwarfare. Their victims are primitive, centralized, static, and reactive in comparison. Informationalized warfare has already seized ground in the IoT.

The next evolution of cyberspace is not without its risks, opportunities, and moral hazards.

Risk and the Internet of Things (RIoT) control is an essential text for comprehending and managing risks within the IoT. Tyson Macaulay masterfully describes the IoT ecosystem at extraordinary depth and sophistication. The anatomy and operating environment of the IoT is contextualized and brought into sharp focus for stakeholders. The book exposes bona fide threats and contagion to our privacy, health, safety, and security. It represents a strategic understanding of the IoT and offers a new integrated risk management framework for the future.

S. Hunt
Chief Technology Officer, Home Gateway Security, Intel Corporation

I recently made a presentation on the cybercrime potential of home IoT at an entrepreneur conference, accompanied by a smart soft toy bear who, to the surprise of the audience, surreptitiously video-recorded the entire proceedings. Later, speaking to the product team of a global white goods manufacturer on the potential exploitation of in-home smart appliances, the comment "It's only a fridge—who wants to hack it?" was made.

The IoT is penetrating our lives at a rate that we could never have predicted. From critical infrastructure, to manufacturing, to the toys our children play with, this market demand and revenue opportunity are being met by new players with little experience of cybersecurity. Particularly worrying is that many of the exploits are the result of common mistakes and oversights that the cyberprotection industry has been aware of for decades.

Tyson's book reminds us of the mature thought processes that go into protecting compute, but applies them to the emerging IoT—topics that have been studied and refined since the beginning of compute, but somehow don't seem to be obviously related to smart toys and factory machinery.

Innovation is to be encouraged, but unless we include the concepts of risk assessment, secure design, and privacy considerations in the rapid development and adoption of IoT, we risk exposing ourselves, our families, and our companies to cybercriminals, and of course, limiting the adoption and success of this empowering trend.

I believe that IoT is going to make our lives smarter and more connected, and I hope through the efforts of thought leaders like Tyson, they will be no less secure.

F. Khan
Chief Security Analyst, TwelveDot
Canadian Chair to ISO/JTC1 SC27 (IT Security Techniques)

Businesses and consumers alike assume that security and privacy have been accounted for in IoT solutions. However, that is not always the case and in some sectors, the shift to use Internet Protocol (IP) and the Internet to backhaul data has significantly altered the threat vectors of these solutions.

With risk and the Internet of Things (RIoT) as the baseline IoT solution, companies have no excuse for not designing and implementing sound security practices into their solution. And no, security does not have to interfere with a positive user experience. When considered at the design and concept stages, security features become embedded into good design, resulting in a solution with better availability and reliability while maintaining user privacy and security.

This book is a must-read for any risk manager who is responsible for IoT. You could consider it a "trusted companion," detailing security requirements that should be considered when performing TRAs) and design assessments against IoT solutions.

As an organization that specializes in evaluating IoT solutions and solution providers, we expend much time and effort attempting to educate both executives and solution architects on how to best approach security and privacy in the context of IoT. Creating risk management practices for IoT is no trivial matter. But in RIoT, Tyson provides a single resource for all the concepts and considerations for implementing secure IoT solutions.

Let's face it—first-generation IoT will inherently be riddled with insecurities. Let's learn from that and begin working on the second generation, to ensure that security and privacy are considered in both business and consumer solutions, regardless of sector. So no more excuses—Tyson's book will help build a safer IoT landscape for generations to come.

M. Burgess
Chief Information Security Officer, Telstra

There is no doubt that connectivity and technology provide great benefit to our society and the economy today. Indeed, the full potential of technology and connectivity to touch and benefit us all has yet to be fully realized. These benefits are accelerated and realized by the IoT trend.

But with these benefits come some risks, and as more of the world embraces technology and connectivity, this risk increases.

There is no doubt that individuals, businesses, and governments already confront and deal with many complex issues and risks; however, understanding the risk of IoT and what this trend actually means can be a challenge.

Most people will understand the need for security at an airport—we can see the scanners, and we understand why we all need to comply with security requirements. But in the intangible world of cyberspace, where the assets we value are not visible and the threats are invisible, it can be a struggle to grapple with what this actually means and how we go about minimizing the risks.

Today, we read or hear plenty about cybercrime, cyberespionage, and hacktivism, and in this regard, it is important to note that in the end, cybercrime is just crime, cyberespionage is just espionage, and hacktivism is just protest. There is nothing new in crime, espionage, or protest, except the increase in connectivity and rapid uptake in technology means that crime, espionage, protest, and even mistakes can happen at a pace, scale, and reach that is unprecedented.

That makes cybersecurity a significant issue—one of global importance that no organization can handle alone.

The IoT trend is leading to an increase in volumes of data being generated, collected, accessed, and stored, and all of that potentially valuable data need to be protected.

This also potentially means that billions of untrusted or unsecure devices on the Internet will intensify the significant challenges that we already face today unless the cybersecurity and risk aspects of the IoT trend are not addressed.

This book makes a timely and much-needed contribution to our collective understanding of this challenge and how we best go about reducing this risk.

J. Nguyen-Duy
Former Chief Technology Officer, Verizon Enterprise Solutions

We first began the security journey by building keeps and walls in a vain attempt to keep the bad guys out and our data safely protected within. We soon discovered that attackers could easily scale, jump over, or tunnel under those walls and moved on to deploy host- and network-based intrusion detection sensors. When that failed, we moved on to dynamic malware inspection and sandboxing, and so forth. Ultimately, we watched over our networks and sensors with security information and event management (SIEM) and log management tools with an eye toward compliance, only to be confronted by a horrific combination of unaware users, vulnerable systems, and highly efficient attackers working in a dark web marketplace that marries tactics, techniques, and procedures to the highest bidder. Accordingly, we no longer think of security in terms of a hermetically sealed environment in which only legitimate traffic can traverse or the passing of compliance audits. Our notions of security now fall within the multidimensional domain of cyber, and the object of the exercise is risk management—which risks should be absorbed, deflected, or transferred.

Today, practically every aspect of the human experience is connected by machines—from consumer to corporate; our lives are increasingly enriched and enabled by billions of inter-connected devices operating quietly throughout our infrastructure and just slightly beyond our consciousness. Indeed, the research firm Gartner predicts that over 6 billion things will be in use by the end of 2016—a 30% annual increase—and will grow to over 20 billion devices by 2020. This Internet of Things (IoT) represents a massive expansion of our ecosystem and challenges already overwhelmed security teams to identify anomalous behavior and understand context across a vast array of users and systems—and to do so at machine speed. And yet in this new dynamic, the familiar themes of threat, vulnerability, and risk management still resonate.

It is easy to be overwhelmed by the sheer scale of the challenge facing us, and readers are well served by my friend Tyson Macaulay's practical approach to framing IoT risk management. A significant portion of Tyson's career has been devoted to IoT security issues, including solutions to protect carriers, users, and infrastructure from emerging vulnerabilities unique to these environments. This broad and deep insight into the strategic operational issues, as well as day-to-day risk management, delivers a refreshing, practical framework for builders and operators of the IoT world.

Preface

This book that has been almost 4 years in the making, longer than I expected. It started as a hypothesis in 2012: will the Internet of Things (IoT) need security and risk management that is different from contemporary and conventional information technology (IT) security and risk management? At that time there was precious little written on the IoT generally, and almost nothing about IoT security. Most of what existed was in the form of industrial control systems and security, which was an excellent starting point but only part of the IoT story. There were also a few stunt-hacks of "things" like video DVRs and some high profile examples of control system hacking, but mostly the IoT and its security requirements, vulnerabilities, threats, and risks was an enigma. Largely, it still is an enigma. This book is a lantern in a very large, dark space.

From 2012 to 2015, I was working at Intel, as the CTO for Telecommunications Security. This provided an amazing opportunity to learn about IoT from a firm driven by its ambitions to develop computing chips to underpin the (bright) future of the IoT. Similarly, my time at Fortinet in 2015 and 2016 provided an platform to continue this work. The efforts of Intel particularly to understand the IoT presented a huge intellectual opportunity to zero-in on IoT security and risk management, and go deep. But that was easier said than done.

Going deep on IoT security was a bit like a game of hide and seek or cat and mouse. What information and research existed in 2012 was tentative and scattered. To go deep meant having to go to people and places—not just surfing through the Internet with clever Boolean searches. The information I was looking for was mostly contained in labs and people's minds, or was simply not available and had to be discovered through conversation or inference based on related work and experiences.

Going deep on IoT security meant taking every opportunity to ask "who is interested in IoT security" whenever I met a large company, especially telecommunications firms (products vendors and carriers). Usually I would get a reference to a person or a group that was starting to ask their own questions about IoT security, so I would seek them out in the hope we could share knowledge and notes. Often this would occur through meetings facilitated by translation: Spanish to English, Japanese to English, Chinese to English, Swedish to English, Australian to English. (Just kidding. Swedes speak amazing English). More than once I used an on-line translation tool to get the gist of some internal planning presentation which was shared with me about IoT service designs, in another language.

The development of international standards (ISO/IEC, ITU-T) around IoT began as I started work on this book. As an active member and contributor to standards organizations, I was privileged and fortunate to get exposed to the thinking and ideas from many different experts and national bodies; conveniently also translated into English! During 2014 to 2016, I convened an international study group on IoT security, which meant long trips to remote places like Borneo, Malaysia, Jaipur, India, London, UK, and even Ottawa, Canada (in summer). Going to such places meant that local IoT professionals who might not have the time or resources to leave the region would attend the local meetings. Invariably, they brought rich insights and unique experiences to the discussion of IoT security, to the benefit of this work of course the standards efforts themselves.

If some parts of this book seem to shift abruptly, this is the result of trying to paint a picture of a galloping horse (the IoT), from its back! The hope is that you see this for what it is: the beginning of the beginning in a new and important field of security and risk management. Optimistically, this is an anthology of a new domain, that will likely split into numerous specializations, in the years to come. In some cases the techniques discussed will rely on technologies that, like the IoT, are merely in their infancy. Some of these technologies and hence the RIoT Control technique may not achieve their early promise, while other may exceed expectations. The bottom line is that this book is a point in time assessment of how to control and manage Risk and the Internet of Things (RIoT Control).

T. Macaulay
CISSP, CISA, Aug 2016

INTRODUCTION—THE INTERNET OF THINGS

The Hitchhiker's Guide to the Galaxy, a space comedy radio series created by Douglas Adams for the BBC, contains the admonition: "Don't Panic."

Good advice when it comes to the Internet of Things (IoT) and its risks, because the state of security and privacy in the IoT in 2016, is frankly not good and getting worse. And it needs to be much better. This is the core reason behind this book.

How bad is it? Here are five samples indicative of IoT security situations chosen from a wide and growing selection of ignominious examples:

Nuclear facilities and power grids. The US National Nuclear Security Administration, which is responsible for managing and securing its nation's nuclear weapons stockpile, experienced 19 successful cyberattacks during the four-year period of 2010−14.[1] Also, as many of you are aware, in June 2010, Stuxnet, a nasty computer worm designed to attack industrial programmable logic controllers (PLCs), was discovered. PLCs allow the automation of electromechanical processes like centrifuges (which are used in separating nuclear material). Meanwhile, in 2015 and 2016, the Ukrainian power grid has been under siege and has become unreliable as presumed Russian attackers continue to pound on it.[2]

Health and hospitals. In an unprecedented move, in 2015, the US Food and Drug Administration (FDA) directed hospitals to stop using Hospira's Symbiq Infusion System because it can be remotely accessed by hackers, allowing the unauthorized user "to control the device and change the dosage the pump delivers, which could lead to over- or under-infusion of critical patient therapies."[3] The FDA—a non-IT organization—is now drafting across-the-board what it calls "postmarket" guidance for IoT medical devices, assuming they are horribly insecure.[4]

Infrastructure. The Department of Homeland Security recently disclosed a 2012 breach in which cybercriminals managed to penetrate the thermostats of a state government facility and a manufacturing plant in New Jersey. The hackers exploited vulnerabilities in industrial heating systems, which were connected to the Internet, and then changed the temperature inside the buildings.

Steel mills. Germany's Federal Office for Information Security (BSI) recently issued a report that confirmed that hackers had breached a steel plant in its country and compromised numerous systems, including components on the production network. As a result, mill personnel were unable to shut down a blast furnace when required, resulting in "massive damage to the system." The BSI report stated, "The know-how of the attacker was very pronounced not only in conventional IT

---

[1]http://www.usatoday.com/story/news/2015/09/09/cyber-attacks-doe-energy/71929786/.
[2]Hackers cause power failure in western Ukraine—http://www.bbc.com/news/technology-35297464.
[3]http://www.securityweek.com/fda-issues-alert-over-vulnerable-hospira-drug-pumps.
[4]Postmarket Management of Cyber Security in Medical Devices, www.fda.gov.

RIoT Control. DOI: http://dx.doi.org/10.1016/B978-0-12-419971-2.00001-7

security but extended to detailed knowledge of applied industrial controls and production processes." (*Makes one wonder if this breach was perpetrated by a former, disgruntled employee. That would bring a whole new (chilling) meaning to the term "going postal.").*

The kitchen. Not normally the place to be associated with lethal cyber-threats, the kitchen is proving to be a very weak link in the IoT security chain indeed! "Smart appliances" are entering the kitchen in the name of both convenience and healthy (or healthier) living, and basically compromising the entire home or office network. Smart refrigerators prove entirely vulnerable to malware, and smart kettles spit back Wi-Fi passwords to anyone who cares to ask. Beyond being incredibly vulnerable to attacks that make them launching pads for attacks on everything else within range, they also malfunction and damage food, actually creating safety issues for users!

Many people recognize the need for this book and supported its development, but many eminent people in the area of security told me that it was a waste of time.

> The IoT is too new! It is developing too quickly to try and systematically secure.
> We don't understand the IoT well enough to discuss security and risk management meaningfully.
> No one agrees on what the IoT is, so you are wasting your time, Tyson.

To those people I must respectfully disagree. The IoT is well underway and we must start making serious efforts systematically to secure it. This book is merely a small contribution to the early process of trying to secure the IoT. It is the beginning of the beginning.

YOU ARE NEVER TOO YOUNG TO START GOOD HABITS

The first mass-produced car, the Model T Ford, had no wheel brakes like all modern cars. The Model T used a highly unreliable form of friction bands made of leather connected to the transmission to stop![5] But at least it had a brake.

Some people argue that the IoT is "too new" or "developing too fast" to have serious discussions about security. This is like telling early automotive engineers working on the Model T and its successors (like the Audi RS7) not to waste time on brakes, because the hydrogen fuel-cell flying car is not ready, so brakes are a wasted effort.

Early attempts at IoT risk management, security methodologies, and standards will absolutely be superseded by better things to come. Eventually, we will have the equivalent of ceramic disc brakes that recover kinetic energy during braking, to charge batteries, and smart driverless cars that automatically avoid collisions to the point that they become flukes rather than "normal accidents." But we have to start somewhere.

WHAT IS THE IoT?

Risk and the Internet of Things (RIoT) is something to manage and control (RIoT control).

The requirements, threats, vulnerabilities, and risks presented in this book represent a superset applicable to the IoT. All requirements, threats, vulnerabilities, and risks apply to all IoT systems and services.

---

[5]https://en.wikipedia.org/wiki/Ford_Model_T.

The point of compiling this superset of security and risk management information for the IoT is to allow system owners, designers, and risk managers to have a comprehensive view of what might be applicable. From that point, they will be in a more informed position to understand how the unique needs and functions of a given IoT service might drive risks that in turn must be managed.

AUDIENCE

This book has been developed for a wide range of readers.

For executives (Chief Information Officer (CIO), Chief Information Security Officer (CISO), Vice President (VP) Risk Management, Regulatory, and Compliance folks), business line managers and/or people not specifically interested in the operational details of IoT security, but want to understand the problem, we recommend in this chapter and in Chapter 2, The Anatomy of the Internet of Things, Chapter 3, Requirements and Risk Management, Chapter 4, Business and Organizational Requirements, and Chapter 12, Threats and Impacts to the IoT. This will provide a basis in the business-level issues, opportunities and threats that must be managed related to goods, services, and systems.

For people such as architects, engineers, security practitioners, and risk managers concerned with the secure development or operations of IoT goods, services, or systems, Chapter 5, Operational and Process Requirements, Chapter 6, Safety Requirements in the Internet of Things, Chapter 7, Confidentiality and Integrity and Privacy Requirements in the IoT, Chapter 8, Availability and Reliability Requirements in the IoT, Chapter 9, Identity and Access Control Requirements in the IoT, Chapter 10, Usage Context and Environmental Requirements in the IoT, Chapter 11, Interoperability, Flexibility, and Industrial Design Requirements in the IoT, and Chapter 13, RIoT Control, are recommended. These chapters will provide insight into specific operational requirements for security and risk management in the IoT, as well as possible risk treatments. (This book discusses the concepts of risk transference and acceptance—but is necessarily focused on what you can do, if you choose to do something inhouse!)

For those people such as researchers, academics and students, journalists, and other security professionals who just need to know more, we hope this entire book is meaningful and accessible to you.

Welcome all!

HOW THIS BOOK FLOWS

The intent of this book to convey as much useful information about security requirements, threats, vulnerabilities, and risks in the IoT as possible, in a context familiar to those who must manage risk. It will therefore follow a format that will be immediately familiar to those who have conducted risk analyses, read threat-risk assessments, conducted them, or even have a broad-based security background that has introduced them to formal risk management.

So how does a risk assessment typically flow? Thusly:

- Asset inventory: What are you assessing or protecting?
- Requirements and sensitivity analysis: To how much damage are the assets susceptible, from the perspective of confidentiality, integrity, and availability? (In other words, unauthorized disclosure, change, deletion, or delay.)

- Threat analysis: Who or what might want to impact sensitivity?
- Vulnerability analysis: Where are the weaknesses that a threat agent might exploit?
- Risk and mitigation: Taking into account the frequency or likelihood that a threat agent will try and exploit a vulnerability, what is the risk? Risk is almost always expressed in a qualitative manner (high/medium/low, for example), and we will not attempt to go beyond this convention. And finally, what can you do about the risk?

In the course of this book, we will hit all these high points and have developed chapters to fit this approach.

This chapter is an introduction to the concept of the IoT, what it might be, and what it probably is not. "Might" because this is a new area, and definitions are not hardened or complete.

Chapter 2, The Anatomy of the Internet of Things, is about the parts of the anatomy of the IoT: component parts and the different stakeholders. This is intended to identify what is in scope when discussing risk and the IoT. This is the first exercise of sensitivity analysis, as described previously.

Chapter 3, Requirements and Risk Management, is the second part of a sensitivity analysis—what are requirements for confidentiality, availability, and integrity from the perspective of business and operations?

Chapter 4, Business and Organizational Requirements, is about threats to the IoT: the "who" and "why" associated with the risks as we understand them now. In Chapter 4, Business and Organizational Requirements, as in Chapter 3, Requirements and Risk Management, we will try and remain at the business and operational level for discussion.

Chapter 5, Operational and Process Requirements, is about vulnerabilities in the IoT at the business and operational process levels, sometimes touching on technical issues. Vulnerabilities, in contrast to threats, are about the "how" of risk. How will a threat agent or entities inflict damage?

Chapter 6, Safety Requirements in the Internet of Things, is about safety risk requirements in the IoT and how they are related to security requirements.

Chapter 7, Confidentiality and Integrity and Privacy Requirements in the IoT, is about privacy, confidentiality, and integrity requirements in the IoT.

Chapter 8, Availability and Reliability Requirements in the IoT, is about availability and reliability requirements in the IoT and the associated risks and vulnerabilities.

Chapter 9, Identity and Access Control Requirements in the IoT, concerns identity and access control risks and vulnerabilities in the IoT.

Chapter 10, Usage Context and Environmental Requirements in the IoT, is about usage context and operating environment requirements in the IoT.

Chapter 11, Interoperability, Flexibility, and Industrial Design Requirements in the IoT, is about flexibility and interoperability requirements in the IoT.

Chapter 12, Threats and Impacts to the IoT, is a broad discussion of threats in the IoT, including a strategy for threat assessment and ranking.

Finally, Chapter 13, RIoT Control, is about treating the new risks in the IoT. It describes some of the potential new management techniques and operational controls and safeguards that might evolve in the coming years.

We have tried to make this book approachable for a variety of readers, not merely risk management and security nerds, so expect to see chapters that might drift into discussions tangential to pure risk management, but helpful to provide context. The IoT is a rapidly developing domain and any aids to memory or comprehension are generally helpful.

WHAT IS THE IoT?

The IoT is about devices at the edge of the Internet communicating to big centralized machines, often making decisions and taking action without people in the loop. It represents billions of devices speaking to each other, often managing outcomes in the physical environment. They do this because it represents an improvement in some sort of outcome of service—presenting either greater efficiencies or a value-added outcome or service.

The IoT presents business opportunities in virtually all industrial sectors. The IoT is integral to the future of goods and services.

But first, let's talk about what the IoT is not.

NOT ABOUT INFORMATION DISSEMINATION PARADIGMS

The IoT is not just a new type of World Wide Web server, with fancier pages and more clever ways of mashing up data so we can consume it. It is not about newsfeeds or emails or any other types of data created by people, for people. It is about data created by machines, mixing and mingling with the data from people. It is about the emerging machine-made information dataset existing alongside the current, human-made information dataset.

NOT ABOUT INFORMATION SHARING

The IoT has little to do with some highly visible trends like social networking. It is not a new way to share information among people. It is, however, a new way to collect and gather information from the world at large, especially the physical world. No doubt it will come to pass that social networking will take advantage of the services delivered by the IoT. For instance, Foursquare is a social networking service that has repurposed geolocation capabilities in smartphones.

NOT ABOUT WIRELESS NETWORKING

The IoT is not just about wireless systems. Wireless networking will play a large part in the IoT and has been the catalyst for the first generation of "things" on the Internet—but that is the beginning and not the end of the story, especially given broadband wireless technologies known as 4G and soon 5G, which bring high-speed data connections capable of supporting everything up to and including high definition video functions requiring gigabits of capacity, or remote manipulation technologies that tolerate only tiny latencies in the milliseconds.

The IoT will be about many types of networks running orthogonally (side by side without touching) and acting as redundant systems for one another: fiber-based systems, copper, even laser-based networking links. The IoT will require many networks—but all speaking the same language of the Internet—*Internet Protocol* (*IP*), or at the very least have access to a gateway that allows traffic to come and go from IP-based networks that will bind the endpoints to the analytics and applications in the data centers.

This point about IoT going beyond wireless is an important concept to bear in mind because at the time of the writing of this book, most of the early precedents of machine-to-machine (M2M) systems are based on cellular wireless. Typically, the cellular data network infrastructure, which supports the ever-growing array of smartphones and tablet computers, also supports connectivity with machines. Wireless has been a huge boon for the M2M industry, because the earliest version of M2M (named industrial control systems—more on this soon) depended on physical, copper phone lines. These lines were very expensive to install, especially in remote locations, and equally as expensive to maintain. Cables and poles in remote locations tend to break and corrode and need regular replacing. And unlike copper phone cables and poles in urban areas, the entire cost of the line had to be supported by the M2M system in question. Costs cannot be spread over a large subscriber base.

Cellular wireless fixed that problem at a single stroke; however, we must not assume that hardline connections for the M2M systems are obsolete. Neither should anyone assume that "wireless" means "cellular" wireless. There are many forms of wireless network available at costs equal to and even lower than cellular wireless, especially for short range (less than 1 km) communications.

THE IoT IS (MOSTLY) NOT ABOUT PRIVACY

Privacy laws around the world have teeth, for good reasons. Without privacy laws, the opportunity for abuse of personal information is virtually unlimited. Lives can be ruined and businesses wrecked because of bad management of personal information. Increasingly privacy and personal information is a target, sometimes for reasons unknown:

- The Ashley Madison attacks in 2015 exposed millions of "cheaters"—those nominally enrolled in a dating service for married people.
- No reason was ever given for this breach other than a suggested moral disapproval.
- Ashley Madison was not about the IoT, but the IoT will afford ever-greater opportunities to expose personal information.

There is much liability associated with poor handling of personal information, with varying degrees of fines, sanctions, and jail time potentially associated with these practices. Prohibitions, fines, and sanctions vary depending on where you are and often the industry in question.

There is a need for careful balance when it comes to defining what is personal and private, versus what might be merely unstructured data with the potential to be personally identifiable under certain conditions. Privacy concerns have been known to slow or stop IoT development, and thereby the IoT itself.[6]

The foundation of this problem lies in the fact that some of the most ferocious privacy advocates are nontechnical, or even luddites; skilled political or legal operators, they know how to slow or stop projects until their demands are met. Unfortunately, imposing uninformed technical or operational requirements can impose costs and complexity that reduce the potential of projects. In some cases, projects become over-budget white elephants.

In the IoT, this risk of privacy-related requirements-creep also represents a danger associated with complexity. As we will discuss shortly, complexity increases risks: operational risks associated with people and processes, technology risks associated with hardware or software glitches and failures, and business risks associated with outcomes and design objectives. The IoT is already shaping

---

[6]https://www.eff.org/deeplinks/2011/05/california-proposes-strong-privacy-protections.

up to be the most complex artifact ever created by man. The necessity to add further complexity must be carefully weighted and balanced.

Personal information is just that—it's about you, or someone else. Personal information must also be identifiably about you or someone else. A piece of data about your shoe purchase that is aggregated with millions of other purchases is not personal information unless your identity is linked back to the purchase and the information is stored and managed together. This is a broad definition and there is much quibbling associated with what "identifiable" means, and unreasonable positions have been taken on both sides of this argument. There will probably never by a uniform definition or protocol. There are guidelines from august organizations like the Organisation for Economic Cooperation and Development (OECD), but they tend to be a starting point for national laws, which then diverge widely.

Most of the data in a given business is not personal. For organizations that try to estimate how much of the data they manage is personal in nature—it would probably come out to less than 5%, even for businesses dealing in retail services where collecting and managing customer data is a core capability. For industries like manufacturing, the proportion of personal data would be even smaller.

Most data in a business is proprietary, internal information about production, coordination, finances, marketing and sales, research, and general administration. Much of this data, again, is unstructured—emails, loose files on servers. The issue is that personally identifiable data will frequently be scattered throughout this unstructured and structured (databases, directories) mass of information. This is where problems with privacy emerge most quickly from a security and control perspective.

Similarly, most data in the IoT will not be personal information, or will not be personally identifiable information. It will be logistics and control data from devices, identified by IP addresses. The linkage between these network addresses and actual human users, if there are any, are typically stored and managed in a completely separate manner. With most Internet services providers (ISP), the IP address management systems are linked to a subscriber ID system indicating level of access only. The subscriber ID system might then link to a billing system indicating the account status, which might link to a different system managing subscriber identities. There are many degrees of separation between what is technically personal information and personally identifiable information.

True, *if* you could capture the data flows from a given device (say a power meter), and *if* you could get the mapping of the device name to a subscriber ID, and *if* you could map the ID to a subscriber's real name, and *if* you could sift out the extraneous signaling and network handshakes from the system payloads, *then* maybe you might have personal information and may have broken a law. Maybe.

Privacy is an important consideration in the IoT, but you must be knowledgeable and keep it in perspective; otherwise, the risk of a white elephant will loom large. This theme will surface several times through this book.

THE "OLD" INTERNET OF DATA, VOICE, AND VIDEO

The current generation of the Internet consists of people-operated devices consuming webs, emails, making phone calls, viewing videos, and publishing the minute-by-minute accounts of the mendicant's mornings. This Internet is composed of servers in the data center storing and managing vast amounts of information, which the devices at the periphery request. The requests are made by people, who operate the devices rather than devices making the requests in any automated manner.

Alternatively, the servers in the middle act as repositories or aggregation points for content developed by users in the periphery, who publish to the data center so that other users can consume. Much of this content possesses questionable value or indiscernible purpose.

This version of the Internet has brought profound changes to the world, created much new wealth, and bettered the lives of millions, if not arguably billions of people in the matter of a few decades.

The IoT includes the old Internet, but is substantially different from the old Internet for at least one very simple reason: the devices at the periphery of the network are not operated by people. These devices may be semi- or fully automated. And they will vastly outnumber the human-operated devices in a short period of time.

The IoT will include the "triple play" of data (Internet), voice, and video, for no other reason than the fact that all the "assets" we will discuss shortly, which are different from the old Internet, will be using the same underlying networking technology. These new assets and the old assets of data, voice, and video are speaking the same language. This does not mean that they will be constantly and unavoidably sharing networks; however, much sharing of networks is inevitable because of the economic efficiency of using technology and infrastructure for multiple purposes.

This book will discuss some of the potential techniques available for managing the IoT for maximum efficiency and security combined.

The IoT promises a great future, but not without risks that must be managed.

THE INTERNET ++

If the IoT includes the old Internet of data, voice, and video; it also contains new assets that take the Internet from being a network of human-operated devices to a network containing many nonhuman-operated devices—the "things." These things go by a variety of different names and have been described in many ways, which often reflected the particular use case or constituency doing the describing. For instance, energy people with practical, near-term, and real-world use cases may speak about the "things" as smart meters in homes. People in manufacturing may consider "things" to be industrial control systems managing production processes. The health industry may consider things to be monitoring equipment for hospital patients or outpatients.

Several different descriptive tools for comprehending the "things" in the IoT have been developed by leading entities, such as vendors and standards bodies. It is helpful to review them to understand the relationship between these tools and the IoT. Are we speaking about the same things?

M2M COMMUNICATION

M2M systems are part of the IoT, and M2M, like many of the terms to follow, can be seen as a catchall term. M2M is not limited as a concept to any specific industry because it encompasses the range of assets outside the old Internet of data, voice, and video. The current generation of M2M applications includes both fully automated and semiautomated systems. For example, today some of the most commonly labeled M2M systems include point-of-sale (POS) and automated vehicle location (AVL) services. The POS devices are semiautomated, in that people must initiate and authorize the transactions (ideally), while AVL is an automated system for reporting the geospatial coordinates of assets like trucks and other delivery vehicles.

One notable characteristic of current M2M systems is that they are largely unidirectional in data flow or service requests. The POS devices start the transaction with central transaction processing systems, and are usually not equipped or intended to support incoming commands. AVL systems push data almost exclusively to central servers, which then display and report to the asset owners. AVL systems are generally not meant to receive over-the-air comments. The advantage of the unidirectional nature of these early M2M systems is that exploitation opportunities are more limited: physical access to the remote endpoints is required, while network-based attacks are lower in probability.

CONNECTED DEVICES

Connected devices is also a catchall term for things other than servers and PCs that are entering the network. Like M2M, there is no hard or fast rule as to whether connected devices are automated or semiautomated, requiring human inputs to complete commands.

If there is any distinction between M2M and connected devices, it might be that bidirectional communication appears to be more frequently present in the cited examples and reference designs. Connected devices may be more likely to communicate with each other, rather than transmit but not receive.

Connected devices as a definition also tend to envision both a centralized management infrastructure and/or a situation where devices communicate on a peer-to-peer basis. For instance, a pair of transportation sensors connect to each other to share data about speed and heading and negotiate right-of-way based on a predefined and agreed algorithm, without referencing back to any centralized system or server. This type of peer-to-peer decision making offers some very large advantages in terms of speed of decision making and reduced loads on networks. Conversely, the potential for oversight and safety controls may be truncated without near flawless design in such autonomous peer-to-peer systems.

SMART-EVERYTHING

There is a lot of "smart stuff" on the market right now—pretty much something for every room in the house and every industrial application. There are smart cities and homes and offices, smart health and transportation and energy, and on and on. This concept, like M2M and connected devices, is contained within the IoT.

For instance, smart cities will have highly coordinated infrastructures, made possible by the IoT. Transport flows because smart cars speak to smart traffic controls about destinations, route optimizations, speed, heading, and so on. Smart roads indicate when they need repair to maintenance scheduling systems. These systems will use unimagined combinations of peer-to-peer and client-server based decision making, ubiquitous networking, and massive amounts of high-assurance bandwidth to move all this data back and forth and archive data, which might later be needed for purposes such as usage billing, urban planning, or forensic accident investigation.

Perhaps the distinguishing feature of the "smart" discussion versus M2M and connected devices is that it tends to be more conceptual and less technical in nature. As a result, many of the discussions around smart things simply assume a network and do not quibble about the nature of the network: is it shared? Is it built on standard technologies and protocols (like IP) or is it a dedicated, proprietary system? Such discussions are frequently out of scope of the smart discussion, if for no other reason than "smart" is a vision more than a solution. Not to say that "smart" is impractical of a distant future, not at all.

"Smart" is part of the IoT and will evolve as a notion, probably in a fractal-like fashion. Small smart systems will join other small smart systems to create larger smart systems. For instance, the smart home is composed of smart appliances, smart safety systems (smoke detectors, carbon dioxide detectors, motion detectors), smart health monitoring for grandma, and the desktop and mobile computing devices of the family. This smart house combines with the smart car in the garage to create a smart domestic power storage system, which becomes a citywide power-storage system, which becomes a national storage system. In this way, a smart city or country will actually be composed of thousands or millions or billions of smaller smart systems.

UBIQUITOUS COMPUTING

More so than any of the other terms synonymous with the IoT, Ubiquitous Computing (UC) is the least concrete and the most abstract and conceptual term. The scope of UC is wide, spread over all areas of computer science, including hardware components (like chips), network protocols, interfaces (such as human or machine), applications, information assets and types (that is, business versus personal information), and computational methods.

In order to realize UC, a wide range of technologies must be combined, such as industrial sensor networks, multi-medium (copper, fiber, electromagnetic [radio], infrared, and so on) networking, radio frequency identification (RFID), M2M, mobile computing, human-computer interaction, and wearable computers.

Though the UC concept involves various technologies, the essence of UC is the intelligence about, and knowledge of, our surroundings (also referred to as *context awareness*). By knowing the surroundings, including the dynamic geospatial relationships involving human users and their tools (cars, elevators, medical devices, and even each other), UC systems can offer useful customized services that drive increased personal and business efficiency.

WHO ARE THE MAJOR PLAYERS IN THE IoT?

Complex IT projects are often accompanied by complex interdependencies among the project stakeholders. And in the IoT, there are often more stakeholders in a given system or service than might be intuitively obvious.

STAKEHOLDERS

Every system has a variety of stakeholders: people or entities that have an interest in the way in which the system itself is operated. Naturally, part of that concern will extend to the security of the system, in relation to the function of the system.

The IoT is a technology system involving endpoints, networks, and in many cases coordinating centralized servers, databases, and data storage systems. The stakeholders in the IoT that will need to be considered from a security and risk management perspective are varied. Not all stakeholders will necessarily be involved in all IoT systems.

Generally, look for the following stakeholders, and their requirements, during all stages of IoT risk management: requirements definition, design, build, operate, and audit.

Many a fine career has foundered on the rocks of unconsidered or unconsulted stakeholders, who come to the table after development is well underway or complete. Some of these stakeholders will bring new requirements, which can generate massive cost overruns or outright cripple projects. In Chapter 3, Requirements and Risk Management, we consider what some of these requirements may be for the emerging IoT. But who are the likely stakeholders?

A SIMPLIFIED VIEW OF THE IoT STAKEHOLDERS: GROUPING BY ASSET CLASS

There are a total of seven stakeholders outlined in Table 1.1; too many for easy remembering and management-level discussions. So let's consider a much simpler formula where we group these

Table 1.1 IoT Stakeholders	
Users	Who is either operating the device in the IoT or depending on the operational assurance of the device?
Application service providers	Who is responsible for the integration of the solution? Many IoT systems will be built from component elements, not a single, monolithic design. Requirements established for the system should be viable in the context of the different vendors' solutions that must be integrated
Manufacturers	Who is building the physical devices that compose the solution? Typically, they will be building for many thousands if not millions of different clients. They are seeking to maximize utility of features and functions and (probably) minimize costs.
Network operators	Who is running the myriad of available networks that may be part of the IoT? Telecommunications carriers will frequently be part of this mix, but so, too, may be entirely private or dedicated networks. The interface points between such networks bears special attention.
Data center operators	Who is operating the physical platforms hosting any centralized servers or storage associated with the IoT system? There are many precedents for who runs the data center, and they can be entirely independent from the other stakeholder with unique requirements.
Regulators	From locale to locale, regulation may differ. In some locales the particular application or system within the IoT may be regulated, and in others laissez-faire. What level of government has oversight? What sanctions can they exercise for regulatory breech? What are the conditions of licensure? Regulators may also be certification and accreditation bodies in a given country, whose role is to test for conformance to national standards related to quality, security and safety.
Interdependent third parties	Who is depending on the users and their ability within the IoT and the given IoT system under assessment? Who are the users depending on to provide necessary goods or services (information) required for the operation of the IoT system under consideration? The interdependencies are ignored at the peril of the project owners.

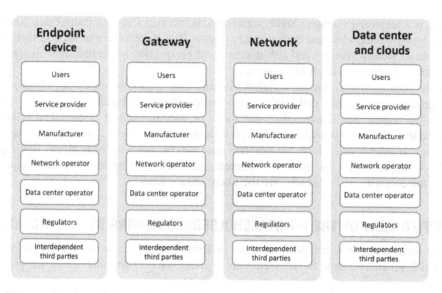

FIGURE 1.1

IoT asset classes.

stakeholders very broadly into four asset classes as per Fig. 1.1: the endpoints, gateways, the network, and the data center. Each of the stakeholders will exist within each asset class, but for the purposes of high-level discussions it is potentially easier to aggregate stakeholder requirements according to asset class—as long as the parties in the discussion understand this is what is happening!

ENDPOINT DEVICE AS AN ASSET CLASS

The endpoint device is the most remote element in the IoT, at the end of the network. These are the computers or simple input devices operated by humans, remotely managed or fully automated devices collecting information or responding to commands issues from centralized control points.

- *Users* in the context of the endpoint may be anonymous individuals (at a point of sales terminal, for example) or may be industrial owners of sensors or meters or control systems, which are dedicated to their purposes. Users will continue to be who we currently understand them as too: people using tools like web browsers on desktops, laptops, and an ever-growing range of mobile devices.
- The *service provider* for the endpoint may be the same as the user in the event that the device is dedicated and managed by the owner. But the service provider may also be a third-party outsourcer, running either shared or dedicated endpoints on a contract basis. The service provider may well specialize in managing devices in the IoT and have many different devices under management, possibly in many *different jurisdictions*—a consideration when managing risk and IoT; where are service provider contracts enforceable? Where is the data associated with service provision (configuration/administration, process state, legal, design) managed?

- *Manufacturers* build the endpoint devices. In some cases they may be service providers, too, as is common in the area of industrial controls. In other cases manufacturers may provide configurable devices into the market and have little knowledge of where they go or how they are used. Typically, such manufacturers would only see their products from a warranty perspective. However, differences will exist among manufacturers of even commodity-type endpoint devices; endpoint devices are not created equally, and the defect rate, mean-time-to-failure, and error rate will vary. Additionally, many questions may arise related to the complete function set of endpoint devices. Are they doing only what they are claimed to do? What is the potential for manufacturers accidentally or deliberately to insert undisclosed control features? From a risk perspective, asking such questions about provenance (who made it and where did it come from?), functional validation (code review and testing), and failure rates is an important practice for risk managers.
- *Network operators* may or may not apply in the context of the endpoint, but do not assume anything until you understand the architecture associated with the systems. Specifically, it may be the case that the endpoint devices are self-organizing and support their own peer-to-peer networking or mesh networks. In such an arrangement, the devices pass traffic through one another until a gateway to a larger network is found. The network operator in this scenario may be the service provider managing the devices, or the user/owner.
- The *data center (DC) operator* likely has only a marginal consideration in terms of the endpoint itself. The DC operator will care about the frequency and size of the data sets that are being generated by the endpoints.
- *Regulators* will have a variety of different sorts of concerns associated with the endpoints, especially if the endpoints are controlling physical outcomes in the real world. For instance, if the devices are controlling transportation or manufacturing systems, the health and safety issues will abound. In the early days of the IoT, it may be the case that the ability of regulators to understand and effectively govern endpoint devices will be subject to change as their regulatory practices evolve. *As a matter of risk in the IoT, owners and operators of endpoint devices should be aware that such regulatory evolution will occur and be aware that regulations may be subject to change.* We will discuss this issue in more depth in subsequent chapters. Regulators will also be quite interested in the manufacture of some devices, especially devices with radios that interface with the licensed spectrum (such as cell phone networks) and devices that have life-critical applications. Regulators do, in some cases, promote "guidelines" for IoT security (though not using that moniker), representing information that all stakeholders in the IoT need to be aware of to manage the threat of guidelines becoming new, punitive regulation.
- Finally, *interdependent third parties* should always be considered in any form of risk management. Interdependent third-parties are those parts beyond the user or owner that may rely on the goods or services (data) created by the endpoint devices for their own production or continuity. Alternately, they may be third parties upstream in the supply chain whose inputs are critical to the production processes associated with the endpoints. In either case, interdependent third parties can represent substantial business or operational risks in the form of liabilities, sanctions, or penalties associated, ultimately, with the performance of the endpoint devices.

GATEWAY AS AN ASSET CLASS

A *gateway* is a new asset class relative to conventional enterprise IT architecture, which speaks typically of endpoints, networks, and data centers. The gateway might be defined as the boundary between two domains of control at the edges of the Internet, or the gateway might be defined as the last hop before the "thing."

Gateways are critical control points in the IoT because they are often the last piece of the IoT system or service with access to powerful processing and memory. Therefore, gateways are the places where you can apply security and risk management controls for devices that lack sufficient controls to protect themselves and their data.

Historically, gateways have been "dumb" devices that were lumped in as part of the network. They just passed packets back and forth, perhaps doing simple address translation from one domain to another, but they possessed only primitive security functions, if any.

This type of legacy gateway will be inappropriate in the IoT: gateways will be too important to consider within the vastness of the Internet and its primary focus on moving a packet from A to B as reliably and quickly as possible.

Gateways will also be as distinct as the network in terms of the stakeholders. The same *types* of stakeholders will exist, but gateways may be manufactured, bought, owned, operated, regulated, configured, and used by entirely different stakeholder entities than the network.

The relationship between gateway and network may be completely independent in the IoT. But gateways may at times also be entirely intertwined with the network, such as in the case of cellular networks and base stations (node Bs and evolved node Bs).

Such relationship does not diminish their criticality or the need to consider them as unique control points. They must be considered uniquely in the context of IoT security, privacy, and risk management.

At the gateway level of an IoT reference design, the initial network connection of endpoint devices may be many different technologies: especially wireless technologies. Some of these technologies may be non-IP in nature. One of the roles of the gateway that is distinct from the backhaul network is to convert data from non-IP to IP packets.

The stakeholder descriptions provided below for "network" are sufficiently similar that we will not repeat them here.

NETWORK AS AN ASSET CLASS

The network is the glue of the IoT. The network backhauls data from gateways to the data center and cloud-based management and storage functions, the effective "brains" of the IoT.

The network, as an asset class, is composed of many sorts of basic connection technologies that support the IP, whether version 4 or version 6 (there will be more on IPv4 and IPv6 in subsequent chapters).

The network backhaul may be provided by many different technologies using IP: for instance, wireless short-range technologies linking to longer-range wireless networks such as fiber-optic networks, which in turn carry traffic at high speed directly into data centers and clouds.

- *Users* in the context of the network are ideally anonymous to the network, in the sense that traffic is not associated with specific users, whether they be enterprises or individuals. The reason for this is simple: huge amounts of information can be extracted from even summary analysis of network traffic. We will discuss this matter later in the book, but an import risk to manage in the IoT is the relationship with the network providers and the terms under which they operate. Again, ideally, traffic in the network will be classified based on packet-by-packet instructions that indicate to the network operators the user's requirements for service levels, any potential issues to the security reputation of the users; in either case, this allows the operators to apply appropriate qualities of services to the traffic.

- The *service provider* may be the same as the network operator (below) or may be distinct for part of the trip taken by the data. While a service provider may manage devices for users, it is entirely possible that they do not manage networks; the devices may simply interface directly with a public or private Internet managed by a telecommunications carrier or network operator, offering general capacity to all devices in the IoT. Another model may be that the users and endpoints initially connect to a private network managed by a service provider, which then uses a third-party network operator for transporting the data over long distances to the data center. While such an arrangement will be common, it also presents risk to the IoT because accountability for network service levels and security in general is split among providers. Given that data is often required to flow in real time or near real time, there is an opportunity for service providers to blame network operators for service degradation, and vice versa. Such situations are never good for rapid problem resolution and effective risk management in the IoT (or any network for that matter).

- In the context of the network, *manufacturers* build the network elements: routers, switches, servers supporting critical services like Domain Name Service (DNS), Dynamic Host Configuration Protocol (DHCP) (for IP address management), RADIUS (for authentication services), and security elements such as firewalls, denial-of-service protection, and network analysis tools. Network elements should be largely, if not completely, transparent to the users, managed by the network operators or potentially by service providers. In most cases, manufacturers will provide configurable devices to the market and have little knowledge of where they go or how they are used. Typically, such manufacturers would only see their products from a warranty perspective. Like endpoint devices, questions may arise related to the complete function set of elements composing the network. Therefore the guidance associated with network element manufacturers remains consistent: asking questions about provenance (who made it and where did it come from?), functional validation (code review and testing), and failure rates is an important practice for risk managers.

- *Network operators* are typically the main players in the network assets class and will frequently be represented by large incumbent carriers (usually the old telephone monopolies, which may or may not have been deregulated), competitive carriers buying and reselling wholesale capacity, new entrants using alternate network technology to that of the incumbent such as wireless networks, cable networks, or even fiber networks using rights of way associated with utilities or infrastructure such as railroads or pipelines. While these network operators may share certain forms of infrastructure such as fiber bundles, rights of way, and radio towers, they will often operate distinct network elements (switches, routers, firewalls, and so on) and make their own selections about manufacturers and suppliers of equipment and services. All network operators are not created equal. Service levels will vary, even if service level agreements appear comparable. Much of the risk in the IoT will be found in the selection and management of network operators; much more on this to following in subsequent chapters.

- *Data center operators* have a vested interest in the network as an asset class because it connects the endpoints to the centralized services provided through the DC. But the DC operators also have a perverse incentive to remain at arm's length from the network operator; specifically, degraded service associated with the give service [M2M, voice over internet protocol (VOIP), Internet, or whatever] is difficult to diagnose if the DC and the network operator are not operating in close cooperation and collaboration. This fact allows for much passing of blame and finger pointing during incidents, and represents a fundamental risk within the IoT: accountability across asset classes. Ideally, from the perspective of the application owner or the user, degraded services should be readily detectable and addressable, especially in the context of physical impacts. However, the frequently unique ownership structures of data centers and network operators can act against these priorities.
- *Regulators* are all over some network providers, and barely touch others. Usually the incumbents are heavily regulated while new entrants, if they are allowed and exist, are comparatively lightly regulated. The regulatory regimes related to just about any incumbent will cover tariffs (prices), lawful access (wire taps under judicial or other government orders), and possibly mandates to service provision (for instance, to rural areas). Usually, regulation is intended to promote access to citizens, and support industrial development broadly. Regulation typically does not get granular in terms of service levels. From the perspective of the network asset in the IoT, regulators are rather benign. Do not anticipate that regulators will facilitate or mandate conditions that will mitigate much risk in the IoT. Regulators in many cases lack the mandate, flexibility, or skills to manage risk in the IoT. However, regulators do, in some cases, promote "guidelines" for security, which can represent a practice about which all stakeholders in the IoT need to be aware to manage the threat of new, punitive regulations associated with the IoT.
- *Interdependent third parties* are a fundamental consideration for network asset owners, because virtually all core (long haul, bulk) carrier networks are shared by many entities and users. Data mixes and mingles as it moves through these shared networks. While this data will be segregated at many levels (link-level, network level, session level, and so on) and in many ways (encryption, compression), it still shares the same basic infrastructure. A broken, slow, or dirty (containing illicit or malicious traffic) "pipe" is a broken, slow, or dirty pipe for all of those who rely upon it. The upshot is that IoT risk management requires a certain awareness of the third parties sharing the pipes; not necessarily who they are, but that they exist and the network service provider has mitigations such that the actions of one users should not catastrophically impact the others.

DATA CENTERS AND CLOUDS AS AN ASSET CLASS

The data center or "clouds" are in part a figurative term for the centralized collection and management point in the IoT. Often the centralized collection point will be a data center with larger amounts of storage and processing power to manage the vast amount of data generated by the endpoints in the IoT. It may also be more of a centralized management point, where information from the endpoints is assessed and instructions based on the aggregated intelligence are issued back out to endpoints, or used for out-of-band (not part of the process specifically) management decisions.

DCs and clouds will come in many forms in the IoT, and already exist in a wide array of configurations from a wide array of vendors. Some DCs will be dedicated to a single tenant or owner, like a bank or government. This is a traditional approach to DCs/clouds. The more modern approach is a *cloud*, where DC resources are managed by a third party in a multi-tenant infrastructure. The applications may be dedicated to a tenant, but the platforms (operating systems) and infrastructure may be shared. Increasingly, organizations are employing hybrid systems, mixing dedicated DCs/clouds with shared and rented cloud resources together. They mix-and-match DC and cloud computing according to matters such as the sensitivity of the data, the geolocation of the data center or cloud, and demand fluctuations.[7]

Stakeholders in the context of the data center assets are more similar in characteristics to the endpoint asset class than the network assets.

- *Users* in the context of the DC may be anonymous individuals (at a point-of-sales terminal for example), industrial owners of sensors, or meters or control systems, which are dedicated to their purposes or major organizations like banks or governments with massive, centralized data stores. Users will continue to be what we currently understand them to be, too: people using tools like web browsers on desktops, laptops, and an ever-growing range of mobile devices. For users, DCs are the asset where they keep large volumes of information, but they may have little idea where the data actually resides. This issue of the physical location of the DC/cloud assets class represents a significant risk to users in the IoT.
- The *service provider* for the DC may be owned and operated by the user (owner) of the endpoints. Historically, users have owned and operated their own, dedicated DCs, but as the size and importance of DCs has grown dramatically over the last decade, DCs and especially clouds are increasingly operated by specialized service providers for all but the largest users. DC service providers are typically third-party suppliers running huge, shared facilities. For instance, Amazon Web Services and Microsoft Azure are two of the world's largest cloud service providers. The DC/cloud service provider may specialize in managing devices in the IoT, but more likely will offer standardized service levels across all IoT applications types. For instance, the DC/cloud service provider supplies heat, power, space, network access, and computing platforms (operating systems), and even fully configured software applications (Salesforce.com is one of the more notable examples, as are the new versions of Microsoft Office and Adobe Acrobat). One of the major IoT risks associated with the DC stakeholders is how they address and report security. This is often a tricky issue to manage because the shared nature of the DC asset class means that security practices and events affect all users within the DC.
- *Manufacturers* in the context of the DC would be the entities that build both the computing platforms and the network elements used inside the DC. Historically, this hardware and network equipment would have been transparent to the user. In some cases, the users may procure and manage their own hardware, just using the DC for heating, power, and network. In either situation, the selection of manufacturers and equipment types has become more meaningful as the linkage between physical location of data and regulation has become more important. This

---

[7]There is much to be explained related to cloud design and different forms of cloud, such as Infrastructure as a Service (IaaS), Platform as a Service (PaaS) and Software as a Service (SaaS). But this book assumes that the reader is aware of these distinctions.

linkage is now manageable because of the advent of auditable security controls that allow data processing and applications to be restricted to specific processors and therefore hardware platforms. The ability to use such emerging risk management controls will be important in the IoT, particularly for information that is especially sensitive or subject to extra ordinary regulatory oversight.

- *Network operators* definitely apply in the context of the DC/cloud, and are an important consideration in managing overall risk in the IoT around the DC, the simple reason being that as large centralized resources, the network is the path to and from the DC. The assurance of the network resources leading to the DC are entirely aligned with the overall assurance of the service, as much as is the DC. A challenge associated with managing DC risks (also referred to as "computing cloud" risks) is managing the risks associated with the relationship and interface between the network operators and the DC providers. The closer the relationships and the better to co-management and monitoring, the generally better the risk may be managed. Conversely, when DCs are provisioned with network resources coming from exclusively lowest-cost providers (with the lowest service levels), then squabbles over accountability of any service within the IoT will rapidly emerge.

  Of course the *data center operator* itself is key to the risk management of the DC asset class. Issues that emerge related to DC operators will include, but will not be limited to: geographic location, data replication practices, security policy, procedures and operations, regulatory environment, financial stability, ownership, audit, and executive oversight. Historically, DCs have not been considered "critical infrastructure" in the way the telecommunication service providers, banks, hospitals, police, and transportation, have been considered critical infrastructure. In the IoT, the degree to which a given jurisdiction comes to recognize the centrality and criticality of DCs in the IoT will definitely affect the ability of users and owners to manage risk. Why? Because industries defined as critical infrastructure are assigned special support and prioritization during times of emergency: very probably, the times when the IoT systems under threat are needed the most.

- *Regulators* in the context of the data center are typically concerned with the data management practices associated with the applications in the DC, rather than the DC itself. For instance, Payment Card International (PCI) (an industry regulator versus government) will have a variety of concerns associated with the management of credit card information by transaction processing applications within the DC. Much of these concerns will be addressed by the application owner or operators; but to the extent the DC provider is supplying the networks internal to the DC, they may be of interest to regulators such as PCI. Certainly, the physical risks to data in the DC (theft of backup media, as an example) will also be of interest to regulators.

  Historically, DCs were lightly regulated compared to networks; however, this has recently changed with the collapse of the Safe Harbor[8] agreement which in effect governed DC/clouds in the US, used by European citizens and companies alike. Regulators are taking an increasing interest in DC/clouds and how personally identifiable information is managed in these assets. The ability of regulators to understand and effectively government DCs will be subject to change as

---

[8]https://en.wikipedia.org/wiki/International_Safe_Harbor_Privacy_Principles and http://www.bbc.com/news/technology-35460131.

regulatory practices evolve. *For instance, beyond Personally Identifiable Information (PII), it may be the case that DCs come to be widely viewed as formal, critical infrastructure under the information technology sector, which already includes network operators and manufacturers of (endpoint and network) equipment.*

- *Interdependent third parties* may be one of the largest risks in the IoT under the data center asset class, the reason being that most DCs are shared resources with many different clients. While the DC may go to pains to segregate the computing platforms and therefore the applications and data within the DC, they typically all share the same networks going into and out of the DCs. Brute force network attacks (such as denial-of-service attacks that simply fill the network with attack traffic) on DCs against a particular client application almost inevitably impact all clients in the DC. Similarly, denial-of-service attacks aimed at computing versus network resources can have the same collateral affects. To the extent that a DC hosts a variety a different clients, management and segregation of data in motion and in use by tools typically under the DC operator's control will have a large influence of risk and the IoT.

WHY DO THEY CARE? STAKEHOLDERS FROM A DIFFERENT ANGLE

Stakeholders in the IoT might be alternately understood as those caring about fundament issues of who, what, where, and how:

- Who are the stakeholders and interested parties?
- What data is being managed?
- Where is the data going?
- How is the data protected?

WHO HAS ACCESS TO DATA IN THE IoT?

Who cares about the data under management in the IoT? The matter of who has access to data and devices in the IoT is related to the range of stakeholders. The simple answer is "a lot of people and organizations."

Some of the stakeholders are the owners of the data, yet many of the stakeholders have business interests related to the management and transport of the data. These managers and transporters have little to no insight into the meaning or type of the data: the payloads are opaque.

For the owners of the data, the concerns are fairly evident. They probably expect that the data will arrive in a manner timely to the application within the IoT (email, medical monitoring, security camera, meter, and so on), unchanged, complete, and confidential. But these data-owners have complete dependence on the device manufacturers, gateways, and network service providers. These manufacturers and service providers are in many ways constrained by the notion of data transparency: they know it is there, but many have precious little context: they don't understand how it is used and what the potential risks associated with degradation in quality or services levels are.

The opaque nature of payloads in the IoT is an important security consideration and is at both times a benefit and a bane. The benefit of data or payload being obscured is that data can be managed and transported in a more-or-less anonymous manner. Do you really want your service providers or manufacturers of devices to know what you are doing? Probably not. And recall that because the IoT contains much data generated automatically or semiautomatically by machines, the data within the IoT is not just emails and web traffic. Data in the IoT will be about home automation, medical devices, transportation, and many other systems. Visibility into this data within the IoT would allow manufacturers and service providers essentially to reconstruct the lifestyles of individuals or the minute-by-minute operational details of organizations.

The benefit of data being opaque for many of the whos in the IoT is personal privacy and at a much larger scale, confidentiality of commercially sensitive information.

The bane of being opaque to the whos of the IoT is that classification of different types of traffic becomes more difficult: classification in terms of how fast is the data shuttled through the network, how much confidentiality control is applied to the data, and how much care is taken to reduce errors or retransmissions of data.

Classification allows manufacturers and service providers to offer tiers of service appropriate to the application and data being generated by the application. This means that applications and data for greater sensitivity can be directed through paths and down pipes that treat it with the care and urgency it requires—according to the users, who will probably be paying the bills in one manner or another.

Classification capability also allows for applications and data with lower requirements for assurance and less sensitivity potentially to use cheaper forms of devices and transport—lowering the costs to the end users. For instance, lower assurance requirements for a given application or data payload could mean that it arrives at a slower rate (speed), potentially taking several seconds or even minutes.

Another distinction in service may be that the data takes a nondeterministic path: a nearly random or unknown path down a wide variety of pipes, according to where capacity is lowest and probably cheapest. See the following section of "Where" for more discussion on determinism.

The bane of data being opaque for many of the whos in the IoT is that it may impede cost efficiency and security overall, and increase risk.

THE "WHAT FOR?" QUESTION OF DATA IN THE IoT

The "what" question is essentially about the data being managed by the endpoint devices and sometimes the gateways, transported through the network and being stored in the central repositories, according to the application or use case under consideration. What is the function in the data in IoT? What sort of information are being collected and managed defines how the endpoint devices, networks, and data centers are specified, built, used, and eventually retired or disposed of.

The IoT users are clearly stakeholders because the data is typically attributable to them; and in some cases, such as personal information, belongs to them. In other cases, such as sensor data, ownership may be less clear-cut. For instance, if data is not personally identifiable with an individual, it is not personal, even though it may be about people. This is important to recall at all times while assessing risk and the IoT: "personal information" must be personally identifiable. Just because data is about people does not mean that it is subject to risks associated with the many and manifest personal information statutes that exist around the world.

To the extent that users, or system designers, suspect or know that personally identifiable information is managed and transported in and through the IoT, they need to be conscious of the "what" related to their data, security, and risk in the IoT.

Businesses, government, and other entities that act as users in the IoT need to be aware of the sensitivity of their data measured on scales that include their entire intrinsic value. Is there commercially sensitive information? For example: is the information financial results, operational indicators, formulae, or even system control instructions? Are there marketing or other commercial strategies? Information associated with national security? Information belonging to other businesses, governments, or other entities for which the first party is accountable to a third party? Is there personally identifiable information? In this instance, the "what" of data will drive resulting risk, when combined with the other elements of who, where, and why.

Manufacturers of endpoint devices in the IoT are clear stakeholders, as are the manufacturers of systems required to interface with the endpoints. For instance, whoever makes the system within, say, automobiles that call out over the IoT, needs to take account of the nature of the data when the security associated with their participation in the IoT is defined. Is the information purely anonymized and statistical data about wear and tear metrics? Or is the data linked to ownership information and geospatially recorded travel patterns needed to predict maintenance and proactively address looming mechanical failures? Both may be legitimate forms of data to push from the automobile, but they are radically different from a security and privacy perspective. Alternately, what if the automobile was enabled with bidirectional communications capabilities, so that the manufacturer could push software patches to the car? This would probably push the security requirements associated with the IoT communications even higher, because of the potential for unauthorized agents to inject unauthorized software that could impact physical safety. For manufacturers, the "what" they intend for their devices in the IoT is fundamental to the risks involved and the risk management appropriate.

Systems integrators, the people responsible for building the IoT from all the pieces and parts, are as concerned with the "what" question as manufacturers and third-party systems because in the end they are on the hook to make it all work.

Manufacturers will generally wish to address as wide a market as possible with their products and will probably build in capabilities to support a range of "what" when it comes to data types. There we can expect that higher and lower risk applications will be supported from a single type of device that may be used in a variety of different applications in the IoT. Therefore it is a matter of the configuration and management of the end devices, network, and DC that will determine the security of the data, and the resulting risk that be managed by the system integrators.

"What" also defines where the device is physically located, its form factor, and the control interface for both people and other machines (assuming there is a control interface for people). Therefore the owners of the environmentally adjacent assets are stakeholders: for instance, private individuals, governments at various levels, landlords.

Because "what" can include data related to environmental or physical safety, commercially sensitive information, and potentially personally identifiable information, regulators may be direct stakeholders, too. In most cases, regulators regulate, they do not run systems. Therefore, the accountability for risk management in the IoT associated with "what" will typically be that of oversight and audit.

Indirectly, there may be other forms of stakeholders associated with the "what" of IoT; insurers, for instance. If the data from a device in the IoT somehow generates potential liability through its unauthorized release, change, deletion, or a degraded state of availability or outright loss, then insurers may well be indirect stakeholders. Possibly, such insurers may be direct stakeholders in the IoT.

THE "WHERE" THINGS HAPPEN TO DATA IN THE IoT QUESTION

The "where" issues related to security and risk management in the IoT include the endpoint devices where data is often created, gateways where data may be normalized, go through preprocessing, get encrypted, are compressed, and then sent to the transport networks and finally the end-of-the-line DC or cloud systems.

The endpoint where the data is created will often be the remote devices in the IoT. These are the devices that in effect start to reverse the flows of the Internet as a whole, as more and more small devices pour data into the network destined for central data centers and storage arrays. There are many threats to endpoints that will be discussed through the course of this book, but the fundamental concerns remain the same: is the data that is created at the endpoint sufficiently protected from unauthorized release, unauthorized change and deletion, and is it created in a timely manner? These concerns, the reader will recognize, are summed up in the reoccurring trinity of "confidentiality, integrity, and availability."

Constrained endpoints might not have the power to normalize and prepare data for transport and backhaul across the network in an efficient or secure manner; gateways might be a place *where* a significant amount of processing is performed, either for efficiency (to remove extraneous or repeated data sets and to perform compression) or for security (the gateway may apply encryption, and possibly also provide authentication for endpoints that cannot support robust identity regimes and need to delegate to the gateway).

The next point is "where" is the network. This is the location of the data after it leaves the originating endpoints and passes through some form of gateway (remote devices or possibly a centralized control systems), en route to the destination (DC/cloud, centralized storage or processing, or, potentially, endpoints, where it will be considered an instruction or other control parameter). The "where" in the network is important because data flowing through a network is always subject to a variety of threats. At a high-level these will include broad threats like eavesdropping, change, and deletion. (Other threat descriptions like "interception" and "masquerade" are related, and equally appropriate for consideration.)

The degree to which the data moving through the IoT is considered sensitive to confidentiality, integrity and availability attacks will determine the amount of determinism that might be required to sufficiently manage risk in the IoT.

NETWORK DETERMINISM IN THE IoT

Determinism refers to the ability to understand and predict the path that data will take through the network: where is the data at any given time? As data moves through Internet-based networks and the Internet itself, this property—"Where is my data?"—is actually not a very obvious value. Beyond the fact that predicting routing on the Internet can be fraught, routing may change from packet to packet of data.

In fact, the default nature of the Internet is to move data efficiently and, more importantly, to route around blockages, slowdowns, and stoppages. In fact, if you go back to the seminal reasons behind the invention of the Internet, you will find requirements for an information network that could withstand complete destruction of some nodes (geographic regions), but continue to support communications with the surviving nodes.

The value of network determinism, from a security perspective, is that physical interception, recording, injection, masquerade, and other attacks become more difficult. You may trust certain paths and pipes more because you know where the physical fibers run, where the routers and switches sit, who owns them, and how secure all these network assets are. The more you know about the "whos" running the networks of the IoT, the easier it is to make accurate risk assessment associated with "where" data travels and dedicate appropriate levels of resources to security. The less you know about the "whos" in your IoT, the more risk you must either accept or treat through other means—also known in the jargon of risk management as *compensating controls*.

The last "where" to consider is about the location of the data when it comes to rest. Two issues associated directly with "where" are related to regulations and to capacity and its derivative costs.

Depending on the nature of the data, the jurisdiction in which the it comes to rest may introduce or reduce risks from regulation, in either its origin or destination domain.

Consider the origin domain first: what regulations governed the data in the area it originated? Are the data personally identifiable, particularly? Certain types of data may not be readily removable from the jurisdiction in which they were generated. For instance, personal information is rarely allowed to be moved across national borders, unless due diligence has been performed and carefully documented; sometimes, personal information may not be removed from its original jurisdiction at all. Alternately, certain types of data may be considered commercially sensitive and associated with production levels and resulting sales and profits. In this case, movement of data from one jurisdiction to another may or may not constitute a responsible (or negligent) management and associated liability. Such matters need to be taken into account before committing to a destination for data moving through the IoT.

The destination dimension of "where" is probably even more important than the origin because, as the saying goes, possession is nine-tenths of the law. When it comes to regulatory issues, the risks most often spoken of are associated with the rights to discovery and search that apply in different jurisdictions. Is the data held in a country with weak or no specific protection from illegitimate search (and possible seizure and destruction)? Or is the data held in a jurisdiction with the same or recognizably similar laws and regulations? In the first case, risks may be elevated and in the latter there may be no impact on the overall risk associated with the IoT.

THE "HOW" QUESTION OF IoT DATA MANAGEMENT

The "how" of risk management in the IoT is about the security applied to systems managing the data and the data itself. How is the data managed at the four distinct parts of the IoT: the endpoints, the gateways, the network, and the DC/cloud.

How risk is managed at the endpoints is as much about the data that is being collected or acted upon from a central control system as it is about the devices themselves. In some cases, it is possible that the continued functioning of the device is more important that the assurance of the data collecting, managing, or receiving. The same might be said of an IoT gateway, which might support a variety of different services, of which the most important, aggregated sensitivity is to availability: they need the gateway up and running above all.

Many of the devices in the coming IoT will be battery operated, will scavenge energy from the environment (for instance, solar or wind power), or will exist in such multitudes that if each one consumed a significant amount of power, the electricity bills would destroy the business case.

In such cases, the ability to secure data on the endpoint device may be limited because the function of the device itself takes precedence over some or even all security-specific functions.

Returning to the trinity of security once again: confidentiality, integrity, and availability, how the device and gateways protect confidentiality will be a matter of good code development as much as the application of encryption and intrusion detection/prevention technologies. Good code development in smart devices and systems ideally facilitates reduced energy consumption, but cryptographic, firewalling, and intrusion-detection systems functions never reduce resource consumption; such technology requires processing power and corresponding energy.

For this reason it is possible that risk management of devices in the IoT leads to the absence of crypto, firewalling, and intrusion technologies in some cases, or the entire delegation of these capabilities to gateways, away from endpoint devices. Similarly, integrity can be protected with careful operating systems and code development and/or software-based algorithms (hashing functions and error checking protocols, for instance) that provide safeguards against integrity risks.

Availability risks associated with data are partially addressed by carefully developed device code and appropriate energy management practices ensuring that the device does not stop running. These availability risks and control solutions are intrinsic in the overall security of the device, while confidentiality and integrity risks may at times be, literally, too expensive to implement in full or even in part on the endpoint device.

How data in the IoT is protected in the network is also an important element of risk assessment and management. We have previously covered the topic of determinism in network communications and how it impacts risk. Namely, that the path (the "where") of the data can affect who potentially has access to that data in order to perform a variety of different attacks. Such attacks may be with or without legal authority.

Within the network itself, a variety of questions might be asked associated with how data is transported, independent of where it is transported. Ideally, if data is transported with much care associated with "how," the "where" risks can be greatly mitigated and reduced. For instance, a variety of encryption technologies are available for network communications. The most popular of these would probably be Secure Socket Layers (SSL), widely used in web services but reusable for just about any form of data. Another very common network-oriented security control is IP security (IPsec) where secure tunnels are created from endpoints to gateways. In the event that encryption is not possible due to endpoint constraints, as we discussed above, then gateways and networks can be designed to provide closed or "virtual" private networks and architectures.

Network segmentation is another element of "how" networks will be managed in the IoT. Segmentation allows for logically closed architectures and addressing schemes that do not allow data to reach other networks, effectively stove-piping the sources and destinations of data in a given IoT system. Such schemes are widely used in enterprises around the world but also in some very large Internet services and DC/cloud infrastructures. Private architectures and segmentation are a form of risk management that will be discussed later, but they are definitely part of the "how" associated with risk management and the IoT.

The last element to be considered from the perspective of "how" is the data center and/or cloud: the central storage, management, and control infrastructure of many IoT systems. How is the data protected in these systems and how are the DC/cloud systems themselves protected?

DCs, cloud services, their underlying storage systems, management systems, and controls systems are complex, and understanding the "how" of such systems is difficult—at the very least because many of the providers of DC/cloud services have developed proprietary software and systems as a point of competitive advantage.

A RISK-BASED APPROACH TO THE SECURITY "HOW" QUESTION OF THE IoT

As a general approach to managing risk in the IoT, consider the manner in which these complex systems are managed from a *business perspective, an operational perspective, and a technical perspective.*

The "how" from a business perspective is about the management support for security and formalized risk management. Are there security policies to guide operational managers? Do the policies take into account issues such as regulatory compliance in a sufficient manner?

The "how" from an operational perspective is about procedures, staffing, training, and auditing. Are things well documented, is the staff knowledgeable and sufficient, is there any sort of third-party confirmation of the sufficiency of the processes? Do the operational procedures support the higher level business objectives and policies?

The "how" from a technical perspective is about the hardware and software that is applied to provide security. Are there multiple layers? Is there centralized or coordinated reporting? Are the technical controls adequately maintained by the operational procedures?

The remainder of this book will look primarily at the business and operational management of risk, touching on technical risk management regularly but not getting into the specifies of individual technologies or vendor solutions.

FINAL WORD ON WHO/WHAT/WHERE/HOW

This section should have exposed that there are many dimensions and stakeholders with responsibility to manage risk in the IoT, and they have overlapping but distinct priorities and perspectives.

Multidimensionality and overlapping responsibility are a recipe for oversight, both willful and accidental. If too many people are potentially accountable for managing risk, then some or even all of them will make bad assumptions. They will assume others are taking care of things, when in fact no one is taking care of risk.

CONCLUSION

The IoT as an issue faces a lot of competition from other trends and popular memes on the Internet, so we started the chapter by trying to sift out what the IoT is and is not about. The IoT is not really about social networking, even though there are sources that would have everyone believe that everything is somehow about social networking. Social networking is firmly in the realm of the current Internet—versus a core of the evolving IoT.

Neither is the IoT about privacy. Privacy is about personally identifiable information. There certainly will be personal information within the IoT, and there will probably be some new privacy challenges created with the IoT; but fundamentally, the IoT is not about the management of personal information. Most information in the IoT will be about transactions, movements, and activities that are not personally identifiable. Privacy, because it is by definition very "personal" to everyone, is well protected in legislation in many places and cases. We most likely have what we need to proceed into the world of the IoT without needing to be overly concerned that privacy will somehow suffer for lack of attention.

The IoT depends on the network very heavily, if not critically, but is not the network itself. The network is an enabler and a risk in the IoT. Lots and lots of attention and investment is going into broadband networks and especially wireless networks at the time of writing. But this investment is being made for many reasons, the IoT being only one of many and probably not the largest driver of network investment. The network is critical to IoT, but not the defining element of the IoT.

The gateway, as the intermediary between the endpoint and the network, will be a much more critical factor with the IoT than it has been in the past, due to its potential to manage resource-intensive functions such as data encryption, authentication, and storage for the often resource-constrained endpoints.

The world has not really made its mind up about what to call the IoT. We, in this book, are calling it the "Internet of Things," which is a phrase coined about 10 years ago and is not original to this book in any way. But others with a variety of different intentions are calling the IoT by other names, yet we are all speaking about the same thing for the most part. At the very least, distinctions are probably small while similarities are very large as you compare strict definitions. Other names you are likely to see include Machine-to-Machine, Smart Systems, Intelligence Systems, Connected Systems, and even the semantically quibbling Internet of Everything. In the end, the risks and issues we discuss in this book will apply to whatever system name happens to be applied.

The IoT is not distinct from the past Internet, it is an expansion of the past Internet that has been dominated for about 20 years by discussions around the "triple play" of voice, video, and data service. The IoT contains all these legacy applications and assets and brings new applications and assets into the mix. All these assets, new and old, are now mixed into the same network. Security and risk management for the old Internet is as important as ever to the IoT. The question from a risk perspective is: what else is there to consider with the new assets within the IoT?

The IoT is about layers of stakeholders and many new service-deployment and delivery options, not like the old days of the previous Internet with simple(r) vendor-buyer relationships that were essentially replicated, with slight differences. In the IoT, there will be many options associated with the endpoint: where the data comes from or goes to; in the gateway: what functions should be offloaded from the endpoints and how; in the network: which media are used and how fast or with what degree of assurance it moves; and in the data center and the various types of clouds that are available to manage the masses of data flowing out of the IoT. This choice enables lots and lots of new and innovative management, operational and technical models, but also increasing complexity.

THE ANATOMY OF THE INTERNET OF THINGS

2

This chapter describes composition of the Internet of Things (IoT). In order to manage risk, you need to understand not only the applications, devices, or services under assessment, but also the other types of devices that will at some point certainly share parts of the underlying infrastructure of the IoT.

WHEN DOES THE IoT ACTUALLY GET HERE?

The IoT is here now and growing every day. In the beginning, the IoT was largely invisible to most people, in the form of smart meters, infrastructures, ATMs, cameras, and so forth. By 2016, the IoT was increasingly a household point of discussion because many consumer goods had been made *smart*. At the same time, the IoT is becoming notorious because security has been done so poorly. This book is full of references and footnotes to consumer devices—not just commercial IoT devices—with poor security.

The IoT is rapidly being deployed in several sectors, as we will discuss shortly, and revenues are being generated for all the stakeholders looking to generate revenue in the first place. It has been a real business since about 2010, but has started to become serious, with accelerating growth reaching 50 billion devices by 2020, or even more.[1]

IPv4 DOES NOT DO IoT ANY FAVORS

There are many reasons why the IoT and machine-to-machine connectivity (M2M) is only taking off now, versus back in the 1990s when the Internet in general was seeing remarkable growth and investment in Europe and North America. At least one of these reasons is that the vision of millions and billions of small devices communicating with each other and with centralized applications was incompatible with the natural limits of Internet Protocol version 4 (IPv4).

IPv4 has approximately 4.3 billion available addresses in total, for everything—for every device on the planet. This meant that using IPv4 would require careful network segregation because a given address would be used over and over again. It would also mean larger and larger operational costs because juggling all these networks within networks becomes fraught. In the end, the lack of IPv4 availability from carriers would have raised the long-term costs and viability of M2M, purely from a network perspective.

---

[1]http://www.cisco.com/c/en/us/solutions/internet-of-things/overview.html.

RIoT Control. DOI: http://dx.doi.org/10.1016/B978-0-12-419971-2.00002-9

27

From an IoT risk-management perspective, this is important to understand because deploying IoT systems on IPv4 may work in the short term, but probably not in the medium to long term. At some point, even if your particular application does not require upgrading, the carrier network will. When a major carrier upgrades, a customer will sooner or later be required to follow suit. Maybe it will not be the next day, but eventually. Making assumptions like "IPv4 will always be available in the next 20 years" is risky. Organizations that want to get into IoT need to assume that even if they have a perfectly functional IPv4 solution today, it is much too unwieldy to last well into the future where amortization formulas reach break even and payback.

IoT IS ENABLED BY IPv6

For the most part, the first generation of IoT has been deployed on legacy Internet technology: IPv4. This situation will not scale into the future of the IoT. Not even close!

Networks based on IPv4 are facing a major upgrade, where network equipment everywhere will require enhancement to handle Internet Protocol version 6 (IPv6).

In February 2011, we ran out of *old* IPv4 addresses; there were none available for dispensation to regional Internet registries. When these regional Internet registries have dispensed their last IP addresses, there will simply be no IPv4 addresses left and any new organization, device, man, woman, child, or beast that needs an IP address will have to get an IPv6 address.

Regional registries are forecast to run out of addresses themselves at different rates, with the Asian and North American registries already having exhausted supplies in 2011. African and Latin American registries are projected to have sufficient address through to 2015 and beyond, but based on past projections around address exhaustion, this could be an overly optimistic forecast.

IN BRIEF: WHAT IS IPv6?

IPv6 is the successor to version 4 of the Internet protocol addressing system that has supported the growth of the Internet to date. IPv4 is the addressing system that most of the current Internet uses, and a majority of internal enterprise networks also use a type of v4 known as *private addressing*, which was reserved within the IPv4 specification for this purpose. (There was an IPv5 for a short while, but it was a very specific sort of protocol within the family of *multicast* protocols and never got out of experimental stage; however, it did manage to occupy an increment in the generation of IP technologies and as a consequence, the lifeblood of the Internet [IP] skipped over to version 6).

IPv6 differs from IPv4 in a number of ways, such as enhanced security and mobility features, but the main benefit of IPv6 is virtually unlimited IP addresses to support the coming IoT. IPv6 comes with the capability of supporting many more addresses: IPv4 has a maximum of approximately 4.3 billion addresses. IPv6 supports 3.4×10^{38} or 340 trillion, trillion, trillion addresses.

WHAT DOES IPv6 MEAN FOR IoT IN GENERAL?

IPv6 means change and change generally means risk. Furthermore, IPv6 is not an option: those who delay planning for the coming of IPv6 will eventually find themselves isolated in vestigial pockets of IPv4 users. Why would managers inject more risk into their IoT future? Because they can't yet see a need for moving to IPv6.

For a manager, IPv6 is terribly technical and best left alone except for the knowledge that you need it! For an engineer, IPv6 is still terribly technical, but this is the price to be paid for its power and scalability. It is a small part of the anatomy of the IoT today; but like dye diffusing in clear water, it will eventually permeate to every facet of the IoT and not only tint but dominate the entire infrastructure. If it were 1910 and Ford had developed the mass production line for cars, would you want to be investing in horseshoe-making machines or tire-making machines? You would probably maintain your horseshoe-making machine by improvising and bootstrapping and transition investment toward machines that could be used for making tires.

Stopgap measures abound for avoiding IPv6, but only because the levels of M2M deployment and the population within the IoT is nascent: it has not yet entered the rapid phase of adoption some call the *hockey stick* of growth, shown in Fig. 2.1. The hockey stick (which can apply to any industry or product and is not unique to the IoT) is characterized by relatively slow growth (less than 50% per year) until an inflection point is reached, at which point growth is measured in hundreds of percent per year.

Although the IoT has not yet reached the inflection point of growth, stopgap measures related to networking continue to be applied. Network managers and those deploying the first generation of IoT denizens are persisting with IPv4 because it is what they know and what their equipment will support without question. Yet they are also making their living more complicated in the future because retrofitting and extending old equipment and technology over and over to business requirements is a fraught process. Sooner or later a point of diminishing returns is reached. The IoT will accelerate the approach of the diminishing returns associated with IPv4.

In the meantime, the IoT as it stands is built, developing, and maturing on the overburdened bones of IPv4. This fact is not yet retarding growth and development, but it will come to that point, and this poses a major risk to the IoT and the many opportunities it presents to the world. There is a potential price to be paid for passing the inflection point in IoT growth while remaining unprepared and un-converted to support IPv6.

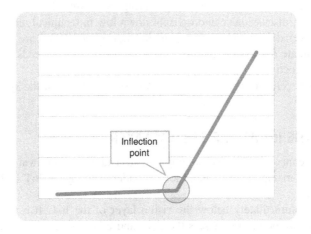

FIGURE 2.1

Hockey stick of growth.

THE ARCHITECTURAL FRAMEWORK OF THE IoT: ENDPOINTS, GATEWAYS, NETWORKS, AND DCs/CLOUDS

It is possible to dive deep, very quickly into *what* specifically the IoT is composed of, but let's start slowly. It is of little value to the world at large if the IoT is only understood in terms that only engineers and technicians appreciate and understand.

Another problem with diving deep right off the start with a topic like the IoT and its associated risks is that it is very easy to overlook important concepts and high-level perspectives when you start your considerations right up close. Starting with descriptions of engineering specifications, protocols, and application interfaces would probably lose some of the most important lessons available about the IoT at this point in its development and evolution.

For instance, the fact that the IoT is not merely about smart little devices cleverly making our lives better can be overlooked. Media hype and technical minutia can attract a lot of attention to the devices operating at the endpoints of the IoT and obscure the fact that the IoT, when considered at possibly its highest level—as we covered in Chapter 1, Introduction—The Internet of Things—the IoT is composed of at least four asset classes: endpoints, gateways, networks, and DCs/clouds.

This concept of the IoT containing at least four asset classes is critical to risk management, because the greatest risk for any manager is accepting risks of which you are entirely unaware. While there will always be risks you cannot know, at least deal with the risks that are knowable!

GETTING BELOW THE VISION LAYER

It is not uncommon for people to talk first about the IoT at the *vision layer*—what is the new and emerging service the IoT will deliver? What will the *smart home* look like? How will *intelligence vehicles* run on *smart roads* and create *connected transportation infrastructure* that will run better, faster, and cheaper? This is the *vision layer*; it is the concept and the idea that drives more discussion and seeds more detailed investigations into things like regulatory affects, business cases, market analysis and focus-groups, and eventually engineering feasibility.

After the vision layer, discussions can drop right down low in technical terms—often to the endpoints: the remote, clever devices again. How should they work? What are the technical requirements? This is a legitimate discussion and absolutely necessary, but it needs to occur in context if risk is to be managed effectively.

Context for risk management in the IoT comes from consideration of the *system layer*.

UNDERSTANDING THE IoT AT THE SYSTEM LAYER

The *system layer* is a conceptual device, as opposed to a tangible, hardware or software element that can be touched and manipulated. It is a tool for understanding the IoT and therefore the risks inherent within the IoT.

The system layer is immediately below the vision layer of the IoT. It is the next-least detailed descriptive tool, which can be used to assess the risks and controls that are appropriate for a given IoT application or service. Descriptions and models at the IoT system layer start to dissect the

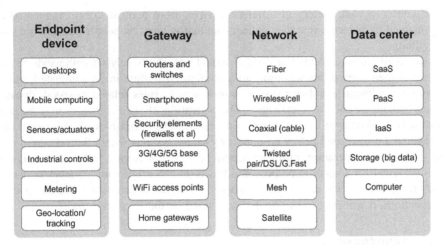

FIGURE 2.2

The IoT at the system layer.

vision into manageable classes that can, in turn, be understood in detailed ways that allow for the treatment, transference, or acceptance of risks.

At the system layer, the IoT is composed of four asset classes: endpoints, gateways, networks, and DCs/clouds. These assets might be more conveniently called by different names; but in the end, the system layer is a very useful descriptive tool because it reduces the amount of potential error due to oversight in risk management: accepting risks unknowingly.

By using models at the system layer, IoT engineers and risk managers can get a better understanding of where threats and vulnerabilities are likely to lie in an end-to-end context. Fig. 2.2 is a depiction of the IoT system layer.

In Chapter 1, Introduction—The Internet of Things, we discussed the four different asset classes in the IoT according to the stakeholders and players associated with each class. *Who, Why*, and *How* they can concern and interests in the IoT asset, and the potential effect on risk and security.

In the following section we are going to go deeper into the nature of these classes, without concern for the stakeholders. What are the properties of the asset class that may be most meaningful to risk management in the IoT?

ENDPOINT ASSET CLASS IN THE IoT

The endpoint asset class reflects the far reaches of the systems comprising the IoT: the things that exist at the far ends of the network; what is at the end of the line, interfacing with the rest of the world? What is collecting the data from the environment, from people or from other machines? What is controlling the logical-kinetic interface? This is the boundary where instructions and ethereal data are converted to movement in the real world. Conversely, this interface is where the real world is converted to digital information by the endpoint.

Endpoints can be a wide variety of different devices, from manual to semiautomated to fully automated—manual in the sense that they collect data that is input by people and that are otherwise not doing anything.

A semiautomated endpoint device in the IoT would potentially rely on commands to initiate a process, which is then carried out according to a configured routine in an automated manner. An example may be a collision avoidance system, which applies rules related to speed, distance, and environmental conditions once it is activated. The activation of such a system may be semiautomated in that it is invoked by a human driver as a new form of old-fashioned cruise control—or, it might be activated a millisecond before an impact by safety systems within the vehicle.

A meter collecting temperature information may be an example of a fully automated device in the IoT. It is designed for a specific purpose and has certain configuration parameters designed by the manufacturer and set by the application manager. Unless those parameters change or the device fails or malfunctions, it will continue to do the same thing on the same basis indefinitely.

ENDPOINT INTERDEPENDENCY

At the endpoint asset class, the IoT will frequently resemble a system of systems where endpoints may interact with each other in a wide variety of ways, with interdependencies based on automated, semiautomated, or manual relationships. These combinations of interdependencies will prove to be one of the most complex and pernicious elements of the IoT to management from a risk perspective.

The nature of the IoT with its distinct asset classes and competitive and fragmented ownership within each asset class will allow services to be formed and reformed from component parts. Because there will often be more than one source available to IoT service providers for any given type of asset (endpoint suppliers, gateways suppliers, network suppliers, and cloud suppliers), each of the different possible combinations will have a unique risk profile. Changing one supplier of software for cloud services supporting endpoint devices, for instance, can entirely change the interdependency risks. While functionality of the endpoints might appear consistent under normal conditions, the real risks will lie in the differences in how suppliers act under abnormal conditions, where interdependency weaknesses will most likely manifest themselves.

Endpoint systems of systems will rapidly become very complex in nature with many paths through the system and many different potential combinations of instructions sets, the final outcome of which are difficult to predict without careful assessment and management.

In some ways, the endpoints relationships in the IoT can easily take on chaotic relationships in the sense that very small changes in the configuration of the interrelated endpoints can dramatically change the functionality of the endpoint system of systems.

By way of a purely hypothetical example of endpoint interdependency in the IoT: motion sensors in pavement and fences communicate with facial recognition (biometric) processors inside security cameras, which in turn speak to light-detection sensors and lighting activation systems (so there is enough light for the cameras to work to see who or what is in the vicinity). Suppose that low temperatures cause the light-emitting diode (LED) lighting system to reach its required illumination more slowly, causing many of the pictures taken by cameras to be too low resolution for biometric analysis? As a result, the cameras activate preconfigured protocols where they continue to take pictures repeatedly until a sufficiently fine-grained image is available. This causes the cameras to work harder, consume more memory and power, and generate more heat. The heat causes condensation in the camera cabinets, which creates humidity and lowers the expected mean-time-to-failure of the cameras by 75%—raising operational costs and ruining the business case. The system operator cannot meet service levels under the contract terms and abandons the contract as soon as it is legally allowed.

These sorts of endpoint interdependencies within the IoT are an essential part of risk management in the IoT. The root cause of this business risk in the IoT is a very specific performance detail for a lighting system, which is integrated with a camera system, which is integrated with biometrics analysis systems, which in turn is activated by motion sensors.

Interdependency vulnerabilities and risks associated with the IoT—not merely at the endpoint—will be a reoccurring topic throughout this book.

SENSING VERSUS PROCESSING

Another useful tool for understanding the endpoints in the IoT is to assess whether the device is a sensing device, versus a processing device. This is how some of the early work from the International Telecommunications Union (ITU) has viewed the endpoints in the IoT.[2]

A sensing device would be simpler than a processing device, but also potentially cheaper and therefore more populous in the IoT. A sensing device would interpret the physical world and relay the information immediately, through the network back to the application in the data center (DC) or a centralized processing point.

Simple sensing devices have the risk management advantage of being relatively easy to assess from the perspective of what can go wrong. However, when a simple device deployed in the thousands or even millions goes wrong, it is a big problem. A simple sensing device might measure heat or pressure and immediately transmit readings on a set basis back to a central application through the network with no preprocessing performed. This presents the potential for compromised or defective sensing devices to become threats to the IoT system, through what amounts to a denial of service (DoS) situation; or potentially the quality of data managed by the IoT service is degraded as a whole due to corrupted events being pushed into the system by such a compromised or defective device. For this reason, significant diligence will need to be applied to simple sensing devices before they go into operational deployment. Alternatively, gateways become the first powerful control point to manage risks from compromised or defective endpoints (see the next section).

At the other end of the spectrum will be more complex endpoints with data processing abilities. Such devices may be very powerful decision-making systems deployed at the periphery of the network to minimize the necessary amount of data "backhaul," and improve system performance. Unlike simple sensing endpoint devices, data processing devices will face a more complex threat environment because there is more to go wrong!

Managing risk in the IoT, from the perspective of the endpoint, will take on a different complexion from system to system depending on whether the endpoints are simple or complex. In all likelihood, the ability to apply controls and safeguards at the endpoint will also vary according to the simplicity or complexity of the endpoints. Simple devices will have limited abilities to enforce security, while more complex devices with configurable parameters, excess memory, and processor power should have a greater ability to support different levels of threat-mitigation according to the assessed risks.

---

[2]ITU Y.2060 – Overview of the Internet of Things—http://www.itu.int/rec/T-REC-Y.2060-201206-I/en.

GATEWAY ASSET CLASS IN THE IoT

Gateways in the IoT are special because they are either the boundary between two domains of control or the first network hop from the IoT device. This makes gateways a critical control point for a variety of security and risk management functions:

- As a boundary: a gateway might be the "edge" of the network managed by a large service provider. Everything past that point outward toward the endpoints in a network domain might be controlled by a different stakeholder, such as in the case of an enterprise or small business network, which is in turn used for local area networking of IoT devices.
- As the first network hop, a gateway might be cellular base stations or Wi-Fi access points in homes. The endpoint devices connect directly to the gateway, which is the way the endpoint connects to the Internet: the gateways are their portals to the networks that transport the data to and from the IoT device.

NOT JUST A PART OF THE NETWORK

Gateways are too important to the IoT to be considered *just* part of the network. In conventional enterprise architectures, the trinity of asset classes is simpler:

- Endpoints (desktops and servers)
- Network (routers, switches, firewalls, and infrastructure like Domain Name Service (DNS)
- DC/cloud services

In IoT architecture, there needs to be an evolution because the *new* IoT endpoints are far more diverse than the endpoints of conventional, legacy enterprise architecture.

IoT endpoints will be much more constrained and unable to protect themselves like desktops and servers can. IoT endpoints will be built to be more inexpensive and disposable than enterprise endpoints. Furthermore, there will be a huge range of IoT endpoint manufacturers and vendors, from toy makers to pharmaceutical firms. They will have hugely different abilities and interests to build secure devices. Even if they have the ability to create secure IoT devices, they may not wish to do so due to complexity and costs (more on this soon).

Gateways are typically much more powerful than the endpoint they support. They have more processing power, more memory and storage, access to power mains versus batteries or scavenging power from the environment. All these things also mean the ability to have access to faster networks. For these reasons, gateways become an information processing point, as well as a security control point in the IoT.

GATEWAYS AS INFORMATION PROCESSORS

Gateways will take information from IoT devices to *normalize* it, which can mean several things:

- To check for errors or corruption and correct these imperfections, or request new data from the endpoint before forwarding, through the network, to the cloud-based IoT service platforms and software.

- To add compression to reduce transport costs through the network.
- To apply encryption on the data before transport across the network to protect confidentiality, including identity and personally identifiable information.
- To remove malformed traffic that might be the result of endpoint compromise or defect.
- To support authentication processes between the endpoint and the cloud-based service platform because the device does not have sufficient resources to engage in strong processes that might be required across the Internet. Instead, the device uses lighter weight identity and access processes to connect to the gateway, which is expecting the devices. The gateway then acts as a security proxy, telling the centralized services that a device is enrolling or connected, based on *LAN-side* communication with the device itself.

GATEWAYS AS LOCALIZED INTRUSION PREVENTION AGENTS

Gateways will be critical security elements for protecting endpoints from threats associated with malicious *local* devices, as well as quality of service degradation due to resources like a local network that is shared with our endpoints.

For instance, the coming fifth generation (5G) cellular networks are broadly considered to support technical specifications such as 1 Gbps of wireless access bandwidth and 1 ms of communications latency.

These requirements in turn will make certain use cases like *smart transportation* (self-driving cars) and remote manipulation (telepresence, remote surgery, remote fine-motor operations, and so on) possible.

But to get to these type of performance capabilities for the endpoints, they will frequently need to be *locally switched* and have *local breakout*.

Local switching means that packets move between communicating endpoints without being passed back into the network, as is typical in many cellular networks today.

The packet comes off the radio, hits the gateways, and it is immediately sent back out the radio to the destination device, which is using the same gateway (see Fig. 2.3). This will be a very important part of the IoT, but it needs a lot of control to work in a secure manner.

An additional feature of the gateway in the IoT is that it will seek the shortest and especially the *cheapest* route to the Internet. This is frequently called *local breakout* (see Fig. 2.4). The importance of local breakout for RIoT is that traffic to and from the endpoint may bypass security that is applied in the wireless network.

NETWORK ASSET CLASS IN THE IoT

The network in the IoT, as shown in Fig. 2.2, will be composed of many different possible physical media and connection technologies (sometimes referred to as OSI "data layer—layer 2"—the layer below the "network layer—layer 3").

It is typical to discuss and describe network communication in terms of layers. Several layering models exist; the most commonly used are:

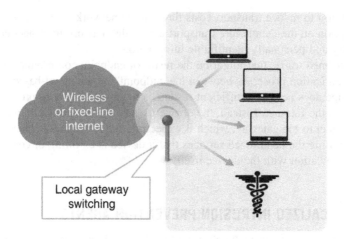

FIGURE 2.3

Local gateway switching.

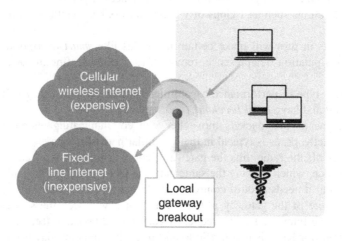

FIGURE 2.4

Local gateway breakout.

- Open System Interconnect (OSI) reference model, structured into seven layers (physical layer, data-link layer, network layer, transport layer, session layer, presentation layer, application layer)
- Transmission Control Protocol/Internet Protocol (TCP/IP) or Department of Defense (DoD) model (not to be confused with the TCP/IP protocols), structured into four layers (link layer, network layer, transport layer, application layer)

A common feature to both models is the concept of *encapsulation*: different layers operate independently from each other; however, these layers are also isolated on a technical level in that they are managed by distinct network elements. Short of technical failures, the contents of any lower- or higher-layer protocol are inaccessible from any particular layer. Going forward, we will frequently refer to the OSI model layers, reflecting industry convention.

OSI REFERENCE MODEL

The seven-layer OSI model shown in Fig. 2.5 was defined in 1984 and published as an international standard (ISO/IEC 7498-1). The last revision to this standard was in 1994.

While this system can appear complex, especially to laypeople, it provides a very useful and practical way to discuss network engineering. After a while, even a nontechnical manager will easily understand the difference between layer 2 (the point-to-point linkages like Ethernet and switching technology) and layer 3 (IP). In fact, you can get a very long way understanding only four of the seven layers (1, 2, 3, and 7). Additionally, some layers have proven to be less crucial to the concept (such as the presentation layer), while others (such as the transport and session layers) have required more specific structure, and possess overlapping and conflicting conditions for some of the protocols widely used on the Internet, such as Secure Socket Layer (SSL).

Layer 1, the physical layer, describes the networking hardware, such as electrical signals; and bits and bytes, such as network interfaces and cabling.

Layer 2, the data-link layer, describes data transfer among machines; for instance, by an Ethernet connection.

Layer 3, the network layer, describes data transfer among networks; for instance, by the IP.

Layer 4, the transport layer, describes data transfer among applications, flow control, and error detection and correction; for instance, by TCP/User Datagram Protocol (UDP).

Layer 5, the session layer, describes the handshake between applications; for instance, authentication processes.

Upper layers	7	Application layer ✓ Message format, human-machine interfaces
	6	Presentation layer ✓ Coding into 1s and 0s; encryption, compression
	5	Session layer ✓ Authentication, permissions, session restoration
Transport service	4	Transport layer ✓ End-to-end error control
	3	Network layer ✓ Network addressing; routing or switching
	2	Data link layer ✓ Error detection, flow control on physical link
	1	Physical layer ✓ Bit stream: physical medium, method of representing bits

FIGURE 2.5

OSI 7 layer model.

Layer 6, the presentation layer, describes the presentation of information, such as ASCII syntax. Layer 7, the application layer, describes the structure, interpretation, and handling of information. In security terms, it is relevant because it relies on all underlying layers.

THE MANY LAYERS OF DIFFERENT NETWORKS

Endpoint devices, gateways, and data centers in the IoT will use every conceivable type of network technology that exists today, and new ones will evolve to meet the emergent requirements for networking in the IoT.

In many cases the nature of the network technologies will be entirely transparent to the IoT application owners. They will "assume" connectivity and that the complexity of network technology will be largely hidden.

But understanding the risks in the IoT requires that managers have at least some notion of the manner in which the network as an entire asset class in the IoT actually works; not at a highly technical level, but at least conceptually. To do otherwise is committing the cardinal sin of risk management: accepting risk you do not understand at all.

Within the home, for example, a device in the IoT might collect telemetry information about an individual's health, initially transmitting the telemetry through a short-range wireless technology, covering just a few meters, to some sort of aggregation gateway. The telemetry might then get relayed to a medium range wireless network, which will extend several dozen meters to a residential gateway device interfacing with a fiber-to-the-home (FTTH) network.

In this example, the FTTH connection is the boundary in the IoT between the notionally private home network and the shared carrier network (more on this shortly). The fiber connection is the long-haul connection, probably moving the telemetry to within a few hundred meters of the application (in a data center) that will process it. Depending on the distance between the IoT endpoint and applications in the DC, a piece of data in the IoT could literally transit through dozens of networks. At the very least, data in the IoT will probably rarely see less than at least two distinct networks at layer 1 (physical layer) and layer 2 (data layer): the network that takes it to the data center where the applications resides, and the network inside the data center itself. Understanding such basic architectural realities is very useful when assessing and managing risk in the IoT.

LOTS OF MEDIA, BUT NOT NECESSARILY A LOT OF OPTIONS

The network is the critical infrastructure in the IoT. The network enables, makes, or breaks all the applications and value-added services within the IoT. And while endpoints, gateways, and data centers in the IoT are many, networks are few—or possibly even just one if viewed from the perspective of layer 3 in the OSI stack discussed previously. Even at layers 1 and 2 there will typically be few options available to any given device in the IoT. This is why the network is so important to risk management in the IoT; contrary to theory there are few options.

Why are there not a lot of options? Because first of all the IoT is made possible by one supereffective and efficient protocol at layer 3 (the network layer): IP. (Though, as previously discussed, it comes in two flavors or generations, v4 and v6, but it's all the same family.) While there might be a wide variety of application-level network protocols that support a wide variety of applications, there is really only one IP. Managing risk requires you get your IP right, because if you get it wrong the effects resonate through your systems and affect everything. Consequences of bad IP management are monumental in the IoT.

At layer 1 (the physical layer), there are usually several viable options available to any given devices, including multiple types of wireless (Wi-Fi, Bluetooth, ZigBee, cellular, satellite, and more), multiple types of fixed-line (phone lines for a digital subscriber line (DSL) and G.fast[3], or even analog modems, copper coaxial, RJ-45, fiber, and more) and possibly even optical (laser, infrared). Yet building and maintaining network interfaces in devices is expensive from both an initial investment perspective and from an operational perspective. Managers will need to balance the risk of losing the network with the costs of building and operating redundant networking interfaces and capabilities.

Many devices in the IoT will probably rely on a single interface to the network, or will at some point pass through a gateway device that relies on a single interface. Therefore the physical network interface is potentially the Achilles heel of some safety-critical IoT devices and applications because building in redundancy is too expensive in terms of capital expenditure, energy consumption, or operational cost. This is a threat, this single interface. More on this in Chapter 12, Threats and Impacts to the IoT.

At layer 2 (the data-link layer), much the same situation exists but is most frequently tied to the selection and number of physical interfaces (fixed line versus wireless interfaces primarily), therefore compounding the issues of capital (one-time) and operational (on-going) costs and energy consumption. It is common for different physical interfaces to support unique layer 2 protocols, which have been developed to support the physical barer network. For instance, a copper phone line will commonly use DSL while a fourth-generation (4G) cellular connection will employ a variant of Orthogonal Frequency Division Multi-access (OFDM). These are, as you might imagine, completely different layer 2 protocols and require their own software and/or hardware. Again, the more resilient the IoT manager or designer makes access to the network from the endpoint, the more expensive it becomes.

IP AND REDUCED-CALORIE IP

At layer 3, the problem of choice is probably less acute than at the lower levels in the protocol stack because there is little choice: it is IP. There are exceptions, however, where different flavors of IP come into play depending on the distance from the network center or the application itself. Basically, at the far ends of the IoT, a *lite* version of IP will be found. These lite versions are designed to consume fewer resources than regular IP, but at a price. Understanding the price of lite IP is also part of managing risk in the IoT.

A variety of different forms of IP-lite will be found at the edges of the network to support resource-constrained devices. These devices will often be sensors that are embedded into specific physical infrastructures and are running on battery power or perhaps scavenging energy from the environment. They might also be disposable devices that are made to be cheap and therefore have minimal capabilities other than their basic functions, such as sensing. Therefore, manufacturers will employ every means available to extend the life and reduce the cost of these devices; this means reducing the processing loads generated by the network stack on the device, which in turn means

---

[3]https://en.wikipedia.org/wiki/G.fast.

making networking protocols simpler. Simpler can also mean less secure and more prone to attack, which is where the IoT risk manager needs to propose the appropriate balance.

Different manufacturers will propose different networking means and ways of getting data from low-power, remote devices to a gateway that speaks *proper* IP and can communicate with the Internet and the get data to the applications probably sitting in data centers. Some of these means and ways will be based on known and documented forms of lite IP, such as 6LowPan from the Internet Engineering Task Force (IETF): IPv6 for low power personal area networks. Other ways and means will be developed by manufacturers as proprietary solutions.

LOW-CAL IS NOT NECESSARILY BETTER

Dealing with the matter of custom-made IP-lite solutions at the ends of the IoT will be a serious problem of risk managers in the IoT. First, how will you know if custom solutions are out there? Manufacturers will probably gloss over this aspect and just call it all *IP networking*, when what they really mean is they have a gateway for their remote devices that is I/O-enabled according to spec, but the side of the gateway facing the endpoint devices is speaking some sort of customized solution. Assuming that such proprietary solutions are out there, how will managers know they are secure of the risks associated with them? It is possible to request security audits and certificates and all sorts of other assurance, but in the end a nonstandard solution is never preferred. IP and the IETF lite-variants have gone through considerable real-world testing, which all drives toward their predictability from a security perspective.

ABOVE AND BEYOND IP

Beyond layer 3, a multitude of choices come into play for application designers and managers. Many of these choices can improve or sabotage the security and therefore the risk in the IoT.

The variety of these choices between layer 4 and layer 5 is substantial, with error controls and encryption typically being applied at this point in the network stack. For instance, TCP, the bread and butter of the Internet protocols, is a layer 4 protocol. But there are alternatives to TCP, primarily UDP, but certainly there are yet more alternatives and of course space for doppelganger, custom protocols, too.

Protocols commonly found at layer 5 include such favorites as hypertext transport protocol (HTTP) and SSL, both of which are well understood and are frequently employed together. But again, it is entirely possible that manufacturers or IoT application developers or integrators elect to use custom-developed protocols, with unspecified risks.

This is one of the main issues with security and risk management of the network in the IoT; what are the protocols being used below layer 7? Because these protocols are often obscured from all but the most technical elements, and potentially managed by different service providers, it is a confusing matter to approach for managers of risk. We will discuss some of these risks further in this book, but the basic piece of information that is required to start managing risk in the network support the IoT is: what is nonstandard? What is customized in this network, between the endpoint and the data center?

AT THE APPLICATION LAYER

What about the application level, layer 7? Are protocols at this level as critical to managing risk in the IoT? First, at layer 7, you don't so much have communications protocols as just data formats. How is information organized so the application can receive and understand it once it comes off the network?

The application level refers to the applications that sit on top of the network and use the networks to get their data from one endpoint to another—such as a server.

While IP is central to managing risk in the IoT at large, where an attack against the network protocols at layers 1 to 5 will affect all applications using the network, application-level attacks will largely limit their impact on the application itself, or, by extension, the operating platforms that the application resides upon. For this reason, responsibility for managing risk in the IoT might be reasonably divided between the network owners and the application owners. While there is no hard and fast rule, it is fair to say that layers 1 to 5 will frequently be in the domain of the network people, while layers 6 and 7 will be in the domain of the application people running the centralized services in the data center and perhaps the application-level security at the remote endpoints.

THE NETWORK IS THE DIAL TONE

Even kids understand what *dial tone* is—for now. Unlike cellular phones, land-line phones play a tone as soon as you pick up the receiver to indicate that the line is working and ready. (Conversely, you don't get dial tone with cell phones because they don't want to waste precious power and radio spectrum until you have actually dialed your number). In the IoT, the network needs to be like dial tone—always there—to the point that we don't even really think about it, much like real dial tone. It is pretty much always there (unless Dad forgets to pay the bill or cuts it with a shovel while digging a new flower bed. But that is his fault, not the network's fault).

Dial tone is something we have come to assume. The IP network, like dial tone, is something we assume (someone else is taking care of it). In the IoT, risk associated with the network connecting the endpoints collecting and generating information to the data center and applications processing and adding value to the information will come in two general flavors: those you manage and control and those you don't manage and control.

THE NETWORK YOU KNOW VERSUS THE NETWORK YOU DON'T

It is better to deal with known evils than unknown evils, the old adage goes: "The devil you know versus the devil you don't." So it is with information technology, including endpoints, data centers, and networks. However, in the case of the IoT, it will very frequently be the case that dealing with the devil you don't know is absolutely required because creating and supporting you own network is not economically viable. For instance, an IoT application looking to gather data even more than a couple of kilometers or miles from the data center will often be compelled to use network services from a service provider. It is how these service providers manage their network that affects risk in the IoT.

Network service providers act as aggregators of traffic and networking business cases, meaning they combine the needs and investment abilities of millions of subscribers to come out with a single menu of services and shared costs. They take the communications needs and requirements of sub-scribers, find the lowest common denominator of service-levels, and then manage and charge according to these service levels. Usually, the cost at which service is provided is so superior to the cost of building a network unilaterally that applications will be designed with the network service levels in mind. This is all very reasonable and rational. And, this is the process and business model that has made the Internet viable after all!

THE NETWORK IS A COMMONS

While local area networks (LANs), in-building networks, and short-hop networks (less than a cou-ple of kilometers) will often be privately owned and operated by your IT staff, the network that joins these local networks will usually be provided by a telecommunications service provider with a business case founded on the shared nature of the infrastructure. Many clients are served through the same network devices The same copper, fiber, or radio links for all. The same switchers, rou-ters, name servers, and network access control system. The same switching closets, central offices, and underground conduits. The same technicians, help desks, and managers all support the vast array of subscribers supported by the service provider. This means that managing IoT risk associ-ated with networks is like sleeping with an elephant.

A former prime minister of Canada said that "living next to the United States of America was like sleeping with an elephant": every twitch and spasm is felt and potentially dangerous. The same can be said about the relationship between IoT application owners and the network asset class that depend upon but have relatively reduced control over the networks that underlie their IoT services and applications.

When things happen to the network service providers, the repercussions can be felt keenly. While this fact may seem elementary, it reflects a disproportionate relationship; for instance, the rapidly maturing expectations and requirements of the IoT around service levels versus the slower-maturing capabilities and sensitivities of telecommunications service providers.

Service providers may not be adequately geared or provisioned to support the IoT, and as a result, will make changes or offer service levels that inject risk into the IoT without understanding this is a consequence: sleeping with the elephant.

When the network is a commons, shared by the multiple and diverse clients of the network ser-vice provider, then needs are aggregated to arrive at service levels that balance the possible with the affordable. What level of service can be provided, and sold to the largest number of subscribers successfully? It is possible from an engineering perspective to build and manage a network with the coveted "five nines" (99.999%) of availability—which translates to just a few minutes per year of excusable delay; but there are big costs associated with this type of service. While there are no clear or definitive models of how costs escalate as service level targets climb toward five nines, the Law of Diminishing Returns is known to kick in beyond three nines.[4] That is to say that the costs of providing four nines will be at least twice (200%) that of three nines, and the cost of providing five nines will be four times (400%) that of three nines, as shown in Table 2.1. In terms of actual,

---

[4]Approximately, the law of diminishing returns states that past a certain point, equal levels of investment yield (very) rapidly declining levels of benefit.

Table 2.1 Availability Targets Expressed as Time			
	Downtime		
Availability	**Per year**	**Per month**	**Per day**
99.9%	8.76 h	43.8 min	10.1 min
99.99%	52.56 min	4.32 min	1.01 min
99.999%	5.26 min	25.9 s	6.05 s

guaranteed service levels over one month, the difference between three and five nines service levels is a few "guaranteed" minutes per day versus less than a second per day.

Bear in mind, too, that the service level guarantee between three and five nines for networks supporting the IoT or any other service does not mean the network will actually be out for the period each day/month/year. Many service providers routinely surpass service levels month after month, without additional charge to clients. But this is essentially luck because the systems are not engineered reliably to provide those service levels.

More importantly for those assessing and managing risk related to the IoT, service level guarantees are not open-ended acceptance of liability from service providers. In fact, it is the opposite. Typically, service levels are backed-up by simple refunds and credits. So even if the service were to fail—whether three nines or five nines—there is little recourse or compensation available to IoT service providers associated with the failure of the network (short of third-party insurance). Having said that, network service providers will typically strive heroically to meet and maintain service levels because the reputational risks of repeated service level failures has a corrosive effect on business. But you get what you pay for, even in the ethereal world of networks.

NETWORK COSTS ARE A BUSINESS RISK, TOO

Few application owners in the IoT are likely to pay willingly for the service levels they want. That is to say, pay for five nines of network availability at 400 percent the cost of three nines; especially when three nines is the worst-case estimate from the service provider. This 400% number is just an estimate, but it reflects the widely known fact that higher availability requires substantially more and more investment and costs the closer you drive to near complete (100%) availability. Achieving 100% availability is for most a theoretical goal, not a real goal. There is always something, some unknown or unaddressed or emergent (newly evolved) risk that will sooner or later bring even the best, most resilient systems down. At the very least, systems will generally need to be taken offline for maintenance at some point during their operational lifetime. Risk managers in the IoT need to understand and factor for these outages, not only because they are bound to occur no matter how much you spend, but the costs of trying to avoid them may make the application or system unviable.

THE NETWORK TIDES ARE CHANGING

The Internet of today is the opposite of the Internet of tomorrow. This reflects the fact that the data flows within the IoT are the opposite of the data flows in the contemporary Internet. The reversal of the network tides has profound effects on the approach to managing risks in the IoT, if for no other reason than many assumptions must be revised about the Internet over what has been an essentially stable model since its birth to the World Wide Web over 20 years ago.

Today, data moves mostly from large centralized servers in the data centers outward, to the endpoints. Desktop and mobile devices operated by people consume information and services. As a result of this model, many of the access technologies in the Internet have been designed with higher download capacities than upload capacities. Similarly, resilience and redundancy efforts have focused on the central elements in the network, the elements further out toward the endpoints would typically become lower and lower in their availability characteristics because they were generally pure consumers of information and data. They did not drive enough value back into the network to warrant significant investment in security and risk management.

The flow of data in the evolving IoT changes for reasons illustrated in Fig. 2.6. The vertical axis represents the characteristics of data associated with cycles or pattern of flow. Is the data constantly flowing or coming in predictable or unpredictable bursts? The horizontal axis indicates the size of the files being moved. Are they large files or small files—large chunks of data representing a "whole" piece of information, or small chunks of data that represent a complete piece of information.

The original "killer apps" that drove the fantastic growth of the Internet were Internet data (web and email primarily), video (YouTube† and other streaming services like Netflix†) and voice (VOIP services like Skype† and Vonage†). These applications are generally composed of relatively large files that were sent and received on demand by human users; therefore the traffic is cyclical—typically during the working day and early evening. For this reason they are in the top right quadrant.

The current and first generation of IoT applications are different from the original applications. Closed-circuit television (CCTV) and other forms of video surveillance and monitoring have found their way onto IP and the Internet and consist of large files flowing from the endpoints into the network on a constant basis. Similarly, POS applications are now widely using the Internet and

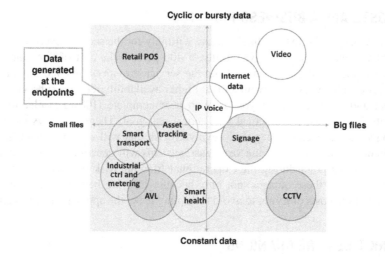

FIGURE 2.6

Data flows into the IoT.

IP-based systems to send relatively small messages about financial transactions, synchronized with business hours typically, with data also being generated at the remote endpoints and flowing into data centers for processing and clearing. A third contemporary form of IoT application is automated vehicle location (AVL). In this case, the endpoints are generating constant flows of some pieces of data (coordinates and identifiers), which go back to centralized applications. Again, the data flow itself is reversed from the original Internet conventions.

The high-growth future of the IoT applications is likely to involve applications like asset tracking of many kinds of devices, not just cars and trucks; all sorts of remote industrial controls and meters, including smart electricity grids and energy management systems; smart transportation, including planes, trains, and automobiles that speak to each other to coordinate movements in a way that is much more efficient and probably safer than having human controls doing everything; and certainly smart health applications, which monitor health conditions and probably apply treatments on a semiautomated or even an automated basis. All these IoT applications will be net creators of telemetry and information about the systems and processes they are monitoring and managing, sending much more data into the network than they receive from the network.

In the evolved IoT, data flows from the remote endpoints toward the central data centers and data processing elements. This is the reverse of what we have grown up with on the Internet. In the IoT, the billions of new endpoint devices on the network become the creators and transmitters of data, not consumers of data. As a direct result, a fundamental new risk condition arises: the entire network becomes much more important from a security and resilience perspective. From the remotest parts of the network to the center, security and risks must be managed in a much more comprehensive manner.

THE NETWORK IS GOING *WHITE BOX* AND *OPEN SOURCE*

Networks to data have been running on open standards and open protocols since the beginning. IP is open, for instance, as are TCP and HTTP. But the operating systems running the routers and switches that are the backbone of the Internet have been closed-source, proprietary solutions based on hardware appliances with specialized chips sets for fast processing. This means that the actual platforms of the Internet have been virtualized. This is changing as network processing is moving to generalized enterprise processing platforms based on Intel server chips.

This is known as *white box*—meaning that the chips and elements in the box are based on known, off-the-shelf components. White boxes are seen to possess many benefits. White box is now possible because general purpose processing has approached the speed and effectiveness of custom processing chips in network processing. The cost of generalized processing chips is much lower due to economies of scale than custom or specialized network processing chips, rendering them a more economical option.

White boxes are claimed to be significantly less expense from a capital perspective than proprietary black boxes,[5] where *black box* means the internals are not known or understood, only the functions are important. With white boxes, because the hardware and processing platform is known and based on the x86 Intel architecture, many people and vendors know how to develop software.

---

[5]http://blogs.gartner.com/andrew-lerner/2014/11/19/britefuture/.

More sources of software means not only many potential alternative vendors and solutions for network software but also the ability to go open source.

Open source in the network can come as open source router or switch software, which means that the cost of the software becomes *zero* as it is publicly developed and maintained. However, there is usually some cost to open source in the form of support services, which are available on a commercial basis. Red Hat is the most famous example of open source, commercial support, where the software is free, but if you need support—which all professional business tends to want—then that must be purchased. Yet the cost of buying open source support is typically well below the cost of buying commercial, closed source software (and the accompanying support).

Open source is also entering the network in the Network Function Virtualization (NFV). We will talk more about NFV later in this book. NFV can refer to network capabilities that are not based on a specific hardware appliance like a router or switch, but are accomplished all in software and managed by a generalized processor that is also used to run applications and software versus special chips. NFV exists in the data center, where software-based networking has existed for a while, but using proprietary solutions like VMware or Microsoft's HyperV.

In the network, NFV and white box solutions are being developed, using open source software platforms like Linux, KVM hypervisors, and software-based routers. The proof that these open source, white box network solutions are fundamentally changing the network can be found in announcements from major carriers like AT&T, which says that by 2020, it expects 75% of its network to be virtualized.

Open source and white box virtualization of the network will come up many times in this book as a boon and bane to the IoT: a boon because it will enable many new forms of security for the IoT in a highly effective and efficient manner, and a bane because it will introduce complexity and a broad new attack surface.

CLOUD AND DATA CENTER AS AN ASSET CLASS

Finally we get to the part of the system layer we are calling the DC or the cloud. The DC need not have a monolithic definition; it can be varied in the sense that it might be both real and physical or virtual. A "virtual" DC is typically referred to as a *cloud* and might be operated by third-party service providers as a shared, multi-tenanted resource. Fundamentally, a cloud or a DC is the place where the *big data* that has been gathered at the IoT endpoints and transported through the network goes to be processed, stored, or otherwise managed. For the purposes of our discussion over the next few pages, we will refer to the cloud, although the asset could in fact be a traditional DC as well.

BIG DATA AND THE IoT

Big data lives in the cloud, and is essentially a cloud problem that is becoming acute most rapidly because of the advent of the IoT. All those smart devices and machines out there collecting telemetry on people, places, and things, and often executing negotiations about geospatial events and movements and therefore (hopefully) logs about these negotiations, are feeding a cloud somewhere. How do we know this for sure? Because these devices are too small to accommodate such data, and health, safety, customer relations, and liability (if not direct regulation) will require that much of this data be saved.

Big data is not a problem for endpoints—they just do their job creating vast amount of *small data* which, when combined, grow into a big challenge. The math is actually pretty simple: if you have one million sensors embedded in streetlights in a state so they can be made energy efficient, and they each produce a half kilobyte (500 bytes) packet of data every minute about their on/off state, energy consumption/brightness, and time to probable failure, then you get 72 GB a day (20 DVDs) of log data just from streetlights. How to manage and store this data is a big data problem.

Big data is not a problem for the network, necessarily. Though moving (for example) 72 GB every day just for streetlight management might seem like an undue load on the network, the network can be flexible in a number of ways. First, adding capacity to the network, through the advent of fiber optics, means reconfiguring or at worst replacing the switches and routers at central junction points; it does not require replacing the fiber, because its theoretical limits are, well, limitless. Light, like numbers, can be divided into ever smaller channels (defined by wavelengths or colors), which all share the same fiber at the same time. The problem with network capacity will most likely lie in getting data from the most remote sensors to the first fiber gateway. Networks up to this first gateway are definitely a challenge to be addressed and will be discussed subsequently as potential operational risks to be considered in the design of IoT applications and services.

DEFINE CLOUD IN THIS DAY AND AGE: CALL IT A DARE

As a risk manager in the IoT, understanding the nature of the cloud in a given IoT application or service is critical for a variety of reasons. The simplest reason of all is that is where your data lives. In many cases the data will represent huge value to organizations; it will be intellectual property, it will be strategy and planning, trade secrets, and to a lesser extent may contain regulated data such as financial information or personally identifiable information.

The data in the cloud may also be more of a record of what has happened in the course of creating value in the IoT. It is a log of the smart transportation operations or the smart health telemetry that led to a certain decision. In these cases the value of the IoT application may lie primarily in the real-time execution of an operation or near-real-time provision of a service, such as a location-based service.

However, even data that is basically a record of what has happened in the course of adding value has plenty of value itself. In this day and age of big data, we have ever-growing analytical capabilities associated with mining massive datasets that reflect what has happened, versus affecting or managing what is about to happen. These analytics and the data scientists who are performing them are finding new value in old data, and this value is stored in the DC.

As a risk manager in the IoT, recognizing the latent value of the contents of the cloud is critical, because that affects the risks that must be managed and can cast the vulnerabilities of the cloud in a different light. In later chapters we will be dealing with the threats, vulnerabilities, and risks associated with the cloud.

In this section we will seek to make the reader acquainted with the broad range of resources that might be considered a DC or cloud and some of the defining characteristics that can produce novel risks.

PRIVATE AND DEDICATED: BEFORE THE CLOUD

Since the beginning of computing up until less than 15 years ago, all DCs were pretty well private and dedicated to a given organization. From huge entities like banks, governments, and multinationals to the smallest mom-and-pop business that used computers, everyone had his or her own DC.

This DC might have been everything we expect a DC to be now—with raised floors and uninterruptible power and heating, ventilation, and air conditioning (HVAC); but it might also have been little more than a corner of a closet where the servers and maybe a network switch sat. In either case, the systems were used exclusively for the business of their owners and all the data on the systems belonged to the people who owned and operated the DC, from the floor tiles to the ceiling tiles. Sure, systems of timesharing on large mainframe computers have been around for a long time, but even those situations were essentially exclusive arrangements to borrow or rent resources from an owner for a specific period and for a specific purpose.

For a risk manager in these days of dedicated infrastructure, the DC was by no means a simple thing to manage. But the fact that it was dedicated to the organization and its data meant that many awkward questions about shared access to physical and logical assets within the DC could be addressed more easily. All the data had the same fundamental owner, and all people with access worked for the same organization. Access controls are still important inside dedicated DCs—much more so now than previously due to the emergence of more rigorous management standards—but certain threat and risk assumptions about security with a single owner-operator are more easily justified.

This situation of a dedicated DC started to change radically in the late 1990s as virtualization first started to take hold. *Virtualization* for the purposes of this current discussion refers to the ability for a computer platform (hardware processor, memory, power supply, and so on) to be shared by many different instances of operating systems, applications, and even network functions running only in software. Previously, it was about one server and one operating system, and whatever applications happened to be installed on that operating system. With virtualization, one server could be used to host many instances of many operating systems and applications, which would appear to the applications and their users to be running on dedicated hardware platforms. In fact they were sharing *virtually* dedicated operating systems. Almost all the same logical isolation principles applied, though shared computing resources meant that it became possible for one virtual system to hog and consume resources to the detriment of the other systems. But this was manageable.

The other element of virtualization that completely changed the DC world and ushered in the world of cloud computing was the ability not only to share processing and memory across many virtualized operating systems and applications, but the ability to add to the horsepower available for processing and memory on the fly. This is the property of virtualization that allows resources to be added without the requirement to reinstall the operating systems because they have been virtualized already and essentially decoupled from hardware. This decoupling of the systems and applications from hardware processing and memory is at the heart of virtualization. For risk managers, it also introduced new threats and vulnerabilities as the old assumptions about a single owner of the data and the infrastructure collecting and managing the data collapsed. For the risk manager in the IoT, understanding the risks associated with the virtualized, cloud-based DC is critical because, given the volumes of data generated by the IoT, there is no prospect of reverting to a much more costly, entirely dedicated DC paradigm.

CLOUDS

When it comes to DCs, it is often a matter of choosing which type of *cloud* that is appropriate for your IoT application. While it is still possible to use dedicated DCs, fewer and fewer organizations are electing to pursue the expense, as the availability, price, and presumably the security of shared cloud environments improve.

Because this is a book about risk management and security, let's quickly home in on the statement about security in the previous paragraph: why is it getting better?

Fundamentally, experience among cloud operators has led to more knowledge about the threats and risks facing clouds, and this knowledge is being fed back into training and standardization efforts. A wide variety of cloud-security training is available from the various self-organizing security-certification bodies, both old and new. On the standardization front, cloud security has been a hot topic for a while and the first generation of truly international cloud security standards are now being published. For the risk manager in the IoT, cloud security awareness and training will be critical.

However, much is happening to confound the assumption that cloud security is improving. While virtualization has become a known technology, it is itself changing:

- *NFV*: More functions are being virtualized, including network functions like firewalls and intrusion prevention systems that were formerly appliances.
- *Internal segmentation*: Internal to clouds, *segmentation* is taking hold, where different tenant machines are logically grouped and separated into distinct control domains.
- *Containerization*: New forms of virtualization known as *containerization* are driving new vendors into the cloud ecosystem and seeing many more small instances of virtual machines being used to replace large monolithic applications.
- *Software-defined networking*: Software-defined networking has entered the cloud, allowing for new forms of automation and on-demand provisioning of services.

All these things will increase the attack surface and generate additional complexity, and therefore risk, in the management of clouds.

APPARENTLY SIMPLE. NOT.

Clouds in the IoT are not uniform or simple in design or functionality. They are available in many shapes, forms, and fashions and the type of cloud purchased for the management of IoT data is important.

The importance in the selection of cloud technology lies in the fact that more or less risk will be transferred to third-party operators depending on what type of cloud is produced. This is a key concept in risk management anywhere, not just is the IoT.

Risk management is about treating risks, transferring risks, or accepting risks. The trick when it comes to the IoT, clouds, and DCs, is to understand what the balance is among those choices when you make a choice to buy. Later is a very quick rundown on what risks lie where in the world of clouds and the IoT. More references will be found in the section on standards.

A basic taxonomy has evolved to describe the different sorts of clouds that might be build or procured. This taxonomy consists of three different genres of cloud: IaaS, PaaS, and SaaS.

Infrastructure as a Service

Infrastructure as a Service (IaaS) refers to the *bare metal* sort of cloud arrangement where a third-party DC provider will supply floor space, heat, power, network, processors, and storage—but little else. IaaS means that you, as the IoT application owner, will be responsible for installing the operating system and any applications you might wish. As is the case with most any type of cloud service, you will also be responsible for account management of the users of any application on the system.

It is most important to understand what is not part of IaaS, which is security. Let's start with the network that provides access to the IaaS, but doesn't have DoS protection—make sure you ask before you buy. And what about firewalls and intrusion prevention system (IPS) on the DC gateway? Is that provided? What about inside the DC itself, including any soft-switching fabric that accompanies most virtualized systems in modern DCs. More on this in our coming discussion of vulnerabilities and risk management in the IoT.

Next, the operating system; this, too, will be the responsibility of the entity procuring IaaS services. The operating system will probably be entirely up to the application owners because most of the IaaS infrastructure is relatively generic in order to host any type of operating system (OS) that a client may want: many flavors of Linux, Windows, and even MacOS. This means that the application owner needs to be very careful to guard and maintain the OS, applying probably the same degree of rigor as if the DC were purely private, especially if the IaaS provider does not bundle any firewall or intrusion detection services with the IaaS itself. As a risk manager in the IoT, OS management in an IaaS environment is something to be monitored carefully.

Finally, the IoT application itself may sit on the operating system that has been installed to support it in the IaaS. As is the case with the OS, the security of the application will usually rest entirely with the owner of the application because the service is only to provide infrastructure. Hardening and securing applications is not necessarily any harder than securing operating systems; however, the more customized the application, the more difficult it may be to assess actual risk because custom applications likely have had less developmental testing and trial by fire than commercially supported applications. In any event, attacks on the application layer of the IoT service can be every bit as effective as any attacks on the operating system on the infrastructure.

IaaS therefore sees risk around the network and hardware performance *transferred* from the application owner to the IaaS provider, while risks associated with the operating system and applications must be treated or accepted by the application owner.

Platform as a Service

Platform as a Service (PaaS) refers to an online capability that will include the infrastructure (IaaS) as well as the platform for the applications (in IoT or otherwise).

The *platform* is code/jargon for the operating system for the most part: Linux variants like Red Hat, SUSE, and Ubuntu (open-source Unix), Unix (closed source Unix-systems like Solaris), various Windows servers, and just about any other form of operating system that can be provisioned within a virtualized environment. The *provisioned* part is noteworthy for risk managers in the IoT because virtualization relies on a key technology known as *hypervisors* that manage the different operating system images that may be sharing a common (IaaS) platform. Not all hypervisors will reliably support all operating systems.

Some large PaaS service providers (DC providers) are also known to customize them or *roll their own* hypervisors to aid in the operational efficiency of their IaaS; unfortunately, this may conflict with an ability reliably to support a wide range of operating systems for the purposes of PaaS. To the extent an application into the IoT wants to take advantage of the economies of PaaS, it needs to be supported by an operating system that comes with service levels from the DC provider or the maker of the hypervisor technology.

Hypervisors can be critical to the assurance and risk within the IoT because an incompatibility between and an operating system and a hypervisor can lead to a range of failures, some predictable and other less predictable. The only way effectively to manage risk is to stay within the warranty of the vendor or support community and match operating systems to hypervisors. For this reason, it is worth mentioning the major providers and products in order to ensure that everyone understands exactly what we are talking about: VMware† from VMware, Citrix† from Citrix Corp, and MSCloud† from Microsoft represent a major portion of the commercial, proprietary market while a kernel-based virtual machine (KVM) is an example of an open-source hypervisor that may be found within third-party DC services.

Software as a Service

Software as a Service (SaaS) refers to an (IoT) application that is delivered to multiple independent *tenants* who will also share the platform and the infrastructure supporting the system. SaaS is a very widely known model that many people's use without understanding what they are using. For instance, Facebook, Google, LinkedIn, and Wikipedia are all SaaS applications.

From a risk management perspective, SaaS often represents challenges because such services are essentially utility services intended to host a large body of users, based on a limited and predefined range of possible configuration choices. This, of course, includes security configurations, controls, and safeguards.

SaaS in the IoT will present opportunities for efficiencies and economies related to the management and processing of the vast data volumes to be generated by the endpoints; however, it will also present risks to the IoT. Specifically, risks that must generally be accepted if the SaaS utility is to be used, or costly alternatives pursued. Much more on this in Chapter 12, Threats and Impacts to the IoT and Chapter 13, RIoT Control.

ARCHITECTURAL AND BUSINESS MODELS OF THE CLOUD

Cloud and DCs (in the virtual sense of DC that we have been using throughout our discussion) have another dimension in addition to the IaaS, PaaS, and SaaS service dimension. The DC, being virtualized, can be distributed *technically* and *commercially* but remain apparently whole and undivided to the end-user and the IoT applications that it supports. This ability to appear as a single entity while in fact being fragmented technically adds complexity to the risk manager's job. The better we become at developing and supporting cloud-based resources to grow and evolve the IoT, the more risks are pushed below the waterline and consciousness of the users and owners of the IoT application or service.

TECHNICALLY DISTRIBUTED CLOUDS

Technical distribution of DC resources means that the processing power behind the services (IaaS, PaaS, SaaS) might be spread across multiple, physically distinct data centers but appear uniform to the applications. In other words, computing resources (infrastructure) that are physically separated but connected by fast networks can appear as a single resource to applications. Applications may be replicated among these locations and data are selectively processed wherever the capacity is most available and latency (due to network transport) is the lowest.

From a cost perspective, being able to separate physical infrastructure from processing requirements offers huge advantages, because work can go where there is excess capacity even if that capacity is on the other side of the world!

From the perspective of the risk manager in the IoT, understanding where your data resides physically is important, especially if there are national borders involved. Depending on the jurisdiction, lawful access requirements may provide for legal but not necessarily authorized access to information and data. In the IoT, this can amount to many different sorts of threats to both proprietary commercial data and personal information.

The other thing to understand about the technical distribution of cloud capacity is that data may travel through a variety of physical networks while it is being *balanced* across DC infrastructure. It is possible that the DC infrastructure would be located in jurisdictions that are amenable and friendly to the IoT application owners and operators, but the transit network owners are less benign. Therefore the route of the data moving through distributed clouds can be as important to understand as the location of the actual processing and storage equipment. For instance, there was a well-documented incident in 2010 where all Internet traffic in the Asia-Pacific region was (accidentally?) routed through China for a short period of time, making all unencrypted traffic visible to putative observers in that country, and definitely making traffic pattern analysis on all senders and receivers possible.[6]

COMMERCIALLY DISTRIBUTED DCs AND *CLOUD BROKERS*

By *commercially distributed*, we mean that while the technology may be the same or at least interoperable, the owners and operators of the platform may be commercially as well as physically distinct. In other words, an application in the IoT may be placed into a cloud/DC that is not only spread geographically, but also operated by different entities.

Why would you do such a thing as spread your application across not only geographic sites but different commercial providers? Because of the cost saving.

Many organizations have large computing clouds that see periods of very low activity and utilization, and they are seeking to get more return on their investments. For this reason, they have started to open their clouds up to third-party applications and processes during low or off-peak periods, essentially renting out their clouds. Examples of these sorts of cloud or DC landlords are universities, retailers, or even motion picture houses; all have significant peak demands for their internal applications, but also regular and even scheduled down time. Rather than keeping their cloud resources idle, they rent them out. However, these businesses are not professional landlords. Like individuals who buy rental properties at ski resorts or in the city, they turn to specialized property-management firms. These cloud-property-management firms are one form of cloud broker.

---

[6]http://www.washingtontimes.com/news/2010/nov/15/internet-traffic-was-routed-via-chinese-servers/.

For the purposes of the IoT and supporting the large data processing requirements generated by the IoT, there are at least two types of cloud broker: aggregating brokers and arbitrage brokers.[7] (There is also a third sort related to managing the identity and access controls to cloud services, which is typically out of scope of even SaaS. However, given that much of the IoT is about machines that possess a single identity—unlike people with many identities and logins—we are not going to dive into the rather large topic of single-sign-on and identity management on the Internet.)

AGGREGATING BROKERS AND THE IoT

An aggregating broker may provide services or software or both, to enable applications to run across a selected set of cloud service providers (CSP). An aggregator may work with an IoT owner to identify the CSPs appropriate to the necessary security and performance requirement of the IoT application and then act as the glue that makes these services appear as a single unified resource to the application itself. An aggregator may also provide additional tools and warranties related to security and risk management that make one of the underlying CSPs security-compliant, where they may not be based just on the standard commercial offering. An interesting example of an aggregating broker is found in the US government, where a single entity has been assigned to validate the security of CSPs and act as the approving brokers for procurement by all federal agencies, for use with public information.[8]

For the purposes of risk management in the IoT, aggregating brokers might be quite useful. They can perform services associated with matching security and reporting requirements with different CSP vendor solutions in a faster and more efficient manner than trying to accomplish the same delicate task with internal resources, which may not be specialized in CSP management and affairs. Also, certain risks might be effectively transferred to the aggregating brokers through service level agreements and other contractual covenants, effectively outsourcing part of the cloud and DC risk to a party potentially more qualified to manage it and adding value at the same time.

ARBITRAGE BROKERS

Arbitrage is seeking the best price for a commodity good or service, among district market places. For instance, if gasoline can be bought in country X for $1 a gallon and in country Y for $1.10 a gallon, then there is an arbitrage opportunity to buy gasoline in X and sell in Y—and keep the $0.10 difference. The same sorts of conditions may apply among CSPs because the spot price for compute cycles and storage may vary from CSP to CSP. These variances might be due to the time of day, prevailing economic conditions, national holidays and festivals, or any other factor that might reduce demand in one place in the world to a point lower than another place. Assuming that the cloud resources are comparable and the network capacity is sufficient, an arbitrage opportunity exists to move processing tasks from a higher cost to a lower cost infrastructure and distribute the savings between the application owners and the cloud brokers.

---

[7]Gartner Says Cloud Consumers Need Brokerages to Unlock the Potential of Cloud Services http://www.gartner.com/newsroom/id/1064712.

[8]http://fcw.com/articles/2013/04/16/disa-cloud-contracts.aspx.

In the world of the IoT, this might amount to heavy data processing tasks being shifted from one CSP to another in a seamless manner as costs change. The savings through such a scheme could potentially be substantial, perhaps reducing operational costs on large processing tasks by many percentage points.

However, as any risk manager knows, when the focus shifts too heavily to trimming a few points off operating or capital costs, it is typical that the security and assurance profiles change, and not for the better. It is not uncommon for the application owner to end up accepting more risk as the services being procured become cheaper. This is not always the case, especially when cost reductions are the result of technical and productivity advances, but risk managers need to be sure. This especially is the case of cloud brokers engaging in arbitrage to reduce costs, where costs are really the driving factor for moving information and processes from one location to another. And, also in the case where high degrees of automation are required to make the arbitrage processes efficient. As we will discuss in the Chapter 12 on Threats and Impacts to the IoT, highly complex systems (like the Internet) overlaid with even more complex systems (like cloud computing arbitrage brokers) create chaotic or difficult-to-predict environments in which to practice risk assessment. Add a third layer of IoT applications on top of the Internet and cloud services and the complexity increases even more.

ONE MORE IMPORTANT THING ABOUT CLOUDS AND DCs IN THE IoT

One very important thing to note about clouds, despite what type you elect to buy, it that brute DoS protection is almost always the scope of the third-party service provider, whether you are consuming IaaS, PaaS, or SaaS. Why? Because the nature of the shared facility means that brute force attacks that seek to disable any given application in the DC and cloud will mean that all tenants of that cloud will be affected; an attack on one is often an attack on all. Therefore, it should be within the scope of the common denominator among the tenants—the landlord—to provide some form of safeguards against these types of attacks.

That said, it is all about the service level agreements. Do not assume DoS attacks on clouds are covered by the service agreements, because many DCs and cloud providers are less than explicit on this fact. Even the means to providing DoS safeguards and controls should be subject to review by risk managers in the IoT concerned about the access and storage of their data. See Chapter 8, Availability and Reliability Requirements in the IoT, and Chapter 13, RIoT Control, for a more detailed discussion on DoS vulnerabilities associated with clouds and DCs.

CONCLUSIONS

The IoT is here now, and risk managers need to get acquainted with what it looks like both technically and conceptually. Technically, the IoT is also a ship covered in barnacles right now; specifically, IPv4 and IPv6 are both in use where only one is appropriate, namely IPv6. IPv4 persists because it has been around since the very birth of the Internet, but it has run out of space; there are no IPv4 addresses left to assign to the burgeoning population of IoT devices on the Internet. The persistence of IPv4 in the IoT will make the risk manager's job tougher because two incompatible networks will coexist for a while to come and will need to be managed. While many of the vulnerabilities between IPv4 and IPv6 are common, there are unique vulnerabilities, too. The vulnerabilities in IPv6 are less well understood than those of IPv4, and will present a challenge going forward.

Conceptually, always consider that the IoT is composed of four key asset classes that must all be managed together, and not in isolation. Remember that risk management is about treating risks, transferring risk, or accepting risks: when it comes to the trinity of asset classes, too often managers implicitly move to accept risks they know nothing about. Be educated about the four asset classes in your IoT system: endpoint, gateways, networks, and DC/clouds.

Endpoints will be either devices that transmit information back to applications, typically within DCs, or they will be devices that can also receive instructions and information in addition to transmitting data. Sensors would be part of the first class of devices; everything from smartphones to banking machines to industrial controls would be in the second class of device. Frequently, devices will be limited in their ability to protect themselves, and security controls in the network or the data center will need to compensate.

Gateways will be the intermediate stage between the endpoint and the network. Taking advantage of greater processing power and storage than endpoint devices, gateways can be used to normalize, compress, and encrypt data, and to perform more robust authorization and integrity checking before the data makes its way to the network.

The network is the dial tone of the IoT. Everything depends on the security of the network because a device without the network is merely an isolated machine, deaf and mute and without any context to make sense of the world. Network for the IoT will vary greatly and will be highly heterogeneous: there will be many varieties of network between just about any endpoint creating or consuming information and the data center where that information is destined or originating.

The tides of the Internet are also changed in the IoT. Whereas before the networks and security assumed that most of the information was flowing from the center of the network (the DC) to the endpoints, this is no longer true. Threats will target the IoT and its data at every point in the ecosystem: the endpoint, gateway, network, and DC/cloud; whereas traditionally they targeted the DCs and clouds at the center of the Internet and the data they hold. In the IoT, more and more data is flowing from the endpoint and gateways into the center. While the center will still be targeted by threats, the endpoints and gateways have significantly more value and will be targeted, too—as massive generators of information and content. The design and engineering of network security can no longer assume that more information is flowing mostly in one direction: from the center outward.

As for the data center in the IoT, it has taken on new and varied dimensions with the advent of not only virtualization and clouds, but layers of service providers supporting different elements of the data center, some managing infrastructure, some platforms, some services, and some acting as brokers and aggregators between the other service provider in a transparent manner. For the risk manager in the IoT, understanding and balancing the many options related to the data center with the associated risks is a complex undertaking.

REQUIREMENTS AND RISK MANAGEMENT

3

What is meant by "requirements" in a security and engineering context, Why are requirements useful for managing risk, and what do Internet of Things (IoT) requirements look like generally? These are the questions we will attempt to address in this chapter. In addition we will demonstrate how requirements are relevent to risk management in the IoT: Risks will manifest themselves in relation to "requirements" or project goals: what do you need to get from the project for it to be considered a success, and does security play a part in the overall success?

A PARABLE FOR REQUIREMENTS AND RISK MANAGEMENT

Bob has had a successful career, to date, in the information technology (IT) department of a large city's government. As a result, he is placed in charge of a new and ambitious project to link the city's streetlights together into a network. The reason for the project is because the city's mayor attended a conference and heard about a similar project in another major city that is considered a leader in modernization. The mayor wants to be a modernizing leader, too.

Bob does not know much about operational issues associated with streetlights, but he does know about IT. The fact that the mayor wants the job done means this is a high-profile task, and obviously important. But other than the executive "requirement" to appear as a modernizing leader, the objectives of the project are unclear, as are the benefits. Nonetheless, Bob kicks off the project by pulling together a project team.

The project team consists of his best IT architects, an electrical engineer from the lighting division, a project manager, and a procurement specialist to help with the preparation of a request for proposals (RFPs). The architects will generate the technical requirements, assess the responses, and assess how they might impact the existing systems. The electrical engineer will provide the specifications of the existing system, and some insight into growth and expansion requirements. The procurement people will make sure that the necessary bid processes are followed. Bob will present the final recommendations about vendors to the mayor's office for approval and budgeting.

Working with his team, Bob develops and releases an RFP looking for a "smart street lighting" proposal. The RFP includes:

- The necessary technical information about the existing street lighting systems
- The corporate interfaces they intend to use for controlling the street lighting system
- A list of the desired control functions related to the lighting system
- All the correct financial and bidding terms and conditions

RIoT Control. DOI: http://dx.doi.org/10.1016/B978-0-12-419971-2.00003-0

From the beginning, things go sideways.

Shortly after the release of the RFP, internal people step forward and ask why *they* were not consulted? The executives from the facilities engineering department had no idea that one of their engineers was developing a multimillion-dollar RFP with the IT department! Who is going to pay for and train its staff to manage this system once it arrives? The union leaders want to know the impact on their members. The city ombudsman wants to know the effect on the privacy of city residents. The Emergency Management staff wants to know if and how the system will react to abnormal (emergency) conditions? The security staff—from another part of the IT department—want to know where a vendor solution will stop and start, in terms of keeping the system secure and who will fund the increased budget they may need to support the online street lighting infrastructure? The mayor's political staff wants to know what the benefits are for the taxpayer, in the simplest terms. And then the local electricity utility comes around with questions about the impacts on loads, and how might the old established demand patterns change? And once the utility starts raising flags, the regulators take notice: will this somehow affect the grid? Will this somehow impact the cost of power at given times and require a review of the tariffs paid by the city?

Finally the vendors start posting questions. Lots of questions. They begin with "Do you want the infrastructure good, fast, or cheap? Choose two of the three." Then the vendors get into more details: how much logging, how much networking, how much redundancy, how much security? One RFP clarification is released. Then another. But the questions about requirements against which to design a proposal keep coming in from vendors, and questions about the "real" benefits start coming in from the media and citizens groups.

Soon the project collapses due to the weight of its own ambiguity and ill-defined requirements. The RFP is canceled and, at best, Bob is considered to have been promoted to his level of incompetence.

Many things went wrong for Bob. Many of these things are not specific to the risk and the IoT—they are general IT and contracting risks. But a few things made this project different from others and amplified mistakes to the point of the project stopping; where many IT-only projects start the same way but end up finishing, even if they limp across the line at the end. Here are three things related to the key lessons of this book:

1. Bob treated this as an IT project. This is not just an IT project because it is dealing with a kinetic outcome (traffic lights turn on or off and provide safety-related services to millions of tons of moving metal at any given time). There is a cyber-physical interface involved. This means that the range of stakeholders has expanded dramatically, flowing toward nontraditional stakeholders and into the supply chain.
2. Bob was thinking of the project in terms of old fashioned data flows, which existed largely in isolation from the rest of the organization. IT may slow or even stop, but production will generally continue. In the worst case, *services* might be impacted, but no people or property are physically damaged. Similarly, dependent external entities are used to IT outages: we deal with them all the time. They can cope with half a day of radio silence from the city, if necessary. In other words, Bob did not understand the service-level changes that occur within the IoT versus the legacy, data-centric Internet.

INTRODUCTION

This chapter describes what amounts to a process called a "sensitivity analysis" within a risk management program. We deliberately refrained from using the word "formal" when discussing the risk management program, because this may imply an unnecessary and elaborate process.

True, you can arrive at many of the conclusions in this book related to the IoT and risk, but that will be a matter of chance, intuition, and luck in many cases. As a risk manager at any level in the organization, relying on intuition and luck is the worst thing you can do.

To understand what you know and what you don't know about risks in the IoT makes a disciplined approach to risk management beneficial, or even necessary. We will get to it in subsequent chapters, but really understanding the vulnerabilities and risks in the emerging IoT merit an approach that we begin outlining in this chapter.

Requirement assessment starts with some basic questions to which, surprisingly, the answers might not come easily or quickly. For instance, why are you undertaking the project? Probably not for the purposes of security or risk management. As a result, risk management is typically not core to the objectives and thinking around the project.

It is common for large and small IT project requirements to be poorly defined and documented. In order to frame a discussion of risk and IoT, it is helpful to illustrate some of the typical requirements associated with IoT, which is what we want to do in the following pages. Risk managers in the IoT will find useful examples of the sort of requirements that might be overlooked by those not trained or concerned with security and risk. This chapter is not intended to be only for engineers and risk managers, because requirements are commonly very poorly compiled and documented.

AUDIENCE

The consequence of badly managed requirements definition and sensitivity analysis is pretty much always cost overruns, and usually not small overruns. Sometimes the consequence is disaster. Weak requirements development also invariably leads to clumsy or only part-right implementation, which slows or delays adoption and dramatically impacts customer satisfaction. For anyone concerned about the total cost of IoT projects or adoption rates, this chapter is for you, too.

The processes and methods we outline should be instructive for anyone concerned about the risk in IoT systems and especially new systems and applications in the area of *smart* systems, *connected* systems, or *machine-to-machine* (M2M) systems, where many of the processes and operational models and applications are essentially new.

FRAMING THE DISCUSSION

In the previous chapter, we wrote about the four key assets in the IoT: the endpoint, gateway, network, and data center (DC)/cloud as the basic classes within the IoT. Each of these asset classes needs to be considered and managed from a risk perspective, whether the management consists of treatment, transference, or acceptance of risks. In many cases, the IoT risk management strategy is almost a fait accompli because some elements—often the network—are entirely outsourced to third-party service providers. In these cases, risk has essentially been transferred through service levels and other contracted agreements, and all that is left to do is audit compliance.

Now that we are discussing more detailed elements of risk management, the illustrative tools of endpoint/gateway/network/DC might be employed again, but overlaid with security criteria. This is how we intend to proceed in the following chapter.

We will start with an overview of the broadly different types of security "requirements" as defined in the long established and applied *800-53: Security and Privacy Controls for Federal Systems* from the US National Institute of Standards and Technology (NIST). While 800-53 is an IT, and not an "IoT" security standard, its methods for compartmentalizing security and risk management processes are well thought out and are applicable to the IoT, even if the specific controls are focused on traditional information management systems.

Why compartmentalize the management of risk in the IoT? Like any large and complex task, managing risk in the IoT is easier to accomplish with clear(er) subtasks and boundaries where work can start, stop, and be delegated. Additionally, the NIST divisions can be useful because they can reflect typically occurring boundaries of authority and controls so that people with accountability for one level of security or privacy requirement may be spared the need to try and inject themselves into other people's domains of controls—either above or below them hierarchically. Nothing obstructs security and risk management like organizational politics.

WHAT ARE SECURITY REQUIREMENTS?

Requirements are the functional properties that an application or system must support in order to fulfill its intended objectives efficiently and effectively. Requirements can be broad and wide ranging, addressing everything from graphical user interfaces to engineering feeds and speeds.

Security requirements are a subset of the overall requirements, but a frequently overlooked subset. Security tends to sit mostly in the background like plumbing; therefore security requirements and the controls and safeguards that meet the requirements can be overlooked and even ignored. Finding a methodical way of managing security requirements provides a great benefit because of this behind the scenes status.

NIST 800-53r4[1] presents three tiers of security requirements and capabilities: organization, business process, and information systems. (Previous versions of NIST 800-53 referred to the tiers as "business," "operational," and "technical." No doubt the NIST had logical reasons for renaming these tiers, probably reflecting changes in scope, evolution in thinking, and even a touch of militarization of the US federal risk management process (consider that merely a casual comment)—but the old titles where perhaps easier to understand, if even they were slightly less accurate under the new definitions.)

As NIST itself says in 800-53r4:

> To integrate the risk management process throughout the organization and more effectively address mission/business concerns, a three-tiered approach is employed that addresses risk at

---

[1]http://csrc.nist.gov/publications/PubsFL.html.

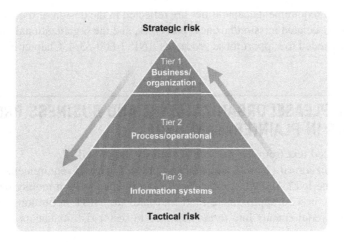

FIGURE 3.1

Security requirement and capability tiers.

From NIST 800-53r4.

the: (1) organization level; (2) mission/business process level; and (3) information system level. The risk management process is carried out across the three tiers with the overall objective of continuous improvement in the organization's risk-related activities and effective inter- and intratier communication among all stakeholders having a shared interest in the mission/business success of the organization.[2]

Tier 1 provides a prioritization of organizational missions/business functions which in turn drives investment strategies and funding decisions—promoting cost-effective, efficient information technology solutions consistent with the strategic goals and objectives of the organization and measures of performance. Tier 2 includes: (1) defining the mission/business processes needed to support the organizational missions/business functions; (2) determining the security categories of the information systems needed to execute the mission/business processes; (3) incorporating information security requirements into the mission/business processes; and (4) establishing an enterprise architecture (including an embedded information security architecture) to facilitate the allocation of security controls to organizational information systems and the environments in which those systems operate.

Determining what parts of the organization's information technology infrastructure demand the implemented of higher assurance security functionality is a Tier 1/Tier 2 risk management activity (see Fig. 3.1 in this chapter). This type of activity occurs when organizations determine the security requirements necessary to protect organizational operations (i.e., mission, functions, image, and reputation), organizational assets, individuals, other organizations, and the Nation. . . . After the security requirements and security capabilities are determined at Tiers 1 and 2 (including the necessary assurance requirements to provide measures of confidence in the desired

---

[2]NIST 800-53r4, p. 7.

capabilities), those requirements/capabilities are reflected in the design of the enterprise architecture, the associated mission/business processes, and the organizational information systems that are needed to support those processes[3] (NIST 800-53r4, Chapter 2, p. 25).

TRANSLATION, PLEASE! ORGANIZATIONAL AND BUSINESS PROCESS REQUIREMENTS IN PLAIN(ER) LANGUAGE

That was a lot of quoted text from the masters of security jargon: NIST.

So what are organizational (Tier 1) and business process (Tier 2) requirements as they relate to risk management in the IoT? And what about Tier 3, information system requirements?

At this point, it is best to approximate (and translate) the NIST definitions for organizational and business process requirements into terms that private sector risk managers might more readily recognize.

BUSINESS/ORGANIZATION REQUIREMENTS

Organization requirements (formerly called "business requirements" by NIST, and variously called "strategic requirements" and sometimes "market requirements" under other risk management frameworks) include the following sort of matters, which are visible at the executive level:

- Regulatory requirements related to laws or industry standards. For instance, industrial regulations about health and safety, financial reporting regulations such as Sarbanes-Oxley, privacy, service availability or tariffs laws, or self-regulating industrial standards like NERC-CIP in the electricity industry.
- Financial requirements for budget, gross profit, or profit margin. For instance, security and risk management have an allocated share of the IoT system investment.
- Competitive requirements such as time to market, price points or cost pressures, product differentiation, product automation, or protection of intellectual property and strategies.
- Internal policy requirements related to organizational directives and mandates. For instance, sustainability as a corporate goal, *privacy by design* as a requirement for all new systems, or automation as a key strategic pillar of the corporate plan.

BUSINESS PROCESS/OPERATIONAL REQUIREMENTS

Once organizational requirements are agreed upon, then business process (aka operational requirements) can be more easily and safely defined. Why "safely"? Because a business process requirement that is not directly and obviously linked to a higher level/Tier 1 organizational requirement is orphaned. How did it get to be a requirement in the first place? Does it have management support if it does not map to an organizational requirement? Are you sure?

---

[3]*NIST 800-53r4 Security and Privacy Controls for Federal Systems*—April 2013, http://nvlpubs.nist.gov/nistpubs/SpecialPublications/NIST.SP.800-53r4.pdf.

Business process requirements should map to one or more organizational requirements, if for no other reason than to show that the system being developed for the IoT somehow supports the most fundamental priorities of the organization.

Business process requirements express a much greater degree of detail and specificity. Business process requirements should possess enough detail that they allow for appropriate technical controls (Tier 3) to be selected by risk managers, but without necessarily being prescriptive—at least about technology (though business process requirements can be prescriptive about operational issues, as we will demonstrate).

REQUIREMENT MATRIX

Organizational requirements may also map to multiple business process requirements affecting risk in the IoT. This means that a *matrix* of requirements will typically develop, as illustrated. (The following section will explain this matrix in greater detail.)

Table 3.1 will be applied later in the chapter to show how the numerous organizational and business process requirements worth consideration might be affected by security and inject risk into the IoT.

Table 3.1 Requirement Matrix		
Organizational	**Operational Requirement Class**	**Operational Requirement Stipulation**
Regulatory—support local laws Internal Policy—support for organization-specific objectives or strategy	Confidentiality	Financial disclosure laws require auditable protection from unauthorized disclosure
	Integrity	Financial disclosure laws require auditable protection from unauthorized disclosure
	Availability	License to operate requires 99.99% availability
	Privacy	Perform privacy impact assessment at IoT system design stage
	Resilience	See "availability" + emergency management teams trained as per legislation

REALLY—WHO WANTS TO KNOW ALL THIS REQUIREMENTS STUFF?!

So, you are a manager or an executive working to deploy a service that depends on the IoT, or have inherited a system that needs to be hardened and made more secure. You go to the trouble of collecting requirements information, but how do you know it is the right information and, more importantly, how do you explain your questions to the people with the answers?

For instance, gathering requirements will typically involve anyone dealing with risk and the Internet of Things (RIoT) far and wide across the organization. It will also mean asking a lot of questions that might appear to be superfluous or just a simple waste of time. This can be the case because priorities regarding security vary at different levels in the organizational hierarchy. To make sense to the top executives and managers, you need to speak their language!

When it comes to security requirements in the IoT, the organizational requirements will be most meaningful at the top of the pyramid; the C suite, as they say.

Organizational requirements are largely about the regulatory environment in which RIoT must be managed or the internal policies established by top management that must be applied under the "internal law" of the organization.

Have you ever walked into a meeting with a top executive, thinking you have all the answers, only to find out that you have been viewing risk from a different perspective? That is probably because the executive had information about risk that you did not.

As a senior manager, there are typically many conversations among executives to which you are *not* privy; especially conversations among the top executives, auditors, and board members who all tend to bring outside, not internal, risks to bear on any RIoT assessment. For instance, auditors will be very concerned about the ability to make clear and strong attestations about the integrity of financial statements.

While auditors will probably work at many different levels in the organization and ask many questions, they will in the end issue a simple option to the C suite: compliant or not? Therefore regardless of with what an IoT system is supposed to be compliant or how it attains this compliance, the simple act of being compliant will drive a lot of attention at the levels that matter most.

From the simple question of "yes" or "no" to compliance, the questions get more complicated—but not that fast! As Fig. 3.2 indicates, even the subsequent level in a normal organizational hierarchy will not be digging deep. Issues like timeliness or reporting and broad accuracy come into play, and eventually costs—but rarely the deeper details of risk.

At and near the top of the organization, organizational requirements might be all that matter. Therefore, being able concisely to name the organizational requirements and the degree of compliance is going to be critical to successfully managing risk in the IoT, because support at these levels determines resourcing; resourcing as in money for RIoT control.

Once you get lower into the organizational hierarchy, the business process requirements emerge as important details associated with the organizational (regulatory/policy) requirements at the highest levels.

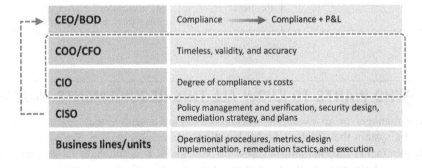

FIGURE 3.2

Reporting risk in the corporate hierarchy.

In the IoT, matters associated with the secure functioning of, say, traffic sensors and therefore requirements for network availability and device resistance to tampering might seem paramount. Yet these are business process requirements that need to be mapped to something bigger to be both understood and appreciated at the top levels. For instance, the chief executive officer (CEO) of the service provider running the traffic sensors for the highway department will be concerned with issues like being able to meet contracted compliance or legal compliance/liability. He/she is probably not willing to get into the details of device tamper resistant. That is too detailed.

Finally, in Fig. 3.2 we have drawn an arrow from the Chief Information Security Officer (CISO) to the CEO/board of directors level. This is to reflect a management transition that is underway and accelerated by the IoT: security as a board-level concern and the CISO as a role with a mandate larger than the Chief Information Officers (CIOs)—and therefore not necessarily reporting under the CIO.

The CISO mandate is growing because of the increasing role of "shadow IT," or the IT systems and services that are purchased by the lines of business directly to support business-delivery yet are independent of the CIO organization. Good examples of *shadow IT* include Salesforce and Dropbox, which offer very useful and widely-used business-support services, but are entirely out of the control of the CIO.

The IoT will drive even more shadow IT. The IoT will necessitate that the CISO manage both the "in house" IT security under the CIO, and the shadow IT that is outside the control (and budget) of the CIO.

RISK, REQUIREMENTS, AND DELIVERABLES

If top management is prone to grant resources for RIoT control based on (accurately expressed) organizational requirements, what does it need as deliverables? If management don't like details, what must you plan to provide to prove the ability to be compliant with regulatory or policy requirements (organizational requirements)?

As is the norm for details at reporting levels, so too are deliverables associated with RIoT differ between the lower or higher levels in the organization.

At the top of the organization, the deliverable associated with RIoT control can be as simple as an affirmation that the system will pass or has passed a compliance audit, and possibly what if any impact (positive or negative) this might have on the organizational profit and loss statements (P&L). At the top executive level there will be little time or patience for much more detail than this unless there happens to be a particular reason to know more. Operational security risks and security deliverables are best appreciated in minimum doses.

Further down the hierarchy there will be increasing interest in the details and nature or degree of compliance, and especially to what the costs of potential risk-reduction strategies will amount.

At the levels explained, the top executive and board of directors, the overall organizational requirements and business process requirements come into sharper and sharper focus, and the deliverables to validate compliance will become more meaningful. Fig. 3.3 illustrates the sorts of artifacts that might be expected through the organizational hierarchy to provide proof that risks are being adequately managed.

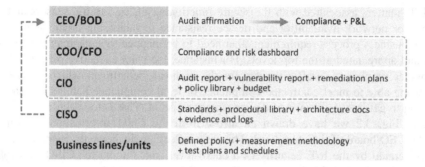

FIGURE 3.3

Risk and compliance deliverables.

TECHNICAL REQUIREMENTS: THIS IS WHERE WE DRAW THE LINE

At Tier 3, technical requirements for endpoint, gateways, network, and DCs/clouds become system-specific, and they are defined according to a distinct sub-process of risk management including their own NIST standard (800-37 – Risk Management Framework), and this sub-process comes into play and formalized processes are applied to selecting technical controls.

This is because each unique IoT system or service will have specific requirements according to a variety of factors, such as the threat level (see Chapter 4, Business and Organizational Requirements) and the sensitivity of the asset, application, or system. Trying to enumerate all such potential combinations is impossible; even trying to generate a "top list" of technical security requirements is a fraught process and more likely to mislead than inform.

For instance, Tier 3 technical requirements to support Tier 3 controls and capabilities will include specific stipulations and metrics. Consider the property of availability: how much up time is required? How short must the recovery period be? How far back must data be recovered?

Alternately, consider the property of confidentiality: how long should cryptographic keys be, given the information managed by the application? (The length of a key will determine how hard is it to crack using brute-force methods of trying to guess every possible key.) Again related to confidentiality: how deep should the background checks go on the users, administrators, and auditors, given the information managed by the application?

> Trying to make recommendations at this level of technical detail (Tier 3) is beyond the scope of this book. In fact, if the reader finds specific, technical guidance about generic, "recommended" technical controls and requirements they should be cautious about adoption of such controls because they lack the context of the IoT system under consideration.

Adopting or even considering technical guidance about security from generic threat and risk profiles can be dangerous because such estimates of security requirements can easily understate as well as overstate a requirement. In the case of understating the requirements, the outcome is easy enough to predict: system compromise. Overstated security requirements lead to the risk that the system is nonfunctional at worst or inefficient at best. It will cost too much to build and run and the business models used to justify the initial investment may be entirely undermined.

By working at the level of organization requirements (Tier 1) and business process requirements (Tier 2), we can provide a broad set largely reusable risk management guidance applicable to the IoT.

For any given system in the IoT, a large proportion of organizational requirements may overlap and significant portions of the business process requirements may also overlap. If not overlapping, the sample of organization and business process requirements supplied here can serve as a pick list for risk managers, auditors, regulators, and system designers. Not all requirements will apply to all IoT systems, but many will apply to most IoT systems.

APPLICATIONS AND SERVICES COMPOSING THE IoT

In Chapter 2, The Anatomy of the Internet of Things, we took a look at the general anatomy of the IoT and started to sketch out the type of applications and systems that will rely on the IoT. Now is the time for a few more concrete examples and use cases for user industries and applications because we are discussing requirements.

We will start with an outline of the IoT applications that are in the here-and-now: stuff that is happening, even if the IoT applications are not entirely obvious to most people. The intent of this section is neither to catalog an exhaustive inventory of what is going on in the world right now, nor to define the limits of possibility. Such a task would be difficult and would inevitably possess significant gaps.

The following is a sample of the applications and industries that will come to populate the IoT and therefore the sorts of requirements that will define them and, eventually, when we get there, the appropriate ways of managing risk associated with these applications and industries as they pile onto the IoT.

In the course of outlining the range of applications and industries that might be found in the IoT, we will focus on two qualities of any given IoT system: the effect on

- Operational efficiency
- User satisfaction

In fact, these are two of the simplest requirements for any application in the IoT. The best IoT applications will provide lots of both operational efficiencies and happy users.

OPERATIONAL EFFICIENCY (AS YING)

Operational efficiency means that by virtue of the IoT, goods or services are created or delivered faster, cheaper, better, fresher, with few defects, and so on. Operational efficiency gains may be so great for a given IoT application or system that this is the only requirement and justification for investment; however, user satisfaction is always important.

Many of the benefits in the IoT and business cases will relate to operational efficiencies, and in turn efficiencies mean that services are delivered with less cost, fewer people, and fewer resources consumed. In many cases, operational efficiency will be the imperative driving the IoT system or service in question, especially if the service is related to not-for-profit entities like government or socialized health care. However, operational efficiency is a virtue in all industries, and it will certainly drive IoT systems for reasons such as competitive advantage.

USER SATISFACTION (AS YANG)

Unhappy users can absolutely derail any IoT project (they can derail any IT project, period)—so this is a major risk in the IoT. User satisfaction should always be considered even in light of tremendous operational efficiency gains, and the minimum objective relative to huge operational efficiency should be a benign impact on user satisfaction. (For instance, "they don't even notice" or "they don't care.")

User satisfaction is about just that: happy, contented users, whether they be corporations, small, home-based businesses, or private individuals. Users of the IoT who believe they are being treated fairly and getting a better product or service will be satisfied and will drive adoption, which in turn will drive the operational efficiencies that, somewhere in the business cases, must assume some sort of adoption rate.

It may be the case the "users" in the IoT will be other IoT systems: machines communicating with machines. In this case a contented user would be one that is getting exactly what it expects, when it expects it. Goods or services or data arrive on time, in the expected format, in the expected volumes and with low or no errors (defects). In this case, user satisfaction might be about being diligent, not about breaking the other systems with which you are interfacing!

INDUSTRY USE CASES, EFFICIENCIES, AND SATISFACTION

One of the best devices for aiding people to understand the IoT are *use cases*. Use cases essentially are examples of how something might be used to achieve goal or purpose, in the context of a situation meaningful to a given industry.

Use cases are also the tool often used to decide whether a solution is able to meet the business and operational requirements of management, before an investment is made.

Use cases can be very simple or very detailed. They can merely outline a situation where a given technology or device might be applied usefully, or they can be very detailed step-by-step instructions that provide engineering guidance and technical specifications.

The use cases presented here are many, but not detailed. The idea is to show the range of different use cases in different industries so that risk managers can see that the key business requirements of operational efficiency and customer satisfaction appear in many ways within and between distinct industries.

Here is a summarized list of the industries for which we have created sample use cases for the IoT. These industries include those that are generally identified as critical infrastructure, as well as industries generating substantial value and economic activity:

- Transportation
- Healthcare
- Government (all levels)
- Public safety and military
- Retail and hospitality
- Food and farming
- Manufacturing and heavy industry

- Entertainment and sports
- Energy and utilities
- Finance and banking
- Education
- Information and communications technology(ICT)

TRANSPORTATION INDUSTRY

The transportation industry stands to benefit widely from the IoT. Smart transportation is synonymous with lots of improvements in the movement of people and goods.

Sample IoT Use Cases

- Smart trains, planes, automobiles, boats, and spacecraft
- Traffic signals and lights that automatically respond to environmental conditions or that can be remotely controlled
- Roads, rails, runways, and piers that report wear and tear and proactively schedule maintenance

Operational Efficiency

- Shorter trips
- Less human oversight
- Fuel efficiency
- Infrastructure utilization improvements
- Lower losses due to delays and spoilage
- Higher productivity due to reliable supply chains

User Satisfaction

- Less tiring commuting and traveling (due to less supervision and higher security)
- Lower personal and corporate costs associated with transport
- Faster time to destination
- Improved safety
- Improved profitability

HEALTH CARE

The IoT is bound to support more and more healthcare applications and services because it represents one of the best, easiest ways to reduce service-delivery costs, which are relentlessly rising everywhere. In addition, health services delivered through the IoT have the potential to create entire new avenues of delivery appropriate to a rapidly aging population (in many countries).

Sample IoT Use Cases

- Remote diagnostics, examinations, and treatment
- Remote patient monitoring, tracking, treatment, and telemetry
- Automation of treatments as a result of remote monitoring capabilities
- Remote surgery

- Prescription management and dispensing
- Medical asset tracking (tools, ambulances, pharmaceuticals)
- Improved accessibility, including multilingual support and aural directions

Operational Efficiency

- Better utilization of scarce human resources
- Better utilization of scarce or expensive tools and systems
- Lower costs associated with facilities, wear and tear, transportation
- Higher compliance rates with prescribed medical regimes
- Higher detection rates in early stages
- Faster and more complete access to past and current medical records.

User Satisfaction

- Better medical outcomes and recovery rates
- Faster diagnosis and treatment, shorter patient wait times
- Less tiring commuting and traveling (due to less supervision and higher security)
- Better information for patients and practitioners
- Larger range of treatment options

GOVERNMENT

Government in this instance does not include public safety agencies (that comes next), but it does include many vital functions such as regulation of important industries (banking, food, health, transportation, telecommunications, and so on) and coordination among private sector stakeholders during times of emergency.

Much of the benefit government will see from the IoT will come in the form of better information to support policy and regulatory decisions and the delivery of day-to-day civil and social services.

Sample IoT Use Cases

- Smart cities (waste management, traffic management, policing: many use cases covered throughout this section)
- Remote service delivery (social services, regulation)
- Accessibility, including multilingual support and aural directions
- Real-time environmental monitoring (air quality, water levels, pollution, earthquakes)
- Municipal water/sewer monitoring and control
- Asset tracking and inventory
- Building/property management and maintenance (office campus, parks, and monuments)

Operational Efficiency

- Better utilization of expensive human resources
- Better utilization of scarce or expensive tools and systems
- Lower operating costs associated with facilities
- More effective monitoring and enforcement
- Higher detection rates of regulatory breaches
- Faster and more complete access to past and current medical records

User Satisfaction

- Enhanced service delivery
- Maintain and improve services without increased taxation

PUBLIC SAFETY AND MILITARY

Surveillance is often the IoT application that comes to mind first when it comes to public safety (police and intelligence, but also fire) and the military. However, these public safety and military organizations can also be expected to employ, if not pioneer, many of the use cases from many of the other domains, such as transportation.

Sample IoT Use Cases

- Perimeter surveillance
- Investigation surveillance
- Asset tracking and location
- Remote asset control
- Weapons tracking and identification
- See *transportation* and other use cases

Operational Efficiency

- Better utilization of expensive (and fragile) human resources
- Access to previously impractical locations
- Automated surveillance capabilities
- Better utilization of scarce or expensive tools and systems
- Higher detection rates
- Faster remediation of incidents

User Satisfaction

- Better security outcomes and higher success rates
- Access to new information, intelligence, and logistics
- Reduced causalities and accidents

RETAIL AND HOSPITALITY

Retail and hospitality are both industries dealing frequently with individual buyers and consumers, but also some large businesses. As a result, they are trying constantly to deliver a personalized experience and at the same time automate and streamline processes as much as possible to gain competitive advantage. The IoT offers many potential use cases for creating new operational efficiencies and at the same time create the perception of a highly personalized experience for the customers.

Sample IoT Use Cases

- Inventory management and logistics
- Highly targeted promotions based on physical location and environmental conditions

- Antitheft and antifraud
- Ticketing and admission management
- Facilities monitoring, and management
- Accessibility, including multilingual support and aural directions

Operational Efficiency

- Lower inventory management costs and losses
- Lower spoilage and returns
- Higher success rate for promotions and campaigns
- Lower customer conversion costs
- Lower inventory shrinkage and less fraud

User Satisfaction

- Higher availability
- Fewer complaints
- Cleaner, safer facilities, and premises

FOOD AND FARMING INFRASTRUCTURE

From the farmer's field to the kitchen table, a wide variety of benefits from the IoT will be found in the food industry. The food industry is not only about supplying supermarkets for domestic shoppers; it also includes restaurants, cafeterias, and food caterers that support major institutions like hospitals, transportation companies, military bases, and business campuses. The food industry also includes the whole distribution business, which acts as the middlemen between the producers and the end consumers or commercial distributors.

Sample IoT Use Cases

- Field and pasture sensors indicating chemical and environmental conditions to producers
- Tracking of produce, livestock, and processed foods for quality and defect management, spoilage, and expiry.
- Tracking of heirloom varieties at risk of being lost
- Access control and monitoring of food processing faculties
- Automation of delivery processes and accounting
- Automation of ordering services and billing

Operational Efficiency

- Lower spoilage and expiry
- Fewer health incidents
- Faster tracking and mitigation of health incidents
- Rapid compliance reporting and evidence to regulators
- Increased automation in wholesale distribution
- Increased end-consumer statistics and feedback about preferences and tastes
- Larger selection of food sources and varieties
- Provenance of origin

User Satisfaction

- Better quality food
- Better information about ingredients and contents
- Safer food
- Reduced prices (due to increased efficiency)
- Increased selection (due to supply chain efficiency)
- Verifiable options related to provenance: genetically modified, organic, and so forth.

MANUFACTURING AND HEAVY INDUSTRY

Manufacturing is no stranger to smart devices and pioneered much of the groundwork for the coming IoT through the field of industrial control systems (ICS) and supervisory control and data acquisition (SCADA) systems, both of which have been around in varying forms for many decades.

Manufacturing is also one of the original risk managers in relation to the IoT, publishing early security standards through organizations like the International Society of Automation (ISA) standard 99.[4]

We can expect that manufacturing from heavy to light industry, from durables to perishables, from highly regulated to hardly regulated industries, will continue to be avid adopters of smarter and smarter systems and IoT.

Sample IoT Use Cases

- Process monitoring and management
- Equipment monitoring and management
- Health and safety monitoring and management
- Inventory management
- Shipping tracking
- Defect and recall management
- Proactive servicing and warranty (a faulty, factory-installed tire is getting too hot, and a new one is waiting at the dealer; this is better than fixing a car/truck after a blowout!)
- Product-service bundles and mating (your couch knows that your car keys have slipped between the cushions!)
- Access control and monitoring for employees, suppliers, and contractors entering premises.

Operational Efficiency

- Higher production uptime
- Lower maintenance costs
- Lower defects and spoilage
- Lower shrinkage rates of high-value components
- Fewer occupational injuries and accidents
- Shorter shipping and transportation delays
- Production flexibility: produce in smaller batches without higher costs

---

[4]See www.isa.org.

- Rapid compliance reporting and evidence to regulators
- Access to expanded markets through connecting with other goods and services (as with the car key example mentioned previously)

User Satisfaction

- More reliable and predictable supply chains
- Better quality goods
- Better information about goods (origin and provenance)
- Lower defects and warranty claims
- Reduced prices (due to greater efficiency)
- Increased selection (due to supply chain efficiency)

ENTERTAINMENT AND SPORTS

Expect entertainment and sport to be a surprising success in the IoT—the recent popularity (and insecurity) of the Fitbit is merely the beginning[5]. Most discussions around IoT tend to overlook these industries because they are service-and-people focused. And how much can you realistically increase tracking, monitoring, tracing, and embed more data in a person? In the end we will probably be very surprised by what the IoT brings to these industries, if for no other reason than the industry, unlike its denizens, is not in the limelight.

Certainly an area of unlimited potential is enhanced or augmented reality, where information about the things in the environment (people, places, fixtures, cars, shops, everything) can be overlaid in an image that combines reality with additional information. Enhanced reality is already available in some game consoles and through the frequently cited, early example of Google Glass.

Embedding sensors and information repositories into objects and clothes allows information about the nature of the object or the wearer of the object to be accessed from online sources.

Sample IoT Use Cases

- Fitness and performance monitoring
- Video capture in first person (e.g., helmet-mounted GoPro or similar devices) or entirely new vantage points (such as cameras embedded into Formula 1 racetracks)
- Drones enabled with video capture capabilities
- Enhanced reality for gaming
  - Role-playing and first-person in real physical environments (*holodeck* type)
  - Educational geography games for school children
- Enhanced reality for tourism
  - Multilingual tours for sites and monuments
  - Simulated physical locations for promotion
  - Embedded promotion and advertising
- Enhanced reality for sports
  - Player stats and health
  - Equipment and materiel descriptions and information

---

[5]https://blog.fortinet.com/post/fortinet-fitbit-threat-research-statement.

Operational Efficiency

- New adjacent service revenues from existing products
- Higher return rates and more repeat buyers
- Production customization and flexibility: produce in smaller batches or unique products without higher costs
- Access to expanded markets through connecting with other goods and services (again, the car key example)

User Satisfaction

- Real-time and granular feedback to encourage goals acquisition
- Positive impressions of personal progress
- Engaging interfaces and perspectives
- New products and experiences
- Wider selection of product features, differing levels of enhancement
- Reduced prices (due to more efficiency)

ENERGY: UTILITIES AND THE SMART GRID

The poster child for the *smart* world and the IoT is probably the energy industry. The ways and means of automating and injecting intelligence into energy systems, whether electrical, gas, oil, solar, hydro, wind, tidal, and so on, seem endless. Placing the many different elements of our interconnected energy infrastructures is a prime objective of many producers, consumers, and regulators alike. You cannot go far into the world of IoT before you encounter an energy application or product.

Risk and the IoT is very often also associated with energy and the potential kinetic (and privacy) impacts associated with malicious control of the infrastructure. Therefore special care is being taken in the development of secure smart grids and other management systems.

Sample IoT Use Cases

- Metering and time-of-use billing for consumer and businesses
- Coordination of batteries and storage systems to balance loads
- Pipelines and transmission lines with reports on status and proactive adjustments to loads and failures
- Generation system coordinated with storage systems

Operational Efficiency

- Flexible billing to encourage savings among consumers and businesses
- Reduced labor associated with billing, service, and monitoring
- Reduced outages lower maintenance costs
- Improved command and control
- Improved utilization of available generation sources
- Integration and coordination with storage sources

User Satisfaction

- Higher service levels (fewer outages of shorter duration)
- More pricing options
- Increased visibility into charges
- Improved public safety
- Integration with home and office automation

FINANCE AND BANKING

If there were any industry that lives and dies by its networks, it is the finance industry. Telecommunications services are the largest single spending point for financial-service entities in the United States and Canada[6], a relationship probably replicated around the world. If you consider spending on a good or service as an indicator of dependence on said good or service, then finance is more dependent proportionally on telecommunications than any other critical infrastructure.

Financial services were among the earliest adopters of the IoT, because so much of their operating costs were in telecommunications. They were and still are always looking for ways of gaining efficiencies through better telecommunications technologies and designs. It was not long after the popular emergence of the Internet that banks saw that it presented an amazing opportunity to connect remote assets to the DCs without expensive, private lines. It also presented the ability to offer a transition from physical, person-to-person services to online M2M services.

Sample IoT Use Cases

- Retail POS terminals
- Remotely located automated teller machines (ATM)
- Online desktop banking
- Mobile banking
- Device-based transactions (i.e., buy groceries from the touch console on your fridge)

Operational Efficiency

- Less capital (storefronts) required to service same number of clients
- Faster transaction processing and clearing
- Reduced theft, fraud, and other losses
- Extended service hours and abilities without proportional cost increases
- Fewer service desk calls

User Satisfaction

- Easier to access banking services
- Wider range of services and extended hours
- More selection of financial services for IoT device makers and service providers
- Faster and more flexible financial-service delivery

---

[6]See Macaulay, Tyson, *Critical Infrastructure: Understanding its component parts, vulnerabilities, operating risks, and interdependencies*, 2008.

EDUCATION

There is no doubt that education has benefited from the advent of the Internet generally, but what about the IoT? Will that make a difference to education and learning? Almost certainly "yes."

A wide variety of learning aids become possible with the IoT, from information embedded and overlaid into real-world objects (similar to the Entertainment use cases) to anticheating technologies; there are many opportunities.

Sample IoT Use Cases

- Enhanced reality for learning
- Real-time empirical data from topic of study (video from marine probes used to study ocean biology)
- Security in schools
- Student condition-monitoring[7]
- Automated identity and access control (to school facilities) services
- Inventory and tracking of valuable educational assets and goods
- Remote education and engagement

Operational Efficiency

- Wider range of information and experiences offered without leaving the classroom
- Better security without additional human resources
- Inexpensive sources of previously rare or unavailable data
- Curriculum customization and flexibility: produce smaller or unique courses without higher costs
- Access to expanded markets through connecting with remote or other students

User Satisfaction

- Better learning experience
- Wider selection of courses and learning materials
- Reduced security burden
- Reduced costs for expanded experiences
- New and varied experiences and relationships
- New collaborative opportunities

INFORMATION AND COMMUNICATIONS TECHNOLOGY

Can the network create new benefits for itself? In other words, will the IoT bring new benefits to itself in some sort of virtuous circle and feedback loop? Well, at the very least the IoT will bring more devices onto the network, creating more demand and (hopefully) more revenues and profit opportunities.

---

[7]See http://www.emote-project.eu/.

The ICT industry, just to be clear, is typically considered not only telecommunications carriers but also various manufacturers of equipment and software. It might also include certain types of service providers like systems integrators and DC operators.

Sample IoT Use Cases

- Physical infrastructure tracking, inventory, automation, remote management and security (wires, fibers, poles, conduits, junctions, telecom vaults, backup power supplies, access controls)
- Device-gateway coordination, monitoring, and management[8]

Operational Efficiency

- Automated network management and service migration
- Automated service-level adjustments and compliance
- Less manpower required to support vast physical infrastructure
- Faster location and remediation of physical faults (breaks, cuts, vandalism)
- More precise management of upgrades, maintenance, and end-of-life replacements

User Satisfaction

- New and more flexible network services
- Better network performance
- More resilient ICT
- Lower ICT costs
- Fewer outages
- Wider range of services and extended hours
- Faster service ordering, deployment, and delivery

SUMMARY

This chapter focused on gathering and assessing requirements for the IoT and especially security and risk management requirements.

Requirements gathering and assessment can be a bit of an arcane process because it is occasionally overlooked entirely, and often done in an incomplete and ad hoc manner. Because of the risks posed by the IoT, which is the topic of the following chapters, poor requirements gathering can have terrible follow-on effects.

Risk managers in the IoT will be no better than the requirements they compile and feed into the application and system development processes. Requirements management will be a core skill for security and risk practitioners in the coming years, more important than previously because of the expansion of the networks and IT to a cyber-physical interface and kinetic consequences.

---

[8]Emerging 5G wireless services will be heavily dependent on IT to coordinate IoT devices in their use of many different forms of gateways, employing different wireless spectrum, and layer 2 protocols. Many of these gateways will themselves be *things* in the sense that they not only directly deliver services to users, but act as proxy gateways for other IoT devices. Smartphones are one example of a device/gateway combination that will be coordinated with 5G technologies.

There are fundamentally three types of requirements that are interrelated and mapped against one another:

1. Business and organizational requirements are typically visible at the top management levels and are key to getting business cases for security and risk management funded. These requirements typically have to do with compliance to regulation, industry standards, or top-level organizational policies set by management. Internal organizational policies might include privacy, human resource policies, or strategic competitive directions for the organization as a whole.

2. Operational and process requirements are used by all management levels below the executive for defining critical aspects such as service levels, performance, and features. Operational requirements should map to and support business requirements. For instance, if an organizational requirement is to support privacy regulations in several jurisdictions, then a clear operational requirement is for privacy processes in design, deployment, testing, and ongoing support.

3. Technical requirements are represented by the hardware, software, and network features that support the operational and process requirements. In this book we will not attempt to discuss or recommend technical requirements because they vary substantially from use case to use case, and the threat, vulnerabilities and controls are even more diverse. The definition of technical controls is best left to the risk manager and security personnel on a given IoT project, using the higher level requirements as guidelines for what needs to be done technically. Alternately, business and operational controls can be used to define what is not mandatory from a risk and security perspective at the technical level—and justify those limits.

In this chapter, we reviewed the two primary use cases related to security in the IoT: operational efficiency and user satisfaction. While it is true that these could be the critical use cases in many projects, they are especially important to keep in mind with security and risk management. Why? Because security and risk management have chronic difficulties in proving their worth and getting the necessary budgets and resources. For this reason, more than just about any other technical discipline, security and risk management efforts need to be able simply to trace back and show how they can benefit both operational efficiencies and user satisfaction.

For every one of the industrial verticals we reviewed, there are multiple instances of both types of use cases that can be applied and cited by risk manager in the IoT. No matter which industry you might be working within, always attempt to show how the IoT system or project will address both use cases. This will certainly mean collaborating with multiple internal stakeholders and perhaps increase the short-term requirements gathering exercise, but will provide much greater long-term project stability because of the multidimensional benefits that security in the IoT can drive or organizations in many different industries.

BUSINESS AND ORGANIZATIONAL REQUIREMENTS

In the course of field experience and researching this book, several very common business-level requirements have surfaced as typical and critical at the same time. Our objective is to outline and explain these requirements so that Internet of Things (IoT) developers, designers, and risk managers can assess at the outset whether these requirements apply to their use-cases and incorporate the requirements into their strategies.

In the previous chapter, we used a parable to illustrate the importance of understanding requirements generally. In this chapter, we will use the same device to explore business and organizational requirements.

PARABLE FOR BUSINESS AND ORGANIZATIONAL REQUIREMENTS

Alice is the chief executive officer (CEO) of a well-established, profitable, and publicly traded company that builds and operates blood glucose monitoring devices for diabetic patients. The company has the best product on the market and has the industry's largest customer base, providing devices of a variety of teams and different monitoring options. The monitoring services exist in basically two forms: either field workers go to the device (for instance in a patient's home) to perform diagnostics, to calibrate the device, and to download records for analysis; or device owners go to a storefront (such as a pharmacy) or doctor's office to get the records downloaded and assessed. The company also has an online portal where patients can login and download their records.

But there is a looming difficulty ahead for Alice's business: blood glucose monitors are being connected to networks so the results can be automatically processed remotely, and results/alerts sent to doctors in realtime. Alice's company is not an information technology (IT) company and does not want to be one, but Alice decides to network-enable (Internet Protocol (IP)—enable) her products because that is proving popular in the market, and she has to respond.

At the same time, health insurers—both public and private—are encouraging service providers like Alice's to participate in information aggregation portals where patient information from many different service providers can be consolidated for the benefit of the patients.

Alice does not like networking her product and resents that she needs to consolidate her product telemetry with information from a host of mildly related service providers like physiotherapists and even personal trainers. After all, the modern treatment of diabetes is well understood and successful. Why mess with the goose that laid the golden egg?

RIoT Control. DOI: http://dx.doi.org/10.1016/B978-0-12-419971-2.00004-2

Eventually, the decision is made to IP-enable a new generation of glucose monitoring devices, which take the form of a disposable, daily contact lens, which has a sensor and a tiny wireless communications chip embedded that relays readings to the Internet through a local gateway, such as a smartphone or Wi-Fi access point. The software development work will be done by an internal team, which will implement IP networking using an off-the-shelf software library. The new online system will see patient information aggregated in centralized company databases. Healthcare providers like doctors and clinics can do online queries or have alerts pushed to them automatically through a variety of different means. The easiest and cheapest choice for networking all the devices together is the Internet, so that is the intended platform. The entire system will be managed by the existing IT staff, with a few additional resources to help with the workload.

At the start of the development phase, the new team sat together in a whiteboard session and laid out the technical requirements for the device, based on years of industry experience and insights.

From an operational perspective, the main concern was battery life on the lens. This meant processing loads, software size, and communications with the gateway devices had to be highly efficient and compact.

From a customer satisfaction perspective, the service itself was the main value. Customers were going to see this as a major leap forward in the management of their condition and a huge benefit to their well-being!

As a result, a variety of less common use cases and requirements were overlooked and the impact has started to weigh on the product. Many users find that performance is degraded due to poor connections and short battery life.

Failure to understand the business and organizational requirements of the IoT system included:

- Targeted and promoted performance requirements established in the labs where not achievable:
  - Users roamed onto unsecure networks all the time—security became partially dependent on third parties like restaurants and coffeehouses. Alternately, many of the workplaces required network access controls (logon with a username and password)—which they did not build into the devices—so the service didn't work in these environments.
  - The monitor was intended to be worn as a contact lens; users of the lens frequently used other wearable IoT devices like wireless earpieces, connected glasses, and smart watches; these other devices frequently interfered with the radio signals and caused battery life to diminish.
- Certain health insurers and clinics appeared to be generating large loads on the centralized database. On investigation, it was due to the fact that they were harvesting patient data in bulk, not just making queries about individual patients. This resulted in regulatory infractions related to privacy and personally identifiable information.
- The reduced performance of the products generated excessive help desk calls, complaints, product returns, and negative reviews: profits did not materialize as a result.
- The poor performance, negative reviews, and impending regulatory sanctions have also created an opening in the market that Alice has created for me-too competitors, who rapidly learned from her mistakes and captured market share.

Alice's failure to look at the entire operational ecosystem from end to end added a lot of unnecessary risk and jeopardized the entire project. She made many assumptions about what the users would be doing, and about the security and reliability of other key providers, such as network providers and third-party stakeholders, in the healthcare system. The real operational environment turned out to be much different from the lab.

INTRODUCTION

This chapter looks at the top-level business and organization requirements that executives and management will need to address as they move their business into the IoT in a safe and secure manner.

There are not many IoT requirements here—but they are critically important and reverberate down through the rest of the requirements process and inevitably the organization.

In fact, the few requirements we will discuss are not exclusive to security, but have a substantial influence on the outcome of security controls and safeguards in the IoT, because they drive the *prioritization* of investment in security and risk management.

More importantly, this is the start of the IoT risk management process. Any defects, failures, errors, or omissions that occur at this phase will only cascade and amplify as time passes and the project matures. Mistakes made at the outset will not be forgiven.

Assessing the business and operational requirements is so important because all other requirements will map to these top-level concerns, which are identified by management. Business and organizational requirements are the framework upon which the rest of the IoT security program hangs.

AUDIENCE

Because this chapter is about business and organizational requirements, it will be of most value to those defining such requirements: executives, product managers, business unit managers, risk managers, and audit and compliance officers.

Those people concerned with the four main domains of business and organizational requirements should read this chapter:

- Regulatory compliance related to statutes, laws, and self-regulation
- Financial requirements having to do with profit and margins
- Internal policies and directives that reflect top management's guidance concerning organizational behavior
- Competitive market requirements for differentiation, quality, brand, and service or product strategy.

BUSINESS AND ORGANIZATIONAL REQUIREMENTS IN THE IoT

We have now come to the part of this book where we are able to discuss some of the requirements that are emerging for the IoT and that will be especially meaningful to the management of risk in the IoT.

Requirements, as we discussed earlier in this chapter, are necessary to a risk management process because they highlight features such as the sensitivity of assets in the IoT to different threats and vulnerabilities.

The following lists of requirements are not specific to any of the industries we profiled earlier, but are intended as a cross-section representation of typically important requirements that may be present in just about any industry. It will really be up to the assets or application owners to determine which requirements are valid in the case of their particular IoT.

These requirements are not exhaustive, but they should be novel to the IoT in that similar requirements may not appear in enterprise IT, or they may appear with different priority. These requirements are included here because they appear to be rather unique to the IoT or different from what you might find in risk management processes in traditional IT systems.

These requirements should be considered more like a sampling of the potential range of requirements for operational and business process requirements in the IoT. Not all requirements will apply to all IoT systems and services, making these more like a superset from which risk managers will draw when considering the specific IoT system under consideration.

ORGANIZATIONAL REQUIREMENTS RESTATED

Quickly recapping our earlier discussion: business and organizational requirements are most visible at the executive level. They include:

- Regulatory requirements related to laws or industry standards.
- Financial requirements for budget, profit, and margin.
- Internal policy requirements related to organizational directives and mandates.
- Competitive requirements such as time to market, price points or cost pressures, product differentiation, product automation, protection of intellectual property, and strategies.

REGULATORY AND LEGAL REQUIREMENTS

There is no shortage of legal and regulatory requirements awaiting those entering the IoT business as stakeholders and users. In a few cases, awareness and proper preparedness for regulatory compliance will make the difference between the success and failure of opportunities in the IoT. Without any doubt, this is the case where redesigning systems and process after the fact can drive up costs beyond the point at which the system remains economically viable. An example is where data stores need to be redesigned completely and developed to compartmentalize and manage information in manners that are not technically efficient, yet meet regulatory guidelines related to privacy (see more about privacy in Chapter 5, Operational and Process Requirements).

What are legal and regulatory requirements in something as difficult to define (at times) as the IoT? This is a very important question because regulatory requirements represent a lowbar of performance that must be achieved, or else sanctions and worse may follow.

What is more, regulatory requirements may well drive operational and technical requirements in directions that have little to do with other requirements. (Though, as previously discussed, issues such as privacy can have the effect of increasing customer confidence and resulting adoption rates.)

PAY NOW, PAY LATER: COMPLIANCE IS NOT AN OPTION

Preparedness and awareness of regulatory and compliance requirements pay *big* dividends—this is one of the largest risks facing managers in the IoT. Being ready to prove compliance in an efficient and effective way will put any organization ahead of competitors in many cases and save significant resources. In some cases it will mean the difference between a system that is allowed to operate and one that is shut down by regulators or by public pressure and lack of adoption by customers.

Failure to design systems from the start to be compliant with the regulatory regimes they will operate in is a mistake—a mistake that has been well learned in many disciplines of telecommunications and informatics, but it is different in the IoT. The reason it is different is the physical-cyber, kinetic interface we have discussed previously.

The physical-cyber, kinetic interface itself does not necessarily bring different regulation or change regulation. But it does result in the potential vastly to expand the range of regulatory compliance statutes and regulations that an IoT system must support.

The mélange of compliance requirements in the IoT will be unlike anything that has been seen previously. This means that especial diligence must be applied in understanding the requirements at the outset, because the costs of failing to address compliance at the design stage will be unlike regulatory remediation efforts seen previously. The cost to go back and redesign IoT systems—from the remote sensing nodes and endpoints at the periphery to the information management in the big data clouds at the center—will be massive. And in some cases, the cost of making changes after the fact will simply ruin the business.

HYBRID REGULATION: LAWS AND INDUSTRIAL STANDARDS IN THE REGULATORY ENVIRONMENT OF THE IoT

In many cases, legal regulations will in turn compel that the industrial standards be applied—a hybrid of state and self-regulation. How hybrid regulation will be managed involves knowledge of security audit and standards, a discussion to follow immediately after this section.

Hybrid regulation will probably be more the rule than the exception in the IoT; risk managers need to be ready for this and be prepared to explain it to top management when seeking resources to secure the IoT systems and processes. The prime reason for the exceptionalism is that the laws and even regulations cannot keep up with technology and especially the IoT, and they will be crafted in a general manner. The laws will rely on the industrial practices and guidelines to be kept current by those stakeholders working day to day in the field and the industrial domain. The more complex and large the IoT grows, the more this will be the case: all the more reason for large IoT stakeholders to participate in the codification of standards that will increasingly provide the necessary details supporting regulatory oversight.

Hybrid regulation and its demands are critical organizational requirements in the IoT, and awareness of the complexity and interdependence of this emerging form of regulation requires careful management and appropriate resourcing.

IoT REGULATORY EXAMPLES AND HYBRIDISM

Let's walk through a few of the major areas of safety and security regulation that will impact IoT systems, either directly or through supply-chain relationships.

Table 4.1 is a small subset of the many examples of how government regulation is mandating and driving industry-specific as well as international standards to fill the gaps that regulations

Table 4.1 Regulation and Security Standards in the IoT

Form of Regulation	Legal Example	Industrial Standard Example
Financial	Sarbanes-Oxley[a]: reporting of financial results requires secure systems to demonstrate assurance.	Payment Card Industry (PCI)[b]—Data Security Standard (DSS) is a proprietary information security standard for organizations that handle cardholder information for the major debit, credit, prepaid, ATM, and POS cards.
Critical infrastructure protection—electricity	Section 215 of the Federal Power Act requires the Electric Reliability Organization (ERO) to develop mandatory and enforceable reliability standards, which are subject to commission review and approval. Commission-approved reliability standards become mandatory and enforceable in the United States on a date established in the orders approving the standards.[c]	NERC CIP[d]: The North American Electricity Reliability Council—Critical Infrastructure Protection is an industry-specify standard for the security of electrical infrastructure, which is turn has been mandated by the federal regulations of the United States.
Healthcare	"The HIPAA Security Rule[e] establishes national standards to protect individuals' electronic personal health information that is created, received, used, or maintained by a covered entity. The Security Rule requires appropriate administrative, physical, and technical safeguards to ensure the confidentiality, integrity, and security of electronic protected health information."[f]	International Standards Organization (ISO)—Information Security Management Systems (ISMS) 27001 is a widely used set of audit scope tools. It is not in any way particular to health, but does have some specific adaptations to certain industries like energy. In addition, there is 27799 health informatics—information security management in health using ISO/IEC 27002.
Workplace health and safety	Workplace health and safety is not just about slips, trips, and falls these days; it includes IT security and protection from cyber-threats such as identity theft, bullying and harassment, stalking and unauthorized surveillance, and potentially other personal losses that may result from inadequate workplace IT security. Liability precedents in this area were established several years ago, and the IoT will only increase the scope.	Industrial standards associated with workplace safety will come from a variety of sources to combine IT and industrial security with privacy controls and compliance. For instance, ISO, NIST and ISACA CoBIT[g] are the three most common standards for IT security. The industrial and manufacture ring world has distinct but recognizably related standards in the converging works of ISA 99, IEC 62443 and ISO an as yet unassigned 27000-series standard.
Privacy	Privacy laws are everywhere and will be highly applicable to the IoT. Privacy laws exist at multiple levels of government and can sometimes even be apparently conflicting. Privacy laws are usually no more prescriptive than other forms of law, in that they provide scope for interpretation. Typically, privacy laws will seek to provide guidelines around what is personal information and how it may be collected, used, and disclosed.	Many of the same organizations that provide standards for the purposes of assessing security compliance also provide guidance about privacy compliance. For instance, ISO (through SC27—Working Group 5).

[a]http://www.gpo.gov/fdsys/pkg/PLAW-107publ204/html/PLAW-107publ204.htm.
[b]https://www.pcisecuritystandards.org/.
[c]http://www.nerc.net/standardsreports/standardssummary.aspx.
[d]http://www.nerc.com/pa/Stand/Pages/CIPStandards.aspx.
[e]As distinct from the HIPPA Privacy Rule—see http://www.hhs.gov/ocr/privacy/hipaa/administrative/privacyrule/index.html.
[f]http://www.hhs.gov/ocr/privacy/hipaa/administrative/securityrule/index.html.
[g]Control Objectives for IT (CoBIT).

cannot effectively address. However, as the IoT grows and includes more and more cyber-physical and kinetic interfaces with machines and networks, the regulatory burden is growing. Without sufficient guidance (such as standards) to provide and effective and efficient baseline, more ad hoc and proprietary guidelines and will develop.

A large challenge of risk managers in the IoT will be creating security regimes that are reusable and easily provable/auditable—especially in the face of potentially conflicting guidance from multiple industries.

Consider our earlier discussion related to the anatomy of the IoT in Chapter 2, The Anatomy of the Internet of Things: many of the stakeholders in the ecosystem will be providing services to many different IoT applications and services. Supporting unique risk management and security standards and frameworks across all or even some of the range of applications will either raise costs disastrously or reduce the use of these guidelines as stakeholders seek to avoid costs. In reality, probably both will occur at the same time if a multitude of security guidelines come to be required through the fiat of regulation.

PROVING COMPLIANCE: THE $64,000 QUESTION

How is compliance attained or proven: with difficulty in many cases, unfortunately; it usually comes down to audit. Sometimes the audit is through a third-party, and other times through self-assessment. In both cases the audit needs to be performed against some form of standard and an agreed scope.

FINANCIAL REQUIREMENTS

The Holy Grail of IoT security is proving it has a business case. (Similarly, CISOs around the world are even now struggling to prove the value of enterprise security in terms that unambiguously support claims of resources.)

It's not that IoT security has no business case: there are definitely many good reasons to invest in security and risk management, and many cautionary tales of what has happened to those who underinvested. But it is never a simple case to make and all too often cases are based on qualitative measurements and statements like, "the reports of attacks are much worse than last year" or "the IT department is constantly in crisis response mode."

In other words, the business case for security is frequently poorly defined. As a direct result, the much better defined, highly quantitative requirements associated with money (finance) will trump. It is very typical to find finance organizations that can directly account for how investment in sales and marketing equals increased sales. Or marketing departments that can tell top executives how much press time (down to the word or minute) they have gotten for investments in events or promotions. Security and risk management rarely display such direct measurements and figures to support requests for investment and more resources.

IoT security and risk management investment can all too easily become dependent on the intuitively justified yet un-measureable and un-definable evidence, against the beady-eyed measurements of simply doing nothing and keeping more or less cash!

Financial requirements will relate to expenses that affect costs and margins, such matters as:

- Limiting the total security investment to a fixed percentage of total IT spend. For instance, security spending is typically between 6% and 8% of IT budget in 2015[1], depending on the industry and the circumstances. (Spending even beyond this percentage is not necessarily out of line, but it is then subject to different justifications.)
- Ceilings on the total allowed growth of the security budget from year to year.
- The cost of regulatory compliance and the matter that can become especially pronounced in the case of matters related to:
  - Lawful access and intercept associated with judicial orders for wire taps or surveillance
  - Privacy management issues and requests for disclosures from user and clients
  - General legal discovery associated with liability and tort cases arising from IoT systems-related injury
- Security audits and the associated remediation:
  - Creation or augmentation of security policies
  - Creation and augmentation of operational procedures
  - Implementation of audit recommendations associated with exceptions within the audit

Make no mistake, the difference between good and badly planned security is easily ± 100 percent, but usually much much more! As a result, the potential to overspend on risk management and security can have a major impact on the viability of any IoT project. And the ability to effectively manage the financial requirements will be especially pertinent given the complexity of the resulting systems.

DO YOU KNOW WHAT YOU DON'T KNOW?

Consider complexity in the face of financial requirements. It is an often-discussed element of the financial world that the complexity of the financial system is poorly understood—or at the very least, we underestimate risk and don't know what we don't know. Such examples as the crises in 1987, 2001, and 2007 are enough evidence of this fact. And some excellent discussion around this phenomenon has been presented by Nicolas Taleb.[2]

As we have stated throughout this book, the IoT is among the most complex things every created by man. Understanding the interdependencies and cascading impacts associated with threats, vulnerabilities, and impacts is a fraught undertaking. Acknowledging that financial requirements (cost versus benefit) need to be taken into account make the risk management process of the IoT that much more complex! How do you understand the cost of ongoing compliance under normal and abnormal situations? The requirements above are a decent starting point for these considerations.

In any event, financial requirements and the degree to which they are well considered are more than enough to make or break the best-laid IoT plans of venture capitalists (VCs) and men.

---

[1]Gartner—http://blogs.gartner.com/john-wheeler/it-security-budgets-rise-as-data-breach-fear-spreads/.
[2]Nicolas Taleb. *The Black Swan*, 2005.

COMPETITIVE REQUIREMENTS

Competitive requirements will change over time, and sometimes they will change very quickly in response to changes in the marketplace. For this reason, tracking and mapping competitive requirements and the impact on the overall management and especially risk management of the IoT system is critical.

Remember this: few businesses are in business to manage risk. They are in business to deliver a good or a service. If the business/organizational requirements suddenly change due to competitive pressures or issues, then operational and process security need to change to reflect this fact. Maintaining a level of security and risk management that is out of balance with the new competitive requirements will lead to disaster.

Sometimes the necessary answers to competitive pressures (requirements) involve accepting or transferring more risk. Risk and security managers hate to hear such things, of course; however, accepting more risk is not necessarily going to lead to disaster and horrible surprises. Understanding the impact of changes in competitive requirements on operational and process controls allows managers at all levels to understand what they are accepting.

This is where much risk management falls down: competitive requirements change fast, but the changes are not mapping to operational controls and nothing changes at the lower levels. In the complex IoT system that will evolve, these failings will have vastly amplified impacts over what we have seen in the past inside enterprise IT systems and isolated process control systems.

DIFFERENTIATION IN THE FACE OF COMMODITIZATION

Many IoT systems are being developed in an effort to offer a new and better way in the face of commoditization of *the old ways*.

How do you keep customers and stop an endless race to the bottom of prices in the face of product commoditization? This is a very common risk in many industries and dealing with it effectively is a particular organizational or business requirement in the IoT, and possibly more so than at any other time in the history of technology! Why?

Because a division is arising between the *thing* and its physical construction. Many things on the Internet are in large part defined by what they are as much as what they do. For instance, a motion sensor is a custom-built and assembled piece of hardware with specialized software that follows instructions from the equipment provider infrastructure. A blood glucose analysis machine is a custom-built platform, too, with customized software.

But what happens when the hardware is suddenly separated from the software, and generic hardware platforms with multiple integrated generic sensors and input ports come around, and the software is separated from the hardware?

This is exactly what has happened with the advent of smartphones. Smartphones have become platforms for a growing list of physical-logical interaction, including health applications and diagnostics—the (once) holy ground of the IoT. But no longer. Anecdotally, when the quality of *baseline*[3] capabilities approaches approximately 90+ percent of the capabilities of the custom

---

[3]*"Baseline"* is intended to mean the bare-bones functions that nearly all users would require and use regularly. For instance, all drivers need rear-view mirrors. But a car will serve many users very well without air conditioning or even a radio, which would be extra over and above the baseline.

devices. But for a small fraction (less than 10%) of the cost a specialized device, a substantial portion of the market appears to move to strong adoption. Not all the market, but enough to sustain those at the low end of the market using generic technologies to provide most of the functionality of specialized technologies, and encourage the generic platforms to further refine their capabilities and better compete. A prime example of this is in the medical equipment market, where cheap forms of ultrasound device coupled with smartphone technology are highly competitive with much more expensive, dedicated devices that are deemed to be better.[4] The IoT is engendering much more of this sort of innovation and competition.

In the IoT, hardware platforms are being genericized, meaning that, potentially, different vendors' solutions could be loaded on the same platform. This makes the ability to differentiate much more problematic because hardware performance is no longer in scope. In addition, because software is much cheaper to create than integrated hardware-software products, competition will go up and margins down—and the dreaded race to the bottom starts.

Alternately, an IoT system maker might embrace the generic platforms and use the opportunity to create new lines of products and services at different prices for different types of customers or entirely new customer bases. In a crisis there is opportunity, as the saying goes.

Therefore a significant organizational requirement in the IoT, and one directly related to risk management, will be maintaining product differentiation in the face of platform commoditization. The risk is whether the entire business can remain a viable, profitable entity.

Ironically, platform commoditization also offers substantial potential for both efficiency improvements and customer satisfaction. Freed from the burden of hardware manufacturing and integration, there are many places an IoT device maker, application developer, or service provider or operator may divert resources for new and better features.

This conundrum may appear limited at this time, and certain industries or IoT manufacturers may think themselves immune, but that would be folly. The markets are clearly moving away from customized platforms for intelligent devices of all types, and the shifts can occur almost overnight.

Finding the sweet spot between the harnessing of commodity platforms and cannibalizing revenue is one of the primary business and organizational requirements within the IoT.

See later in this book for a further discussion of the threats (Chapter 12, Threats and Impacts to the IoT) and vulnerabilities (Chapter 13, RIoT Control) associated with this requirement, and potential risk management techniques.

MOVING FROM VERTICAL MARKETS TO ECOSYSTEMS

The IoT will be about new applications and services created by multiple suppliers and vendors combining together yet interchangeably. Any given application in the IoT will have many potential stakeholders and contributors, as we discussed in Chapter 1, Introduction—The Internet of Things. This reflects the move from a traditional single provider of a consolidated suite of services to many services combined according to the preferences and specific requirements of the application owners and their clients. Variety of choice will in part define the IoT, and the emergence of ecosystems of suppliers and vendors drives this choice.

---

[4]*The Economist*, Dream of the medical tricorder; http://www.economist.com/news/technology-quarterly/21567208-medical-technology-hand-held-diagnostic-devices-seen-star-trek-are-inspiring.

For instance, there may be competing providers for endpoints, gateways, networks, and datacenters or cloud services. What is more, there might be many different suppliers or vendors within any of those asset classes, competing and differentiating themselves on many different features: service levels, throughput, up time, support, regionalization, customization, and so forth. There are many ways to cut the IoT cake to create new products and services efficiently and in many ways not seen before.

Therefore a major organizational requirement for managing risk in the IoT will be managing how an entity interfaces with the ecosystem of suppliers and vendors that will inevitably surround it.

This interface will essentially be a business or operation requirement, but at a technical level. It might be simply defined as the support for application programming interfaces (APIs) that allow other participants in the ecosystem to call for functions or jobs to be run, or information to be provided from the service provider. APIs allow these calls to be expressed in a predefined and standardized manner so customization is not required. There is basically an instruction manual that can be reused by anyone. Potentially, the service provider requires little to no knowledge of the third-party calling these functions, and this paves the way for automating the ecosystem.

An API works in the other direction, too: a service provider can make calls to another service provider in order to make certain functionality or information available for its own value-added operations and processes.

Without APIs, the IoT efficiencies and business cases will be greatly impeded by the need for customization. In such a case, every provider of goods and services has to form a bilateral relationship in order to interoperate with other providers of good or services. It simply cannot scale to the demands of the IoT.

The requirement to manage risk is related to the bidirectional nature of APIs. First, the requirement is related to the creation of APIs that allows third-party access to functions. Second, the requirement is related to using APIs for your own service delivery and therefore putting APIs on the critical path of your own organizational production, whether this be goods or services.

See later in this book for a further discussion of the threats (Chapter 12, Threats and Impacts to the IoT) and vulnerabilities (Chapter 13, RIoT Control) associated with this requirement for API and more open ecosystems, as well as potential risk management techniques.

INTERNAL POLICY REQUIREMENTS

Internal policy requirements may be about what the company expects from the IoT systems, above and beyond the financial, regulatory, and competitive requirements.

Internal policy requirements are *company law* and approved by management. Often company law is, in turn, derived from what is required according to the edicts of the industry or perhaps a trade association. These are things not part of legal regulations and requirements but may take on the same force as regulations because they have been mandated by top management. What specific internal policy comes about may ultimately be related to other organizational requirements such as competition and strategic market placement.

For instance, here are some internal policy requirements that would be recognizable around the world because of their pervasiveness or industry profile:

- As discussed earlier in this chapter, the NERC CIP requirement involves electricity infrastructure protection. This is a quasi-regulatory requirement in that it is not a law or a formal regulation associated with a law, but is required indirectly through regulation. In some cases, NERC CIP takes on an element of extraterritoriality by imposing regulatory obligations of entities not from the United States—specifically Canadian electricity entities with a high degree of cross-border integration with US producers. In such cases, top management of the Canadian producers need to establish a strong internal policy to retain business alignment with critical partners.

- PCI DSS[5]: involves PCI security standards for processing credit card payments. PCI DSS is a strong example of a quasi-standard established by an important community—the payment card community—which must be applied in order to retain transaction privileges. If an organization wishes to act as a merchant with the ability to process credit-card transactions (as an example), then PCI DSS comes into play. There are various levels of PCI DSS according to what degree of processing is being performed (value, clearing operations), but minimum levels of attestation are required, which are *not* enforceable under law. Possessing the ability to accept payment cards is a business privilege, not a right, and therefore compliance with PCI DSS is done in accordance with internal policy established by management.

- ISO 27001: Information Security Management System (ISMS) is widely adopted for auditing purposes by banks and government. Later in this chapter, we will discuss security audits and risk management in detail; however, suffice it to say at this point that audit is a resource-consuming exercise that is made easier through the application of standards-based security and risk programs. However, the upfront effort of creating a standards-based security program can appear more resource-intensive than just going for an ad hoc approach to security. For many reasons, this is a false assumption mostly because ad hoc security systems raise the price of audit and invariably leave more security holes that result in more incidents and associated (large) costs of remediation. But getting past this upfront pain of applying standards to internal operations rarely happens without management establishing and internal policy mandating the application of a security standard, such as ISO 27001.

- The National Institute of Standards and Technology (NIST)[6] 800 series of standards includes risk assessment and security controls that represent government-wide policy in the case of the US government. NIST is worth mentioning distinctly from other security standards both because of its excellence and its wide-ranging impacts through the vast supply-chain relationships of the US government. As a major procurer of goods and services, any company wishing to address contract information and communications technology (ICT) security requirements from the US government might wish either to apply a NIST-based security program as a matter of internal policy or, alternately, mandate that regardless of which security standard is applied internally to support audit and contractual compliance that a "mapping" to NIST be part of the security

---

[5]Payment Card Industry—Digital Security Standard (PCI DSS).
[6]US National Institute of Standards and Technology (NIST).

program. (*Mapping* is jargon for maintaining a list of which of the numbered security controls under NIST equate to the (numbered) security controls from the standard being applied, such as ISO 27001/2).

- In heavy industry and manufacturing, security is different. As a result, they have different or *adjusted* security standards. The easiest way to express the difference between typical enterprise ICT security and industrial IT security is that the order of primacy is changed. By convention, the enterprise considers security according to: confidentiality, integrity, and availability. In the manufacturing or industrial world, the primacy is typically availability, integrity, and *then* confidentiality. Manufacturing has its own security standards in the form of the converging ISA 99/IEC 62443/ISO 270xx (number still to be defined) as an IT security standard for manufacturers dealing with industrial control systems. The sum is that any industry or company dealing with the manufacturing of goods will potentially adopt an industrial standard over an enterprise standard and establish internal policy on that basis.

- At a national security level, organizations with elevated security and risk management requirements will opt for the sort of security benefits supplied by the employment of code-level controls like Common Criteria (CC[7]), Federal Information Processing Standards (FIPS[8]), or ISO 27034[9]. These types of controls are very granular in nature and the appreciation of them typically requires engineering training and know-how. They also tend to be very expensive because they apply detailed engineering examples and can create cost overhead to products and projects that—in the best case—provide no additional functionality or profit. However, the oversight provided by a CC or FIPS review brings accessibility to a variety of exclusive marketplaces, such as the US government.

AUDITING AND STANDARDS IN THE IoT

Auditing and standards will be critical to the IoT because they enable interoperability. From a risk management perspective, they enable business interoperability.

Without standards, the effort to get independently developed IoT devices, systems, and services working together will be a much more difficult process involving an infinite number of point-to-point relationships that simply do not scale.

Without standards the IoT will evolve more slowly, it will be more expensive, and it will ultimately possess lower quality and higher risk. The higher risk part will start with the business risks we discuss in this chapter, but extend to the operational risks we discuss in the next chapter and to an unlimited range of technical risks that we do not attempt to address.

The reason the IoT will be unmanageably risky without standards is due to the additional complexity that will come when standards are not present. Already the IoT will be the most complex and intricate thing ever created by mankind, with billions and billions of (literally) moving parts connected by ubiquitous and heterogeneous (many different types of) networks. From a risk management and security perspective, no standards mean each IoT system will need to have individual and unique security investments and assessment.

---

[7]http://www.commoncriteriaportal.org/.
[8]http://csrc.nist.gov/publications/PubsFIPS.html.
[9]http://www.iso27001security.com/html/27034.html.

If each IoT system had individual and unique security, then each interface or connect between each system would have to be established through a slow bilateral processes. Such an approach to IoT service development would be uncontrollably expensive and violate one of the most common business requirements of the IoT: that the IoT create value through efficiencies or customer satisfaction, not destroy it.

Without standards, the alternative to an expensive, bilateral system of security and risk management is simply to accept unknown risk—the worst type of risk management decision that can be made, and in many cases counter to regulation and law.

STANDARDS HAVE FLAVORS

Like requirements, security and risk management standards come in essentially three flavors: management (business), operational, and technical.

Management standards provide guidance for the policy frameworks, libraries, the legal/contractual elements, and the audit regimes associated with security and best practices. Many of the existing security standards work can be applied successfully to the IoT, but also gaps exist and are being created, as we will shortly discuss.

Operational standards typically flow out of the management standards and provide guidance related to how security controls should be applied as processes and technical controls involving hardware and software. Operational standards give broad guidance about what sort of processes should be in place and how they should be managed to ensure they are consistent, repeatable, and that risk is effectively managed. Operational standards like management standards will tend to have wide applicability across IoT systems.

Technical standards relate to how things are built. Technical standards allow technical interoperation, interchangeability of components and competition in supply changes—they have many merits. Technical standards are also specific to the IoT system (or any system in fact) under consideration and are either in or out of scope. For instance, if you don't have any radio frequency identification (RFID) assets in your IoT system, then the RFID standards simply don't matter to your risk management program.

DEFINING AUDIT SCOPE IN THE IoT

Much has been written about defining audit scope. Auditors themselves have written plenty about the best practices associated with audit scope generally. The intent in this very short section is to identify the techniques related to auditing in the IoT that may make that process more manageable and effective for all involved.

Scope in a security audit refers to the boundaries of investigation. What processes, practices, technologies, and assets will be examined in the process of assessing whether a degree of compliance has been achieved for a system?

Scope is *not* about establishing a comprehensive target list of everything that might impact the assurance of system. That is impossible because of the complex and un-guessable interdependencies that flow across all systems. Trying to set a scope that addresses all possible threats means you understand all possible threats.

In an IoT security audit, scope will be especially important because of the potentially large number of suppliers and stakeholders that were defined early. For the most part, all these players and stakeholders will have some sort of impact on security. This is especially the case with third-party suppliers of services related to endpoint, networks, and data storage and management. If the scope of the audit is set such that it closes over the many and various service provision boundaries in the IoT, it will drive the costs of the audit up and up, and potentially make the whole process nonviable due to delays and concerns about the way audit results will be used.

Audit in the IoT will therefore be a compartmentalized affair. Each of the various players will need to make independent attestations about his/her own role in the system. Managing and trusting these attestations will be the job the IoT application owner and his/her risk management functions. It is also reasonable to assume that generating audit results for IoT systems might amount to mostly collecting attestations from suppliers about the security of their systems. Conducting actual, formal, internal audits might be a small affair relative to what might be found in large vertically integrated systems where everything is owned and operated by a single entity.

Security scope in the IoT will necessarily be limited to whatever process and assets are actually under the control of the application owner. For instance, if the process of owning and managing an IoT system such as traffic monitoring systems results in just about everything being outsourced to a collection of specialized service providers, then regulatory compliance evidence is about the process of contracting and contract monitoring. In other words, due diligence evidence related to IoT security is about the proper crafting of service agreements to include the necessary stipulations about security (for compliance reasons) and then provisions for monitoring that the security stipulations are being applied by the service providers. Are monthly reports about security required? Are suppliers required to present some sort of audit result of their own to provide that their internal processes live up to their contracted obligations?

This is where the notion of third-party versus self-assessment and the notion of standards become critical to a successful audit within a practice and legitimate scope.

SHORT-TERM PAIN, LONG-TERM GAIN: THIRD-PARTY AUDIT VERSUS SELF-ASSESSMENT

Before discussing standards and their role in streamlining security compliance in the IoT, let's discuss the two basic types of audit that might be used by an organization to provide proof of compliance to regulatory requirements: third-party audit and self-assessment.

Third-party audit

Third-party audit is performed by an independent entity ideally according to internationally accepted auditing standards. Auditing standards are distinct from security standards. Audit standards outline "how" to perform and audit, while a security standard would define "what" to audit.

Typically, a third-party auditor is a consultant of some sort, commonly a professional, certified auditor (usually of financial records). This is the role that many of the largest accounting firms occupy and from which they generate a substantial portion of their revenue. These firms will be retained by the subject of the audit to gather evidence within the organization related to whether security *controls* are in place, are effective, and reflect the policies and commitments (regulatory or contractual) that the IoT goods/service provider is obliged to meet.

A third-party auditor usually comes into an organization with the support of top management and proceeds to pull the covers back and examine the inner workings of a business, according to the *scope of the audit.* This can certainly be an intrusive process and usually consumes significant amounts of time and money in both consulting fees and internal overhead (people time). Third-party audit is not usually something an organization submits to willingly; it is often a matter of explicit requirements or a clear need to prove beyond a reasonable doubt that the results are objective and legitimate. Self-assessment is often the chosen path where it is available.

> "Scope" is a critical element associated with all third-party audit and assessment, and an area where illegitimate manipulation of results can occur to the detriment of the users and consumers of a given good or service. The IoT will be no exception, and in some cases may be more vulnerable to audit scope manipulation because of the stratified and outsourced nature of IoT service composition. We discuss audit scope manipulation in the next section.

Self-assessment

Self-assessment as a form of audit is an internal matter; insiders gather and assess evidence of compliance according to much more ad hoc systems (not necessarily applying auditing standards). Self-assessment is a widely used form of audit in many industries and is permissible under some form of regulation in some industries.

Self-assessment is often preferred over third-party audit because of the fact that it can be far cheaper to run a self-assessment with internal resources than to use an independent third-party. However, self-assessments are also widely acknowledged to be a lesser form of evidence of compliance to regulatory or other requirements. Self-assessments are also more susceptible to "shaping" by internal interests to gain a favorable outcome and audit opinion. For instance, it is not unknown for organizations to perform self-assessments with high scores, only to suffer massive security incidents days later.

In such cases it is usually not a matter of fraud or even bad faith. The self-assessors simply see the most optimistic interpretation of the evidence they gathered to award themselves a pass where an independent third-party might have objectively been more circumspect.

WITCHES BREW: STANDARDS AND THE ART OF THE AUDIT SCOPES

In the following section we will discuss international security standards. But first a quick discussion on how standards play an important role associated with the business requirement for risk and the IoT and how that is helpful.

Audits are used to prove or demonstrate some sort of assurance that a system is operating at a reasonable level of security, according to a well-informed assessor. But, performing audits is expensive and not something to be done in an ad hoc manner. And what can create an ad hoc audit that is both costly and nonrepeatable? Creating a scope of analysis (audit scope) that is itself ad hoc. This is where standards enter.

International security standards can remove much of the perceived and real arbitrariness of an audit scope by providing a baseline set of things that should be done in a security information system. While it is still possible for those being audited to pick and choose which parts of a standard to apply, and to pass audits against those standards, at least the list of available security controls is defined.

With a list of defined security controls from an internationally developed and ratified standard, audits can become repeatable within organizations and comparable across organizations. While there will always be variances in quality of audits and the veracity of the findings, this comparability goes a long way to making risk management in information systems and the IoT easier.

That is basically what standards do for the IoT and especially risk management in the IoT: they make Risk and the Internet of Things (RIoT) control easier.

STANDARDS BODIES IMPACTS ON THE IoT

There are standards, and then there are standards. Similarly, there are standards bodies, and then there are standards bodies. In other words, there are many standards and some are more widely accepted and applied than others. And unfortunately, there is not a lot of control over who can say what a standard is. In security and risk management, this is as much the case as in any industry.

Let's take a look at the origin of these various standards because that often has an impact on the benefits of using those standards for securing IoT systems.

Standards come in a few different forms—some of them carrying more weight than others. At a high level they can represented as:

- Those defined by governments, such as ISO
- Those defined by nations for their sovereign domain, such as NIST
- Those defined by industry groups and associations, such as the Institute of Electrical and Electronics Engineers (IEEE), 3rd Generation Partnership Project (3GPP), and the Internet Engineering Task Force (IETF)
- Those led by vendors to promote a proprietary technology (AllSeen Alliance)

Of these, probably the most important to the IoT will be those based on blessing and faith of national governments and those based on the blessing and faith of industry groups, because the IoT will cross national boundaries in a transparent manner—as does the Internet itself—and will be interoperable across all vendors wishing to play a viable commercial role.

STANDARDS BODIES BORN OF GOVERNMENT

Standards bodies derived from and funded by national governments are common and include nation-specific and international organizations. Often, nations will support both national standards bodies and associations with international bodies.

An example of a national standards body would be NIST or the Korean Standards Association (KSA). Both of these entities would be accountable for generating standards specific to their own countries. These are merely two examples of dozens of nation-level standards organizations.

Another, broader type of standards body would be an international standards body, which would be composed of the nation-level bodies plus representatives from other sources, like industry standards bodies.

Two examples of international standards bodies are the ISO and the European Telecommunications Standards Institute (ETSI). ISO is a global standards organization, while ETSI is nominally European in nature but its specifications are so widely adopted and influential that it is almost global in practice.

Standards bodies born of government are different from those born of industry in ways not dissimilar to the differences between government and private industry; however, there is one particular difference related to security standards and therefore risk and the IoT that is worth understanding clearly. *Standards backed by governments tend to have more weight in law, regulation, and liability than standards from industry organizations.* This is a key point for risk managers in the IoT to be bear in mind at all times when dealing with standards for the purposes of managing risk.

Standards that have standing in law can come in many forms. On one hand, a government is entirely within its power to declare a standard that has been developed at a national or international level, in effect, the law of the land: *this is how it shall be done.* This sort of approach to standards in the IoT, and technology generally can be used as a leveler of the playing field or as an anticompetitive device.

A more typical approach is that a given standard, once supported by a national government through participation in group like ISO, can be written as a term into contracts by government and private industry and not be contested as ad hoc. In other words, the standard can take on the force of law through legally enforceable contracts.

Managing project risks in the IoT will certainly require an awareness of both international standards and their relationship to national standards and contract law.

STANDARDS BODIES BORN OF INDUSTRY GROUPS AND ASSOCIATIONS

The other way standards tend to be developed in the world of technology is through the collaboration of industry players with a mutual interest in quality and interoperability.

The sorts of players that get together will generally include manufacturers, service providers, liaisons from other standards groups, and often regulators from interested national governments. Together these players will often represent a good cross-section of interests.

Industry standards tend to support quality in products and services because good quality encourages adoption and endows a good reputation among users and clients. Lack of standards generally drives lower quality and a poor reputation for the good or service and hurts the overall business proposition. This is why the application of standards and branding with industry standards is a sign of quality. For instance, there were several different variants of wireless local area networks (LANs) in the early days, before the IEEE 802.11b specification became the original (but since surpassed) standard and a mark of a quality wireless LAN.

Industry standards also tend to drive technical interoperability, which in turns drives market growth by making room for product and service alternatives and therefore choice among users. Interoperability also means that users can avoid the trap of becoming tied to a proprietary solution. The risk of such solutions is that you either have to pay what the supplier demands or scrap your investment in order to move. Another risk associated with poor or no interoperability is that if the supplier disappears, you are stuck with a technology investment for which spares and support are unavailable. Interoperability is generally good for everyone, which is why industry standards explicitly promote it.

Distinct from the government-sponsored standards bodies, industry groupings tend to move faster and have been known to eclipse governmental bodies because of a drive to get to market. Conversely, industry-sponsored standards have been known to take occasional shortcuts to get to market, or (accidentally?) overlook certain public interest matters that conflicted with fast or efficient product or service introduction.

For instance, privacy issues in the IoT may not be a highlight of an industry-led standard, whereas it may be a major element in a government standard. In some ways this may make sense because public interest will vary from nation to nation and jurisdiction to jurisdiction. An industry standard would logically seek to remain policy neutral as far as possible. The danger in this approach is that functionality is insufficient to support whatever privacy or security functionality a regulator elects to apply.

Also, it is not common to find standards developed by industry associations to be adopted into law (though they may be augmented or adopted by a national standards body for that purpose). However, industry standards are very commonly written into contracts because, as mentioned previously, they act as a brand of quality and help manage risks associated with interoperability.

IoT STANDARDS IN 2016

At the time of the writing of this book (2012−16), the standards world, both government-born and industry-born, were in the early stages of standards development. Governmental standards bodies such as ISO/IEC/JTC1 WG10[10] and ITU-T SG 20[11] have started looking specifically at IoT security through study groups and even nascent IoT security efforts. Meanwhile, industry-led groups like IEEE[12], Industrial Internet Consortium (IIC)[13], and IETF have also done good work on IoT security specifically; though in the case of IETF, much of the effort is under protocol-specific topics under the term *constrained*.[14]

That is to say, there are not yet definitive standards related to the IoT, if you consider the IoT to be a system for which the sum is greater than the component parts of endpoints, networks, and DCs/clouds. Because most people believe this is the case, it is fair to say at this time there are no IoT standards. Yet.

There are standards for most of the underlying technologies in endpoints, gateways, networks, and DCs/clouds, but the *how* of piecing them together so the IoT services have a better chance of reusing elements and processes is not yet there. For example, some of the existing standards touch directly on the IoT, but do not address it as a whole.

---

[10]http://www.iec.ch/dyn/www/f?p=103:14:0::::FSP_ORG_ID,FSP_LANG_ID:12726,25.

[11]http://www.itu.int/en/ITU-T/studygroups/2013-2016/20/Pages/default.aspx.

[12]http://iot.ieee.org/.

[13]http://www.iiconsortium.org/.

[14]See examples in https://datatracker.ietf.org/wg/core/documents/ or https://datatracker.ietf.org/wg/ace/charter/ or https://datatracker.ietf.org/doc/rfc7252/.

Here are a few examples of burgeoning IoT standards, all of which touch on security at a high level; however, none of these standards define or address the IoT as we do in the book. Instead, they all tend to address a subset of the IoT.

- ITU-T Y.2221: Requirements for supporting Ubiquitous Sensor Network (USN)
- ITU-T Y.2060: Overview of Internet of Things
- ITU-T Y.2002: Overview of ubiquitous networking and of its support in NGN
- ISO WG7 29182-3: Sensor Networks: Sensor Network Reference Architecture (SNRA)
- ISO JTC1 WG10: Internet of Things Working Group
- ISO JTC1 SC27: IoT Study Group
- IEEE Internet of Things Initiative
- ETSI TS 102 690: Machine-to-Machine communications (M2M)
- 3GPP TS 22.368: Study on Enhancements for MTC
- 3GPP SA3: Security
- IoT: Architecture[15]
- IoT: Initiative[16]
- IoT@Work[17]
- M2M: oneM2M[18]
- NISTIR 7628: Guidelines for Smartgrid Cyber Security[19]
- NIST Cyber-physical systems group[20]
- ETSI TC SmartM2M
- ETSI TS 102 690: M2M
- Open Geospatial Consortium - Sensor Web for IoT[21]
- ITU-T
  - JCA-IoT; seehttp://www.itu.int/en/ITU-T/jca/iot/Pages/default.aspx.
- ISO/IEC 29182 Sensor Networks: (Part 1−Part 7)
- IETF Constrained Application Protocol (COAP)
- Industrial Internet Consortium—Security Working Group

For those managing security and risk in the IoT, this is a problem because the IoT will not wait for standards—it will be driven forward in a necessarily ad hoc manner by imperatives affecting both private and public institutions and businesses: customer satisfaction and operational efficiencies.

Additionally, many standards competing to provide guidance on different elements of the IoT will create conflicting guidance for implementers and confusion. Where there is confusion, risk and impacts will follow. Sometimes this risk will be a result of the actual conflicts themselves among standards, where costs are driven up or systems become impossible to operate due to overhead of partially applied controls. In other cases, the confusion of multiple standards will result in none of them being applied, for fear of using the *wrong one* and having to uninstall controls after the fact, at great cost.

---

[15]http://www.iot-a.eu/public/public-documents/documents-1.
[16]http://www.iot-i.eu/public/public-deliverables/.
[17]https://www.iot-at-work.eu/.
[18]http://www.onem2m.org/.
[19]http://www.nist.gov/smartgrid/upload/nistir-7628_total.pdf.
[20]http://www.nist.gov/cps/.
[21]http://www.opengeospatial.org/projects/groups/sweiotswg.

In part, this book is intended as an aid to fill this gap related to standards and formal guidance related to the IoT, and the evolution of the first generation of the IoT security standards, which should probably not be expected before the 2018 timeframe—maybe later. And even then, they will be first generation standards, subject to revision and tuning over subsequent years.

A caveat to the above point is related to highly parochial IoT applications and systems. In areas like *smart meter* and *smart grid*, a significant amount of effort has been applied to develop security standards.[22] Though even in these early cases, the standards have played catch-up with the deployment of the actual systems. And while these standards are highly useful within their specific application domain, they have less applicability generally to many different IoT use cases that are out there.

WHAT TO EXPECT FROM SECURITY STANDARDS IN THE IoT

And what will IoT security standards contain once they are released? What will an IoT security standard look like? Expect to see at least three useful things that will support organization requirements related to policy: terminology, reference designs, and use cases.

TERMINOLOGY FROM IoT SECURITY STANDARDS

The IoT standards as they exist in 2016 are rife with overlapping terminology, synonyms, and even antonyms that can confuse system owners, managers, and developers, thus creating substantial risk.

One example is confusing terms about a fairly basic concept: the network. In some IoT-related standards, the network is referenced but considered out of scope—not part of the specification—though it is referenced as a critical support infrastructure for the rest of the system.

In other IoT standards, the network is absolutely in scope for the security and controls stipulated and therefore integrated into the designs produced under such standards. Because so much security capability and risk can reside at the network level, whether or not to design and utilize security from the network will have a large impact of the IoT system and processes.

In these cases the terminology associated with *network* is vastly different: one is a theoretical construct that is not part of the specification, the other is an active element of the specification. The key difference associated with risk and these terms associated with the network is about what is assumed.

If the term *network* is used as a theoretical construct for something out of scope, then the assumption is that whatever security controls not mentioned or related in the standard must be compensated for in other places in the IoT system. Conversely, if the term *network* refers to an in scope asset for the standard, then security controls associated with the network should be mentioned. The assumption is that any missing controls will have to reside at much higher levels in the design, such as within the application layer. This is a nuance that might easily confuse designers and security professionals alike.

---

[22]For example, NISTIR 7628—Guidelines for Smartgrid Cyber Security—http://www.nist.gov/smartgrid/upload/nistir-7628_total.pdf.

REFERENCE MODELS, REFERENCE ARCHITECTURES, AND THE IoT

Reference designs, reference models, and reference architectures frequently mean different things to different people and especially across standards. Sometimes a standard will possess all three and make a distinction among what one is versus the other by way of the view that they offer to the reader.

A reference model might be a very abstract presentation of the different elements of a solution (in the IoT or otherwise), which is really about understanding the system end-to-end, and its parts in a broad way. Such a model is most useful in that it educates the new and inexperienced on the basic range of issues and players that might exist.

A reference design also serves to avoid major oversights by establishing the basic scope of organizational requirements: what needs to be considered. Not all elements in all reference models necessarily need to be part of final system designs, but they should be considered. In the IoT, with its inherent complexity and broad range of stakeholders, reference models have utility by aiding comprehension of the system and where security might be required and why.

By comparison, a reference architecture could be substantially more detailed than a reference model. A reference architecture might assume that the information from a reference model is available and part of the decision making process already: the user is already aware of the reference model. A reference architecture for the IoT might include information about the connectivity among different technical elements, and potentially provide some technical specifications about the elements themselves or their functionality. For instance, the ability of elements to process data, the type of interface they support (human, machine-only, both) and the way they communicate with the large I/O system as a whole (wireless, fixed-line, through gateways, and so forth).

Reference models and architectures aid in establishing boundaries for the discussion related to the standard—what is in and out of scope—meaning, what is out of scope needs to be addressed elsewhere, if there are security implications, because the controls within the security standard are not intended to address all potential risks.

Reference models and architectures serve to educate on the range of considerations when developing an IoT system and especially considering the security of the system. In the IoT there will be many stakeholders and players in a typical IoT application: from hardware vendors to service platform providers. A reference point provided by a standard indicating what sorts of controls might commonly exist provides a critical baseline from which to start questioning stakeholders about what they do, and what they assume related to risk management and the IoT.

USE CASES IN THE IoT

Earlier in this book we had a discussion about some of the sample use cases that will likely appear in the IoT. Standards should support and enhance the understanding of the IoT by employing use cases to explain the need for security and how the range of security controls that the standard promotes is applicable within use cases. More importantly, use cases should outline why a control is important and what sort of risk it might address.

In this way, use cases within standards start to expose a little more about the threats that controls can address or the type of risks that are being accepted when IoT system developers and owners elect not to employ certain controls and safeguards.

PUT IT ALL TOGETHER: STANDARDS AID RISK MANAGEMENT IN THE IoT

As we have said before, accepting risk is a legitimate form of risk management, especially if treating or transferring the risk ruins the operational benefits or customer experience associated with the IoT system or application.

Standards, through the provision of terminology, reference models, reference designs, reference architectures, and use cases, provide a level base for making risk decisions in the IoT. Standards aid in understanding the scope of the security requirements, the range of potential and recommended controls, and examples of how they might be applied.

Most usefully, standards allow risk managers to understand better which risks they are accepting and balancing against other requirements beyond security.

SUMMARY

In this chapter, we have reviewed some of the most common business and organizational requirements that can have different impacts on risk management in the IoT. These imperatives may possess different weights from industry to industry but should always be considered, even if they are assessed to have little importance in the final analysis. Short-circuiting this process of assessing business requirements is extremely dangerous from an IoT risk management perspective because oversights committed at this stage will resonate throughout the entire IoT system.

Business and organizational requirements need to be actively communicated by management, whether they be about financial requirements, regulatory requirements, internal policy requirements, or competitive and marketplace requirements. These are the top-level requirements to which all other security and risk management should map so that as many of the top-level risks to the IoT system as possible are considered.

Regulatory requirements in the IoT will come from many different directions, depending on the industry, but a few common regulatory burdens will impact most if not all IoT systems. Privacy issues will be frequently discussed, even if there is no personally identifiable information under management—there will always be a need to quickly identify and address demands related to privacy. Compliance is not an option but managing the hybrid mixture of governmental and industry regulation can be a fraught proposition.

Financial requirements associated with risk management and security will have a profound impact on the development of the IoT. For instance, the need for security and risk management to be balanced against costs appears as an obvious statement, yet the business cases for security in many organizations are often poorly stated. We have no reason to believe this situation will automatically change with the arrival of the IoT. Even in publicly funded IoT systems (for instance, some health services) where profit motive is not part of the defining organizational requirements, security will not be a blank check. Using tools like the one discussed in this book will aid in making sure that security and risk are managed in accordance with financial and all top-level business requirements.

From a competitive perspective, managing risk in the IoT will be about the balance of complexity with the ability to keep security effective! The IoT will not be about the best widget, but about the best combinations of widgets and supporting services, interfaces, and support features—probably being supplied partially (if not entirely) by third parties. Competitive drivers will force IoT service providers constantly to morph and expand their means of delivering services, making the security and risk posture a constantly shifting target as a matter of a top-level business requirement.

Internal policy is another form of business requirement that should be taken into account when designing IoT security programs and systems. What does the business expect from the system over and above regulatory, financial, and competitive pressures? The answer may be quite a lot, especially when the regulatory environment is vague about what compliance actually requires! Then internal policy will step into place: *internal policy requirements are where executives will manage the ambiguity associated with regulatory requirements.*

Closely associated with regulatory and internal policy compliance will be auditing and security standards in the IoT. Auditing will be a mandatory business requirement in the IoT to prove not only security and regulatory compliance but also the risks associated with the cyber-physical interface and dangers to personal prosperity and privacy.

Auditing is not something any manager looks forward to, and auditing the IoT will be a difficult process at first. Auditing will consume scarce resources during the deployment and early adoption phases of IoT, but can rapidly gain in efficiency if done correctly and is supported by standards. Side-stepping audit is a recipe for long-term failure for short-term savings. For instance, side-stepping the use of comprehensive international standards in favor of lighter homegrown standards is a recipe for long-term failure when those internally developed standards are found to be an insufficient option for other reasonable and well-informed third parties. Additionally, audits performed against homegrown standards may not pass the approval of regulators, who do not have an interest in independently assessing each homegrown security regime and its policy set. They would rather know that an audit has been successful against a recognized standard, and you both face less professional risk by accepting those results.

OPERATIONAL AND PROCESS REQUIREMENTS

In this chapter, we consider Internet of Things (IoT) requirements that will directly drive design decisions and affect the security of the IoT: operational and process requirements.

Recall from earlier chapters of this book that each of these requirements should map to one of the higher-level business and organizational requirements that are established by the management leadership.

Our goal in this chapter is to provide a framework and starting point for the assessment and development of operational requirements, while the subsequent five chapters will each deal with a specific operational requirement category.

The intention is that each IoT operational requirement category will be meaningful to any given IoT application, system, service, or use case. However, this relevance will be in different proportions for each IoT system, service or use-case. Similarly, not all the operational requirements presented in the chapters after this one are applicable to all IoT applications, systems, services, and use cases; however, all the requirements are worth reviewing by system designers, managers, and engineers to determine if they should be included or excluded, and prioritized accordingly.

Below the level of operational requirements, we have technical requirements. The granular details of capacity, speed, power, and many other quantitative metrics that make detailed product selection and system design possible. Keep in mind that the range of potential for technical requirements in the IoT is near infinity, so we do not attempt to enumerate them in this book.

PARABLE FOR OPERATIONAL AND PROCESS REQUIREMENTS

For one final time, we will use a parable to illustrate the importance of understanding requirements generally.

Bob is the founder of an IoT startup with a product in the automotive and transportation industry called SocialRide. It has developed an application that links social networking apps on the driver's smartphone to the car's navigation systems. SocialRide allows drivers to locate and navigate to family and friends with a seamless, one-click interface integrated into the vehicle navigation system. SocialRide is a free app that must be installed on the user's smartphone and interact with the user's social networking accounts to find friends and promote SocialRide to them. SocialRide takes global positioning system (GPS) coordinates from the phone on which it is installed and uses them to enter address information into the onboard navigation system.

SocialRide has managed to get itself into a testing phase with a large automobile manufacturer, after about 18 months of development and sales efforts. In the course of testing, the automobile manufacturer starts to report back the following unaddressed operational requirements they have noticed with the product.

First, data protection requirements: SocialRide had some security built into its apps in the form of encrypted network connections back to the central company. But mostly the application relied on the native security of the in-car wireless services and operating systems, and whatever the user had for security on his/her devices. However, SocialRide also had undisclosed (though perhaps not specifically hidden) features that skirted privacy guidelines contained in most regulation and parochial legislation. For instance, SocialRide copies all contacts from both the local address book and any social network apps, and transfers them back to the SocialRide server. This functionality is key to the value proposition of the app, consequently no ability to limit the transfer of this personal information is available. Similarly, the SocialRide app automatically disclosed the user's GPS location at all times; there is no option to limit how or when location information is disclosed.

Second, identity and access requirements: the SocialRide in-car application memory copies the user's contacts and caches them locally. These contacts are available when the car is turned on, so the assumption is that if you have the car's key, you have permission to access the SocialRide contacts even if the smartphone is not present. Additionally, the in-car application only allows contacts to be removed through a complex series of commands that are hard to find. In the event the car changes ownership (or is rented) it is likely that personal contacts will remain behind.

Third, context requirements: unlike most in-car navigation systems, the SocialRide in-car app lets drivers configure searches while the car is moving; it does not attempt to detect whether the car is in motion. This is a distracting feature and conflicts with the safety feature in many in-car navigation systems that require the car to be stationary before complex user inputs will be accepted. This is a physical safety requirement, and in some places a legal one as well.

Fourth, system flexibility in design requirements: SocialRide comes with limited help and instructions for starters, but also has no ability to change the size, color, or transparency of the location overlays it applies to the navigation systems. The icons it displays for the location of family and friends are fixed in shape and size. Not only does this tend to obscure other elements of the map that users might value (like street names), but basically makes it impossible for any other sort of third-party app to use the navigation system display for any other value-added service.

Finally, availability and reliability requirements: the SocialRide app on the user's smartphone operates and runs well within the normal parameters of most apps but occasionally hangs and needs to be restarted. SocialRide estimates that restarting the app takes about 3 seconds, and is required on average once or twice per week if it is left running constantly. However, when the app on the user's smartphone hangs, this causes the location of friends and family in the navigation system also to freeze. The result after user testing by the manufacturers is the perception that the car's navigation system is malfunctioning. This affects the perceived quality of the manufacturer's brand.

All of these shortcomings are where things that could have been addressed in development, except they were operational security and risk management requirements that SocialRide had not accounted for, mostly because it did not engage in a formal or methodological requirements assessment process in the beginning.

The manufacturer provides the above comments to SocialRide, but also loses interest in the product. After 2 years and about $1M in seed financing, the company misses its window of opportunity and fails.

INTRODUCTION

When we were discussing business and organizational requirements in the previous chapter, we were talking about executive-level concerns and issues.

At the operational level, we move down at least one level in the business hierarchy to those managing business units and *horizontal* assets within an organization like information technology (IT), finance, and human resources (HR), and possibly sales and marketing and even more functions that might be shared by different business units, but these structures vary widely from organization to organization.

This chapter is about the operational requirements to be considered when establishing a complete risk management program for IoT service. We have not limited ourselves to the operational requirements that might be directly and clearly associated with security audits and compliance, for instance. That would be very easy, but would also leave many gaps from the enterprise perspective.

This enterprise-level perspective of requirements is what we intend to discuss, with a view to risk management. More directly, we are presenting requirements with the enterprise risk management of the IoT, not merely the requirements associated with operations of software, hardware, people, and security processes.

AUDIENCE

At the operational level of the IoT, we categorize requirements into five areas, which are described next and are each the subject of entire chapters to follow.

But there are said to be five different *personas* with different but interrelated requirements from the IoT.[1] These five personas are:

- The Device Trackers
- The Data Insight Seekers
- Device Custodians
- Real-Time Data Analyzers
- Security Fanatics

The requirements that we are about to review are intended and written for what has been unlovingly termed the *Security Fanatics*. Fortunately, everyone knows that without security in IoT systems, there would be no IoT: without security any and every IoT system would run for a short time, then fail spectacularly.

There is nothing more fanatical about requiring security in the IoT than there is about wearing a seatbelt or cooking meat before you eat it. So there!

Nonetheless, the other personas concerned with the operations of the IoT and therefore the management of Risk and the IoT are worth understanding. *These personas will be allies and collaborators for security and risk people. Your requirements will frequently be their requirements, and opportunity to leverage common goals to get necessary resources and executive support.*

---

[1]Frog Design, September 2014 Intel Executive Summit presentation.

THE DEVICE TRACKERS

The device tracker persona is composed primarily of end users of IoT, the system integrators and field engineers who make decisions related to the services dependent on the IoT endpoints being tracked. They represented about 16% of the populated sample in our referenced source and tend to come from large organizations and enterprises.

"Device Trackers care about locating devices, protecting them and predicting when they will run out of power. However, they don't care about ongoing general maintenance and diagnostics. This group is currently using tools to receive and store real-time data on the location and health of their devices. But they still are looking for more complete data, cheaper alternatives, and less complexity in IoT solutions."[2]

DATA INSIGHT [SEEKERS]

The data insight persona are roles such as product application developers and field engineers building the system to support the IoT service. They are interested in which specific features and functions are in demand and how they might be best applied to maximize customer satisfaction. Those seeking data insights for product applications represent about 20% of the personas in the IoT and tend to come from smaller (entrepreneurial?) firms who also look to shared platforms and cloud service for intelligence.

"Data Insight Responders care about taking action on data insights remotely. They employ data sharing and search to gather data and look for relevant insights. Then they use the data insights to take action such as inform security or predict and manage failure. They want application development tools and public cloud integration but care least about scalability. This group has a large range of tools they currently use as well as current pain points. That is because they are looking for a complete end-to-end solution that captures all the data available."[3]

DEVICE [CUSTODIANS]—LONGEVITY SPECIALISTS

Device custodian personas will be found in system integrators and operational managers, the sort of people who develop, apply, and potentially enforce service level agreements. They are the persona in the IoT with the smallest probable population, according to the research at hand. They account for about 13% of the personas. (However, device custodians have the strongest affinity with the security fanatic persona.)

"Device [Custodians]—Longevity Specialists care about device monitoring and management – keeping devices up and running smoothly. If a device does fail, this group of mainly System Implementer and System Managers places extreme importance on backing-up and recovering the device data. Device Longevity Specialists don't display many unique characteristics in terms of current tool usage behaviors. They also have needs that are commonly expressed by all five segments around themes of process automation, standards, security, employee training and price."

---

[2]Frog Design, September 2014 Intel Executive Summit presentation.
[3]Frog Design, September 2014 Intel Executive Summit presentation.

REAL-TIME DATA ANALYZER

The real-time data analyzer persona in the IoT is largely made up of those doing the engineering integration of the IoT service from end to end (device, gateway, network, cloud), or those providing the platforms and applications that manage the data from the IoT devices *en masse*. Not surprisingly, these people come from the wide range of small to medium-sized organizations providing cloud-based applications and platforms for the IoT. They also represent the largest population of personas, at 27% of those involved in the research.

"Real-Time Data Analyzers care about receiving a constant stream of processed data linked to their devices. They use this data to maintain a continuous status report and send feedback back downstream to the device. The ability to use this wealth of current data in order to predict future states is also highly valued. Although analytics is key, this group is currently using data analytics and real time data streaming tools an average amount compared to other segments. Therefore, there is an opportunity to delight this segment with real time analytics solutions."

SECURITY FANATICS

Security Fanatics (also known as security folk and risk managers or merely *smart people*) tend to come overwhelmingly from groups of either end users of the IoT services and devices or the managers of the IoT systems (probably service vendors in some instances). The represented 17% of the surveyed population and come from a range of small to large business. In truth we are all end users, but the security fanatic population is drawn from the range of explicit stakeholders in the IoT.

"Security Fanatics care about the security of data transmission from devices. In fact, they value security so highly that three of the five top utility scores across all segments are for security-related attributes in this segment. Having analytics tools to predict future device needs are also important to this group. Made up primarily of End Users, this segment uses cloud services the least, although they express medium-to-high value for IoT Platform as a Service (PaaS)."

OPERATIONAL AND PROCESS REQUIREMENTS IN THE IoT

Finally, we have come to the part of this chapter where we will set the stage for the next five chapters of this book, where we enumerate operational and business process requirements that are emerging for the IoT. These requirements have been selected because they will be especially meaningful to the management of risk in the IoT.

Requirements, as we discussed earlier in this chapter, are necessary to a risk management process because they highlight the sensitivity of assets in the IoT to different threats and vulnerabilities.

The operational and process requirements in this book will not all appear as obvious security requirements in all cases. These requirements will in many cases be central to many non-security use cases; nonetheless they have been included here because they will have a significant security and risk management impact.

The following lists of requirements are not specific to any of the industries we may have profiled in previous chapters, but are intended as a cross-section representation of typically important requirements that may be present in just about any industry. *They are a superset of IoT operation and process security and risk management requirements.* It will really be up to the asset owners, field engineers, service providers, and/or application owners to determine which requirements are valid in the case of their particular IoT use case.

These requirements are not exhaustive, but they should be novel in the sense that they have been compiled specifically as IoT risk management requirements. They are not merely security, but risk management in the sense of enterprise and organizational risks (discussed in the Chapter 4, Business and Organizational Requirements). They should be considered more like a sampling of the potential range of requirements for operational and business process requirements in the IoT. These requirements are selected because they appear to be rather unique to the IoT or different from you might find in risk management processes in more traditional IT systems.

ORGANIZATIONAL RISKS AND REQUIREMENTS

Quickly recapping our discussion from Chapter 4, Business and Organizational Requirements, of this book: business and organizational requirements are most visible at the executive level. They include:

- Regulatory risks and requirements related to laws or industry standards;
- Financial risks and requirements for budget, profit, margin;
- Internal policy risks and requirements related to organizational directives and mandates; and
- Competitive risks and requirements such as time to market, price points or cost pressures, product differentiation, product automation, protection of intellectual property, and strategies.

The requirements we present here each support at least one of the business-level and organizational requirements in a clear and demonstrable manner. Depending on the industry and IoT use case, the same operational requirement may support different business and organizational requirements. For this reason, we are not going to attempt to create a mapping from operational to business-level requirements.

Generally, operational and process requirements will have to do with:

- Policies that govern specific behaviors of people or processes
- Procedures that provide detailed guidance about how a policy might be implemented or how a process is correctly applied
- Designs and architectures that support the business and organizational requirements for assurance

THE REMAINING CHAPTERS IN THIS BOOK

The requirements in the chapters that follow in this book have been organized into five major categories. In some cases, the placement of a given operational requirement within a chapter was not clear cut; there may have been more than one category where it would have made sense.

Some of these chapters will be very familiar to people with a risk or security management background, while other chapters may appear to these same people to be new or *none core* to traditional security and risk management. But that is the point! The IoT is expanding the requirements for risk management by blending physical and logical systems, manual and fully automated systems, and linking them together via a common network technology. Please resist the temptation to skip one category of requirement!

A major purpose for this book is to try and expose the fact that risks and security change in the IoT. New and unfamiliar issues and requirements affect the risk manager in ways that would not be commonly seen in a more basic, enterprise IT environment. This is an important part of Risk and the Internet of Things (RIoT) control: acknowledging that requirements need to be considered that in a disconnected, not-IoT world just might not matter nearly as much.

Safety. This chapter will review a critical requirement often not associated with enterprise IT systems and the contemporary Internet, safety: What is the effect on risk in terms of (physical or logical) damage if the IoT system fails or performs in a defective or out-of-spec manner?

Confidentiality, Privacy, and Integrity. This discussion will be familiar to security and risk people. It will be about two of the three key properties of security: confidentiality and integrity, with privacy addressed at length as a specific function of confidentiality.

Reliability and Availability. The third key property of security is availability, and requirements associated with availability are presented in this chapter. Availability deliberately has been broken out from confidentiality and integrity because it is at least as important in the IoT as confidentiality and availability; whereas in the enterprise IT world, it is traditionally seen as lower profile requirement.

Identity and Access Control. Identity and Access (I&A) is a critical security and risk management control that is often outside the scope of security and risk management people. I&A services and assets are often run by entirely distinct operational groups, separate from the rest of security. Is some ways, I&A is to data protection and reliability what whales are to the rest of the mammalian world: related but unknown to each other. I&A resources and assets often exist in a security vacuum, rarely seen or touched by the other security assets, using technologies and techniques that are not seen outside the I&A domain. Being aware of this particular species of mammal is critical to RIoT control.

Usage, Context, and Environment. In this chapter, we are getting beyond the range of typical security concerns and into IoT-specific requirements related to risk and security. These are the sorts of requirements that makes the IoT different. These requirements reflect real risk to IoT systems, in the event they are not considered as issues affecting security and ultimately business-level requirements driving efficiency and customer satisfaction.

Flexibility of Design. This last area continues to push the boundaries of awareness for risk and security practitioners. The interconnectedness, cascading impacts, and unprecedented speed of action and reaction in the IoT will take attributes typically left to industrial design and bring them to the attention of risk managers. This may be an uncomfortable innovation for some, but a necessary innovation for comprehensively managing risk in the IoT.

Each of these organizational and process requirement areas will be explored in its own chapter of this book.

SAFETY REQUIREMENTS IN THE INTERNET OF THINGS

6

This chapter discusses safety risk requirements in the IoT and how they are related to security requirements.

Safety is a distinct requirement/characteristic in the IoT, having to do with areas not typically addressed by IT, but critical in the IoT given the cyber physical, logical kinetic interconnections. Safety is more about physical-device (vs software-system) resilience, and predictability of performance and failure (logically and physically).

Safety is intertwined with security and many of the other chapters will discuss requirements that have as much to do with safety as it does with security. For instance, safety is absolutely related to matters such as availability of confidentiality, but also the industrial design and usage context of an IoT system or service.

Safety will also be as much a part of the risk management associated with matters like supply chains, provenance, and the complete life cycle of a product or system, whether the product or system is to be used in the workplace, in the household environment, or for recreational activities.

Safety in the IoT might be seen more prosaically as something that is a physical outcome of a logical or *cyber* event. The following sorts of events might be considered a safety impact for humans:

- Explosion and burning.
- Allergic reactions, for instance to wearable things or to environmental conditions that change as a result of things like climate control systems.
- Sensory impacts (degrade or harm hearing, or especially sight), such as augmented reality systems and services that temporarily or even permanently degrade senses because they are too intense or close.
- Infections and tumors, again related to wearable or implantable devices in the IoT used for therapeutic applications.

The goal of this chapter is to highlight elements that are associated with security but are more typically discussed in a safety context. Put another way, this chapter is intended to introduce IoT risk managers to requirements that may be unfamiliar to those coming from an enterprise IT security environment, versus an industrial environment.

Finally, the IoT safety requirements defined in this chapter will take on different complexions depending on the intended use case of the IoT service. For instance, different types of end users will have greater or lesser understanding of safety and may require different design assumptions around the need for automation of safety functions. Similarly, different operational environments,

RIoT Control. DOI: http://dx.doi.org/10.1016/B978-0-12-419971-2.00006-6

such as home, office, factory, or rugged-outdoor systems, will require more or fewer layers of supplementary safety and security systems, depending on the use case. This indicates that broad-based assumptions about safety and security will not work in the IoT, because in some cases a failure in one security or safety system may be compensated for in other adjacent systems, and in other cases it may not.[1]

SAFETY IS NOT EXACTLY THE SAME AS SECURITY

Ask any industrial control system (ICS) engineer whether enterprise IT security standards and processes are useful in their environment, and he/she is likely to say "partially but definitely not completely." ICS security practitioners have for many years rejected the overtures of *IT security* experts and standards, claiming that ICS is not the same and has different requirements.

They were right. They are right! The lessons learned from those early encounters between ICS and IT now extend to the IoT—which has *combined* the two practices inextricably:

$$ICS + IT = IoT$$

To try and summarize it: ICS and IT have different performance and reliability requirements. ICS especially uses operating systems and applications that may be considered unconventional to typical IT support personnel. Furthermore, the goals of safety and efficiency can sometimes conflict with security in the design and operation of control systems (for example, requiring password authentication and authorization should not hamper or interfere with emergency actions for ICS).

In a typical IT system, data confidentiality and integrity are typically the primary concerns. For an ICS, human or property safety and fault tolerance to prevent loss of life or endangerment of public health or confidence, regulatory compliance, loss of equipment, loss of intellectual property, or lost or damaged products are the primary concerns. The personnel responsible for operating, securing, and maintaining ICS must understand the important link between safety and security.

In a typical IT system, there is limited or even no physical interaction with the environment. ICS can have very complex interactions with physical processes and consequences in the ICS domain that can manifest in physical events.

Safety as an IoT requirement also addresses one key aspect of system behavior: protection against entropic (random) faults of an unintentional nature.

The following safety requirements might overlap and be interdependent with other requirements to follow in this book, but they are worth understanding independently because of the critical nature of safety in the IoT.

PERFORMANCE

Information technology (IT) is full of false claims about performance, which will represent a large safety risk to the IoT. Vendors of IT hardware and software alike will publish claims about

---

[1]ISO EIC Guide 51—*Safety Aspect—Guidelines for Their Inclusion in Standards*, third ed.

performance metrics that simply cannot be replicated. This is all too common; however, industry has learned to adapt to this chronic overstatement of performance by discounting vendor claims, requiring (expensive) trials and proof-of-concept demonstrations, and generally over provisioning infrastructure.

Customers often buy a network device expecting that it will perform at 1 Gbps, for instance, only to find that once they configure it the way they need its performance drops to half or even less! Similarly, organizations invest in software expecting that it will handle (again, just an example) 100 transactions per millisecond, only to find that the vendor performance claims are supported only with very specific hardware configurations that are not appropriate to the customer environment.

In the IoT, where the logical-kinetic/cyber physical interfaces predominate, performance will be about features and metrics like: time criticality, delay, or jitter—reliability of performance; whereas some of the IT-related metrics like maximum throughput might not be important. We will discuss such performance metrics subsequently in this section.

In the IoT, performance of endpoint, gateway, network, and cloud/data-center elements needs to be as advertised by product and service vendors.

Clarity of performance in products and services is an essential requirement of the IoT. When it comes to performance in the IoT, both product and service vendors need to be aware that fudging the numbers or being deliberately vague or deceptive drives untold risks.

RELIABILITY AND CONSISTENCY

ICS includes safety instrumented systems (SIS), which are hardened information elements built for high reliability and associated with failing safely and predictably. This is what the IoT needs.

Conversely, IT elements from the enterprise network and data center (DC) environment are typically not built for high reliability; they are integrated into *high-availability* (HA) pairs and clusters. HA is a cheap substitute for hardware and software reliability because it is assumed that even with poor reliability, most (or at least half) the elements will remain functional after a failure in one element.

IT design conventions related to high availability and clustering do not extend well into the more remote parts of the IoT, such as gateways and endpoints, where the economics (business cases) just do not make sense and the services cannot be deployed based on safety techniques that rely on doubling up on infrastructure.

Many ICS processes are continuous in nature and must therefore be reliable. Unexpected outages of systems that control industrial processes are not acceptable. ICS outages often must be planned and scheduled days or weeks in advance. Exhaustive pre-deployment testing is essential to ensure reliability of the ICS.

In addition to unexpected outages, many control systems cannot be easily stopped and started without affecting production and safety. In some cases, the products being produced or equipment being used is more important than the information being relayed. Therefore, use of typical IT strategies, such as rebooting a component, are usually not acceptable solutions due to the adverse impact on the requirements for high availability, reliability, and maintainability of the ICS.

Similar to the requirements for performance, reliability in the IoT needs to come with more significant and robust specifications with regard to reliability. Measures like *mean time to replacement* (MTTR) or *mean time to failure* (MTTF), which are common in the network and DC world, will need to be extended out towards the edges of the network, in which devices cannot be deployed in HA or clustering designs.

Overall, safety in the IoT will require that gateway elements especially, but also endpoints, become more reliable and consistent in stand-alone performance.

NONTOXIC AND BIOCOMPATIBLE

Much like concerns today about batteries, compact florescent lights, mercury thermostats, and ozone-depleting air conditioning units, a substantial safety risk in the IoT will be associated with the impact of materials used to build IoT devices.

The IoT in many cases will be about devices that are destined to be absorbed into the environment or embedded into living tissues and bodies. For instance, environmental sensors might be deployed with the expectations and business assumptions that once they cease working, they will be left in place to simply decay and disappear. Alternately, the current generation of *wearable* technologies will inevitably evolve into other devices that will be placed more directly on the skin for longer periods of time or will be embedded. The implants of today will certainly become connected, for the purposes of better monitoring, diagnostics, and management.

IoT devices will need to be designed with environmental safety in mind. Devices made of toxic materials will probably engender rougher regulation and monitoring of their distribution, use, and disposal—raising costs.

Safety of the IoT will have a lot to do with not only how the devices act and respond to commands, but what they do to the environment in which they operate, both during and after their useful life.

The need to start engineering devices with newer, specially developed biocompatible materials will potentially mean that other safety features such as reliability and predictability may suffer because the world of information processing and computing is very demanding in terms of physical stresses. Moves toward more environmentally friendly, safe materials in the construction of IoT endpoints will absolutely have effects on the data processing and management assurance of those devices, if for no other reason than that it will reflect a change in the system.

Understanding the safety and risk trade-offs associated with the use and adoption of new, safe materials in the IoT will be critical for risk managers.

DISPOSABILITY

Related to the issue of toxicity in IoT safety is the matter of safety and disposability. What happens when the device reaches end-of-life, is made obsolete, no longer wanted, or is defective and cannot be repaired? From a safety perspective, the environmental issues are clear—but the linkages between safety and information security associated with disposability may not be apparent at first glance.

In the security world, hardware and software disposal is a well understood security process and requirement. Device, system, and service owners in the IoT all must be sure that information is destroyed in the process of disposal of IoT devices, and unauthorized access is not granted to personal or proprietary information (operating systems, configurations, designs, and so on). Many spectacular information security breaches have occurred due to poor or missing disposal practices.

There are disposal issues around safety, too, that will have cascading impacts to IoT security and risk management overall.

Disposability will affect safety in the IoT in relation to elements like the biological and environmental toxicity of the IoT endpoint and edge devices. Will they poison the users? Will they become hazardous once they reach landfills or incinerators in the thousands or millions, or once they get decommissioned but left in place, whether embedded into asphalt or embedded into living flesh?

For instance, in the case of wearables or devices that might get embedded into objects or people, there will evolve clear requirements for mechanically and environmentally stable materials such as:

- Batteries and energy collection and conversion parts
- Conductors/wires
- Processors and memory
- Insulators
- Packaging, housing, and monitoring and control interfaces
- Substrates and functional materials

While safety may dictate that certain materials be used and others be avoided, the impact on information security may be hard to balance as a requirement. For instance, tamper proofing or tamper resistance of information processing or storage parts may require materials that do not meet safety and disposability criteria! Or, disposable battery types may not support the availability requirements and service levels of information security.

SAFETY AND CHANGE MANAGEMENT IN THE IoT

Change management is paramount to maintaining the security of both IT and IoT systems, and is also applicable to both hardware and firmware. As every student of information security knows, patch management required to fix vulnerabilities and other security-impacting flaws is a major supplicant to change-management processes.

Unpatched systems represent one of the greatest vulnerabilities to an IT system. Software updates on IT systems, including security patches, are typically applied in a timely fashion based on security policy and procedures intended to satisfy compliance (organizational) requirements. These procedures are often automated in enterprise IT, using server-based tools and auto-update processes.

Yet, software updates in the IoT cannot always be implemented on an automated basis. In the IoT, each software update may have safety-critical dependencies associated with it, whether it be associated with downtime for patching or the fundamental stability and performance of the IoT system after patching. IoT updates will need to be thoroughly tested and sanctioned by the potentially multiple stakeholders, such as the various equipment, application, and service vendors, as well as the user of the application.

The IoT system, as a whole, may also require revalidation and certification as part of the service level agreement (SLA) and compliance processes stipulated in contracts to high-assurance clients like governments or banks.

Change management process from IT might be the basis for change management in the IoT, but wholesale adoption would be inappropriate and such practices would represent risk to an IoT system or service.

DIVISIBILITY OF SAFETY AND SERVICE DELIVERY UPDATES AND LONGEVITY

There are conflicting requirements between safety and many of the other risk management requirements discussed in this book! Where possible, an upgrade path and methodology for safety functions versus service functions should be separate.

IoT system or device owners should be able to update or upgrade service-related software without impacting safety-related software. Where both capabilities require upgrade or patching, these processes should be divisible.

Not only should safety versus service patches be divisible, but safety patches (unless related to a critical flaw) should be forward compatible with service patches indefinitely. For instance, a safety patch should never be mandatory unless it is related to a critical flavor vulnerability related to performance, reliability, or efficiency of safety systems.

It is possible that evolving technology and design flaws in both hardware and especially software impact information security and risk management requirements, without impacting the safety systems and requirements. The safety system, due to simplicity and clarity of requirements and purpose, may continue to work just fine in the face of a failed service-delivery platform!

Therefore, IoT safety can be more difficult to manage if it is inextricably linked to IoT security management, such as updates. Here are a couple of examples where information security upgrades to the system might be delayed due to safety-critical services and functions:

* Old systems that can't be patched or upgraded without risk to the safety systems
* Old or expensive IoT systems might not have the luxury of development and test environments, so patching in operational system means risking not only the service and production processes, but associated safety processes too. (For instance, a patch works and the service platform is upgraded but the safety processes become unreliable!)

STARTUP AND SHUTDOWN EFFICIENCY (MINIMIZATION OF COMPLEXITY)

From a safety perspective in the IoT, the ability to start and stop a process quickly will be a major risk management requirement. This in turn will implicate not only the design of the IoT endpoints themselves, but the gateways, networks, and cloud services that support them.

The ability to start quickly will be important for IoT devices involved in kinetic motion and movement control. For example, where they may not be active until a person or object comes into range for the purposes of saving power, or where they only become active after sensing an abnormal physical condition like an imminent collision or change in the physical environment. However, once the device is called into action it must be available very quickly—potentially meaning that it must move from a dormant state to an active state in milliseconds.

Under these conditions, an IoT device might be required to forgo security controls that would otherwise be built into the device, gateway, or network communications. Encryption technology on the device is a good example. If the time and energy it takes to decrypt an instruction set on a small, constrained IoT device will take the startup time from 2 to 4 ms, it is possible that service level requirements will be missed!

Very much related to this matter of startup will be the gateways that might support bootstrapping of IoT devices at startup or installation, and the networks and cloud systems that will provide provisioning information and configuration details. If these systems cannot support the startup safety requirements in terms of performance, alternatives will need to be found!

The ability to shut down quickly will similarly have significant safety effects in the IoT and will be a function of not just the endpoint devices, but also the gateways, networks, and clouds that they rely upon for instructions and connectivity.

Shutting down quickly is not so much a matter of the performance of the IoT, but about *failing safely*, and reporting a shutdown in a timely manner to centralized management tools. As another example, when a device is deemed to have breached its stipulated performance parameters, it needs to shut down quickly and allow a redundant system to assume the service functions. Or, in the event that there is no redundant system, it needs to fail safely. (See the next section.)

Consider a health monitoring system. It will probably need to be capable of monitoring a patient's pulse rate or blood pressure very accurately. If the IoT system or service starts to see anomalous readings indicative of an impending device failure from one set of sensing devices connected to the patient, those devices will need quickly to shut down so not to contaminate the pool of good data already collected by the systems in place.

Alternately, in an ICS managing thousands of tons of molten metal, or a transportation system directing thousands of vehicles moment to moment, once a defective device is detected it needs to be removed from the system as quickly as possible.

Failing and defective devices must be stopped quickly and fail safely for one final reason—the complexity of the IoT and the interconnected systems means that bad data and inappropriate operations by even the smallest of devices can have untold effects. Chaotic effects.

As with startup requirements, shutdown and failover requirements may supersede information security requirements for things like encryption, platform validations, device authentication or logoff, clean session termination, and so on. In turn, the lack of these information security controls can make a device more prone to a variety of attacks such as man-in-the middle or masquerade.

Startup and shutdown safety and its relationship to IoT information security is yet another safety balance to be sought by risk managers in the IoT.

FAILING SAFELY

Failing safely means that a system element will stop working in a predictable manner: a manner that has been accounted for in the service design and will result in a physically or logically safe state, post-failure. In other words, physical damage or system disruption is minimized, controllable, and foreseeable.

For most IT devices on the Internet, we really have no idea how they will fail. The hardware platform manufacturers and the software typically do not collaborate to anticipate a service-to-device failure, let alone report it to users.

Even if there was a will to determine how a given IoT device or system might be developed to fail safely, it would be impossibly complicated and expensive given the range of software vendors and hardware vendors for things like servers in the DC, network elements (like routers, firewalls, domain name servers), gateways, and endpoints. As a result, when IoT devices fail, it is very likely that their state will be unpredictable and therefore not predictably safe!

Frequently, devices will freeze and lose data and cutoff connectivity. Sometimes, they will be set to *fail open*, meaning, that is, they stop working, and then any information management operations (like security) they performed cease—but data will continue to flow. In other words, they are designed to continue to pass untreated or insecure data rather than stop the data flow altogether. Sometimes, this makes lots of sense. Sometimes, it does not.

A possible outcome is that some IoT devices will continue to function, but will become *zombie* devices that are no longer responding to external commands from owners and administrators—they just keep doing whatever their last instruction told them to do. In a way, this is worse than failing; this is a runaway train scenario!

In the industrial control world, *failing safely* means something. It means that if a device is no longer behaving the way it is expected to behave, it can be shut down into a predetermined state. That state may be open, closed, or perhaps limp home, where it curtails all functions except the most basic in order to minimize collateral impacts until help arrives.

More attention needs to be paid to failing safely in the IoT and what this means from an information security perspective, especially on endpoints and gateway devices, where security will be first applied.

ISOLATION OF SAFETY AND CONTROL FROM SERVICE DELIVERY

To the extent possible, maintaining isolation of IoT safety systems from operational process management systems is the way to go. This is long-standing best practice in the industrial control world. The difficulty with this requirement for the IoT is the competitive drive for low cost, and the related need to remain efficient in operations. Requiring endpoint devices or gateways to have logically or physically distinct safe versus administrative interfaces can add substantially to costs, both capital and operational.

Safety systems often use the same technology platform as the IoT service-delivery systems, meaning that IoT service vulnerabilities may well be common-mode failures to safety systems, allowing an attacker to compromise both service delivery and control, and safety logic at once or using the same tradecraft.

For instance, an existing issue is that engineering workstations are used to configure both IoT (and industrial control devices) and safety systems—which means that a threat agent could compromise the IoT assets and the safety systems by gaining access to a single workstation. This issue is amplified by the prevalence of *commodity* operating systems, which may have potentially thousands of known vulnerabilities that require only modest amounts of skill of which to take advantage.

In order for the IoT safety systems to function properly, they must also be connected in some way to the IoT service-delivery functions in order to monitor performance, and determine whether safety logic must be invoked. As such, there really is no such thing as a disconnected safety system for the IoT.

From a requirements perspective, it is important for system designers, engineers, and managers to understand that combining safe and service-delivery functions without a thought to any form of isolation creates significant risks. Here is a scenario: knowledgeable attackers could bypass or suspend safety logic without touching service-delivery functions in anyway: business as usual. At that point, they merely wait for a *normal accident* to occur on a random schedule and allow the situation to unfold as it would without safety systems in place.

SAFETY MONITORING VERSUS MANAGEMENT AND SERVICE DELIVERY

Safety systems in the IoT are generally designed with a single purpose in mind: avoiding dangerous situations in the environment (logical-kinetic/cyber physical) by stopping or shutting down services and processes if unsafe conditions develop. Additionally, safety systems are typically implemented as compensating controls for known or anticipated hardware or software failure rates. These failure rates are established through recognized and generally accepted good engineering practices adopted by both asset owners and vendors, driven by industry standard such as ISA-84, IEC 61508, IEC 61511, and others.

In this regard, safety monitoring functions and capabilities in endpoints, gateways, networks, and cloud services in the IoT will be developed for watching safety parameters, not managing or administering safety systems. Actually, management and administration of safety services, functions, or systems in the IoT will be strictly limited.

Therefore the requirement for safety and monitoring is that as far as practical and possible, segregation and access controls the software and hardware used for safety versus service-delivery management is required.

The opposite condition would be to allow any stakeholder who has access to a service-delivery function to have access to safety functions at the same time through the same interface. For example, there is one interface used to for both safety monitoring and service-delivery management.

This single-interface design could be typical for a low-cost IoT device; however, the problem comes in when this single monolithic interface fails and takes both safety monitoring and service management with it at the same time—meaning that control is not only lost, but safety-critical visibility and awareness is gone in the same instant.

RECOVERY AND PROVISIONING AT THE EDGE

In a typical IT system, the primary focus of security (and especially recovery) is protecting the operation of centralized IT assets, such as the assets in the DC or the cloud: databases, file systems, servers, and the like. In the IoT, this condition may be reversed for safety reasons. In the name of safety, an edge device may take on more priority in the recovery process and procedures relative to the centralized assets.

In many IT-centric, conventional Internet architectures, information stored and processed in the DC or cloud is more critical and is afforded much more protection than information stored and managed at the edges. For IoT systems and services, edge devices (such as gateways) need carefully to be considered in business continuity prioritizations because they may be directly responsible for controlling the safety-critical functions and services to endpoints. The protection of the central services is still very important for safety because the central server itself might contain critical instructions for safety management.

Recovery of gateways may involve a number of processes, which amounts to re-provisioning a device in the field either physically or logically. While provisioning will be a critical factor in the development of IoT services, the service levels associated with provisioning may only be factored in within the context of new devices coming into the system. In the IoT, a safety requirement might exist in a given service or system that associated specific service levels for recovery and re-provisioning of gateways. (Re-)provisioning may be as much about safety and merely turning up the service for the first time.

MISUSE AND UNINTENDED APPLICATIONS

In Chapter 7, Confidentiality and Integrity and Privacy Requirements in the IoT, we will discuss documentation and reporting as a security requirement in the IoT. But it is also a safety requirement related to misuse that must be considered at the same time as the security requirement, because such misuse can have dramatic safety implications for the IoT and cascade from information security impacts to physical safety and security impacts.

Without fail, it will come to pass that IoT devices, systems, and services will be used for unintended purposes, in the manners unimagined by designers and service providers. This is known human behavior and should be considered in the design process for safety as well as for security. People will misuse IoT services for all manner of reasons, from mischief to fraud to negligence to laziness to ignorance, due to handicaps, misunderstandings, environmental conditions (see Chapter 10, Usage Context and Environmental Requirements in the IoT, on context),or simple errors and omissions.

The known habit of people applying weak or no passwords to protect system configuration has to be accounted for in safety discussions. While it might be improbable or even inexplicable that an IoT device might be configured by the users in a way to harm the users—it should be expected, and safety documentation and warnings incorporated carefully.

For instance, home thermostats are rapidly coming onto the IoT because of the potential savings associated with energy management. Yet most of these thermostats have rather weak safety features when it comes to malicious or accidental misconfiguration. The furnace is accidentally turned off in the middle of a Canadian winter while the family leaves on vacation; resulting in massive structural damage to the home due to frozen and exploded water systems. Or the heat settings are adjusted by a user thinking he/she was using a Fahrenheit scale when Celsius was applied, resulting in a hugely high setting that forces the furnace to work to the point of failure (and huge gas bills).

Good usage instructions and technical safeguards will be a requirement for, and complement to, information security controls in the IoT.

SUMMARY AND CONCLUSIONS

Safety in the IoT is related to IT security in that it is concerned with intended use and reasonably foreseeable misuse, failure, and malfunction.

Where safety differs from security is in key areas such as the need for:

- Availability over confidentiality in performance.
- Being reliable and consistent in performance under normal conditions as well as failure conditions.
- Management of toxicity and disposability; this will heavily influence IoT device design in the future, potentially exposing the IoT to security threats such as tampering, tapping, or service levels.
- Management of change management conventions in IT; these do not translate well into the IoT or process control worlds.
- Starting and stopping service levels introduced as requirements in a way not typically seen in IT systems.
- Failing in a manner that does not jeopardize safety requires much more engineering—where failing has ad hoc outcomes in many IT systems.
- IoT safety and monitoring systems that should be isolated or at least developed in stovepipes (as far as practical) from IoT operational and management systems—including at the endpoint.

Safety in the IoT is as much related to consumer protection and risk management as security. It is part and parcel of determining the risk posed by consumer and business products and services. Consideration should be given for IoT products and services that are intended for, or are used by, vulnerable consumers who are often unable to understand the hazard or the associated risk. But at the same time, in making devices safer (from a safety perspective), they potentially become less secure.

On the other hand, the interests of the service providers and device makers may lie in the area of security due to business risks, but a balance with safety must be addressed and risk managers must consider both safety and security at once, as a whole.

CONFIDENTIALITY AND INTEGRITY AND PRIVACY REQUIREMENTS IN THE IoT

7

The trinity of information technology (IT) security is confidentiality, integrity, and availability. *Privacy* is sometimes discussed as a separate property, but to security purists, privacy is an expression, or use case, of confidentiality.

This book is all about Internet of Things (IoT) security and risk management, and how it is substantially different and evolved from established IT security. For this reason we have deliberately broken the security trinity into pieces, and added a whole lot more around it to boot! This is intended to express the evolution of security and risk in the IoT: applying old, conventional IT-based frameworks to the IoT presents its own risks.

In this chapter, we will look at confidentiality, integrity, and privacy together because in our analysis they still possess a lot of affinity in the context of the IoT. In Chapter 8, Availability and Reliability Requirements in the IoT, we will tackle availability as a stand-alone topic with regard to the IoT security requirements that might fall under it.

DATA CONFIDENTIALITY AND INTEGRITY

At the start of this book, we mentioned a few basic properties related to security and risk management: confidentiality, integrity, and availability. These are often very technical matters to discuss and as a result are often described in technical requirements rather than operational and process requirements. However, it would be an obvious omission to discuss requirements without touching on these fundamental matters.

Data protection neatly describes most of the key properties of security in a couple of words. Certainly, it implies confidentiality and keeping information flowing around the IoT safe from unauthorized disclosure. Data protection can also support the critical but perhaps less famous property of integrity—preventing unauthorized change, including additions and deletions of data.

The last major property of availability might also be included in data protection, as indicated by how much time might the system or service or device be nonresponsive or nonfunctional, or how much latency can be tolerated; however, unlike confidentiality and integrity, availability is really a matter to be dealt with by the IoT system as a whole (endpoint, network, cloud, or data center (DC)). In the case of confidentiality and integrity, these properties are often most defined and controlled at the edges of the IoT system (endpoint and clouds) where data starts and stop moving.

RIoT Control. DOI: http://dx.doi.org/10.1016/B978-0-12-419971-2.00007-8

What follows is a series of operational requirements concerned with confidentiality and integrity, whereas the following chapter will focus on availability and its unique influence on risk management in the IoT.

CRYPTOGRAPHIC STABILITY

For systems that need to use cryptography to protect data in motion or in storage, the rate at which keys must be changed or updated will affect many related and critical technical elements like power efficiency, device longevity, and cost.

While the detailed technical requirements and specifications will certainly come out eventually, from an enterprise risk perspective, it is helpful first to assess coarse-grained requirements related to cryptographic stability and get to the details later. For instance:

- *Stable IoT systems.* This may a static device topology with known parties or devices not changing keys ever, or very infrequently. This may be characterized by symmetric (shared) key cryptography, with keys built in by the manufacturer or assigned by a service provider at the time of deployment or at maintenance intervals.
- *Unstable IoT systems.* Devices are in dynamic device topology with fairly regular changes as new devices come and go. Devices need to authenticate based on mutually trusted sources, so asymmetric (public key) cryptograph may be employed. The key management is not ongoing so the cryptography might be done in software because the computational and energy costs are not prohibitive for occasional changes.
- *Highly unstable IoT systems.* Dynamic devices have a topology with constant change being a hallmark of the systems; communication with many devices and parties. Cryptographic operations are very frequent, to the point that operating efficiency makes hardware-based cryptography acceleration a probable requirement.

The nature and stability of the cryptographic system may drive critical choices about the device manufacture itself. Or, more likely, the device manufacture will limit the options available related to cryptographic systems. A mismatch between the device abilities and the cryptographic system could have dramatic effects; for instance, the device fails early due to enhanced loads, or perhaps the system owner is forced to turn off an unduly heavy crypto-system to make sure the device lasts as long as required.

AGING OUT: CONFIDENTIALITY THAT LASTS THE TEST OF TIME

Related to cryptographic stability is the concept of *aging out*, which refers to the process where the passage of time makes the security features built into an IoT system obsolete and vulnerable. For instance, the cryptographic key lengths that can be used by a given IoT device maybe hard-coded into the software or maybe limited by the processing power of the device, which is fixed at the time of manufacture.

In such cases, there may be no way to use longer, and therefore stronger, keys. The problem arises when a key length is considered secure today because brute-force attacks (trying to guess the keys by trying every possible combination until you find the right one) are not viable. However, it is an established precedent that keys that were once considered secure are overtaken by the march of technology and processing power, and become insecure.

Once upon a time, around the year 1995, a 56-bit symmetric key length and an algorithm called DES were considered military grade. Today (20 years later) you would not trust your grocery shopping to such a key for security reasons because computing power allows such keys to be trivially broken by rank amateurs. If IoT devices such as industrial devices have 20-year amortization periods, it is very possible that the security of today will be useless before end of life is reached. What then?

UNTAMPERED DATA—PROVE THE INTEGRITY OF THE DATA AND AUTHENTICITY

Control versus user data

Data in the IoT will essentially exist at two levels:

Control level: the data that is used to control the IoT system infrastructure. Generally, this will include service provider configurations, administrative paths used by service providers, out of band device communications used for maintenance and manufacturer logistics, command-and-control and network/gateway signaling data, devices logs, and events.

Usage/user level: application data that results from the actual service being delivered by the IoT system. This may be all manner of user-generated data, or data generated as a result of sensing or actuating by an IoT device. It maybe be user or device services (vs network) logon credentials, user identity, video, voice, Internet/web traffic, or whatever else is being collected at the end point, transferred through the gateway and network, and then processed/stored/managed in the service-DC or service-cloud.

Risk and the Internet of Things (RIoT) control will require understanding what the requirements are at each level, because they may be different! It may be that control-level data is consistent, but different applications and use cases at the user level have different requirements for integrity.

Integrity of data in motion

The IoT system should support evidence that changes have not been made to data, not only in storage (at rest) but also through transmission; including at intermediary *smart* elements like gateways, which perform security functions for some classes of constrained device.

IoT data, both control and user data, must possess some assurance that it has not been subjected to unauthorized change, additions, or deletions, including tags and metadata that come to IoT devices from external services in the IoT service chain. This should include chain of evidence (see below), so that if trust is inherited from a gateway, or a third-party service, there is an ability to understand why a gateway or service is considered as trusted and untampered with in the first place.

PROVE DELETION AND DECOMMISSIONING

Data in the IoT will often be considered highly sensitive for a variety of business reasons: intellectual property, privacy, market intelligence, criminal value, and so forth.

As devices and systems are changed, upgraded, decommissioned, or sold, trusting that information as actually having been deleted, redacted, or anonymized is a functional requirement that will lower regulatory compliance barriers and encourage user adoption. This will include indication and confirmation that data has been deleted—much like we get confirmations that data has been sent or saved in typical email and other messaging systems.

Decommissioning will exist in many forms and might not mean that the device itself is being taken out of service; for instance, the device might merely have been rented for a short period. However, when the service (versus the device) is decommissioned, explicit confirmation that all user or application data has been removed from the device, which should be accounted through as a functional capability of the device or service.

CHAIN OF TRUST

In many cases, IoT devices will execute operations (in the logical and physical world) based on trust inherited from intermediate devices or services, such as gateway devices. In complex systems, how can we have any trust in the IoT application if there are multiple layers of *inheritance*? The answer is to account for requirements associated with chains of trust: "I will trust you because I understand why you trust your counterparties—even if I don't know them myself."

Logs of sufficient detail and with sufficient protection are advantageous to track and understand how a complex series of instructions related through potentially many IoT devices can remain trusted.

For devices that might be provisioned as utilitarian devices that learn their roles in a system, they must also learn who and what to trust. Surely such devices cannot be expected to trust everything...? So they may instead have the ability to recognize certain chains of trust, based on the applied cryptographic techniques or perhaps the roots of trust communicated in key material like public certificates.

For risk managers in the IoT assessing entire systems and services, understanding where the blind spots in their chain of trust exist is a good starting point because there will often be blind spots. Because risk management is about treating, transferring, or accepting risks, accepting the risk will be a useful option because the alternative is a complex system of audit and review that may not be viable in the complex ecosystem of IoT service delivery.

But the key to all risk management is understanding the risk you accept.

ATTESTATION OF CAPABILITY AND FUNCTIONALITY

Devices, gateways, networks, and cloud-based applications may be required to make high-assurance statements to relying parties about their abilities and functionality: another way to say this is that they must state their attributes in a way that can be quickly trusted, or at least in a way that can be stored for later review in the case of some sort of dispute about who was supposed to do what. (This is related to chain of evidence.) This requirement might just as easily be associated with availability as confidentiality and integrity.

For instance, before a device selects a particular gateway among available choices (based on different networks available such as 3G, 4G, 5G, Wi-Fi, and Ethernet), it may wish to understand which of several available gateways has the best bandwidth. It may query the gateways about the service levels they support and the costs they charge for those services levels, and then select a gateway accordingly. The providers of the gateway should provide those attestations about their service-level attributes with some form of nonrepudiation. Cryptography such as public key signatures or even shared keys can allow for such attributes to be communicated quickly such that only trusted claims and devices are used, wherever possible. If no trusted claims related to attributes are available, but untrusted claims from third-party gateways are available, the IoT device or system may apply a different internal logical about whether to use the gateway and if so how.

A further example related to attestation may be the available routes that a given gateway or network will take to move data from an endpoint device to a DC or cloud. In some cases, certain networks, while cheaper or offering sufficient QoS, may not physically possess the needed assurance for the data under management. Perhaps the IoT device is currently being used for monitoring the movement of a government VIP—a national security issue. Maybe connectivity through a low-cost Internet service provider (ISP) with unpredictable routes is not sufficient? Perhaps a higher cost ISP with deterministic (predictable) routing is required while the VIP is in range of the gateway?

Finally, devices themselves may be required to use secure booting techniques which rely on cryptographically secured identifiers at the hardware level contained in trusted platform modules (TPM). As part of joining the IoT system or service, a device may be required to attest to its authenticity and the integrity of its firmware or operating systems based on evidence provided by a TMP.

See the following requirements for further discussion on the idea of trusted routing.

TRUSTED ROUTING OF DATA

Routing of the data has to do with several critical issues related to security and risk management in the IoT. It can be an easy assumption to make that once the data leaves the endpoint device, it will automatically find its way to the destination in a correct and secure manner. But managing risk in the IoT requires that such assumptions should be tested from time to time. For instance:

- Is the device sending data *to the right gateway, even if the final destination is the same?*
- Is the device sending *through the right network?* Network selection can impact not only the types of entities that might observe and access the data, but also the tolls and service levels that are applied.
- Is the device sending to the right place, through the right network, *at the right time?* It is entirely possible that routes will be more or less appropriate for a variety of security and risk management reasons throughout the day, such as threats from eavesdropping, interception, masquerade, or unauthorized change.
- In the right *quantity of service available in the routing selected?* The quality of service required by the IoT application may change over time (hourly, daily, monthly, and so on) as may the quality of service guarantees of different network options.
- In the event that "mixed" networks containing Internet Protocol version 4 (IPv4) and (Internet Protocol version 6) IPv6 are in use, and various forms of network translation are applied (IE. NAT64, NAT46, NAT464, NAT646, etc.), is there any means to trace back sources and destination across such heterogeneous networks?

ERASURE CODE AND DATA GRAVITY

The amount of data being generated by the IoT must sooner or later have some proportionality to the amount of data being deleted or redacted from the IoT. Otherwise information holdings will be both costly and unmanageable to the point where we derive little or no value from it any longer.

This is sometimes referred to as *data gravity*: so much data is generated that it creates its own forces that distort and influence all the other applications and assets without adding any value, or at the very least without adding proportional value to the cost of managing the *gravitational* forces.

Erasure code refers to a system (operational method) or program (automated software) that is intended to delete structured data (logs and events) and unstructured data (messages or files) when certain criteria are met. For example:

- Regulatory retention periods are over
- Policy (privacy) changes require deletion
- Legal covenants end, requiring information to be deleted
- Research has been performed and is completed
- Copies have been made for long-term storage (see next requirement)
- No commercial benefit is to be had

The point of erasure code relative to data protection and integrity is that it manages the risk of *unwanted* and *unnecessary* data storage and retention, which we will discuss in later chapters.

COLD STORAGE PROTOCOLS

Related to the concept of erasure code is the notion of *cold storage*[1]: less accessible, long term storage of structured and unstructured data for reasons related to compliance, legal agreements, and long-term trend analysis and research.

Cold storage has been around a long time. Tape archives and other forms of high-latency (not quickly retrieved) access to these archives are part of any decent IT security program, because the cost of maintaining all archives in a *hot access* capacity is too high. But in the IoT, it will be different because erasure code has acted as a *prescreening engine* and redacted what is not required in cold storage—only what *must* be stored will be stored in cold storage.

While cold storage might be considered a form of availability requirement, we have placed it in this section because the process of redaction involved in cold storage affects the integrity of the IoT data assets.

Cold storage in the IoT: accessible in minutes

The difference for risk managers in the IoT is that when it comes to cold storage protocols, historical forms of cold storage took days to weeks to access, whereas cold storage for the IoT will be measured in minutes to be acceptable. Why minutes? Because the volume of data in the IoT will push more data into cheaper, more cost-effective cold storage *sooner*, but at the same time it will possess significant criticality associated with forensics, law enforcement, system management, complexity, and interdependency analysis.

---

[1]Milini Bhadura, Intel—America Movil brief, August 2013.

INTEGRATED REPORTING: ENDPOINT, GATEWAY, NETWORK, CLOUDS, AND DCs

Reporting across all the assets in an IoT system will be critical to support many business and operational requirements. Why is integrated reporting important across all the main assets in the IoT service ecosystem? Because of the *negative* obligations associated with proving *confidentiality and integirty*: you don't have to prove you are secure—you need to prove you have not been breached.

This integrated reporting means that some sort of capability must exist not only from the assets and devices managed directly by the IoT service provider, but also from the services outsourced to third parties.

In Chapter 3, Requirements and Risk Management, we discussed the anatomy of the IoT, which explained that the IoT is, in fact, a giant system of specialized service providers who are fragmenting horizontally. IoT systems will in themselves be systems of a few or even many specialized service providers. Each of these providers will have a default preference to keep reporting and events *internal*: for the purposes of protecting information associated with internal management practices, customer data, and especially internal security events. But that is counter to the interests of risk management in the IoT system that rely on these providers. (RIoT control!).

The IoT takes on a pronounced *industrial* profile relative to the legacy, IT-oriented Internet, and sees elements like *availability* take on a degree of sensitivity and importance that can exceed *confidentiality* in many cases; however, a simple truth remains: the regulatory sanctions and recriminations will mostly be enforceable around perceived flaws in confidentiality and data protection (privacy) breaches. This is why we place integrated reporting under confidentiality, integrity, and privacy requirements: reasonable visibility can equate to reasonable care and compliance. Meanwhile, attempting to shift blame to service providers on the basis of opaque service level agreements (SLAs) that don't provide any form of timely reporting will potentially be seen as negligent!

Integrated reporting across all assets involved in the IoT system will be highly beneficial to confidentiality and integrity, as well as availability and reliability. Without a doubt. However, due to the negative obligations associated with regulatory breach and the need to prove innocence, it will be a higher profile operational requirement with confidentiality and integrity.

KNOWING VERSUS LEARNING IN PROVISIONING

Devices can either be provisioned with information about where their critical resources are located, or they will learn where critical resources are located during bootstrapping processes at initialization. The integrity of learned-provisioning or bootstrapping information is especially critical to security and risk in the IoT. In addition, the confidentiality of provisioning information itself might represent valuable intellectual property.

For instance, a device might be provisioned and hard-coded with information about its own network address, where to go for software updates, where to send data, and where to find shared services it might need—like domain name services (DNS)or directory services. The integrity of this information is essential because a change in provision information might completely alter the functioning of a given IoT device or gateway.

Conversely, a device might learn all these things because it is provisioned as a blank slate with generic processes for acquiring its initial network address(es) and then *calling home* to a control point for everything else about its role and configuration. For instance, a gateway device is plugging into a network and learns its address, gateways, name services, and where to get information about its role. Eventually, it is taught to become a gateway managing a smart parking system, applying the security properties and managing the endpoint sensors.

There are differences between knowing versus learning in provisioning, related to vulnerabilities, threats, and risks. Understanding what sort of IoT system is under consideration will influence many of the designs considered and costs related to IoT risk management. In many cases, the answer may be that both types of devices are supported. The devices come with some information set at manufacturing and other elements must be learned to be completely provisioned. For example, is the device provided a unique identifier by the manufacturer or by the owner? In such cases, security and risk management will need to employ a fairly wide range of controls and safeguards to support a wide range of provisioning use cases.

HORIZONTAL LOGGING: ACROSS THE LIFE CYCLE

Horizontal logging as a requirement refers to long-term logging of events associated with an IoT system or device, such that security incidents—once detected—can be traced back to their beginning. Implicitly, such logs must possess integrity—they cannot be changed or deleted without the proper authorization.

After a security incident, the second question an executive asks is, "When did it happen?" (The first question is, "What happened?"). Usually, the second question is a lot harder to answer. In fact, the second question is often impossible to answer with any precision at all!

In security systems today one of the largest challenges is retaining the necessary logs to perform root-cause analysis and forensics on a breach. All too often there are no logs, and if the logs are there it is often the case that they don't go back far enough to really know when the breach occurred! And if the time associated with the compromise cannot be established, management *must* assume the worst case: often as a matter of legal obligation.

In the IoT, with automated and semiautomated systems, cyber-physical interfaces, and industrial controls, the issues associated with liability and possibly regulatory compliance, will make horizontal logging a significant requirement.

Fig. 7.1 illustrates the requirements for horizontal logging by showing the relationship between the sensitivity of an asset and the duration of the exposure to a given vulnerability. As the matrix illustrates, this is usually not an all-or-nothing formula: the longer the asset is exposed, the more information leaks or the more damage can be done.

This is not a formal model for risk assessment because it is possible for significant or even maximum damage after a short time, the extended exposures being rather meaningless—the horse has left the barn. However, in the case of threats associated with data theft and exfiltration, it is common to see a relationship between the duration of the exposure and final impact.

Fig. 7.2 illustrates what often happens after a security breach or impact in any informatics systems, IoT or otherwise. The circle illustrates the risk that must be assumed by any reasonable auditor or regulator, without horizontal logging being in place. The sensitivity of the asset that has been

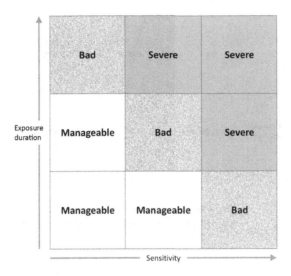

FIGURE 7.1

Exposure-sensitivity matrix.

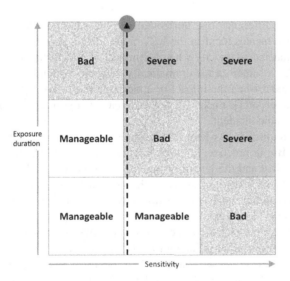

FIGURE 7.2

Sensitivity only—no duration.

compromised is understood because that can be established either proactively (before event) or retroactively (after the event).

In effect, without knowledge of the duration of the compromise, the only reasonable assumption from a risk management perspective is that the exposure has existed long enough to inflict the maximum risk and damage.

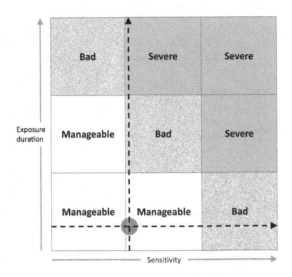

FIGURE 7.3

Risk considering exposure and duration.

Fig. 7.3 illustrates the difference that horizontal logging can make to risk management in general, but especially to risk management in the IoT. In the image, horizontal logging allows the incident response team to understand exactly when the impact or attack started.

The risk that must be assumed drops dramatically with the evidence associated with horizontal logging: you can understand when the impact or attack occurred! The ability to isolate the start and end points of the impact or attack makes all the difference between an assumed catastrophe and a manageable and measureable incident.

Clearly, there are circumstances where the duration of an exposure is irrelevant to the risk: an instant is long enough. But in practice, duration has a lot to do with the final impact. It can determine the amount of data lost and the length of time a system is disrupted.

Over and above all these issues associated with understanding when a system or device might have been potentially compromised is ownership transfer: if you are selling the system, how can you show with legitimate evidence that it does not come with *bugs*?

In the IoT, we must assume that the system containing thousands and even millions of devices and assets will be fully transferrable: sellable property, like a building or an airplane or a company. In such a complex system, the buyer will have a lot of interest in understanding the current security profile of the asset they are buying. Or, they can demand a big discount to buying assets as-is. Risk managers in the IoT need to keep in mind that their duties also include not only the operation of assets, but also the transfer of assets.

DEVICE FEEDBACK: "IS THE DAMN THING ON OR OFF?"

Many of the devices that are likely to be introduced to the IoT will be related to supporting people-oriented activities and transactions; therefore one of the most fundamental means of managing risk associated with these devices is to understand their state. Are they actually on or off? Are your movements, actions, or some form of biometric being electronically perceived and possibly recorded? Are you part of the IoT or not, at this moment and point in time? Should you be concerned about confidentiality?

Device feedback about basic performance parameters like *on* or *off* will go a long way to allowing people to protect themselves and their data from risk. Device feedback about state (on/off) will allow them to understand what sort of security may or may not be required beyond that inherent in the endpoint device at hand. Will you act the same way (more or less formally) depending on the state of an IoT device? And if the device is on versus off, will you look for the presence of additional security because of the risk? For instance, do you look for the seatbelt when sitting in a parked car?

Of the many IoT applications and services evolving, many will have tangential monitoring and recording applications, such as the camera in bank automated teller machines (ATMs), often used by police to understand who passed by at a given time. The ATM cameras are not built or intended for that purpose, but they have proved invaluable in solving many serious crimes. Similarly, it is reasonable to expect that many IoT sensing and recording applications will have ancillary applications related to surveillance and law enforcement.

In some cases, ancillary or tangential functions associated with surveillance will be nonnegotiable: they cannot be turned off without disabling or crippling the service. But, in many cases, there will certainly be distinctions established between *on* versus *recording and transmitting*.

Human-readable feedback about IoT device-state (telling people they are on, or what they are doing) is a boon to adoption. To date, many people tolerate the foibles of laptop microphones that never really tell you they are on or off, or cameras that might indicate on or off—but how do you really know? Or camera phones that appear to activate and snap pictures a little too easily. But as these sorts of capabilities become almost ubiquitous everywhere in our lives, tolerance for these foibles will erode.

As devices in the IoT spread and become more and more a part of people's lives, they will come to want a greater understanding of whether the devices in their proximity are powered and operating. At the very least, many users will want to have this option.

Device feedback about state will have operational benefits in addition to the element of customer satisfaction. For instance, in a smart lightbulb, has the bulb blown out (failed), or has the circuit breaker gone? Such feedback might save hauling out a ladder when a trip to the basement breaker box was required instead. Alternately, various types of IoT state-feedback might reduce incidences of help desk and support calls because of the ability of users to understand better the IoT devices around them: lowering costs and improving satisfaction.

Such consideration about conveniences might also generate significant competitive advantages related to consumer satisfaction and reduce business-level risks.

Finally, IoT state feedback will help reduce risks of users accidentally turning off IoT devices or misconfiguring them in some way that impacts the IoT service assurance. Potentially, if IoT devices are turned off or misconfigured by users, the system they are part of might become unpredictable in performance and therefore a security risk.

In the IoT devices that will be interfacing with people or used directly by people, feedback will become a significant means of risk reduction related to operational requirements.

PRIVACY AND PERSONAL DATA REGULATIONS

We covered privacy as a business and organizational requirement in previous chapters, but privacy is an operational Achilles heel to any IoT service or system, so much so we will touch on the matter of privacy regulation again here.

REGULATORY AND STATUTORY PRIVACY

If you look around the world, privacy regulations are a kaleidoscope. They differ in both subtle and substantial ways from country to country. In some places there are none. In other places they will hamstring an IoT service to the point that the business case is invalid in that jurisdiction.

For some additional guidance on the operational management of privacy requirements, we direct you to a recent book from Michele Dennedy and Jonathon Fox, *The Privacy Engineer's Manifesto*[2].

It is a fundamental requirement at the start of any IoT service-design process to understand what the inalterable requirements are for privacy support and what is perhaps arguable. (There'll be more on the matter of *arguable* later in this book.) Once the clear regulatory requirements are understood, the process of assessing the operational controls can start.

The good news is that most privacy regulations do not provide vast amounts of operational guidance; they don't tell you *how* to apply privacy in any detail.

Privacy laws are typically about guidelines and discuss broad matters related to collection, use, and disclosure of personally identifiable information, as we discussed in Chapter 5, Operational and Process Requirements. However, there are some places where privacy laws and statutes are followed up with more detailed regulations, and your operational requirements may be impacted by these regulations.

NONINTRINSIC PRIVACY

Privacy is not intrinsic to the IoT. That is to say: where you find an IoT system or service, do not assume there is a potential privacy violation lurking.

Privacy—like any other potential requirement or vulnerability in a given IoT system or service—is something to be assessed rather than assumed. As we will discuss later in this book, the potential to inflict damage on the IoT related to establishing inappropriate, hard-and-fast privacy requirements is big.

The massive amount of data present in the IoT as a whole, across all its elements and services without regard to difference of ownership and management, physical and logical storage, means there is no question that the IoT, en masse, is potentially, massively personal. If you can access, correlate, and associate identity with activity logs and events in the IoT, you will pretty much be able to write a biography that will shock mothers and end marriages. The issue is that this is easier said than done. More on this to follow.

---

[2]ISBN: 978-1-4302-6355-5.

While there is plenty of risk associated with privacy in the IoT, this risk needs to kept in perspective and most importantly understood in the context of the requirements derived from both regulation (not a great source of requirements, in reality) and customer expectations (probably more important than regulation, in effect).

ILLUSTRATION: PRIVACY AND SMART HOME AUTOMATION

As an example of how difficult extracting personal information from the IoT can be: consider electrical power monitoring in a home.

If you could isolate and capture the data flows from a specific meter from all the other meters sharing the network, and

if you could sift out the extraneous signaling and network handshakes from the service payloads (the real data), and

if you could get the mapping of the meter's IP (network) address to a subscriber ID held in a distant usage database, and

if you could map the ID to a subscriber's real name held in a different, even more logically distant customer management database,

then, maybe you might have personal information about an individual (a bachelor perhaps?) living alone. And then, maybe, you may end up exceeding the scope of the IoT service agreement and perhaps have broken a law. Maybe.

That is a lot of *ifs*. But more importantly, it assumes that all this information—already segregated for business reasons unrelated to privacy—can be brought together without obstacle.

The first requirement for managing risk associated with privacy in the IoT is keeping the risk in accurate perspective: is any proposed investment in privacy-enabling technology balanced with likelihood of occurrence, operational costs, and impacts on customer satisfaction?

Resisting the temptation to repurpose data

The pressure toward repurposing operational data collected from IoT services, for reasons not explicitly associated with the initial collection of the data, will also be a general business temptation that must be managed with care because of the risks it can present to business level requirements like regulatory compliance and customer satisfaction.

Due to the proliferation of increased amounts of data in an IoT environment, the opportunity to use that data for purposes beyond those for which it was collected becomes a serious pressure and possibility. If the repackaging of data from individual transactions can be resold for additional revenue, business and service providers will consider doing it.

Repurposing of data can be in the cards even before data collection begins, for example law enforcement authorities or intelligence agencies may seek access to data collected by service providers for reasons of lawful access, yet seek to extend the use of the same data to other areas of surveillance and public safety once access if granted.

The impact of repurposing is a major risk because it can easily be perceived as a violation of individual rights to privacy and impact on wider social and public acceptance.[3]

---

[3]IoT Privacy, Data Protection and Information Security, Digital Agenda for Europe, February 2013, http://ec.europa.eu/digital-agenda/en/news/conclusions-internet-things-public-consultation.

In fact, in 2016, this repurposing risk was the source a major dispute between Apple and the US law enforcement agencies, which wanted iPhone cryptography circumvented to support investigation of a particular egregious act of terrorism in which 14 people died.[4]

Design requirements for privacy in the IoT

"[Risk management], information security, privacy, and data protection should systematically be addressed at the design stage. Unfortunately, in many cases, they are added on later once the intended functionality is in place. This not only limits the effectiveness of the added-on information security and privacy measures, but also is less efficient in terms of the cost to implement them."[5]

For this reason, a few operational requirements to support privacy are good to consider as overall project requirements are gathered and compiled:

- *Anonymity*. The ability to subscribe to a service in such a manner that identity is untraceable and usage cannot be linked to an identity. For instance, a user can agree to pay for an augmented reality information service through a third party, which provides blinded payment information and transaction clearing services and making the identity of the subscriber transparent to the service provider.
- *Unlinkability*. The act of ensuring that a subscriber to a given service may make multiple uses of the resources without others being able to link these uses together without oversight and appropriate authorization.
- *Unobservability*. The act of ensuring that a subscriber may use a service without others, especially third parties, being able to observe that the service is being used without oversight and appropriate authorization.
- *Verified deletion*. Applications and services can generate evidence associated with the removal or deletion of personal data, so that individuals can have proof of compliance with requests.
- *Right to be forgotten*. Similar to erasure code discussed earlier in this chapter, this is code or a service that will delete all personal information after a certain period of time. Ideally, the right to be forgotten should be adjustable as a matter of service subscription, where some subscribers have shorter or longer retention time.
- *Data portability*. The ability to access all personal information and logs and transfer en masse to a different service provider, or merely to archive the information for another unspecified purpose.

CONCLUSIONS AND SUMMARY

This chapter took liberty with conventional IT security dogma: it broke apart the established trinity of confidentiality, integrity, and availability (CIA)—putting availability alone in the Chapter 8, Availability and Reliability Requirements in the IoT. We did this because of our belief that:

1. The conventions of IT security do not apply cleaning to the IoT.
2. There are more, newer classes of security requirements that risk managers in the IoT need to balance, beyond CIA.

---

[4]See Tim Cook's Open Letter to the Federal Bureau of Investigation, February 2016, www.apple.com.
[5]OpSit. IoT Privacy, Data Protection and Information Security.

As for confidentiality and integrity themselves, we have reviewed multiple requirements, which include:

- Cryptographic stability—how frequently you can practically rotate or change keys in the IoT
- Cryptographic *aging-out*—how long your key lengths can be considered secure
- Untampered data that is provable throughout the system, not only in storage but also in transmission
- Decommissioning processes and protocols that are established and verifiable
- Chain of evidence—for the purposes of liability and compliance, how *provable* must the source and destination of information be?
- Attestation to capability—can the devices support the mutual assumptions related to security? Or should they seek different associations with different devices?
- Routing of data—does the network transport path support the prescribed assurance qualities?
- Erasure code and data gravity—deletion of data in a timely manner
- Cold storage—more data means more efficient storage, but it must also be accessible quickly
- Integrated reporting—across IoT asset classes, not only from the assets controlled entirely by the service provider
- Knowing versus learning—if a device must bootstrap itself in the field, how can we be assured it bootstraps with the right information?
- Horizontal logging, which means long-term management of events for security-related purposes.
- Device feedback about on and off states to protect confidentiality and privacy

Privacy requirements at the operational level revolve around:

- Anonymity
- Unlinkability
- Unobservability
- Verified deletion
- The right to be forgotten
- Data portability

AVAILABILITY AND RELIABILITY REQUIREMENTS IN THE IoT

8

Availability is a security concept that will be very familiar to people acquainted with enterprise information technology (IT) security and risk management. It is part of the founding trinity of properties: confidentiality, integrity, and availability (the previous two of which were discussed in the Chapter 7, Confidentiality and Integrity and Privacy Requirements in the IoT).

In the Internet of Things (IoT), availability rises in stature. In the Internet and enterprise IT systems, confidentiality and integrity tend to be the most important properties from a risk perspective. Unauthorized disclosure of change can lead to both regulatory and financial breaches and losses. However, availability requirements are not typically part of regulation, and the Internet itself is not designed for quality of service. The Internet of old is a *best effort* network and no guarantees are provided about the latency of traffic because there are frequently many independent and autonomous networks involved.

Availability issues will force the IoT to change the way the Internet is run because IoT requirements for availability will be more stringent and expectations among users and service provider higher because of the criticality of the *things* under management.

While this might seem an impossible request to place on a network of independent networks, what choice do we have? Build a new Internet to support new availability requirements in the IoT? No. That will not work.

What we as IoT system designers, and risk managers need to do, is better describe the operational requirements associated with the IoT so that we can communicate these requirements to the system and network managers seeking solutions and appropriate service levels.

AVAILABILITY AND RELIABILITY

One of the major themes in this book is how the risk associated with the IoT is different from the risk associated the conventional enterprise IT environment—basically the Internet of yesterday: desktop and laptop and smart phones talking to local servers or software in the cloud.

To use the IoT for service and life-critical applications, systems, and services, the components must meet requirements for reliability and availability, which can broadly be defined in terms of robustness and resilience—terms familiar to industrial systems engineers and foreign to most IT system engineers and managers.

- *Robustness*: an IoT system should provide the ability of a service to resist change due to external perturbations without modifying the service configuration.

RIoT Control. DOI: http://dx.doi.org/10.1016/B978-0-12-419971-2.00008-X

- *Resilience*: an IoT system should provide the ability of a service to respond to change due to external perturbations and return the service to its desired configuration.[1]

What follows are some more specific requirements related to reliability and availability that should be considered by risk managers in IoT services and systems. These requirements are not always unique to the IoT, but may take on a different complexion in the IoT—which is what we will try and draw out.

SIMPLICITY VERSUS COMPLEXITY

Simplicity is one of the most important counterbalancing operational requirements associated with Availability and Reliability in the IoT. Managers should bear this in mind as they go through this book and start to look at new and novel security requirements for their IoT system.

Whatever list of requirements you come out with at the end of this book, take a step back and consider the overall degree of complexity each requirement will generate, and whether added complexity is worth the added risk: complexity is not the friend of security and risk management.

The IoT is already an incredibly complex place. As we will discuss in the chapter on threats to the IoT, complexity injected by security and risk management is very serious. The simpler the IoT security and risk management requirements, the better, because they have:

- Less to go wrong
- Fewer costs associated with design, implementation, and management

NETWORK PERFORMANCE AND SLAs

In the IT industry, service level agreements (SLAs) with network service providers of many sorts are typically measured or quantified in:

- Speed in bits per second (bps)—how fast is the connection? At least on the segment up to the point where the data may get dumped onto the Internet (which has no SLA).
- Latency in milliseconds—how much delay will the latest packet experience on average?
- Loss as a percentage—how many packets gets lost or corrupted along the way?

Network SLAs in the IoT will probably contain the same sort of baseline metrics, but are also likely to require additional and new metrics that reflect the different nature of security and risk in the IoT—specifically related to the availability of not just the network, but the impact of the otherwise perfectly safe network on the availability of the device itself! [2]

- *Bits per joule*: how much energy must the IoT device (running on batteries?) use for the amount of data sent? While this might be a function of the device design, it might easily be a function

---

[1]Eric Simmons Contribution to SWG IoT 5 AH4, April 2014.

[2]http://www.fiercewireless.com/tech/story/intel-exec-5g-will-redefine-how-we-measure-network-performance/2014-04-04?utm_medium=nl&utm_source=internal.

of the network too; for instance, if the network provider supplies only marginal network coverage for some devices, they will exhaust their energy reserves much faster trying to transmit to a distant gateway. Devices closer to the gateway will get far more bits per joule than devices at the edges of coverage.

- *Bits per hertz:* how much data can be sent for a given unit of wireless spectrum? Generally, there are two types of spectrum: licensed and unlicensed. The unlicensed wireless spectrum is crowded and full of applications and *noise* because radios that operate in this spectrum can be built and bought by anyone. Wireless LANs, microwave ovens, doorbells, and CCTV cameras often all operate in this shared spectrum. Licensed spectrum means that the frequencies are reserved for applications and services that are granted licenses to operate without interference and noise from other services. Cellular phones, television, and police radios are examples of licensed spectrum. Getting more or fewer bits per hertz will certainly drive decisions pertaining to the use of licensed versus unlicensed spectrum, among several factors. In the context of availability and especially latency, bits per hertz will be a critical decision associated with probability of impact and risk.
- *Bits per square meter:* how much data can be managed by a given IoT device, most probably a gateway. In other words, if a gateway is servicing 1000 square meters of area around it, the amount of data it can receive per second will govern how many devices can be located in the given 1000 square meters! The data-management rate (bits per square meter) will in turn be driven by factors such as the power available to the gateway to run the radios and the spectrum and associated interference and noise associated with the spectrum. Again, ill-considered specifications and requirements related to bits per meter will affect availability and reliability of IoT systems.

ACCESS TO IoT DESIGN AND DOCUMENTATION

The operational controls associated with various forms of business and organization requirements will spawn at least three different dimensions of design documentation that will be required to manage risk effectively in the IoT:

- Application and system design documentation
- User interface design documentation
- Documentation and reporting documentation

All too often, systems are being built with poor or marginal documentation. In the IoT world, with cyber-physical interfaces and safety-critical systems, poor documentation or out-of-date documentation drives an enhanced risk profile. Therefore, risk managers should consider at least the following classes of documentation when reviewing whether what has been created by the development and operations teams is sufficient for the IoT service in question.

APPLICATION AND SYSTEM DESIGN

Application and system design refers to the software and logic that is running on the endpoint, the gateway, in the network, and within the data center (DC) or cloud where the service information is ultimately stored and managed.

Requirements to limit the collection, use, and disclosure of personal or otherwise sensitive data should be built directly into the design from the start to minimize IoT risks not only related to regulation compliance but also to liability (for regulatory breach) and unplanned costs associated with late or postdeployment reengineering.

USER INTERFACE DESIGN DOCUMENTATION

Many devices in the IoT will have no user interface whatsoever—they will be "headless." These services will be deeply embedded into applications, systems, and service and not intended for physical administration by users on the spot.

However, as we discussed in Chapter 7, Confidentiality and Integrity and Privacy Requirements in the IoT, sometimes even the simplest devices will have fundamental requirements for basic interface features, such as indicators of state: on/off, recording/not recording, network up/network down, and so on.

As part of showing due care in the IoT system design process, simple decisions related to user interface, or its absence, should be recorded and managed as part of the service data set.

In the case of IoT devices intended for management by people on the spot, interface design will be a critical determining factor in the overall satisfaction of users and the adoption rate and general commercial success of the service. Interface design and documentation will play a role in managing risks associated with administrative and user errors and oversights. How to create a user interface properly is beyond the scope of this book, except to highlight the importance of this process to risk management in the IoT.

REPORTING AND SYSTEM DOCUMENTATION

From the perspective of a client or a subscriber to any logical service, whether IT or IoT, there is no such thing as security without good reporting of results and system documentation to prove operational proficiency.

Reporting performance and security will be a critical feature that must be supported during any IoT design processor, not as an afterthought.

All too often the metrics and key performance indicators needed to show that a system or service is secure are not easily available after deployment. While it is usually possible to cobble together the necessary logs and indicators eventually to create adequate security and system reports, this is a costly process that also inflicts operational inefficiency and certainly dissatisfies the customer. No one likes asking for security reports only to find they don't exist—meaning that security is probably inadequately monitored all around.

SELF-HEALING AND SELF-ORGANIZING

IoT networks will be reliable and remain available in part according to their ability to fix themselves when they change or when part of their system breaks. Such change and breakages or failure will most probably occur with the highest frequency in the part of the network that is both the most populous and the most dynamic—the outer ranges where the endpoints access the network and gateways.

IoT designers and risk managers should account for the following requirements: determine whether they are small, medium, or major concerns in their IoT service, and determine to what extent resources are available to address these requirements.

How often is the access network changing for the endpoint device *or* for the gateway device, which might support dozens or even hundreds of endpoints? For instance, the topology of a sensor network is not always fixed. Additionally, IoT networks may have to adapt to the availability of communication links between either devices or gateways that might be using a combination of peer-to-peer mesh network and star topologies connecting to hubs or gateways. IoT network topologies will often make the requirements to be self-healing and self-organizing for some of the following reasons over and above the mobile nature of may IoT services.[3] IoT devices might experience changing network topologies due to factors such as:

- Entry and exit of devices: IoT network topologies have to be capable of handling nodes leaving or joining the network without unmanaged degradation of sensor network performance.
- Available power and battery levels (e.g., a device may slow down, reduce functionality, or even drop out as its battery runs out).
- Changing of the role of a device as the environment changes (e.g., the sun comes up and the streetlight goes out).
- Maintenance state (some devices turn off or are rebooted as they go through some form of maintenance—leaving other devices to take up their loads).
- Security state: certain types of traffic may require a high level of assurance associated with network service levels or the trusted nature of gateways and nodes.

Fundamentally, the risk associated with an IoT network will be partially determined by its ability to self-adapt to accommodate changing conditions, especially at the access level of the service. This means the ability to support specific requirements that drive dynamic topologies and derive the appropriate level of robustness, reliability, and availability to optimize resource management and functionality.

REMOTE DIAGNOSTICS AND MANAGEMENT

A major element of reliability and availability will be linked to touchless maintenance and operation. IoT devices and gateways especially will need to operate for long periods of time without physical (hands-on) maintenance or technical support to resolve problems. The only alternatives to hands-on servicing are either self-diagnostics and repair or remote diagnostics and resolution by the system itself or by human operators.

In all likelihood, remote diagnostics and management will be a combination of automated and semiautomated capabilities that are supplied by multiple, coordinated parts of the IoT service. For instance, different capabilities will need to come from different service providers in order to effectively discover and trace problems.

---

[3]ISO/IEC 29182-1.

> Access to diagnostic and reporting information from the many different parts and service providers in any IoT is a critical requirement, and this access should be built into agreements and SLAs by customers. Otherwise, tracing problems associated first and foremost with availability and reliability will be difficult, expensive, and time consuming. This is a major point of evolution in IoT requirements from traditional IT requirements, where disparate reporting from different service providers is the norm rather than the exception.

Today in IT systems it is very common to encounter a system problem, and, in the course of trying to resolve the issue, the different service providers (both internal and external) will simply point fingers at each other as the clock runs. The application guys blame the server (platform) guys. The platform guys blame the network guys. The network guys blame the carrier. The carrier blames all the others. And nothing gets fixed because there is no consolidated reporting from all these systems and service providers rapidly understand to where the fault actually occurred.

As often as not, the system fault is due to cascading and converging issues from multiple systems—to fix the problem you need to adjust two or more systems, neither of which in or of themselves actually appears to be failing!

This is a major risk to any IoT service: the effective and efficient diagnosis and tracking of system problems when there are multiple service providers and manufacturers.

In any complex system involving multiple providers, it is a well-known condition that *service failures and degradations are first blamed on the interdependent service providers. The buck gets passed.* Without good remote diagnostics, it becomes very difficult to be conclusive about where in the service a failure has occurred, and without good diagnostics to prove a failure has occurred in a given part of the systems (endpoint, gateway, network, cloud), getting providers to assume responsibility will be very difficult and inflict delays.

A significant operational requirement in the IoT will be defining sufficient diagnostics capabilities for all parts of the system with enough detail to manage interdependencies in the service efficiency without inflicting too much additional cost. Because most diagnostic tools and logs can create more information management requirements and data storage demands, it can raise costs.

Risk managers in the IoT must break down the different elements of the IoT services and understand what diagnostics are required and available from each distinct element and/or service provider (see Fig. 8.1). Even within the major IoT element categories, there will be subservices. For instance:

- Endpoint devices: define the remote diagnostics and maintenance capabilities
- Gateway devices: define the remote diagnostics and maintenance capabilities
- Network
  - Physical network platform: define the remote diagnostics and maintenance capabilities
  - Network as a service platform: define the remote diagnostics and maintenance capabilities
- DC/cloud
  - Infrastructure as a Service (IaaS): define the remote diagnostics and maintenance capabilities
  - Platform as a Service (PaaS): define the remote diagnostics and maintenance capabilities
  - Software as a Service (SaaS): define the remote diagnostics and maintenance capabilities
- Logging and aggregated reporting across all service elements

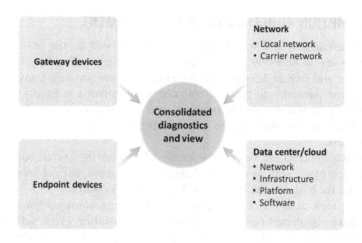

FIGURE 8.1

Diagnostic data sources in the IoT.

RESOURCE CONSUMPTION AND ENERGY MANAGEMENT

Energy efficiency is a major requirement in the IoT, directly affecting reliability and availability and often the general operating lifetime of the IoT device—especially endpoint devices. As product managers will seek to add features and capabilities to make the IoT devices and associated services as marketable as possible, risk managers need to understand the total impact of resource consumption under both normal and especially *abnormal* conditions, and how things like SLAs might be impacted.

For instance, what is the longest possible period the device might conceivably be required to operate without a recharge or energy refresh? Due to climatic conditions? Evacuation conditions due to environmental hazards or terrorist threats? Labor actions? Fuel shortages or other supply chain disruptions?

IoT endpoints and gateways with real-time operating systems are often resource-constrained systems that usually do not include typical IT security capabilities: there may not be computing resources available on the *things* to include substantial or perhaps any security capabilities. Additionally, in some instances, third-party security solutions are not viable for after-market integration even if the IoT system integrator wanted to do so: license and service agreements may prohibit such *upgrading* of IoT devices and break support agreements. Loss of vendor support can occur if third-party applications are installed without vendor acknowledgment or approval.

Energy efficiency and device energy management is important in many sensor networks where the sensor nodes are battery-operated and it is desirable for the network to be operational for as long as possible. Energy harvesting technologies may help with energy management and extending network lifetime, but may vary in effectiveness according to seasonal and other external conditions.[4]

---

[4]ISO/IEC 29182-1.

ENERGY CONSUMPTION ADJUSTMENT AND MANAGEMENT

Another energy consumption and management requirement will be the ability to change and adjust consumption levels remotely; for instance, by slowing or disabling features to reduce energy consumption and extend lifetime. As an example, network data transmission might be moved from real-time telemetry to batched uploads of information to save power from radios. Another example may be that device sensors may reduce their environmental sample rates from every one tenth of a second to every one second, or lights for human interfaces might be dimmed to half strength or less.

These sorts of requirements are very likely features that drive the overall business base for the IoT system in the first place, such as off-peak demand management, but risk managers should also consider them useful for Risk and the Internet of Things (RIoT) control.

Another way to look at IoT risk management with energy consumption techniques is that many industries have significant options for production scheduling given sufficient notice, but they can seldom respond to unplanned energy shortages by simply reducing their short-term demand across the board. Unlike typical consumer applications where loads can be reduced by adjusting heating, cooling and domestic lighting, it is often critical that energy supply be kept within carefully engineered parameters. Additionally, some types of production, once started, cannot be stopped without damage to product quality or equipment. Deviation from planned energy-availability levels can have devastating impacts on production quality, plant safety and security are maintained.

As a result, the IoT criteria used to respond to unplanned energy demand and fluctuations must differ from that of regular IT systems, which for the most part are made to fail and recover once power is restored.[5,6]

WILLS

Wills are essentially instructions from endpoint to a gateway or cloud services about how to act in the event it disappears, due to failure, extended shutdown, or end of life. For some IoT services, the proper definition of wills for an endpoint device or gateways can make a major different in the risk associated with the service.

Often, the notion of wills will be something that is implicitly contained and managed by the different service elements. Or, they may be configured and established by vendors and engineers rather than service owners, product managers, or even risk managers!

To the extent wills exist, they may often be incorporated into gateways rather than endpoint devices. For instance, after a period of time of unresponsiveness, a gateway may send an alert about a given endpoint to a central facility. This means that if multiple services are running on the endpoint device, they might all share the same will regardless of the application.

---

[5]IEC New Work Item Proposal 65/519/NP.
[6]http://www.theregister.co.uk/2014/07/08/standby_consumes_more_power_than_canada_iea/.

A more flexible and likely requirement in the IoT will be for endpoints to communicate their wills to gateway and cloud services, rather than a one-size-fits-all approach. The will message will probably stipulate requirements and parameter about the device, such as:

- Topic or service name,
- Default will (the baseline)—instructions for response and data management *after death*, including metadata such as:
  - Quality of service (QoS) requirements for the device and network, in event that another endpoint device is assigned the role of the dead device
  - Data latency, loss, caching, and retention parameters
  - Error and warning forwarding instructions (who gets the logs)
  - Will lifetime and expiry
- Ephemeral will (context-specific wills)—circumstances and conditions under which the default will is superseded, and the associated metadata

For risk managers in the IoT, it is not necessarily a requirement to all services to support device wills; in many cases these features may be too expensive to implement. However, at the design stage, the ability to express the requirement to support wills may open the service up to more deployment options and potential services, reducing the business-level risk of outright service failure!

FLOW CLASSIFICATION AND QoS

One of the defining requirements of the IoT is that availability risks are amplified; they are more serious than would typically be the case in historical, business IT networks. This was discussed in earlier chapters. Therefore one of the operational requirements associated with the IoT is that QoS capabilities be available for IoT services, where they are needed.

From the perspective of a network provider, QoS is usually technically possible and a functional feature of the network. However, depending on what sort of network subscription has been planned and procured by any one of a number of different service providers at different levels in the IoT service stack discussed in Chapter 2, The Anatomy of the Internet of Things, it can be hard to know what QoS is actually available.

All traffic on the Internet today is *best effort* QoS. The Internet of today is about getting packets to destinations, mostly without regard to the order or latency. As long as the packet gets there, the Internet has done its job. This will not be sufficient in the IoT and requirements related to QoS need to be spelled out.

For instance, alarms and alerts from IoT devices that are sensing physical and kinetic events often have high priority, if not the highest priority. *Best effort* as a design requirement will not pass muster in the event of injury or damage, and issues of liability and guilt comes into play. Even if users and subscribers are formally notified in the fine print that best effort is all the service is intended to provide, there will still be mutterings (or worse) of negligence or indifference to damage when push comes to shove. Can you hear the lawyer now: "How could you design a physically critical IoT service, based on 'best effort networking' and expect nothing ever to happen?"

Chapter 4, Business and Organizational Requirements, discussed the role of the regulatory and the need to take into account the requirements contained in regulations that may pose a risk to the IoT service. An example of such a risk, especially in the context of flow classification and QoS, is the notion of *net neutrality*: that all packets on the shared Internet are equally important and giving priority to one form of traffic over another is *discrimination and anticompetitive*: presumably because certain service providers might get favorable treatment on the network, which places competitors at a disadvantage. But net neutrality flies in the face of the IoT requirement for flow classification and QoS from end to end. We will discuss this matter further in Chapter 12, Threats and Impacts to the IoT.

When it comes to applying QoS to IoT services, one way to look at accomplishing this is to place all the QoS intelligence in the network, or to share it between the network and the endpoint devices and/or gateways.

FLOW CONTROL AND QoS IS THE NETWORK

An established means of applying flow controls and QoS in the network is to use *tunnels* and segregate traffic with different levels of QoS. This means that any traffic in a given tunnel is treated the same. A related approach, if tunneling is not appropriate, may be to apply QoS based on gateway addresses (sources or destination of the traffic). In either case, the tunnels or gateway addresses will be based on point-to-point layer 2 (e.g., Ethernet) connections, not layer 3 transport (e.g., Internet Protocol (IP)); this means that unless the network elements can relay QoS requirements from one to another at each "hop" (such as with multiprotocol label switching (MPLS)), the QoS is lost at the first hop, such as a router.

For risk managers depending on end-to-end QoS applied by the layer 3 Internet protocol network to fulfill reliability and availability requirements, some serious questions about where QoS capabilities stop and start are required!

FLOW CONTROL AND QoS IN THE ENDPOINT OR GATEWAY

A more granular approach to relying on the network to make QoS decisions and then support them is to divide the duty. Let endpoint devices and/or gateways decide on QoS requirements based on *contextual* information (time of day, volumes, environmental conditions—rain, snow, earthquake—and so on).

Allowing the endpoint to establish QoS requirements is not a new idea and is actually supported already in both Internet Protocol version 4 (IPv4) and Internet Protocol version 6(IPv6) through a variety of packet options and packet flags, such as Type of Service (ToS) in IPv4 and Flow Control in IPv6 (See Fig. 8.2). The problem is that routers on the IPv4 Internet of today have been entirely set to ignore the ToS flags and even IPv6 devices will ignore QoS flags unless explicitly configured to do otherwise.

Given the granular nature of the IoT service options that will be necessary to support in the name of efficiencies and service specialization, QoS set by the endpoints will be something that would best be fixed on the Internet as a whole. But that is not going to happen anytime soon.

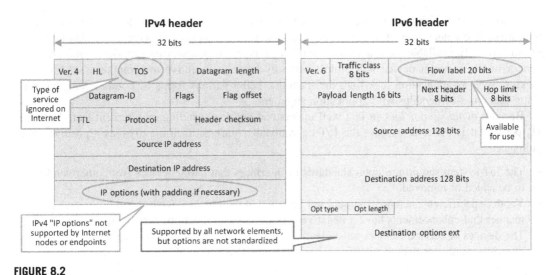

FIGURE 8.2

IP (v4/6) IP header options for staining packets.

This means that IoT system engineers and risk managers may have a requirement to procure QoS through specialized services or network-as-a-service providers who buy bulk QoS from carriers and carve it up among subscribers.

INTERCHANGEABILITY AND VENDOR-NEUTRAL STANDARDS

Interchangeability and vendor neutrality are not a requirement novel to the IoT—it has long been a goal of business IT systems to acquire the benefits associated with being able to mix and match solutions from different vendors, and avoid being locked in. Yet after close to 50 years of business IT, it can still be fiendishly difficult to avoid vendor lock-in, if for no other reason than the fact that all vendors conspire to achieve lock-in! It is good for business!

We have place interchangeability and standardization under availability and resiliency requirements because of the pernicious effects that even apparently small issues can have of the ability of a complex system to meet service level objectives. (Some practitioners would consider that this requirement might even belong under the business and organization requirements section, and they could well be correct).

In the IoT, the requirement for interoperability and standardization is heightened because the number of potential vendors and moving parts has increased from the business IT world: there are more devices, more gateways, and more network services available from many different potential providers and applications available from many different as-a-service providers. From a risk perspective, vendorlock related to one supplier in the IoT system might have a cascading effect into the other suppliers, resulting in lock-in with all of them.

As an example: if the endpoint devices—say some sort of sensor—are made only by one vendor with a specific patent, then it might require specific sorts of network support and technology that are in turn only available from a limited number of network-as-a-service suppliers. Similarly, the vendor of the endpoint device will almost certainly have an incentive to promote other forms of locking, such as application lock-line, the incentive being various forms of commissions, partnerships, and cross-ownerships with application suppliers.

Because *avoid vendor lock-in* is a well understood and longstanding requirement from business IT, perhaps it is better to express the IoT operational requirement differently—as a positive form guidance:

- The IoT system should use open standards or interfaces that allow devices from other vendors to be added or removed.
- Vendor-specific enhancements should not be bundled with basic devices services in such a manner that enhancements have a negative impact on basic functions if they are not deployed.
- The devices or service vendors must clearly publish the technical standards used or state where proprietary enhancements to standards have been applied that might limit interoperability.

LIFETIMES, UPGRADING, PATCHING, AND DISPOSAL

Expressing the design lifetime is an important requirement that risk managers must understand because the intended functional lifetime will have a major impact on the security and risk associated with the IoT system. How long should we expect the device to remain available and predictably reliable?

The longer the lifetime, the greater the potential that the device may be subjected to attack, compromise, or both. This is a simple matter that the longer a target is available to adversaries, the better their odds are of eventually compromising. Additionally, issues such as cryptographic *aging out*—discussed earlier—and vulnerabilities that crop up in software and firmware over time will enable attackers even more! The longer the lifetime of a given IoT device, the more care should be taken to understand the potential difference between the device security profile at the start of its life and the end of its life.

Upgradability (improving the software/firmware) and patch-ability patching (fixing flaws) is a fundamental dimension of device risk and its relationship to device lifetimes. For larger, more powerful devices in the IoT, upgrading is taken for granted as an option to address security and risk associated with ageing out and software vulnerabilities. But for many of the more remote, constrained, or smaller devices in the IoT, this ability to upgrade/patch has a huge impact of risks of all types: financial risks in the form of upfront design and development costs, and ongoing operational costs.

An alternative to focusing on requirements for upgradability is the option of disposal and disposability. If the device is disposable, then the option is to not to try to upgrade it, but to discard and destroy it if and when it is not longer considered secure, is suspected of compromise, or cannot be upgraded or patched any further. Clearly, while we are using availability and reliability as the main context for these requirements, it applies to many of the other risk management classes we discuss in this book.

HEARTBEATS, CENSUS, AND INVENTORY

For an IoT system under design, consider the granularity of what you need to know about the population of devices under management: do you need to know from minute to minute which devices are functional? Hour to hour? Or do you deploy maintenance resources simply when you encounter extended periods of *darkspace*—logical or physical regions that should have no data coming out of them—they have gone dark.

There will be many different techniques for assessing the state of the device population and performing inventories, but probably they will come down to systems of proactive or reactive heartbeats or beacons from devices.

A proactive heartbeat and beacon may be generated repeatedly by a device on a consistent or a scheduled basis. This can be a resource-intensive form of monitoring that reduces the lifespan of a device.

Alternatively, the heartbeat or beacon may be something that happens in response to a *paging* signal from a gateway asking all devices in listening range to announce their status—a reactive approach.

Of these two systems, the reactive approach is widely used in systems such as cellular phones to make sure power and scarce radio frequency spectrum are conserved. The downside is that minute to minute it might be difficult to understand what device is where physically—if they are mobile. So, depending on the location-based characteristics of the IoT application under consideration, proactive announcements about status might be the actual, operational requirement.

DOCUMENTATION AND TRAINING

Documentation and training can be an important requirement in the IoT not only in terms of operations process but also because of its effect of controlling risk under normal and especially abnormal conditions. We touched on this requirement in the previous section on user interface design and its effect on availability and reliability.

Documentation and reporting can be critical to user adoption rates and customer satisfaction because it plays a role in determining to what extent an IoT service is available and reliable for use—regardless of the system's condition. Is the system comprehendible and trustable (via reporting and documentation) for users?

Training and education is another way to talk about documentation and its merits. Explaining to users the implications of what they are allowing and disallowing goes a long way to showing the necessary good faith in the IoT to drive adoption and growth. Similarly, backing up such information with a degree of transparency through logging and reporting of data events, volumes, and frequencies provides the evidence that can address many otherwise costly appeals and investigations before they start.

Risks to the IoT are not all about hardened threat and technical vulnerabilities, they will also be soft, illdefined, and political. Trust will be critical to the advancement of the IoT, and much trust may be earned by properly accommodating for the emotional needs of the end users and even the managers and administrators of IoT systems. These needs are fairly simple in that they want the ability to know something about the system: they want documentation and training to be available (even if they never touch it). In this case, the soft, political risks we are referring to would be that users reject IoT applications and systems not based on merits but on perception.

Availability and reliability of the system as a whole is improved by good documentation and training. Users and administrators will ultimately be the weakest link in the security and risk management chain. Errors and omissions are ultimately only addressable by well-trained and informed users and administrators, and their ability to influence functioning of the IoT system or service.

THE DISCOVERY-EXPLOIT WINDOW AND CYBER-INTELLIGENCE

The discovery-exploit window is the time between when a vulnerability in a system is discovered and the time it is exploited. Clearly, this window is not fixed and will be influenced by factors such as who discovered the vulnerability, and how it was disclosed. But one consistent characteristic of the discovery-exploit window is that is it constantly shrinking as information dissemination becomes faster, and the tools for exploiting vulnerabilities are either free, automated, or commercially available.

Cyber-intelligence is a predictive security function, where bad addresses, URLs, domains, autonomous systems, traffic flows, and files are described and reputations assigned. Cyber-intelligence systems are then queried by devices for information about what is known about connections and data—and presumably applying controls according to the reputational scores that come back and the organizational policy related to such scores.

The discovery-exploit window is often measured in mere minutes! Certainly, once a vulnerability is publicly announced on the Internet it takes very little time before it is being activity exploited with pre-made tools. The Heartbleed OpenSSL vulnerability in a widely used web security platform is a good example of this discovery-exploit window: by the time even the largest and best security-practitioners knew about the vulnerability, tools for exploiting it were already circulating.

In one instance, a teenager with only basic computer skills defeated the security system of the federal government's revenue and tax system—a system known to spend vast sums on IT security. The teenager used Heartbleed exploitation tools that he did not understand but could run as a *script kiddie*. This script kiddie operated inside the discovery-exploit window and compromised hundreds of citizen tax records and identities. He was also so naïve and unskilled that he left digital traces that resulted in his arrest and prosecution.[7]

This means that security systems need to remain dynamic: updating their intelligence about vulnerabilities in order to detect and stop attacks. Essentially, the signatures of attacks and malware need to be disseminated as quickly as possible.

In the IoT, certain device-like gateways, large and small, will probably include dynamic security elements. Some endpoints in the IoT will also include dynamic security, but many will not, for reasons of power consumption, network capacity and connectivity, processing ability, and memory. For devices with the ability and requirement to support dynamic security, the next question will be about how often to update, as well as the freshness of the updates themselves. This is where the

---

[7]http://www.cbc.ca/news/politics/stephen-arthuro-solis-reyes-charged-in-heartbleed-related-sin-theft-1.2612526.

availability and reliability requirements of system components such as cyber-intelligence and updates needs to be carefully assessed by the IoT system designers and risk manager.

The temptation will be to make the refresh intervals for cyber-intelligence as long as possible because refreshing comes with costs. It will require the device to turn on—at the very least. Refreshing will require bandwidth and network—consuming more power and possibly generating tolls. Finally, dynamic security means that there is more to go wrong during the refresh—increasing log sizes and memory needs, administration and support costs, troubleshooting, and maintenance. The issue is that if a discovery-to-exploitation window is 10 minutes in size and a refresh interval is 24 hours, then the resulting *vulnerability window* is pretty big.

Balancing the costs of small vulnerability windows against the risks of large vulnerability windows will be a critical matter for managers of security in the IoT, particularly because it will affect the availability requirements under normal conditions and abnormal conditions alike.

SUMMARY

Here, we have looked at availability in the context of the IoT and found that requirements are different from enterprise IT and general Internet environments.

Basically, the IoT has requirements that are more central to the value proposition of the system as a whole and are less variable.

Service levels for availability in the IoT will vary greatly. In some cases they may be lower than those seen for common applications like web services—which is saying a lot because from a network perspective, most web services have very low availability service levels. Conversely, IoT devices may have very high service levels—such as those found in industrial control systems or high-frequency trading systems in finance, where milliseconds count!

The variability in IoT availability requirements derives from the broad range of new performance and risk management requirements. This chapter has attempted to expose some of these requirements that might not be apparent in typical IT systems, so that IoT system designs might better consider the service levels needed for availability and express them with a greater level of precision and rationale.

IDENTITY AND ACCESS CONTROL REQUIREMENTS IN THE IoT

9

As an observation: identity and access (I&A) control is to the rest of information technology (IT) security what whales and dolphins are to the other mammals: related creatures from a different world! You can be a full-time I&A person dealing only with I&A all day long like user directories and password resets, for your entire career, and have little to nothing to do with the rest of security or other security people.

I&A tends to ride over the top of other security and function independently. For instance, firewalls and intrusion prevention system (IPS) people usually have nothing to do with I&A people. Desktop, server, or data center (DC) security people will carry on regardless of whether or not the I&A system is functioning, usually. While many of these systems will have interfaces to the I&A systems, and possibly interdependencies with the I&A solutions, the contrast and boundaries will be as obvious as sea versus land.

Under a typical IT security-oriented discussion, I&A control is considered a matter of confidentiality; it is about prevented unauthorized disclosure, mostly. I&A control may also share certain elements with integrity, like unauthorized change or deletion. But in both instances, I&A control are mere use cases within the bigger requirements.

In the Internet of Things (IoT), the matter of I&A should be considered one of the *big requirements*; it is independently important for a number of specific reasons:

- There will be far more things than people, which means the scale of the challenge is much bigger in the IoT and a critical success factor.
- I&A will not be performed merely once per logon, as was common in an IT systems—it could be performed multiple times at multiple levels. For instance, a device might undergo I&A at the network, with a gateway, then again to a network service provider for service level subscriptions, then again to an application provider. And within all this may be I&A performed by the human user to the system as a whole. That is a lot more I&A than just logging into your PC on the corporate network!
- Systems will simply fail if I&A fails. While desktops, laptops, servers, and smartphones will usually possess a wide range of functionality even if they fail I&A, or I&A services are unavailable. But in the IoT, due to bootstrapping and network dependencies, many IoT devices and services will be dead in the water without I&A. I&A will be the spark of life for many IoT systems.

The following discussion will take a more detailed look at some of the less frequently discussed elements of I&A in the IoT.

RIoT Control. DOI: http://dx.doi.org/10.1016/B978-0-12-419971-2.00009-1

INTEROPERABILITY OF I&A CONTROLS

Interoperability is broadly considered one of the highest priorities for IoT systems and devices. Interoperability is frequency cited as the #1 challenge of the IoT.

Interoperability refers to the ability of IoT devices and systems to work with other devices and systems from different vendors, service providers, and legal jurisdictions. For instance, a device from one manufacturer is able to speak both a common, standard network language and/or a diversity of network languages to allow it to work in many different places.

So why are we placing interoperability under I&A control, in our discussion of risk and the Internet of Things (RIoT)? Because of the major security requirements in the IoT, I&A control will probably face the greatest demands in terms of interoperability: the ability to bootstrap and adopt I&A to the available environments and to the actual purpose for which the devices were deployed.

For instance, a device deployed for a military sensing application may have a very high degree of assurance associated with the I&A, while the same sensor from the same manufacturer might also be purchased and deployed for a home security application by a consumer—in which case the I&A requirements may differ significantly. Ideally, the same device could support both applications, though perhaps detecting and then applying different I&A processes.

It would be possible to spend this whole chapter on interoperability; entire books have been written on the topic generally. In the case of IoT standards, some have been developed focused entirely on interoperability and everything they bother to say about security is focused just on interoperability of security control at the technical level. Because to get into technical requirements would be beyond the scope of this book, we direct the reader to other sources.[1]

MULTIPARTY AUTHENTICATION AND CRYPTOGRAPHY IN THE IoT

In the IoT there will be far more *multiparty* transactions occurring than in the Internet of old, where most transactions were intrinsically peer-to-peer or point-to-point in nature.

For instance, today many transactions involve a client and a server, where the client authenticates to a server because an application or service is being provided by the server. This might be a consumer-to-business (C2B) service like banking, or a retail purchase or a government service like filing a tax form.

But what happens when the application is a new generation of IoT service involving more than two service providers coming together in the process of delivering the service? And trust and security of communications must be quickly among three or more parties?

The traditional way of dealing with nominally multiparty transactions is to look to the service provider (the server) to aggregate most or all of the suppliers and counterparties into a single relationship for the client—and charge a fee as part of the overall price of the service.

This is what a retailer or a travel agent might do: they have relationships with many suppliers and pull together a package of goods and services for the one client. Or sometimes they merely procure the good or service in bulk (wholesale) and distribute to clients. They then charge a markup

---

[1]See oneM2M (http://www.onem2m.org/) or Industrial Internet Consortium (http://www.iiconsortium.org/).

or margin for this service—this is a well-proven model going back to the emergence of the very first merchants and retailers, probably thousands of years ago: buy from multiple vendors and suppliers so customers can have a one-stop shop where they pay a single aggregator for goods from many suppliers. This is what grocery stores, Amazon (online), or Walmart (bricks and mortar) does today.

But the IoT and the technology underlying it allows for new and even dynamically assembled services to be created from component parts: aggregating merchants are not necessary. Or it involves a service that requires the participation of literally thousands of different devices where aggregation is neither efficient nor viable.

For instance, location-based services around detection and tracking will create many opportunities for services in the IoT. But the services and devices used to establish location will be constantly changing as a person or a device moves around. While it might be possible, it would be expensive and complicated for a third-party aggregator or merchant to try and broker all these location services for a given client. Additionally, such aggregation creates a potential information base of personally identifiable data that you may wish not to create in the first place!

Alternately, for an IoT service or a good derived from different suppliers and vendors for differing prices at differing qualities at differing times, clients or users might wish to rearrange their IoT supply chain regularly or even automatically to take advantages of small differences in service profiles, resulting in more efficiency. This is a significant element of the evolving IoT anatomy—stratification of the supply chain into greater specialization and efficiency, with competition at many different *layers* of a service stack: physical device, physical network, network as a service, software as a service (SaaS), service management, and so on.

A major challenge with getting this degree of efficiency and stratification is that trust relationships must be established among multiple parties very quickly, in a manner that is cryptographically as light as possible to save processor, power, memory, and time!

To maximize the potential of these IoT opportunities, new forms of multiparty authentication are needed.

WEAK OR EXPENSIVE: THE OLD CRYPTOSYSTEM AND TECHNIQUES DON'T SCALE TO THE IoT

There are two main models for authentication used on the Internet: one is weak and breakable (shared key) and one is computationally resource intensive expensive (public key), and neither will address the full range of identity nor access requirements in the IoT.

Secure Sockets Layer (SSL) and Transport Layer Security (TLS) are the most widely used security systems on the Internet today. Both systems use a combination of public key and shared key models to create a secure channel between two endpoints, such as a web browser and a website.

Shared keys are essentially shared secrets known to two or more parties. Parties authenticate themselves to each other by proving their knowledge of the shared secret to the other party (or parties) and the other party (or parties) verifies knowledge of the shared secret. Shared secrets can be passwords, biometric samples, personal identification numbers (PIN), images, gestures, and symmetric cryptographic keys. In simple terms, this authentication model asks the question, "Do you know the secret?"

In the shared key model, only trusted peers have the key or can get the key. If the device can show it has access to the shared key by encrypting or decrypting a token, then it is trusted. Shared key is weak because if the key is exposed, then all the devices and all the services relying on that key are vulnerable and considered compromised. In the IoT, with billions of devices pouring onto the network, the ability physically to access a device and extract the key increases substantially. Also, with more and more devices potentially sharing the same key, the impact of a single key being compromised is big. Shared key is weak not because of the cryptographic algorithms, but because of the vulnerabilities introduced by the management of the shared keys in the IoT.

The other widely used identity and authentication mechanism is known as public key and is too expensive for most of the IoT from the perspective of computation, memory, power, and storage.

Public key involves, in fact, two keys: one for encryption (the public key) and one for decryption and signing (the secret key). Every device employing this scheme needs its own, unique key pair. The public-key systems involve a challenge-response protocol typically restricted to two parties only. One of the two parties possesses the public key (not secret, publicly disclosed) and the other party possesses the private key (not disclosed, held as a secret). One of the parties goes first and encrypts a random message with his secret key-half and sends it to the other party, the other party uses the sender's public key-half to decrypt it and sends the decrypted message back (possibly re-encrypted with the receiver public half). The sender authenticates the receiver if and when the received message matches the original message. In simple terms, this authentication model asks the question, "Can you decrypt this?"

Public key pairs—because of their utility—are much larger than symmetric keys—often 10 times longer. This means that the devices that attempt to manipulate public keys must perform significantly more resource-intensive cryptographic operations for every secure transaction, plus be able to generate, regenerate, and store their own private keys. This is very expensive from a device capability perspective: power, processor, memory, and tamper resistance. The expense of public key manipulation and management may make an IoT device itself nonviable economically in many instances.

Public key is too expensive for some of the IoT because it requires unique, point-to-point authentications for each device with its own unique key pair. This is a massive burden on the network (especially constrained, industrial, or sensor networks) and an even bigger burden on any cloud-based system and services that must maintain secure, authenticated sessions with thousands or millions of devices at once. Also, in the event of peer-to-peer secure communications that rapidly changes, public key will also take too long and/or too many resources or too much network bandwidth.

For instance, as a smart car travels down the road, passing road beacons used for speed and distance safety every few milliseconds, public key authentication of those beacons would probably not happen fast enough without a mini-server at each beacon, which is too expensive both computationally and from a financial cost perspective too!

MULTIPARTY AUTHENTICATION AND DATA PROTECTION

Multiparty authentication and data protection can be expressed simply as a $2 + N$ relationship, meaning that "more than two" approving or participating entities are required to come together to authenticate a transaction. These systems are known as *key splitting* systems and were developed in the late 1970s,[2] which were themselves based on even older mathematics from the 1780s known has polynomials.[3]

The crux of these multiparty systems is that each participate can *recreate* the keys involved in the cryptographic operations by providing his/her share of the split key, versus sharing persistent keys under either symmetric or public key systems.

Multiparty authentication is not necessarily a novel requirement for access to date; there are many use cases where more than two entities need access to a secure resource of an information database.

For instance, dozens of public safety personnel need access to the secure, encrypted radio channel. However, trying to secure these channels using symmetric or public key systems becomes much less secure or exponentially more expensive as the number of participating parties grows. In the case of symmetric (shared-key) systems, the more copies of the keys that are distributed, the greater the potential a copy *leaks* or is disclosed in an unauthorized manner and compromised the entire system. In the case of public key systems, encrypting the channel may mean managing many unique keys: one for every participant!

In the IoT, with all its wealth of personally identifiable data flowing around, there will be an operational requirement to be more explicit about what information is available to whom. For instance, you may grant access to your health information to your doctor working from a hospital system; but not your doctor working from her home systems. In practice, the combination of your permission plus the doctor's consent, plus the hospital system's approval may be required to unlock your information in the data store. In this case, three parties are required to collaborate in a cryptosystem to unlock your health record or the patient, the doctor, and a device must be located within the hospital, for instance.

Another example of a multiparty operational requirement might be identical nodes operating in unison such as a critical sensor network; or they may be highly interdependent elements performing different tasks. In either example, it may be the case that having an adequate fail-safe means to cease operation as soon as one of the elements fails, stops sending data, or stops responding to a heartbeat or beacon. Because masquerade attacks against these systems would be a major vulnerability, authenticating each node related to their response to a heartbeat or beacon may be required. A multiparty authentication system based on a single key that can be *recreated* among all participants would be far better than a system based on a common key *shared* among all participants, or worse, a massively expensive public key system.

A consumer-oriented operational use case could relate to something like photo sharing among friends. Rather than trying to encrypt the same photos for multiple public keys, encrypt it once using a key that can be created strictly by the $2 + N$ participants—who can recreate the secret key when they come together.

In this model of multiparty authentication and data protection, the best elements of shared key and public key are retained, while the weak or expensive characteristics are left out. No storage of keys is required on the endpoints—just enough memory initially to derive a common key, split it, and distribute the pieces among multiple parties. To do so requires only a small amount of memory

---

[2]Shamir key splitting; https://en.wikipedia.org/wiki/Shamir's_Secret_Sharing.

[3]Mathematics to support such authentication and cryptographic systems have long been known. See Euler's work from 1779 on polynomial theorems. The effort now required is to convert these theorems to the entropy sources.

and processor power—enough to generate and split a common key. The only requirement is an awareness of how many parties are actually included in the *multi* part of multiparty: how many peers or participants are needed to recreate the key?

Multiparty horizontal authentication and data protection

One form of multiparty authentication that will be useful in the IoT is *horizontal* in nature: that is, the system can scale to an unlimited number of equally privileged participants, where some but not necessarily all must come together to recreate the symmetric key that was previously split up. All that needs to be understood upfront is the minimum number of participants needed to create the key. For instance, a key that requires three participants to recreate could have unique *fragments* sent to 10 participants—but only three of these authorized 10 need to agree for the key to be recreated and used to authenticate a transaction or possibly encrypt/decrypt information.

Horizontal refers to the ability of an unlimited number of peers to *derive* a common shared key, but from unique credential properties. This is like shared key, but the key is derived versus embedded or stored. Attempting to replicate such functionality under a public key system would require that a shared key be uniquely encrypted by each horizontal peer—which is too expensive for many types of constrained IoT device.

Multiparty cascading authentication and data protection

Related to horizontal authentication and data protection is multiparty cascading authentication and protection. The distinction in this case is the ability to split the key (credentials) assigned to one of the participating entities into further pieces a number of times. Splitting credentials means that an IoT element (person, device, service, whatever) can take its peer-to-peer, horizontal credential and split it in *n*, for the purposes of further controlling usage *from* a group of hierarchically lower peers. Or, an entity might delegate its own credential in a system to several *internal* peers. As in the horizontal model, a minimum number of these internal peers must contribute their fragments to recreate the original fragment. See Fig. 9.1.

For example, using health information as an example again: a hospital encrypts medical records with a key derived from merely two credentials: one from the patient and one from the hospital. To decrypt and access this record, the IoT system needs the patient key fragment (credential) and the

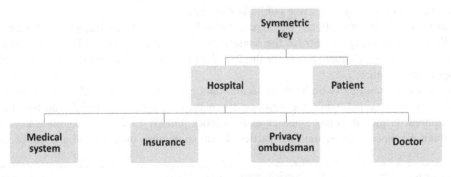

FIGURE 9.1

Hierarchical key splitting for the IoT.

fragment from the hospital. The hospital then splits its own fragment many times, requiring that a minimum of two or three or four or possibly more fragments must be brought together internally, to recreate the hospital original fragment to unlock a patient record.

In one scenario, for the patient records to be accessed, at least two of the four medical stakeholders must supply their unique fragment or credential to generate the single hospital credential, which is then combined with the patient's own fragment or credential to create the key and decrypt the patient records. In an alternate scenario, the crypto-system designer may require that a minimum of three out of four or more internal fragments must be brought together in this cascading hierarchy in order to generate the higher level key half.

MASS AUTHENTICATION AND AUTHORIZATION

A surge in access requests by many devices to enroll or join the network or service in a short period of time is one of the challenges that can face networks and online services today—both fixed line and wireless. A significant requirement in the IoT will be to find ways to support mass authentication events without undue service-level disruptions.

This can occur when a power is restored after a power failure, or perhaps after cellular services are resorted after an outage. It might also occur when many devices enter a service area suddenly, such as a parking lot during a special event; or when many devices suddenly want services at the same time, such as during a crisis when everyone tries to make emergency calls at the same time.

In the IoT, the sheer potential concentration of thousands of tiny devices in a relatively small area will make enrollment, authentication, and authorization service exhaustion a real risk or a major expense that will burden the system with higher operating costs.

When authentication service exhaustion occurs, a virtual denial of service (DOS) condition will prevail, where devices and the IoT cannot function. This DOS will potentially trigger an almost unknowable range of cascading impacts on not only the IoT system being considered, but interdependent systems.

Directly related to the previous discussion about multiparty authentication is group authentication and authorization: the ability for many devices to make individual requests to enroll in or join a network or services, but act on a shared credential that is nonetheless secure from interception or attacks that seek to extract a stored, shared key from a constrained device.

For many IoT devices, the option to manage symmetric keys can be both a risk due to the threat of a single disclosure compromising thousands of devices that may share the same key, or the cryptographic system might be too computationally expensive for the IoT systems and devices in question.

Technologies such as key splitting may offer a solution worth considering, where, for instance, thousands of devices might recreate the same key using entirely different stored fragments. This would allow efficient communications among these devices using a common key, but would also allow devices to be excluded from the ecosystem based on the fragment they provide. Suppose a device is known to be defective, and a hash of the key fragment used by that device is known. When a device attempts to authenticate to a mass-authorization system, part of the enrollment process may make sure the fragment, which is tied to the device, is considered good. If the fragment has had permissions revoked, the authentication is denied.

A variation on this same method for mass authentication may be simply to keep hashes of all key fragments belonging to members in good standing. If a fragment is presented in order to generate the shared key used in mass authentication, but it is not present in the registry of known, good fragments, then authentication is denied—regardless of whether the fragment can create the correct, shared key when combined with an authentication-system fragment.

AUTONOMICS (SELF-CONFIGURING, INTELLIGENT ADAPTIONS)

Many devices entering the IoT will have a basic business requirement to come online and start functioning with a bare minimum of instruction and a high degree of interoperability. They will need to do this in systems owned by as wide a variety of service providers as possible, therefore be as generic as possible in their assumptions about the environment. This ability to self-configure can be referred to as *autonomics*.

Autonomics may include several abilities, and managers in the IoT need to understand from the outset what these abilities might be and their intended operation. Like anything, autonomics will probably mean that more *intelligence* will be required within the device so that it can make sense of whatever environment it finds itself in, and configure itself correctly.

Autonomics will have a substantial security element, because the failure to properly self-configure, or to be duped into inappropriate self-configuration systems, could render the device useless, and at worst it may allow the device to be compromised or even threaten the IoT systems as a whole. Some security-critical, autonomic configuration parameters that might be part of a IoT system include:

- Device name—Does it acquire and assign the correct identity?
- Ownership and membership
- Networks to use, including redundancy and multihoming
- Service levels to seek, and expect, from available providers
- Contextual performance information—What is appropriate performance given parameters such as time of day, location, user profile, and so on

From a risk management perspective, the requirement related to autonomics is that the discovery processes have the appropriate degree of authentication and authorization, so that configuration parameters are obtained and updated from the authorized sources.

DEVICE AND OBJECT NAMING

With the huge number of new devices entering the IoT, hierarchical identification schemes will likely be required to support the identification of devices across possibly millions of different service providers (of networks, software, operating platforms), by country or region, by constituency, and among very different endpoints and devices.

Naming will need to be both flexible and interoperable among many vendors and service providers if the IoT is to reach its full potential. Flexibility of naming and the ability to move and relocate devices from one domain or directory will enable the creation of entirely new services by mixing and combining devices in ways never considered previously.

In addition, as discussed previously, flexibility of naming will make activities such as ownership transfers of devices possible—which in turn further enriches the potential of the IoT because assets become transferrable; transferrable in the face business events like sale to the highest bidder, or divisible in the event of a bankruptcy or the need to split up a company for competitive or regulatory reasons.

The dominant object naming service today is the Internet's Domain Name System (DNS), which allows machine addresses (i.e., IP addresses) to be rendered as human-readable words (www.example.com). DNS also allows the resources behind these services to change IP addresses and move throughout the Internet without the DNS name changing, allowing users to locate the service easily no matter where it might have physically or logically moved.

DNS also stores other types of information about the online service, such as the list of email servers for a given Internet domain, and lists of all the services that might be under a given address (books.example.com, cars.example.com). By providing a worldwide, distributed naming service, DNS has become critical infrastructure on the Internet. When DNS fails, the Internet fails for the most part!

Similarly, an object name service will also be one of the essential elements in the IoT, which can be used for translating the *thing-friendly* names of objects, which maybe belong to a technical discipline and name space (e.g., a long number such as a product code, uCode, or any other self-defined code) on different networks, such as a transmission control protocol/Internet protocol (TCP/IP) network or a constrained network into their corresponding "thing-friendly" addresses to allow other things—and people—to address information to the resource easily.

For instance, if a car manufacturer wants to build smart transportation systems into a vehicle that communicates with highway traffic sensors, wouldn't it be better if there were a standard way to address traffic sensors, rather than cars trying to learn and support unique addressing and naming schemes in each country? State or Province or Canton or Parish? By manufacturer?

Finally, different identification schemes may be required for different types of assets—again— like traffic or transportation sensors versus books or medicines or food. Another reason that different identification schemes might be required is that different IoT assets and things will have different properties associated with fundamental characteristics like lifetimes. Food things will be added and removed from an object naming directory very quickly; durable goods and industrial goods might be added and removed only infrequently. Therefore object name destruction—not just creation and maintenance—will be as much part of IoT operational requirements as will be object registration and creation.

From a security and risk management perspective, the requirement becomes clear: if naming and directory services will be critical to the IoT, the need to protect these systems is evident.

We need look no further than the naming and directory system of the current Internet to understand why: DNS services are critical infrastructure on the Internet and are under constant attack. Successful disruption of DNS basically cripples users. It makes it impossible for most users to find even basic resources like websites on the Internet, impacting the current generation of IoT services in a like manner. They fail, too.

In the IoT—the equivalent, evolved system that comes into play to support interoperability, asset transfer, combination, division, and discovery will be the target of attacks.

DISCOVERY AND SEARCH IN THE IoT

Every IoT endpoint or object can be a source of information, and in many cases it may be more efficient to query or search a directory or database for information about an endpoint rather than querying the device itself. Or, the devices might be too constrained to support queries—and to the extent that any information is available about the endpoint or object it *must* come from a directory search.

Directory searches for IoT devices will be performed for more than just a simple mapping of object name to network address—like DNS. In the IoT there will be a requirement with some applications for much more context related to the device—because device behavior will often be governed as much by context of usage and operational environment as any other factor. For this reason, IoT directories and searches will be required to manage semantic and context information, such as the following sorts of context information:

- On, off, dormant
- Load levels
- Geo-location: Close? Far away?
- Ownership? Usership? Lease length?
- Manufacturer?
- Peers in reach? Status of peers?
- Gateways in reach? Status of gateways?
- Available network service level agreements (SLAs)?
- Available services? What services are the device subscribed to?
- Condition of use? Recreational devices? Professional devices? Law enforcement and judicial order only?

AUTHENTICATION AND CREDENTIALS REQUIREMENTS

Authentication refers specifically to verifying the identity of a device, or perhaps the device and the device user or owner, or maybe even all three at once. This is different from authorization, which is about what a known device (+user + owner) may or may not be allowed to do: authorization as an IoT requirement is touched on shortly.

Authentication standards are a major requirement to efficient operations and development in the IoT. As of the writing of this work, standards development was underway but also incomplete relating to authentication techniques to support the IoT. Ironically, there are several competing standards, none of which seems to be dominant; while the efforts are in good faith issues related to interoperability may yet arise. For instance Fast Online Identity (FIDO)[4] alliance and oneM2M[5] are both propagating authentication and access architectures intended for all IoT markets.

---

[4]http://chipdesignmag.com/sld/blog/2014/07/14/security-levels-the-iot-device-and-server-landscape/.
[5]http://www.onem2m.org.

Authentication and credential management services in the IoT will need to support a variety of different relationships at different levels in the service stacks. For instance there are potential requirements for a given IoT service to support:

1. *Endpoint device to (centralized) application*: Example, an airplane authenticates to an air traffic control system.
2. *Endpoint device to application gateway*: Example, an airplane authenticates to an airport-specific security gateway to establish network connectivity before any data about air traffic control is passed.
3. *Endpoint device to application network(s) and network layers*: Example, an airplane joins a global air-traffic-control-specific network, which in turn is a layer on top of a (nominally) private IP network with services for air traffic control. Perhaps this is a network built on top of regulated spectrum, access to which is also based on specially licensed radio equipment using government-issued credentials for spectrum authentication. (If the radio does not possess the right credentials, it cannot speak to other legitimate radios in the spectrum—though it might still interfere with them by broadcasting in the same spectrum illicitly).

ANONYMITY AND AUTHENTICATION OF IoT DEVICES

An additional potential requirement associated with authentication in the IoT is *anonymity*: a device has its authenticity verified, but pseudonyms and aliases may be used. For instance, as an airplane moves from route to route it might change its identity like it changes its flight number. The reasons to support anonymity services related to authentication extend beyond those that might be imagined for privacy purposes; there are many security reasons not to want device movement to be traceable over long periods of time and space. Work related to IoT identity protection is underway in a number of forums, such as the Internet Engineering Task Force (IETF).[6]

Anonymity will also be an important requirement for the evolution of cyber intelligence systems that involve the IoT. If IoT devices become sources of reporting and events that are gathered and assessed by cyber intelligence systems, there will be conditions under which anonymity may be a condition of participation.

Consider a group of devices such as cameras inside cars. It will one day be possible to aggregate massive amounts of data from these sources for doing everything from traffic monitoring to accident statistics and avoidance technologies. However, car owners may not want to participate if their vehicles can be identified because they fear that insurance companies will simply use the information to raise rates. Alternately, car manufacturers may not want to enable their cars to participate because they fear that competitors will analyze the resulting data to generate statistics related to breaking or steering performance, to the disadvantage of the manufacturers participating in the analytical exercise.

While we can make all the promises in the world about how data will be managed and who will have access, these assurances mean less and less in the new world of mass data leakage and insider disclosures. Much more assuring is the ability to apply anonymity to a device identity for participation in certain groups and functions.

---

[6]http://tools.ietf.org/html/draft-urien-hip-iot-00.

A further example of the requirement to support anonymous authentication may be where a device is identified as a privileged device, but the unique identity of the device is deliberately obfuscated. The reason for anonymous connections for devices can be various:

- The system is used to gather intelligence in a *crowd source* scenario, at a large event or campaign. The information needs to be gathered from unique individuals and their devices, to prevent *voting* more than once. But at the same time, personal privacy issues might inhibit participation unless the anonymous nature of participation can be assured.
- In another situation, the regulatory issues associated with logging and knowing the identity of devices or users creates a data management load that increased costs past the point of business viability. The margins associated with the IoT system cannot support the necessary security to manage information about identifiable devices, and anonymous participation is much cheaper—because regulatory burdens are reduced significantly!

The operational requirement will be not just be for anonymization techniques and services, but also in order to have standardized and accepted means of applying such techniques in a way than can be easily audited in a manner generating consistent and repeatable results.

TAMPER-PROOF, HARDWARE-BASED AUTHENTICATION

Going in an orthogonal direction to anonymity is the concept of credentials built into devices at the hardware level that are used for authentication and cannot be replicated or duplicated, even by the manufacturer. These capabilities exist in some forms of trusted computing (or equipment) environments.

Hardware-based authentication might be required where services must only be performed by authorized equipment, because the geo-location of that equipment or the physical protections around that equipment are unknown.

A good use case for hardware-based authentication services is related to the processing and management of certain types of personal data. In some instances, regulation requires that if personal data is collected and placed into virtualized systems, the processing and storage of that data must be understood: it cannot be moved in an uncontrolled manner to unapproved processing and storage, which may be physically located in unapproved locations—like a different country! One useful control is to limit and link certain forms of information processing to specifically identifiable hardware platforms. If the application managing the restricted or controlled data set attempts to move on to unapproved hardware platforms (or unidentifiable hardware platforms), it shuts itself down.

For IoT risk managers, hardware-based, device-specific authentication coupled with physical geo-location may become a make or break service feature!

AUTHORIZATION REQUIREMENTS IN THE IoT

Authorization is a property of I&A management that focuses on the *access management* element, as opposed to *identity*. Authorization is about what the users, or devices or subjects (which can be either) can do after they has been positively identified. What are the privileges it has related to applications, networks, data sources, and other objects?

In the IT business data world, there commonly are requirements for two sorts of authorization: *subject authorization* and *role authorization.*

- *Subject-based authorization*: a specific identified (authenticated) user or device is given a unique set of privileges, which are probably applied or selected in a manual or semiautomated fashion by an administrator or requested by the user or device according to their preference, objectives, or context.
- *Role-based authorization*: a privilege or set of associated privileges that are applied to a position that may be occupied by more than one *identified (authenticated) subject* at any given time. A subject may have more than one role and may have a set of privileges that is a combination of subject-specific authorization and role-based authorizations.

In the IoT world, we need to add a requirement for a third form of authorization: *attribute-based authorization.* While attribute-base authorization is certainly known in the IT world, its prominence will likely change substantially in the IoT.

- *Attribute-based authorization*: a set of privileges granted not on the basis of previous instructions or configuration, but based on the usage context and characteristics of the subject. Attribute-based authorization may be combined with subject and role authorization, or may stand alone—meaning that given the necessary attributes, an authenticated device may access the services. More on this to follow.

The mixing and mingling or subject-specific permissions overlaid with possibly many roles makes I&A management in the business IT world tough! In the IoT this could be even tougher with the addition of attribute-based authorizations!

ATTRIBUTE-BASED ACCESS CONTROL (ABAC)

Attribute-based authorization in the IoT may at times be orthogonal to role-based systems, overriding them or being simply independent replacements. For instance, under emergency (abnormal) conditions such as a fire, perhaps the employee access control cards will open the emergency exits without consideration for role, because the attributes associated with the usage context demand the door open without triggering additional alarms.

Another example is the contemporary configuration of most cellular phones while roaming: even if a user's phone does not have permission to use a cell network, it will often be granted access to make emergency calls like 911 or 999 calls. In this case, the carrier recognizes the importance of environmental attributes (an emergency) that is completely opaque to the system itself— only visible to the *sensors* on the location—in this case the human operator!

Role-based access controls (RBAC) by themselves may not suffice in the IoT because they are not flexible enough. An RBAC-only system would increase risks in IoT systems and services that that possess the following characteristics:

- *Unpredictable environments*: IoT services within unpredictable environments, such as those environments dealing with many people at once. Where crowd dynamics and emotions can create responses to different conditions that are very hard to project.

- *Contrary functions*: IoT services with dramatically different, or even opposite, functional requirements under abnormal versus normal conditions—for instance, a fire door during an actual fire (abnormal condition) that must open, versus the same door under non-fire conditions that must sound alarms and not open easily.

RBAC cannot effectively account for these sorts of properties alone, and in the IoT, with the increasing prominence of the logical-kinetic/cyber-physical interface, attributes will play an important role in authorization exercises.

ABAC OVERVIEW[7]

Although attitude-based access control (ABAC) has no clear consensus model to date, the approach's central idea asserts that access can be determined based on various attributes presented by an end point or subject, or possibly detected from the environment in which the subject is present. These attributes can modify the rules and conditions under which access is granted or denied.

The major terms used to describe ABAC in Fig. 9.2 are as follows:

- *Attributes* are characteristics of the subject, and the environmental conditions and context that are both predefined by an authority or may be extracted in real time from the environment because they may be dynamic in nature (for instance, weather conditions).
- A *subject* is a human user or non-person entity, such as a device that issues access requests to perform operations on objects. Subjects may possess one or more attributes.
- An *object* is an IoT system resource for which access is managed in part or in full according to identity, role, and context. Examples of objects may include: other devices, applications and services, files, records, tables, processes, programs, networks, information stores, and domains containing or receiving information.

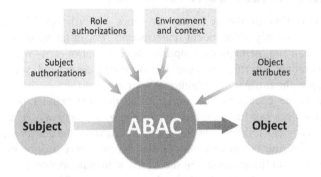

FIGURE 9.2

Attribute-based access control (ABAC) and the IoT.

[7]ABAC is a concept introduced to the author through oneM2M, and this section is derived from, but not identical to, standardization efforts within oneM2M. See onem2m.org.

Fig. 9.2 is a conceptual model of an ABAC where subjects (the entities requesting access to a service or asset) send requests to perform operations on objects or services in the IoT. They are granted or denied access based on assigned attributes and roles of the subject, and they are assigned general attributes of the object and a set of policies that are specified in terms of those attributes and conditions:

- *Environment and context conditions* are the situational framework in which access requests occur and the basis for ABAC. Environmental conditions are detectable environmental characteristics. Environmental characteristics are independent of subject or object, and may include the current time, the current day of the week, location of a user, or the current threat level.
- *Subject authorization* is the set of subject-specific attributes and authorizations. For instance, authorizations granted to a specific individual based on personal skills or qualifications, or to a specific device based on performance specifications.
- *Role-based authorization* is assigned to groups of subjects and may include standardized sets of privileges for groups of individuals or devices with the same requirements, duties, skills, or capabilities.
- *Object attributes* may reflect the environmental or contextual attributes associated with the access request from the perspective of the object. For instance, is the request coming from a subject that reflects a higher or lower priority request according to the service level agreement in place for the time of day, season, or other contextual variable.

One qualification associated with Fig. 9.2 and ABAC: it is not necessary that all forms of authorization be available to gain access to an object. There may be attributes associated with context and environment that will require access, regardless of subject or role authorizations. Again—the situation that comes to mind is abnormal or emergency conditions, where any device might be granted access to the object (certain services or functional permissions) because life or property is imperiled.

Chapter 10, Usage Context and Environmental Requirements in the IoT, builds substantially on this concept of ABAC, looking at the different variables that might reflect attributes, which in turn define the operational context of the IoT systems and the different risks and risk management techniques that are appropriate.

WRITING VERSUS READING IN THE IoT

Related to access controls for subjects and roles in the IoT is a change to a common form or data access and permissioning: that *read-only* reflects the most common privilege. *Read* in this instance, to provide clarity for anyone that has not had the pleasure of dealing with file and system permissions, means that a file or information source can be seen and the contents consumed, but the information or file cannot be changed or deleted or moved in any way. Read-only is the dominant form of data permission for which most people and most things will have experience; for instance, a web page is usually a read-only resource in the Internet of browsers.

Write is the file or data privilege to make changes to the information, to add to or change the file or data sources, and to delete from the data source. Write will often include the ability to change the name of the data sources or filename. Write permissions are typically only given to some sort of privileged user, an account holder or someone who has status on the system. (However, write permissions are often extended in controlled manners for purposes like commenting on web pages in anonymous manners or other sorts of social engagement.)

Granting write permission without read permission is usual before the IoT, outside the world of industrial controls. Why would you need to add to, change, or delete something you could not see in the first place? How would you know you are making the correct changes? This is a requirement that changes in the IoT.

Many devices will be pushing data to the IoT services and applications from the edge of the network. In many instances these devices will have limited processing and storage capability. They may be basic sensors or other devices that are not intended to understand the context of what they are doing, they just do it. In this case, all they need is *write-only* permission.

By convention, write permissions are accompanied by read permission. In the IoT, the requirement for read permissions should be strictly separated and assessed in relation to write permissions; otherwise a variety of risks associated with regulation, data privacy, and intellectual property could hobble a system. For instance, a device with write-only capabilities is substituted for, or masqueraded by, a device with the ability to also read—and this device uses conventional permissions to read data in the data store in an unauthorized manner.

CONCURRENCY PRIVILEGES BECOME UNCOMMON IN THE IoT WORLD

Concurrency means you are allowed to login to a service from more than one device or location at the same time. Google and Facebook and most corporate IT departments allow concurrency up to a limit by *default*—and in some cases the level of concurrency is undefined. Log in as many times as you need to from as many devices as you need to!

Concurrency makes a lot of sense in the business IT world. It is a questionable privilege in the IoT.

Increasingly, I&A control will be about semi- or fully autonomous endpoints, which have no reason to require concurrent connections at the *service layer*. The service layer is the logical layer at which sematic information is exchanged for the provision of specific services, like smart metering or smart health applications.

These devices of endpoints only exist *once*. They do not use different physical devices for the same purpose. They don't attempt to use a smartphone and then three different desktops to do personal banking! They are custom-built for a specific purpose and connect to a service one instance at a time, perhaps two or even three under different and exceptional use cases, but concurrency will not be the same as for personal devices on the Internet, which set the bar for operational requirements.

In the IoT, the risk manager will find that the requirements associated with concurrency will be, by default, *not* allowed, and that specific use cases will be required in order to provision IoT devices for concurrency.

UNIQUELY ADDRESSABLE

In some instances, the network address of the endpoint device or gateway will function as its de facto identity, at least for the purposes of some forms of provisioning or bootstrapping. Therefore, the ability to secure addressing and make sure that addresses are as unique as the service design assumed are important to IoT risk management.

Many IoT system will require that endpoint devices or the gateway they rely on, for unique identifiers (UID), where the uniqueness of the address is important for routing and traffic flows. Conflicts can result in service disruptions and outages.

UID might also themselves be directly associated with products, brands, manufacturers, and specific lots and batches of good. UIDs can easily and are regularly absolutely unique: they are applied to a single device or good only. The requirements and the ins and outs of UIDs are a huge topic, and excellent discussion can be found from sources such as ISO JTC1 SC32—Data Management and Interchange.[8]

Even for endpoint devices that are sitting behind gateways and not directly using the Internet for connectivity, uniqueness of address or identifier can still be critical for billing, auditing, and maintenance.

The ability to tamper with uniquely addressed devices can have a variety of attractions for those willing and interested in committing fraud or trying to damage systems: again, the ability to have uniquely addressable devices is linked to the ability to understand how secure these devices are from address tampering and what the potential for address conflicts and tampering actually happens to be.

The main requirement for uniqueness of addresses for risk managers is to understand what the actual risk is to addressing, and whether to treat, transfer, or accept these risks.

BOOTSTRAPPING IDENTITY

Devices and especially endpoints in the IoT may actually require two sets of identities: an identity that is *disposable* and used during startup—bootstrapping and installation—and another identity that is a more permanent identity used for service access.

Bootstrapping refers to a process where only the immediately local resources can be depended on, and a device has to make do with these resources for the purposes of initial operation. In the case of the IoT, a bootstrap identity is probably a very simple identity that acquires basic permissions on the local network in order to *call home* and start a more pronounced identification and authorization process, where it acquires an identity that can be used for a prolonged period of time and to access service applications and resources.

For instance, a device may have a bootstrap identity that is used the first time it is run. The device knows enough to find a gateway, get an address, and call back to the manufacturer home—that is all. It may not have more than a basic operating system that can do nothing more than support this bootstrap identity. Once the device is able to call home, it is associated with an owner

---

[8]http://jtc1sc32.org/.

(buyer) by the manufacturer and then logically redirected to that owner's network presence. Once the owner of the device receives a query from the bootstrapped device, it might proceed to provide it a full-scale operating system and identity, including both authentication and authorization credentials.

The use of bootstrapping identities can have a significant impact on design, development, and deployment costs. In some cases a bootstrapped identity for an endpoint device may be much cheaper to apply than trying to pre-provision devices from a manufacturer. But, at the same time, a bootstrapped identity means that devices that are coming and making requests are largely or at least partially unknown to the system; therefore the IoT system itself needs to be able to escalate authentication requests according to different factors and manage the risks of bootstrapped authentication according to standardized processes.[9]

Badly designed bootstrapping will open devices and IoT services to all manner of threats and risks associated with theft, loss of control, and loss of view. For devices that are deployed in remote locations, using basic plug-n-play installation skills and techniques, bootstrapping design is a major risk management requirement that even executives should ask questions about. A weak bootstrapping process would be akin to buying a car that starts without an ignition key and no door locks—and then being surprised when it gets stolen!

INTEROPERABILITY AND NEW FORMS OF IDENTITY LOOKUP

Will the IoT system need to interoperate with other IoT systems? Will it be taking information from or sharing information with other IoT systems? Will part of the IoT service rely on third-party service providers of automated services, like transaction processing?

If any of these design considerations are true, then part of the IoT system requirement will have to do with the ability to lookup device identities and associated metadata and attributes from a directory system of some sort.

On the legacy Internet, interoperability and third-party service provisioning is very common on the World Wide Web; whether for the provision of advertising services, site analytics, or transaction services. All these services are provided with the support of the directories in the form of DNS, which all have a service address (network location) to be looked up by the inquiring endpoint (usually a smartphone or desktop computer).

The IoT will certainly make use of the same DNS services, but will supplement with a variety of other lookup services. Some of these services might come from manufacturer consortiums—much like the bar codes are today looked up from manufacturer consortiums.

In the IoT, devices might lookup the ingredients in a food product or the viscosity in engine oil from third-party sources and make automated decisions based on the results. Decisions about allergic reactions or mechanical failure points may also be made this way. The fidelity of the information coming from manufacturer or supplier directories and metadata repositories related to IoT devices and services will be critical to the assurance of automated services and the risk associated with cyber-physical interfaces and outcomes.

[9]As of 2014, oneM2M has developed such a reference process.

But much like bar code systems of today, rogue or imposter directories can pose a series risks associated with misdirection and misinformation.

Risk managers in the IoT will need to understand the operational requirements that come with IoT systems for referring to outside directories and lookups, and managing those risks accordingly. They are substantial risks![10]

OWNERSHIP TRANSFER

IoT risk managers need to account for the possibility that an IoT system might one day be sold, split up, outsourced, or subject to some other management-level change that will require ownership transfer of fractional parts of the IoT system.

Example: a sporting goods company is acquired. It makes a range of footwear and garments and has developed *smart hats* that are worn by various athletes to monitor physical conditions during training and competition: body temperature, hydration, pulse, blood pressure, pH, and glucose levels in perspiration, and so forth. Hats are best for this because the head is a rich source of strong physical indicators. The shoes and garments also have *smart features*—but the sporting goods company is more about inventory management, not ongoing services. In the sale, the group is split and the hats go to one buyer, a healthy lifestyle company, and the garments go to a fashion label. Ownerships of all the *things* now need to be split and re-allocated.

Ownership traffic will require some form of re-provisioning of the endpoints (shoes, garments, and hats). Additionally, these endpoints probably leverage different third-party providers of external systems and services. For instance, perhaps a third-party software provider supplies the free, cloud-based reporting and archiving system for the hats. (Actually, they make money by selling advertising to the health conscious.)In this case, the device authentication and authorization systems that are used within the system may change to accommodate the new owner. Perhaps during ownership transfer, the systems are reset to do a full manufacturer reset, bootstrapping the hats, so that they are entirely re-provisioned.

Ownership transfer might also require that information that had been previously gathered as part of the IoT service also be extracted from data repositories and transferred to new repositories (cloud services?)—for instance, account holder information and activity logs. In the past it has been common for Internet-based services to be bought *lock, stock, and barrel* where all the assets are transferred to the acquiring party.

In the IoT, with increased service stratification, it may come to pass that services take on the same divisibility as old brick-and-mortar conglomerates, which have been so often split up and sold for more as parts than as a whole.

In the same way, a successful IoT service might be sold or acquired, and the component parts are split off. For instance, the endpoints go to one acquirer, the gateways to another, and the cloud-based applications to yet another specialized acquirer. In this case, the transfer of ownership will require that the service be cleanly partitioned and assets be transferred to different owners.

---

[10]See "Data Quality and the Internet of Things"; http://blogs.mcafee.com/business/data-quality-in-the-internet-of-things.

SUMMARY

I&A control used to be a practice apart in IT security, a field that was largely independent from the other security controls that might be found in the endpoints/desktops, servers, network, or DC. There is obviously a relationship, and even and interdependency, but the practices tended to be stove piped and isolated. This situation prevailed because it was relatively simple compared to what is looming related to I&A in the IoT.

In the IoT there will be a lot more I&A to perform, and it will be done multiple times due to service stratification and to fragmentation.

By reading many of the evolving IoT standards or even the general IoT technology media, it becomes apparent that *interoperability* is considered one on the major challenges to the vision of the IoT: and interoperability of I&A will be premier among all interoperability challenges.

Another major requirement and challenge for the IoT will be to evolve cryptosystems beyond the techniques that have served us so well since the dawn of the Internet. Multiparty and mass authentication and cryptography involving well understood but little-used mathematics such as polynomial interpolation and key splitting will need to emerge if IoT systems are to be both secure and efficient in nature. This emergence will probably not be a rapid process, if for no other reason than the old systems continue to work: but change will comes as costs and business risks force further innovations. Standards for anonymization of metadata in certain situations to prevent misuse will also be critical.

At a more functional level, this chapter reviewed requirements that will drive many forms of new or different risk in IoT versus IT systems. For instance, the ability to name billions or trillions of devices uniquely, apply attributes that also change occasionally, transfer ownership of these devices individually or en masse, and anonymous devices and devices that must also be identifiable for lawful purposes; all these requirements will be present in the IoT related to I&A. However, not all IoT systems will need to support all requirements.

As before, the selection or mooting of a given requirement is the job of system designers and risk managers. We are merely trying to create a superset of requirements for them to pick from, as appropriate to the system under consideration.

USAGE CONTEXT AND ENVIRONMENTAL REQUIREMENTS IN THE IoT

Usage context and the operating environment is the next form of requirement we propose as Tier 1 security requirements like Confidentiality, Integrity, and Availability. This is because of the vast number of IoT devices that will be entering, leaving, and sharing networks and infrastructure all at the same time, where managing the I&A in such a system is a critical security requirement. This is potentially radical because usage context is not even known in the earlier world of IT security, or at the very least is rarely discussed or represented in the various standards.

Why context was not a widely discussed security requirement before the IoT is purely speculative. But in the age of threat intelligence, ubiquitous encryption, and constant foraging for clues/indicators of compromise, context is everything!

It is possible that because the IT systems of old did not possess a logical-kinetic, cyber-physical, real-world interface and did not necessarily measure or control the physical world in any immediate or automated manner, they were simply unable to posses an awareness of context. As a result, the IT systems of old where designed with many assumptions about the IT devices, such as:

- they will be used indoors or at least under shelter
- by healthy people
- by calm, rational people
- people who have access to all their senses
- people who posses the necessary language skills
- people who can probably wait until the system reboots, if necessary
- and finally, not operated by *dumb* machines that are prone to make logical but hugely inappropriate decisions under some conditions

These assumptions don't play out in the IoT. IoT devices will range dramatically in what they do and the roles they perform. They will also be designed for a huge variety of rugged environments, by healthy, sick, and panicked people, who might be handicapped or injured or offended by noise or blinded by light or be in pitch black darkness; they might be using a device built far away by people speaking a different language, and the ability to manage or attend to the IoT system might be a second-to-second matter of personal preference, convenience, loss, injury, or even life and death.

RIoT Control. DOI: http://dx.doi.org/10.1016/B978-0-12-419971-2.00010-8

Context can matter in the IoT. It can matter much more frequently than it ever did in the legacy world of IT. Context can matter so much that its requirements will drive significant design, security, and risk management decisions.

INTRODUCTION

Chapter 9, Identity and Access Control Requirements in the IoT, discussed security requirements in the IoT related to I&A controls. There is a relationship between I&A controls and usage context, where I&A provides many of the fundamental security attributes needed to manage devices in the IoT, but *context* provides the finer layer of control to system developers, service providers, and risk managers in the IoT.

In the IoT, context is about situations and conditions under which an endpoint device or gateway is communicating, or is being used or accessed. Context might also influence how a network treats and manages traffic and/or how an application in a cloud service processes and managed the data coming from and going to an endpoint or gateway.

Context is important because there will frequently be more than one context, or use condition, that a system must support. While context may be a technical sounding term, it is ultimately an organizational policy that will define which contexts are acceptable for usage, which require additional security, which conditions might raise the costs of service-delivery, and which conditions might be forbidden—for instance, because they represent too much business risk associated with regulatory compliance. This will be a large role for risk managers in the IoT: defining the security requirements associated with context.

Context is independent of identity and authorization in the sense that possessing the right identity and credentials does not necessarily entitle anything (including a person) to the access available IoT service features and functions at all times. This is a major difference in the IoT from the enterprise IT, where users typically expect to have full access to all features and functions at all times, under all usage contexts.

Context also influences access control in ways totally distinct from enterprise IT and the old Internet. Possessing and then proving the right identity will certainly be important to many of the systems and applications in the IoT—but no longer will it be the only thing required for access. And this does not just apply to people, it also applies to the things on the Internet and especially the mobile things: if they prove their identity, is their context appropriate to the activity they are trying to perform under the given environmental conditions (context)?

Context and usage condition will be defined by at least three potential attributes: the access device, the location or network, and the state of the IoT application. Organizational requirements must either take context and condition into account, or clearly define what the single, acceptable context represents.

THREAT INTELLIGENCE

Cyberthreat intelligence broke out into popular, mainstream discussion in 2015, though it had been around for much longer. Threat intelligence is very much about the context and environment of usage for an IoT system, because threat intelligence can change substantially according to factors such as technologies in use, geographic location, language, region, and demographics.

Threat intelligence is generally about source Internet Protocol (IP) addresses, domain names, Uniform Resource Locators (URLs), files, or payloads that are known to be bad or suspected of being bad. This translates into a *reputation* score that can be looked up by security infrastructure, which in turn can enforce a policy of treatment; for instance, when traffic or files are received via an incoming smtp (email) network connection from an Internet address known for sending spam, the dubious traffic or files might be denied by messaging servers based on a poor reputation of the source—without any processing of the payload. This amounts to proactive blocking of threats before they reach their targets and in this example before expensive processing is spent on accepting the connection in the first place.

In the IoT, the use of threat intelligence will become an important requirement for system designers to consider because IoT systems will be too expensive, fragile, or constrained to be expected successfully to field all attacks. IoT systems, including both IoT endpoints and the big centralized data centers, will need upstream security elements to take action against threats, risk, and suspected intent based on intelligence.

From an operational perspective, an IoT service provider may be receiving data from a health-services device in a home with a single home gateway. If the reputation of that gateway were suddenly to degrade because it had been observed consuming virus-laden malware or engaging in attacks over the Internet, the provider might wish to respond to the intelligence. This response might take many forms, such as, e.g., alerting the health-service subscriber to the dangers of having health-care devices in the vicinity of an infected device (in the same home network). The IoT service provider might do this to preserve customer experience, or as part of a service-level stipulation intended to manage liability: service may be denied if malware is present in the home, or all liability and service levels are in abeyance until the home is cleansed of malware.

SOURCES OF THREAT INTELLIGENCE

Threat intelligence is available from a variety of sources. Security boutiques composed of a single-talented individual or a handful of security experts might create and sell intelligence *feeds* or lists of bad addresses on the Internet; places that you never want to see traffic to or from, entering your domain of control (home or business). Vendors will create and infuse their products with intelligence about the changing reputations of IP addresses, domain names, and malware files; updating the intelligence on a regular schedule—often minute to minute. Increasingly, network providers will use their management capabilities to track down infected or malicious devices based on network behavior. Choosing the source of threat intelligence will again be related to the usage context and environment of a given IoT system. For example: if you are building a smart city in China full of *things*, threat intelligence from an American firm might not include the necessary granularity when it came to malware written for Chinese language users, or IP addresses located in China. In such a case, context requires a degree of regionalization for better results and better risk management.

Along the same lines, industrial control systems often use rare or arcane protocols on top of an IP, or encapsulated inside the transmission control protocol (TCP). Not all vendors of threat intelligence will understand the operational environment, let alone the protocols, necessary to create threat intelligence (or signatures) for industrial systems.

CONSUMING THREAT INTELLIGENCE

Risk management in the IoT will also be about the ability to consume and use threat intelligence in a timely manner.

Threat intelligence has a high decay rate—probably measuring half-life in a matter of hours versus days. This is so because threat agents will shift their Internet bases of operation quickly to avoid detection. And malware has become polymorphic and nondeterministic: polymorphic meaning it will spawn and respawn itself in slightly different shapes and sizes to avoid detection, nondeterministic meaning that the initial shape of the malicious initial attack payload will be not be easily related to the final installed version.

For these reasons, IoT systems that can benefit from reputational threat intelligence will also need systems that deliver the intelligence almost as soon as it is released (discovered), but also injected into security infrastructure of application as soon as possible. *This means automation of the processes for deploying threat intelligence.*

WHERE TO APPLY THREAT INTELLIGENCE IN THE IoT

As we have stated throughout this book, there are four broad asset classes in the IoT: endpoints (devices) and gateways; networks; and data centers (DC) or clouds. Security in the IoT is about controls within all these points to support the IoT services and systems—not about security capabilities in a single place.

Threat intelligence in the IoT can be applied and consumed in all the asset classes in the IoT, but probably the simplest places to apply threat intelligence will be on the borders between *domains of control*—such as the dividing points between public domains like the Internet, and domains where the infrastructure is dedicated to a single owner's purposes. Under this model, the starting points to apply threat intelligence to IoT risk management will be the gateway and the data center. Fig. 10.1 is an end-to-end overview of an IoT system architecture at a high level, showing a variety of devices and services in a single picture: from endpoints to shared or dedicated gateways, to a common-carrier transport network, to dedicated or shared/cloud DC services. While DCs and clouds come in relatively uniform descriptions, gateways come in a variety of forms, many of which barely recognize themselves as gateways for the IoT, yet.

(Our assumption is that the IoT system under consideration is not some sort of highly segmented system, with traffic that never shared assets like routers, firewalls, or even DCs, with other systems or services. To one degree or another, most IoT systems will share some assets with other services and systems, and some of those will certainly be Internet-based in part or in full!)

HOW MIGHT YOU USE THREAT INTELLIGENCE?

Because threat intelligence is about reputations of payloads and places on the Internet, an IoT system might set a policy that maps reputation to usage policy and service levels.

For instance, an Internet-based IoT service for car warranty might connect to customers' automobiles for maintenance, updating, and preventative monitoring. If the customer's home

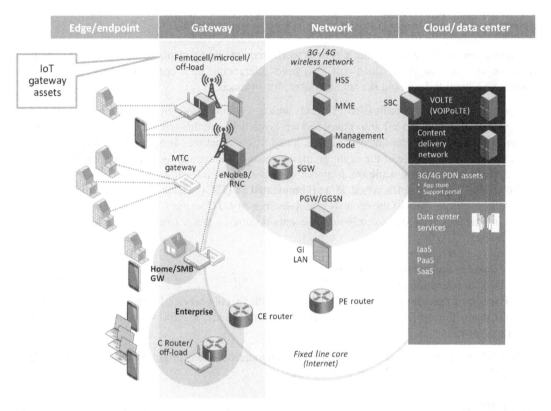

FIGURE 10.1

Places to consume threat intelligence in the IoT.

(via the gateway) suddenly acquires a low (bad) reputation according to threat intelligence, the IoT services provider (car dealership, perhaps) may suspend all service and notify the customer of its policy in this regard.

Why suspend an IoT service because of threat intelligence? Because a poor reputation on the IP address being used to consume the service indicates that something is not right with the IP address or the devices that sit behind it in the home, office, or other location. Whatever is causing that IP reputation to fail might also be attacking and probing all the other IoT (and other) assets in the home: making them unreliable and subject to failure or compromise.

No service provider wants to be held to account for service levels and quality assurance on devices and assets that are under attack by third parties. The providers might get blamed for something they have nothing to do with! So... they cut off the service due to poor reputation with threat intelligence.

Threat intelligence, if derived from a quality source and used in a timely manner, is fantastic context for service delivery in the IoT!

In Chapter 13, RIoT Control, we will discuss some techniques for utilizing threat intelligence.

ACCESS TO AND AWARENESS OF DATE AND TIME[1]

The interaction of the IoT with the physical world requires components to be aware of context, in the form of date and time. Time will also need referencing to a common source; otherwise, a number of critical tasks would become unviable, for instance:

- Synchronization and coordination of events among systems managed by independent parties—the stratification of the IoT into many service layers will see this frequently. Synchronization can also have *monumental* effects on health and safety functions. Imagine if the streetlights turned off in the middle of the night on highways? Or if a cooling system in a foundry went into maintenance mode while the furnaces were running at full capacity?
- Access to Coordinated Universal Time (abbreviated as UTC) will be a critical requirement for synchronization—as will the security and assurance of UTC sources itself.
- Record keeping related to exactly which events occurred when for reasons such as:
  - Billing
  - System debugging
  - Forensics and lawful investigation
  - Dispute resolution and litigation
- Service-level management—for an IoT system with varying service levels by time of day, the exact moment at which a service level changes can have major impacts on service quality and billing/costs.

The following are specific characteristics of date and time that might be requirements within a given IoT system, and introduce or address risks.

TIMELINESS

One of the critical characteristics of the IoT system is its capacity to operate in real time, responding to events as they happen. Because real time is dependent on the specific application, it is more appropriate to use the term *timeliness*.

Timeliness is the characteristic of providing a service within a specified time. Timeliness is necessary to deal with a range of functions at different levels within the system. The cyber-physical nature of IoT requires the components to act within the time specified to process a constant stream of data from the sensors and act on that data back in the physical world. The delay between the sensing and the actuating must be kept within the required time. If the underlying system is much faster than the application requires, time stamping may be sufficient for implementing real-time control.

TIME STAMPING

Accurately associating a time with a measurement or activity from the physical world is an important aspect of IoT components. It is needed accurately to combine or associate data from multiple sensors and data sources for a wide range of factors, including:

- billing
- health and safety
- service-level tracking and compliance

---

[1]Eric Simmons, contribution to SWG IoT 5 AH4—April 2014.

Both the time value and accuracy of the time value are needed properly to assess whether a specific component can perform the requisite task.

Time stamping is typically a trusted operation, is managed by a trusted source, and can even involve cryptographic signatures. Just calling something a timestamp may be misleading and have security and safety implications because of the assumptions of relying parties to the service.

If time stamping is a requirement for an IoT services, then the specifics should be defined with clarity. For instance:

- Are cryptographic stamps are required, or not?
- What is the accuracy of the time stamp?
- What is the format of the time stamp?
- What is the time source?

PRESENCE OF PEOPLE (LIVING BEINGS) AS CONTEXT[2]

The presence of people or potentially any living beings can be a critical element of IoT context because at a stroke it may engage health and safety issues, and well as regulatory issues beyond health and safety such as privacy issues.

Are people around? Are they part of the IoT function set? In other words, is there still a service if people are not part of the equation? For instance, a financial transaction service might not be possible without people there to authorize it or to deliver the goods or service in exchange for the transaction.

Does anything about the device indicate that people are around? If the device is in use, does that indicate that there must be a person around it? Are there any privacy impacts associated with that knowledge? For public areas, probably not; but in a home? It is directly implied by the application itself, as in the case of a medical monitoring application, or might it be inferred by the application, as in the case of an elevator control system?

The presence of people may have significant impacts on operational requirements related to state: on/off, fast/slow, warm/hot, and so on. The degree to which an IoT system spends more or less time in a particular operational state may have a major impact on the investment returns of the system. As an example, building systems turn off the lights when people are not on the floor or in the room, rather than leaving them on all night long just for cleaning and security staff.

The ability to understand whether people or living beings are present might also provide risk managers an opportunity to reduce costs or even free resources for other value-added tasks. Consider smart transportation systems: if a series of cars (taxis?) are traveling without people inside, they might elect to travel closer together, stop and start faster, and save energy in ways they might not otherwise employ because the ride would be too uncomfortable with people inside!

Also, consider the potential to free resources for other value-added services, if people are not around. Processing and memory in the endpoint, gateways, and network might all be curtailed without the need to satisfy the environmental requirements of people—and this excess and unused capacity might then be resold in a spot market or pool of resources. This is already happening in

---

[2]IETF IoT concept statement.

the DC and cloud computing world, where capacity is sold on a minute-to-minute basis. The advent of virtualization out into the network and endpoints will allow for similar sorts of resource brokering and arbitrage.[3]

DEVICE TYPE AS CONTEXT

The type of device(s) in an IoT system provides valuable requirements to the risk manager related to simple monitoring and control use cases.

Device type provides context because the nature of the device will frequently provide a good indication of the usage conditions associated with this device. Use cases related to context might include the type of network traffic that such a device should be allowed to generate and receive. Context about the device might also provide obvious use cases, like whether or not that device is mobile or not, and to which network locations it might be expected to send data.

The endpoint device will affect context and risk because different devices are subject to different vulnerabilities and threats. For instance, mobile devices are more prone to loss, theft, or observation (shoulder surfing) than a typical desktop access device. Small, inexpensive, or disposable devices might have very little available resource for "extras" like security and are therefore prone to attacks that might be otherwise easily repelled.

Sometimes the device type provides very helpful context as to what can reasonably be expected to appear on the network coming from that device. A shared kiosk or terminal will generally have a very limited allowable feature set and can be expected to remain rather immobile.

An endpoint device might also be known to use an operating system and have a performance profile that is able to support better, or worse, security controls and counter measures. There are many ways to determine a lot of information about the access device—and this information will impact on the context of the operation being requested from the IoT application.

It is entirely possible that the same identity may be functional across multiple devices types, but that the ability of that identity is also related to the device type. In other words, the application becomes context-aware.

Banks—always leaders in online security—have been using device types as context awareness for the security of online banking for many years. In these cases, if the software detects that you are attempting to login using a previously unused browser or operating system, you may find yourself going through an escalated challenge-response requirement. The same can be said about banks and the location or network from which a user tries to login. This brings us nicely to the second potential element for context and risk in the IoT.

CONTEXT VERSUS STATE OF IoT APPLICATION

The state of the IoT application can refer to the operations it is expected to be undertaking coupled with the potential sensitivity of those operations. For instance, is the thing in an operational state or

---

[3]See ETSI's NFV web site for use cases, reference architectures, and security problem statements: http://portal.etsi.org/tb.aspx?tbid=789&SubTB=789,795,796,801,800,798,799,797,802.

a dormant state and do the commands it is receiving make sense in the context of that state? Is it sending telemetry or in the process of receiving command and control information? What is the owner of the asset or thing trying to do with it?

The state of a thing on the Internet can have an impact on not only the risk of the security context but also on the basic operational costs and efficiency of the object. Consider something like streetlights. Are the control systems associated with streetlights as critical during the day as at night? Do you pay for one-minute response times for alerts from the streetlight systems on a round-the-clock basis? Or perhaps just between twilight and dawn? Clearly, such organization guidance around contextual requirements can have a certain impact on overall efficiency and is a core elements of risk management in the IoT.

Some typical states that an IoT risk manager might consider for an IoT system when assessing monitoring, detection, and response requirements are:

- On or off: while this might appear obvious, the ability to understand if an endpoint device—or any device really—is on or off can depend on the ability of many different systems and a network to function correctly.
- Dormant or listening: many devices and assets will move into power-saving modes when not in use. These states might make them appear to be *off* or even lost/destroyed unless the requirements associated with monitoring these states are clearly distinguished. These are problems that have been addressed in the network world long ago for wireless devices, but such a technical approach may not be appropriate at the IoT service level.
- A third possible stage is between *on* and dormant, which is paging or polling. This is a state where a device is either leaving a dormant state for a fully active state, or might be primed to do so. Paging and polling in the wireless world means that the device or gateway is trying to access a resource and is calling that resource and waiting for a response before doing anything further, like sending data. Paging and polling are relatively expensive from a resource perspective because the device is in a state of alertness and waiting for action. This is not a good place to get stuck for any device in the IoT because you are waiting for services and burning resources, but not necessarily getting anything done.

This notion of context and state of IoT systems is also reflected in privacy related work and potentially the sort of business and organizational requirements we discussed in Chapter 4, Business and Organizational Requirements. For instance, The Future of Privacy Forum's code on Mobile Location Analytics[4] calls for the use of in-store signage to advise consumers that IoT systems are active and information about them is currently being collected. The code also calls for the store to provide contact information in the event an individual wishes to opt out of the system. Exactly how this might happen is far less clear—but the thinking is an early indication that *state matters*.

LOCATION, LOCATION, LOCATION

Location tracking and geolocation is a significant operational requirement for many of the use cases in the IoT and can come into play for both endpoint devices and gateways especially because they might both be mobile or easily moved.

---

[4]Future of Privacy Forum, "Mobile Location Analytics Code of Conduct," October 22, 2013.

> Additionally, location tracking and geolocation, as system bound to information technology, have obvious linkages to requirements associated with safety, but follow under the categories of confidentiality and integrity. The ability to manage location tracking and geolocation securely will be very significant to the assurance of the IoT.

Location tracking typically refers to the ability of an IoT system to understand factors not only about location but also with the movement of a device—such as its heading, speed, distance traveled, and elevation. In location tracking, these characteristics might be provided from the device itself as telemetry, or possibly inferred from geolocation information. Location tracking is typically associated with some form of geolocation—but not necessarily. For instance, an IoT system might not care—or want to know—where a device is, merely how the device is moving and, therefore, functional and perhaps that its operational *context* is also normal.

Geolocation is about the actual coordinates of a device or object relative to establish waypoints or markers. Geolocation is *not* necessarily about the ubiquitous global positioning system (GPS), which has been incorporated into so many public and commercial applications. Geolocation can certainly be accomplished without the aid of GPS, as we will discuss. Geolocation may or may not be associated with location tracking, especially if the device or asset being located is a landmark that never moves!

Without a doubt, location and the ability to track devices will have a major impact on the context of the device or object: is it physically too high or low relative to something else in the IoT system? Is it in the right position? Is it where it is supposed to be at noon on Monday, or has its context changed from the usual pattern?

Because location and tracking requirements are so important, we have included a review of many of the different location and tracking technologies available that will need to be assessed for risk.

The reason we have gone deeply into this area is to impress upon the IoT risk manager that there are many ways to address the operational requirement for location finding and tracking, and many of these technologies will have strengths and weaknesses from a security and risk management perspective.

CONTEXT AS A COMBINATION OF LOCATION INPUTS

Many IoT systems and devices will be defined by their ability to understand where they are and report positions back to the system owners. Other devices and IoT systems will find that their context can be defined by information from location and tracking services, and the context will be a major determinant of features and functions available and the interpretation of events in the physical world and commands from the logical world (network). There are many ways to address the operational requirement for location finding and tracking, and many of these technologies will have strengths and weaknesses from a security and risk management perspective.

In the IoT, some objects will move independently (like wearable technology on a person or a vehicle). Other IoT objects will move as a group—that is, they will coordinate movement relative to their objective position in the world and their subjective position relative to other objects around them. Traffic and transportation management systems would clearly fall into this system.

Therefore, according the IoT system under consideration, different and multiple tracking methods may be required. Part of requirements analysis associated with location and tracking will be determining not only *if* but also how many location and tracking systems might be required.

The physical location of a thing, and the network it is relying on to access the IoT application or service, will have a tremendous impact on the security context and the associated risk. For instance, should the device or object be moving or stationary? Should it be located in Germany or Argentina?

Location and tracking requirements will also aid in telling whether the device or object (the thing) is situated in a location that is known to be secure, not secure, or ambiguous because little is known about the location? If the thing is attempting to communicate from a location that is known to be secure or from which is it know to communicate regularly without apparent secure lapse, then the risk might be lower(?). Similarly, if the thing is suddenly communicating from a location that is entirely new and unknown (ambiguous) or known to be associated with malicious devices and network attacks, then the risk might be higher.

Increasingly, organizations are applied *geo-tagging* elements into application communication systems and protocols in an attempt to get greater situation and possibly predictive information related to the thing. Geo-tagging might be accomplished in a variety of ways. Frequently, it is done based on things like IP addresses and the known geographic locations of Internet provider points of presence (POPs). Also, smart devices increasingly have GPS utilities built into them, and coordinates can be simply accessed to feedback to the application.

The higher the assessed risk associated with the location and gateway or network in use, the more compensating controls organization policy may require around tracking and location.

GEOLOCATION AND ELECTRONIC TRACKING POLICY REQUIREMENTS

Successful risk management requires policies. Policies will necessarily cover location and tracking of IoT devices and provide internal and external guidance about the fact that tracking is underway and how the information associated with tracking will be collected, used, and disclosed. It is likely that IoT systems will require distinct tracking and location policies, much like distinct privacy policies exist now.

Tracking and geolocation policies may be wrapped up and contained in existing policies like privacy policies, which are a standard feature of most online services. However, privacy policies exist primarily to manage regulatory and compliance matters (business-level risks) by providing operational insights to users about the collection use and disclosure of personally identifiable information. Users can then extrapolate privacy risks, based on this information.

The same may apply to tracking and geolocation policies, which may emerge in the IoT: they will be intended to provide operational guidance related to the use of tracking and location technologies in IoT systems, to address or inform risk management around IoT systems.

In the area of regulation of tracking and location, little appears to have been attempted at the time of writing, perhaps because the IoT is still so new, and the potential risks that might cascade from the compromise of tracking and location systems are still unclear. Risk managers should anticipate a degree of regulatory ambiguity, in which case internal policies make even more sense by showing due care and attentiveness to a poorly regulated domain.

Policies related to IoT tracking and geolocation will also provide some immunization against claims of reckless management of personal or other forms of information in environments where regulations are either nonexistent or conflicting.

By way of example, the following policy level requirements are summarized and expanded from work done by ISO in the area of location and tracking technologies[5] and should be considered for inclusion in both internal and client-facing IoT system policies.

When tracking and geolocation as *optional* for basic service delivery:

1. IoT device or object geolocation functionality must be "off" or disabled by default.
2. The IoT device or object must store geolocation data only for as long as is necessary to provide the capability to which the user opted in.
3. The app/service must provide some obvious, visible indication that geolocation data use is enabled.
4. The app/service must provide the user a simple, easy-to-use mechanism temporarily or permanently to disable the app/service use of geolocation data.
5. The IoT device or object must provide an explanation of the geolocation functionality and ask the user for explicit opt-in consent.
6. The IoT device or object must provide some visible indication of current geolocation functionality status, that is, geolocation functionality enabled (*on*) or disabled (*off*).
7. The IoT device or object must provide a mechanism to disable (turn off) geolocation functionality until the user decides to change the setting.
8. IoT device or object *ingredients* (for example, hardware, software, or firmware) must honor user configuration settings.
9. Where possible, the app/service should provide users with a choice regarding the granularity, or precision, of the location information used. For example, the user could be offered the choice to select between allowing the app/service to use country-level, postal-code−level, or precise GPS coordinates.
10. Where possible, the IoT service should provide users with a means to control when location information is used. For example, the app/service could be designed to only use location information when the user checks in, as opposed to being always on.
11. The IoT device or object should, where possible, provide the user a simple, easy-to-use mechanism to remove geolocation data stored on the device or within the IoT service.

    Regardless of whether tracking and geolocation is optional or mandatory for the IoT service:
12. The IoT device or object must appropriately secure any geolocation data stored on the device.
13. The IoT service should not collect or store personal identities with associated unique identifiers (UIDs), such that personal information is created with location data.
14. If collection and storage of UID and location data is absolutely necessary, the data must only be stored for the minimum amount of time necessary to fulfill defined business and legal requirements.
15. The app/service update process should prompt the user to review current app/service privacy settings.

---

[5]ISO 18305—Real time locating systems—Test and evaluation of localization and tracking systems.

16. In the event that the app/service wants to use geolocation data for a new, different purpose, the app/service must provide the user with an explanation of the proposed new purpose and ask the user for explicit opt-in consent prior to using the geolocation data for the new purpose.

17. App/service must provide information about what personal information will be accessed, collected, or used; what personal information will be stored (on the device or remotely); what personal information will be shared, who it will be shared with and why; how long personal information will be kept; and finally, any terms and conditions that may affect a user's privacy, prior to user download/installation.

18. Where possible, the app/service should provide users with a means to control whom their geolocation information is shared, such as, e.g., by allowing users to designate with which of their friends they want to share their location information.

19. Where possible, the app/service should provide a simple, easy-to-use mechanism to disable geolocation data use according to the users preference, such as disabling geolocation data use outside specified hours.

MAPPING IoT SERVICE REQUIREMENTS TO LOCATION AND TRACKING TECHNOLOGIES

The array of available tracking and location technologies is greater than most people think, and offer powerful contextual abilities to system designers, engineers, and managers.

Understanding the options available for location and tracking is critical to the work of product managers and engineers, but not necessarily front-and-center for IoT system designers and risk managers who might be selecting devices from a list of limited manufacturers, or perhaps just one manufacturer.

Location and tracking is such a critical function in many IoT systems, even if the system owners themselves do not understand fully the central nature of this function. For instance, while location and tracking might not be core to IoT service under consideration, it might have operational benefits that make the business case stronger. Consider the ability to understand the location of endpoint devices, making maintenance and replacement more efficient.

The following discussion is (again) extracted from excellent work done in the International Standards Organization (ISO) under ISO 18305, "Real-time locating systems—Test and evaluation of localization and tracking systems."

LOCATION FINDING

Finding location involves a wide range of techniques, and outcomes: from globally precise locations to locations that are meaningful only in the context of the question (how far am I from home?).

Different operational requirements related to context and location finding will be addressed by different techniques. From a risk management perspective, the operational choice location-finding techniques may affect a range of business level risks, as well as generate operational vulnerabilities associated with other operational requirements beyond location finding and tracking.

The following is a sampling of the different location-finding techniques that are already common and are sure to be mainstays in the IoT.

RECEIVED SIGNAL STRENGTH (RSS)

Most radio frequency (RF)-based location and tracking services rely on the availability of a number of RF transceivers, known as anchor nodes. An anchor node could be a cellular base station, a Wi-Fi access point or gateway, a Bluetooth device, an radio frequency identification (RFID) tag/reader, etc.

In most cases, an anchor node is stationary; and because its position is fixed and known, it is possible to work out the relative position of other devices around the anchor node. In certain applications, one may encounter mobile anchor nodes that are equipped with their own reference location device that accurately estimates the location of the anchor node on a continuous basis.[6]

In its simplest form, the location of an RF anchor node is taken as the estimate for the location of a receiving device; when either the device "hears" the RF signal transmitted by the anchor node or vice versa. To hear means to be able to receive data packets from the transmitting entity and know its identity. An RF receiver may be able to hear an RF transmitter from afar if the transmission medium between the two acts like a waveguide, which would be the case if the two entities are in LOS of each other in a corridor or tunnel.[7]

PROXIMITY (i.e., RFID)

A proximity system would be a form of coarse-grained location finding where the service requires only a general idea of where a device is located, relative to a known fixed location. RFID is an example of this capability.

Even though proximity-based localization could, in principle, employ any wireless communications standard, RFID is the most widely used choice in such systems. RFID systems including RFID tags may possess (or lack) a variety of security safeguards against certain forms of attack. An awareness of what type of security controls are assumed for an RFID system is important.[7]

TIME OF ARRIVAL (TOA)

If the time at which an anchor node transmits an RF signal and the TOA at the tracked IoT device/object are known, then the Time-of-Flight (TOF) is simply the difference between the two. The TOF can be used to estimate the distance between the device and the anchor node, if one assumes the propagation speed for the RF signal is the same as speed of light. This process is called RF ranging. The role of the anchor node and the tracked device (likely an endpoint of a gateway) can be reversed; that is, the device could be the transmitter and the anchor node the receiver.[7]

---

[6]The italic text is derived from ISO 18305.
[7]Adopted from ISO 18305, "Real time locating systems—Test and evaluation of localization and tracking systems."

TIME DIFFERENCE OF ARRIVAL (TDOA)

Consider a situation where a device/object/and two anchor nodes, for which locations are known, receive this signal and record the times of reception. If the clocks of the anchor nodes are synchronized, then the TDOA can be computed.

If it is further assumed that the RF signal has travelled at the constant speed of light—an assumption that we know is not true when the signal travels through objects—then one can compute the difference between the distances from the device to the anchor nodes.

If the plane in which the device and the anchor nodes reside is known—e.g., if it is known that all three are on a particular floor of a building—then the location of the device might be reasonably assumed to be the horizontal distance from the anchors, on that floor. If that plane is not known, i.e., when we are looking for an device that could be anywhere in the building, then the location of the devices involves a complete sphere of potential locations around the anchors.[7]

SIGNALS OF OPPORTUNITY

This category of location sensors offers an alternative to satellite-based systems like GPS, when such signals are weak or totally unavailable, for example deep inside buildings. Yet another motivation for this approach to localization is the fact that satellite systems are highly susceptible to jamming and spoofing. The signals that could be used opportunistically for localization purposes include digital audio/video broadcast signals, analog TV, AM radio, medium wave (MW) radio, and cellular base stations.

The techniques that could be used for localization based on signals of opportunity include those discussed above, and more! Naturally, it is essential to know the location from which these signals are transmitted in order to be able to do any localization.[7]

ACOUSTIC SENSOR

Acoustic sensors are used for determining the distance between an emitter and receiver pair using the time or angle of arrival of the emitted ultrasound pulse(s), or the time difference of arrival between concurrently emitted pulses. Acoustics could provide geolocation as the position of the receivers was known precisely, but integration between this form of range finding and geolocation is not implied or guaranteed in any way. Typical solutions on the market can achieve ranging precision of few centimeters.[7]

IMAGING

Various types of imaging that can be used in location finding can be classified in several ways:

- Three-dimensional (3D) imaging captures a 3D image of the environment at which it is looking. For example, a scanning lidar[8] or laser camera system can be used to build a 3D model of the environment and estimate ranges and locations based on software models that use the known

---

[8]Lidar is a remote sensing technology that measures distance by illuminating a target with a laser and analysing the reflected light.

location of the scanning device as a form of anchor for the relative or perhaps geolocation-specific estimates.

- Non-line-of-sight systems are imaging systems that can see through walls, clothes, shipping containers, ground, and other objects. One example is an infrared or thermal imaging camera that can track energy or heat signatures passing through walls. Another example is an ultra wideband (UWB) imaging system, which can be effective in detecting metallic objects that are behind walls or some other (nonmetallic) objects. System of ground-penetrating radar are frequently used in geology and mining, and may even have practical applications in the IoT.
- Line-of-sight imaging can employ normal photographic still/video cameras that capture luminance and chrominance on an image sensor to acquire distance and range, so long as the light levels in the area are understood.[8]

MOTION TRACKING

Motion tracking is frequently but not necessarily linked to location finding. Motion tracking might be deployed in an IoT system alone and used for a variety of purposes without location finding; for instance, athletic applications that measure distances moved and speed.

Identifying the specific requirement for motion tracking will often lead IoT system designs toward a particular technology. Each technology may possess idiosyncrasy vulnerabilities and risks that should be taken into account and either accepted, treated, or transferred as appropriate.

The following is a comprehensive (but inevitably incomplete) discussion of some motion-tracking technologies that will provide fundamental services in the IoT[9]:

- Accelerometer: An accelerometer is a device that measures acceleration relative to gravity. This is not necessarily the coordinate acceleration, but the acceleration associated with the phenomenon of weight experienced by any test mass at rest in the frame of reference of the accelerometer device.
- Magnetometer: Magnetometers are sensors that can measure magnetic fields. The most popular application of magnetometers in personal electronic devices is the electronic compass that can determine the orientation/heading of the device using the Earth's magnetic field as reference.
- Pedometer: A pedometer is a sensor used to count the number of steps to estimate the distance a person has walked. In the past, they were typically implemented as electromechanical solutions leveraging a swinging lead ball pendulum. Today, modern pedometers use inertial sensors that deduce the step count through software processing of acceleration data. Modern devices exhibit typical accuracy of $\pm 5\%$ in counting the steps.
- Inclinometer: An inclinometer is an instrument for measuring angles of slopes or tilt, elevation, or depression of an object with respect to gravity acting as a perpendicular reference. It is also known as a clinometer, tilt meter, slope gauge, gradiometer, level gauge, declinometer, and pitch and roll indicator. It measures both inclines (positive slopes as seen by an observer looking upward) and declines (negative slopes as seen by an observer looking downward). There are different types of inclinometers, including mechanical and electronic.

---

[9]Source: ISO 18305

- Altimeter: An altimeter is a sensor used for measuring the altitude of an object, and altimeters have been reduced in size and price to the point that they can be found in many low-cost devices. The most popular operating principle for modern altimeters is pressure sensing. In modern personal electronic devices, the pressure sensor is typically implemented by leveraging the piezoresistive effect on gauges that can detect the strain due to the applied pressure. This technology is suited for implementing sensors that measure absolute, gauge, vacuum, and differential pressures.

In the IoT, it is important to understand that triggers like motion sensing are critical inputs to location and tracking, and the associated risks. The interdependencies of these systems with location and tracking may influence the degree to which such systems are secured from logical as well as physical attacks.

AUTOMATED ACCESSIBILITY AND USAGE CONDITIONS

This IoT requirement could have easily been covered in Chapter 11, Interoperability, Flexibility, and Industrial Design Requirements in the IoT, but we elected to keep it under context because accessibility is something that needs to be at least semi-automated under many IoT use cases, not something that must be configured through lots of granular and finicky user configuration options.

The distinction is that accessibility should be automated as far as possible, because users should not be expected to understand all the features and functions of a given IoT system that can make the system easier for them to use.

The IoT system should be aware of and respond to accessibility issues as far as possible or proactively offer accessibility options based on contextual observations.

Accessibility is often, wrongly, associated with wheelchair ramps and big buttons on calculators and hard-wired phones at my grandmother's house—making products and services available to those with special or different access requirements due to age or disability.

In the IoT, accessibility takes on a whole new meaning, and it has risk and security consequences. Accessibility—as an operational requirement—must be part of the IoT design process, but not for reasons that we usually associate with the word; for instance, accessibility for the aged or those with disabilities.

Accommodating technologies for users will definitely be part of the IoT, such as for IoT devices associated with health and aging: *smart health*. Features such as larger control screens and buttons, auditory instructions in lieu of written instructions, and multilingual capabilities (both written and verbal), will all play a role in making IoT devices widely accessible, which in turn drives adaption rates up, efficiencies up, and aggregated costs down.

Another interesting form of accessibility will have to do with environmental accessibility: being able to read screens in the sun, or in the dark, in the rain, as noise levels change (as you move from your office to a train), or when you must move from visual/touch-screen controls to verbal controls because you start to drive a car, and so forth—IoT devices will be everywhere and we should not assume that the environment will be clean, dry, and well lit for typical consumer usage.

To maintain accessibility, IoT devices will need to have integrated sensors that detect the environment and communicate the conditions back to the application over the network. The various DC and cloud-based applications that manage the many devices in the IoT then make a decision about which form of command and control is best for the conditions and provide the necessary information (how much backlight to use, subtitles in the appropriate language or subtitles *for dummies* vs experts) back to the device back over the network; otherwise the device must maintain all that information locally—and keep it up to date. That type of capability—locally stored and managed accessibility features—would raise the cost of IoT devices and IoT service substantially, given the range of accessibility requirements emerging in the IoT.

Accessibility must also work across heterogeneous networks—you should not be limited according to the network that you have roamed onto—for instance, subtitles should not disappear from the video controls because you move to a new network.

Therefore, accessibility users/consumers, administrators, technicians, law enforcements, regulators, and the full range of potential stakeholders will be enabled by the networks that carry the critical instructions and information for different types of controls and human-machine interfaces (HMIs).

This is where security and risk enter. Poorly designed devices could have their critical control interfaces tampered with over the network (Internet) if poorly secured. Similarly, a poorly secured gateway or network could be slowed or disabled such that IoT devices could not update their user interfaces, resulting, for instance, in voice commands not being available when you need them, or a screen you could no longer read as you move from a dark room to the car. The risks could also be associated with critical infrastructure management; for instance, a novice technician when trying to reconfigure a device like a pump is sent a falsified command interface when he asks to transition out of the expert mode. Or, perhaps due to network availability and element of security, only the expert mode is available and a wrong command is issued out of inexperience.

A few specific sorts of operational requirements related to IoT that will affect risk management for the system as a whole are:

- Age-sensitive and disability sensitive: larger fonts and easy to see interfaces due to aging populations and the increased use of devices to service these populations: smart health. Recall that this is not just about usability: it is also about security. *User and administrative errors increase as the accessibility of the IoT system approaches the limits of the users of the system.*
- Environmental: IoT devices will be everywhere and we should not assume that the environment will cooperate. Other environmental accessibility issues will include:
  - Temperature
  - Lighting
  - Humidity and wetness
  - Dust, particulates, and environmental hygiene
  - Air quality and environmental hazards

  Being able to deliver environmental modification to many IoT devices will rely on the gateways and networks, and their security.
- Heterogeneous networking: Accessibility will not only be about human users, but endpoint devices and gateways themselves. Enabling IoT endpoints and gateways with more than a single

networking interface addresses many of the potential risks associated with resource exhaustion, jamming, and regulation that can affect the networking and communications ability. Multiple different technologies like combining a Wi-Fi interface with a fixed line Ethernet interface port and perhaps a Bluetooth interface will allow devices and service more than one option for a critical requirement: *to remain connected.*

• Service provider and route accessibility: accessibility must work across many network providers—to the extent possible. This means that standards-based network and large system of peering and interoperability are preferable over small *clubs*—even if discounted network access charges is a lure. At the same time, service routing should be transparent and ideally communicated in some automated manner such that devices can make decisions about whether the routing will support the context and related service levels of the context.

SUMMARY

This chapter has proposed that usage context and the operating environment have become as critical to security and risk management in the IoT as confidentiality, integrity, and availability are in the legacy IT world.

Many of the assumptions that underpinned security and privacy in the IT world do not hold in the IoT. Most IT systems were developed with vague service levels, and the intention that they will be used from the safety of a desk or at worst a smartphone from the couch; IT will work exactly the same by day or night, hot or cold, in Japan or Lesotho, and the worst that can happen is large-scale fraud and financial losses. IoT devices will be used everywhere, will be directly respond to both their physical and logical environments, and will sometimes have pronounced effects on physical safety.

Among the requirements we covered in the chapter, threat intelligence was one of the most complicated and important. Threat intelligence is still in its early days and tends to be a siloed product with a wide range of qualities. Ideally, threat intelligence will one day become a commodity that is generated through the collaboration of many hundreds or even thousands of security entities—outputting a well understood, standardized reputation score for any entity using the Internet and sharing information across domain of control and services. But there is a long way to go before we get there!

Other aspects of context and the operating environment will also come into play in the IoT and managing risks: systems and services will need to be more aware of date and time, whether people are near or far, and to a certain extent even a degree of awareness about what type of device and service they are to begin with.

Devices, especially endpoints and gateways, in the IoT will also have potentially more than one context that they support: for instance, normal context and abnormal context (emergency situations?). Being able to understand how context influences security and operational requirements will be important to risk management in the IoT.

Location will play a huge role in the development of the IoT and will be one of the strongest pieces of contextual data that a system or service might have at its disposal. Location will provide context in many ways—including the actual geographic location and whether the device or person is in motion or stationary, as well as whether that is a normal or abnormal condition. Additionally, there are many different location finding and tracking technologies available: the choice of technology will certainly have an impact on the security, privacy, and risk associated with a given IoT service. While the instinct will invariably be to adopt the location technology that is the most convenient, simplest to deploy, or cheapest to integrate, care should still be given to the longer term, post-deployment effect of these location technologies on risk.

Finally, we concluded with a review on accessibility—but accessibility defined differently from typical definitions that seek to accommodate personal handicaps. In the IoT—where devices are developed for multipurpose applications, for a worldwide market, with the intent that they can be re-provisioned, can have their ownership transferred, and can be repurposed in the field—accessibility is also about changing interfaces and device feedback according not only to the users' but the applications' location, time of day, and any other contextual variable that may come into play. Accessibility requirements and risks in the IoT are really about considering not only the intended users under the intended conditions, but about the unplanned users and unintended usage context under which the devices and IoT system will be asked to perform.

INTEROPERABILITY, FLEXIBILITY, AND INDUSTRIAL DESIGN REQUIREMENTS IN THE IoT

11

This is the last chapter on requirements in this book, and it continues to push the boundaries of awareness for risk and security practitioners in the Internet of Things (IoT). In fact, some of the topics in the chapter are decidedly forward-looking, but will also introduce unprecedented opportunity for interoperability, flexibility, scalability, and industrial design: information executives, security and risk managers, system designers, and engineers need to be ready!

The interconnectedness, cascading impacts, and unprecedented speed of action and reaction in the IoT will take attributes typically left to manufacturing processes and bring them to the attention of information technology (IT) and generalized enterprise risk managers. Interoperability, flexibility, and industrial design is the third and final class of requirement we are proposing as novel, emerged security characteristics of the IoT, along with safety and usage context. (The other requirement classes we discussed reflected a needed reordering and reorganization of previously understood security characteristics.) This is the last of the major categories of IoT requirements that we will explore in the context of security and privacy in the IoT.

This may be an uncomfortable innovation for some, but a necessary innovation for comprehensively managing risk in the IoT.

INTEROPERABILITY OF COMPONENTS

Interoperability is frequently cited as the number one concern among IoT system vendors and service providers.

Everyone is worried about IoT interoperability: devices and services in the IoT should be readily decoupled or loosely coupled, while also being able to become tightly integrated and coupled according to the system designs. The IoT should be both divisible and interchangeable without sacrificing efficiency or security.

The design of the IoT system should allow composition from independent, decoupled components for flexibility, robustness, and resilience to changing situations. Use of independent and interoperable components allows for ease of composition and the ability for reuse in new and different systems and contexts through their interfaces. Decoupling should also exist between vertical level of the IoT stack to allow each level to be modified and replaced without affecting the other layers.

RIoT Control. DOI: http://dx.doi.org/10.1016/B978-0-12-419971-2.00011-X

There has already been much ink spilled about interoperability in the IoT, and the risks associated with poor interoperability: high costs, inflexible deployments, rapid aging of resources, and poor utility.

One important thing to bear in mind when you hear that "Interoperability is the top concern among service providers and vendors": they are not the target users!

Ask the IoT users, the customers, the average consumer, driver, patient, or parent what their number one concern is? It is *not* interoperability. After value for money, it is *security and privacy*. They don't care about interoperability—they assume it.

Don't forget that as a risk manager in the IoT you can address that interoperability issue flawlessly and the customer will mostly be unimpressed and will generally not give it a thought. They *will* ask about security and privacy, however. So will regulators.

ABOUT INDUSTRIAL DESIGN

Industrial design generally refers the applied art and engineering associated with esthetics, user attraction, ergonomics, functionality, and/or usability of a product—typically a physical product versus a logical (software) product. Industrial design may also be a major factor in the product's marketability, operational abilities, and production.

The ability of the IoT system to adopt, or be adopted, to a wide range of different service providers and usage contexts will have an impact on the risks associated not only with the business success of the system, but the security and assurance of the system, too.

The following requirements affect the ease with which a given IoT component (endpoint, gateway, network or data center (DC)/cloud) can be built, maintained, extended, integrated, or broken up and sold as pieces. These are all desirable capabilities from a business perspective, though a variety of regulatory or other matters could have a strong influence on flexibility.

SELF-DEFINING COMPONENTS AND ARCHITECTURE

Elements in the IoT will often need to describe themselves in order to maximize interoperability and flexibility, and to achieve *plug-n-play* capabilities that can be efficiently and effectively secured.

The IoT system will regularly connect a set of heterogeneous components to perform differing functions based on stakeholder needs. The IoT will be all about mixing and matching different subservices to create entirely new services, like selecting items from a closet to create different and new outfits each day.

Many different devices, assets, and stratified service providers may be involved in supporting a given IoT system, much like many different designers and clothing manufacturers will be found in any given wardrobe.

To this end, the IoT system design should provide components for which characteristics and behavior are well defined and described; e.g., providing self-identification or provisioned in such a way that a central and accessible repository can provide significant details about the element, if provided with a unique identifier such as a serial number or media access control (MAC) address.

Such centralized systems for identifying IoT elements and their properties in turn need to be open and accessible, providing descriptions using standardized semantics and syntax. Components should use standardized component/service definitions, descriptions, and component catalogs.

From a risk management perspective, the flexibility of the IoT system will change according to whether or not the manufacturers of the elements (services and assets: endpoints, gateway, networks, DCs/clouds) support some easily applied process for understanding the properties of their devices.

Communicating the functionality of a given device does not necessarily have to require a *lookup* against a central repository, it could be that properties are communicated by the device itself after a poll of uni-cast (one-to-one) query is received. Of course, this means that the device has to support the network functionality to respond to such a poll or query—ideally in a manner that is nonproprietary.

What matters when it comes to security and risk management in the IoT is that the properties that are communicated in automated fashioned—to drive flexibility and utility of the devices—is done in a manner that can be trusted. More to the point: properties cannot be intercepted, forged, changed, deleted, or delayed in a manner that can result in risk to the IoT system itself.

DEVICE ADAPTATION[1]

IoT devices and objects should be able to adapt to the situation where they find themselves. Right now, when a cell phone user roams from one country to another, it is largely assumed that the phone will be compatible and a roaming agreement will exist. Similarly, when a person with a smartphone enters the user's home, it is typically configured to "offload" its data services from the cellular network to the home Wi-Fi network automatically. Again, when it reaches the office environment, it adapts to the corporate network settings, again offloading data services.

Adaptation in the IoT for many services and applications will be far more complex and important. Adaptation will not be limited to the endpoint devices and service objects, it will extend across the assets classes within the IoT: endpoints, gateways, networks and DCs/clouds.

In the emerging world of fifth-generation (5G) wireless, which is expected to enter some markets as early as 2018 and 2020, adaptation will play an even greater role because it is central to most interpretations of 5G: devices will not only roam to wherever the best connectivity is to be found, but will also combine different wireless technologies at the same time to get aggregated bandwidth. For instance, your carrier's fourth-generation (4G) connections plus your in-home Wi-Fi together give you wireless 500 Mbps combined. Under such conditions, the route of data through the network will be almost nondeterministic (unpredictable).

For risk and security managers in the IoT, the trick will be to understand what connectivity adaptations are available and how they might be used and balanced to improve risks (including business risks, like profitability) and security at the same time.

---

[1]Concept derived from Gyu Myoung Lee, "Internet of Things—Concept and Problem Statement," IETF July2012.

Because adaptation is probably available from a variety of points in any given IoT system, the question for system designs is where to apply which adaptations to greatest benefit.

> It is up to the risk manager to decide whether adaptations and their presumed benefits in fact reduce risks across the board, rather than address one sort of weakness or risk and greatly amplify another.

Let's look at a few example adaptation requirements and how they might be balanced for the purposes of risk and security management:

- *Endpoint devices*: Example: in-building security motion detection in areas that are high traffic during the working day, but very low traffic off hours.
  - *Adaptation*: Power-saving objectives mean to go dormant during working hours? To record and cache data versus real-time transmission? To stop recording altogether?
  - *Assessment*: The power and network savings might be a legitimate business reason to turn off real-time motion detection, but other reasons like personnel security and liability management might make caching data for later upload to a storage server a sensible approach.
- *Gateway device*: Example: providing Internet access to the subscribing endpoint devices in range, for a traffic monitoring application that reads licenses plates.
  - *Adaptation*: Which access network should the gateway use? There might be four network choices available to the gateway: local fixed-line Ethernet, locally provided Wi-Fi, third generation (3G) cellular, and 4G cellular.
  - *Assessment*: different technologies have different costs, service-level commitments, contractual commitments, business-level risks, performance parameters (operational risks) related to confidentiality, availability, and integrity. The risk manager needs to make choices taking into account all requirements and provide a recommendation.
- *Network device*: Example: a router operating on the edge of the service provider network, offering connectivity to several dozen gateways from different gateway-managed-service providers, inside an enterprise—as well as general enterprise Internet connectivity for the servers and desktops.
  - *Adaptation*: Which service level to provide to what data? Different IoT services might require different service levels for different properties, like availability (latency), integrity (loss), and confidentiality.
  - *Assessment*: Different service levels will have different costs from the network provider(s), and typically the least cost service meeting the service levels requirements should be used; yet different routes through the network may represent different risks to all properties for reasons such as distance and network control and provenance.

INCLUSIVITY OF THINGS

The definition of the things that makes up the IoT should be flexible and open-ended. Rather than restricting what a *thing* is, focus on accurately describing the characteristics and behavior of a thing.

In the standards world, formal definitions for *thing*" are typically inclusive, but not always. For instance, some definitions will try to restrict things to industrial sensors or machines that run on an automated or semiautomated basis.

Restrictive definitions of *things* induce risk into IoT systems, because they deny some basic truths and drives inaccurate assumptions about the IoT that system designer, engineers, and risk manager must bear in mind:

1. The IoT uses shared networks. Even if the network from the device to the gateway is dedicated and proprietary, it will be very rare for an IoT service to forego any form of shared network—like the carrier networks. This means that all manner of devices, from the oldest Internet-enabled Windows 3.1 (or even pre-windows disk operating systems!) desktop machine to the newest wearable technology will be using the shared assets at some point. The sharing may only occur deep in the telecom carrier core or it might occur at the first hop in the network like a home gateway—but it will always be there, and probably for most of the geographic distance the data is transported.

2. The IoT uses shared technologies. One of the risks of the IoT is that it is a "monoculture" in many ways: it is built on a common platform of Internet Engineering Task Force (IETF) protocols (Internet Protocol (IP) being the big one); and many of the IoT systems will use common computing platforms (hardware chips, memory, storage) even though the devices and gateways may appear completely distinct.

Inclusivity as a design requirement does not mean making space for all manner of devices and services inside the IoT system being developed. Inclusivity means understanding that the IoT is a great big place and interdependencies exist because of shared network and technologies, and risks much be managed accordingly.

No IoT system exists on its own, in true, complete and unique isolation.

Much like our planet, everyone and everything in the IoT has some degree of inclusivity whether acknowledged or not.

SCALABILITY

Scalability in an IoT system needs to support as large a range of applications, devices, workloads, and complexity as possible—balancing business requirements like cost efficiency with operational requirement for flexibility and the ability to reuse components for different services. For instance, the same components that are used in a very simple application should also be usable in a very large, complex distributed system. Ideally the components can be adjusted and scaled quickly (even during runtime).

Scaling may mean adding more and more endpoints to the IoT system. It may mean increasing the rate at which data is flowing to or from or being processed by endpoints, or scaling might be related to the number of semiautonomous IoT systems that are being managed from a single infrastructure. For instance, a multitenanted solution might allow many customers to share a single service or infrastructure, versus having to operate a dedicated service or instance of a service for every new customer: a far less scalable solution.

Poor scalability drives many risks in the IoT, including impacts to availability resulting from lack of capacity and an inability for the management system to cope with the populations under management. Because these features are more complex than issues of uptime and unauthorized deletion, we have placed them in the requirements class of interoperability, flexibility, and industrial design.

Additionally, an IoT system might be designed with scalability as a basic requirement, but get the details wrong due to an incomplete perspective and appropriate use cases upon which to base assessments.

As an example, a common mistake from Enterprise IT is to develop software or hardware for a given task in an isolated environment, assuming that no one will ever attempt to use the data, software, or hardware in a different environment or for new, operational, or value-added applications and services. But lo and behold, a few years later someone finds a clever way to use the data or the software in a totally unanticipated manner, but in a different, less isolated, and less secure environment. Because the software was never designed to operate in a *less hygienic* operating environment, the consequence is a functionally operational but insecure system.

The critical perspective about IoT scalability is anticipating what you have not yet imagined. Are there technical requirements that might make integration of the IoT system at hand with other systems easier? It may be that scalability might not be about your system, it might be about the scalability of a different system that wants to interface or leverage your system.

It will be very difficult to predict how an IoT device or asset (software, hardware, system, or service) will be bundled, repackaged, tweaked, leveraged, and repurposed once it is launched. Small changes to software may enable entirely new services and interfaces with systems that were not anticipated during system design, transforming a putatively small, niche-oriented IoT system into a massively large IoT system.

What do requirements for management in a massively scaled environment—one beyond any practical business case that anyone has thought about—look like? Maybe a little extra reporting capability? Maybe a little extra firmware memory? Perhaps it is a matter of allowing generic or undefined variables in application programming interfaces (APIs) or network headers?

For a security or risk manager, recommending devices, assets, tools, and platforms with extra undefined functions that can be populated at a later date might have significant value as well as scalability.

NEXT GENERATION WIRELESS NETWORK REQUIREMENTS

At the time of writing, *next generation network* was synonymous with several different meanings, but especially the rapid evolution (and hype) associated with 5G.

The term 5G refers to the newest effort from cellular mobile standards bodies. The fate of 5G and the IoT are closely linked, because the IoT is the basis for many of the use cases that drive 5G adoption. For people concerned about risk in the IoT, understanding the basics of 5G is essential to understanding the environment for IoT operations and requirements starting around 2018 or 2020.

At the time of writing (early 2016), 5G standards have not been ratified; they are a work in progress. As a result, the requirements presented here are not only generalized but also forecast—the final specification for 5G may either exceed or fall short of these requirements for a wide variety of reasons that are well past the scope of this book.

Many of the generalized design requirements for 5G are derived from IoT requirements. By *generalized* we mean that they have been aggregated across a range of envisioned IoT use cases, with the idea that 5G must suppose as many as possible.

The following are some of the generalized requirements for 5G, which in turn are considered IoT requirements for wireless, cellular networks:

- *Capacity*: This refers to the ability to manage both higher volumes of wireless traffic with 5G and also more devices within a given area: high density.
- *Speed:* 5G is envisioned to provide far greater speed than 4G systems, with targets starting at 1 Gbps and going up to 10 Gbps, depending on the vendor and variables such as cell size and device characteristics.
- *Latency*: One of the keys to the importance of 5G to IoT security is latency, with a targeted latency of less than 1 ms for information traveling between the mobile endpoint using 5G for access and whatever else is at the end of the communications, such as, for instance, another endpoint in the local cell zone that is collaborating in some form of traffic or transportation coordination.
- *Efficiency*: As we see evolving now with 4G[2], 5G will have special features for IoT devices that will make their communications and associated power consumptions substantially better than with typical cellular technologies today. In addition, greater bandwidth and lower latency will mean that a given amount of data might be moved much faster and therefore require less power for radios, which can go dormant faster.
- *Reliability*: 5G will look to achieve a perception of *zero downtime*, through a combination of multiple overlapping wireless technologies and alternate means of access to the Internet. If one cell goes down or is at capacity, an adjacent cell will compensate. If one particular radio spectrum technology is at capacity or experiencing degraded services (for instance a licensed cellular technology), then a different radio spectrum can be seamlessly accessed as an alternative access (such as local Wi-Fi hotspots).
- *Agility*: 5G system should be able to adjust to not only the conditions and locale, but to the types of traffic and especially the types of devices on the network. Certain device types may get different service levels for their data, different routes through the network, and access to different services, such as security.

We will come back to a much more detailed discussion and description of 5G in Chapter 12, Threats and Impacts to the IoT, and Chapter 13, RIoT Control.

STANDARDIZED INTERFACES

In order for the IoT system to integrate different components, the interfaces to these components should be based on well-defined, interpretable, and unambiguous standards.

---

[2]See Narrowband LTE reference: http://www.fiercewireless.com/story/new-lte-standard-internet-things-gets-push-3gpp/ 2015-09-22.

The IoT in a way is eponymous with regard to interoperability because it is named for the IP—the ultimate standardized communication system.

Further, standardization of interfaces will allow for easy provisioning of various components by any systems envisioned today and into the future.

Lack of standardized components and interfaces has advantages that some manufacturers and service providers may elect to pursue, like proprietary systems of old. Going in the opposite direction of standardization might create some perceived competitive advantages early on and up front, but not in the long term, given the IoT flourishes based on openness.

Many of the technologies supporting the IoT are open, not closed. They have been developed by *special interest groups* (SIG)—quasi standards groups formed by voluntary industry consortia:[3] coalitions of the willing. SIGs have been a large part of the Internet to date and will be an even larger part of the IoT.

One major example of a standardized interface is that which is required for hardware or machine-based authentication—an element of identity and access control. We have previously discussed the different forms of access control in Chapter 9, Identity and Access Control Requirements in the IoT, and how they represent risk-management requirements in the IoT; however, we did not discuss the standardization elements of human-less/machine-based authentication.

In the human world there are a variety of operational and technical techniques that are considered *standardized*, but really they are conventional. They are well understood, agreed upon, and widely used; but also they are generally accepted as legitimate. Techniques such as password and password rotation, two-factor authentication techniques like biometrics, and random number tokens are well understood and relatively simple. Not only that, but the processes are common across product vendors, and authentication technologies will be reusable. SAML, OAuth, and Kerberos are a few examples that utilize a range of configurable, well-regarded cryptographic algorithms.

In the IoT, authentication will frequently need to be undertaken solely by the device, without any human providing any previously shared secret or biometric (such as a fingerprint). This means that the hardware will need some way of preserving or generating a unique identity and passing that identity in a secure manner to an IoT service provider(s) in a manner that cannot be stolen or duplicated or otherwise broken.

There are currently no accepted conventions for interfaces or processes for machine-type/hardware-based authentication, and this is a major gap in the requirements and risk in the IoT. (However, there has been standards work done on unique device identity, which we will review as potential RIoT controls in the final chapter of risk, chapter: RIoT Control.)

LIMIT OR MINIMIZE BLACK-BOX COMPONENTS

There is often a tension between the desire to keep proprietary and competitive advantages secret and the benefits of being flexible and interoperable with other products.

---

[3]Just a few examples from the networking world include Bluetooth, Zigbee, and Weightless—all critical endpoint-to-gateway communications protocols.

In the IoT, the risk of *black-box* components, whose inner workings are opaque or unclear, rises for some issues well understood from enterprise IT systems:

- *Complexity.* Complexity is a hallmark of IoT systems because many devices and objects from different vendors and service provider mix to create infinite possibilities for new and better goods and services. Complexity means that faults in a black-box system can have many more cascading effects. Managing complexity risks requires better insight into the working for the discrete parts of the system, not lots of little secrets.
- *Troubleshooting and debugging.* Debugging faults in complex systems becomes harder and harder the more objects within the system are black boxes. The IoT accrues tremendous advantages for being flexible and applying standardized interfaces and communications protocols; openness needs to apply to the software and firmware that runs devices and objects, as far as is possible. The more black-box devices and objects in an IoT system, the more unproductive finger-pointing will occur when something goes wrong.
- *Vendor lock-in.* Efficiency is smothered with vendorlock caused by proprietary, black-box devices, and objects. This is anathema to the IoT and something to be avoided. Black boxes have the effect of reducing flexibility and increasing costs in a system whose key benefit is driving new efficiencies: better ways of doing things.

> The overall requirement is for less complexity, and therefore more transparency in IoT platforms and solutions.

Accordingly, the movement to *open source* components will increase and the software business models will increasingly shift toward supporting open-source products, not proprietary code. Two excellent examples of this movement in the enterprise IT world can be seen in the success of the Red Hat[4] Linux-based operating system, and the Helion Linux-based system from HP.[5]

For IoT system and product companies contemplating a black-box strategy to preserve competitive advantage, consider the risks imposed on partners and customers, and the impact of adoption. What good is a secret sauce if no one buys it?

For those developing or assessing the security of IoT systems and products, understand the black-box risks and as far as possible try to quantify them. As we have discussed in detail elsewhere, intuition is a terrible risk management tool.[6] Do not trust intuition with regard to complex risks in complex systems. At the very least, understand what you don't know about the black-box products.

LEGACY DEVICE SUPPORT[7]

Legacy devices and systems are those that were designed and deployed in the past. For instance, it is typical that industrial control systems will have planned lifetimes that exceed those of business

[4]http://redhat.com.
[5]http://hp.com.
[6]Macaulay, Tyson. *Understanding Critical Infrastructure Threats, Vulnerabilities, and Risks*, Elsevier 2008.
[7]Ric Simmons. *Contribution to SWG IoT 5 AH4*, April 2014.

IT systems by five times or more! A 20- or even 30-year planned lifetime means that products deployed in the 1990s might easily see service well into the 2020s—when the IoT has become far more prevalent and important than it is at the time of writing (2010s).

These legacies have aspects (including devices, systems, protocols, syntax, and semantics) that exist due to past design decisions, and these aspects may be inconsistent with the current architectural requirements.

Engineers and risk managers need to assess carefully to what extent the IoT systems and architecture should support legacy component integration and migration. In the course of this assessment, be careful about the potential for new services and products to be envisioned after deployment through integrating outside systems of legacy technology. You never know where the IoT will go!

New IoT components and systems should be designed so that legacy aspects of an interconnected system do not unnecessarily limit future system evolution. A plan for adaptation and migration of legacy systems must be established to ensure legacy investments are not prematurely stranded.

The requirement is that legacy components should be integrated in a way that ensures that security and other essential performance and functional requirements are met. This will start with an inventory of the security capabilities of all devices in the IoT service under management. Some of these devices may be older and inherited, bought or repurposed for use in the *new* IoT system.

> To the extent that these legacy devices have limited or no security capabilities, elements like the IoT gateways, network, and DC/cloud services will need to be considered as compensating controls.

UNDERSTANDING WHEN GOOD IS GOOD ENOUGH

Cheap memory and powerful processing are driving software developers to add complexity to IoT systems that might not be required. As we continue to state: complexity equals risks—operational risks of software/firmware bugs, but also financial risks associated with product costs in development and testing, and liability costs in the event that an overly complex systems with bugs get through quality assurance (QA) because the bugs are obscured in the complexity.

In the IoT, many systems dealing with the physical world do not require specifications and parameters to the fourth or even the first decimal point because the environmental variables and other inputs themselves might not be measured or managed to that degree of specificity.

In some cases, a margin or error $\pm 20\%$ might be good enough to make a decision in an IoT system. Creating and maintaining software and firmware that is not constantly gathering, averaging, and correcting readings well beyond the required operational parameters is an important requirement to continue to be aware of.

A good discussion related to this topic came about after Toyota was found negligent in its design of acceleration control software for the Camry model in 2014.

> I have worked with several programmers who have written support code for the analog circuits which I've designed. In most of these cases, I have had to tell them, 'slow down, why are you adding all this code which isn't needed?' The reply is always something like, 'memory is free so

we choose to add a lot of complex stuff just 'cause we can.' For example, if a parameter is only required to have 20 percent accuracy, why are we introducing interpolation between each sample point, then calculating the result to 16-bit accuracy? I wanted 10 lines of code. I got a thousand. Another example: For closed loop control of a motor drive, the software I had to work with was monitoring so much stuff that I couldn't get the calculations done before the next sample time. Many of these were parameters within an inner loop, which could have been completely ignored since the outer loop corrected for these. Remember open loop gain G/(1 + GH)? G can vary by a large amount and the final response will still be $\sim 1/H$. You don't need 0.0001 percent accuracy to calculate G. The programmer didn't know this because he had never taken a feedback theory course, or he forgot it. I'm thinking of the reply to my question of why it takes tens of thousands of lines of code to read the position of a gas pedal. Rathbun explained to us all the items he has to put into his code. He's probably a pretty smart guy and does what the systems engineers want but, is this all necessary? Are the systems engineers 'over-designing' it?

Darrell Hambley, Consultant—Power Electronics Specialist[8]

Therefore a requirement for good risk management and security in the IoT will be diligence related to over-engineering and introducing complexity. It will not be easy to understand where the point of diminishing returns is for quality of confidentiality, integrity, availability, service-levels, accuracy, and measurement in the IoT; but the first step is to understand that there is a point of diminishing returns that is also the point of escalating risks.

NETWORK FLOW REVERSAL AND DATA VOLUMES

Recall that the IoT will have four different assets classes, each of which will have distinct demands and will see different changes in these demands as the IoT truly comes online and grows: the end-point, gateway, network, and DC/cloud.

Focusing on the network in this instance, the requirement will be for differences in traffic-pattern profiles that must be supported. Fig. 11.1 is an example some research from Alcatel-Lucent related to patters from different IoT use cases: medical, energy, and transportation.

The significance of the chart in Fig. 11.1 lies not necessarily in the differing requirements placed on the network (such as the reversal of network flow—where more traffic is headed *downstream* into the Internet than being consumed *upstream* from the Internet) by the IoT services, but also in the effect of the network requirement for flexibility on other requirements like safety, integrity, and availability/resilience.

It is not just the devices and the application that need to adjust to flexibility requirements in the IoT, it is also the networks supporting the IoT, namely the large carrier networks that join all the smaller peripheral or *capillary* networks (enterprise networks, home networks, DCs, and clouds) together.

And as the networks adjust to the changes introduced by IoT, so will the security requirements of the networks.

---

[8]http://www.edn.com/design/automotive/4423428/Toyota-s-killer-firmware--Bad-design-and-its-consequences.

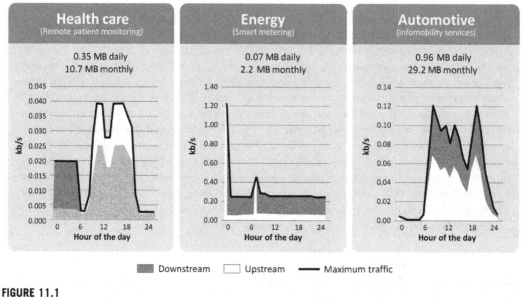

FIGURE 11.1

Network profiles of different IoT services.

Alcatel Lucent Bell labs.

IP ADDRESS TRANSLATION: IPv4 AND IPv6

In several of the earlier chapter we discussed Internet protocol version 6 (IPv6), and how it will be increasingly present in the IoT. To recap: we have exhausted the Internet protocol version 4 (IPv4) address space that contained roughly 4.3 billions addresses. IPv6 is the next generation of IP address and has an address space that is logarithmically larger. It is difficult to imagine exhausting IPv6 address space—as long as we are limited to the planet earth, or even our solar systems, as our networking domain. But who knows?

It is very common for carriers to support both IPv4 and IPv6 in parallel and in serial; for instance, IPv4 and IPv6 running end to end beside each other on the same layer 2 transport. Or IPv4 being translated to IPv6 (NAT46), IPv6 translated to IPv4 (NAT64) or even tunnels where IPv4 might be backhauled through an all-IPv6 core and then dumped back out onto a different carrier IPv4 network closer to the destination (NAT464). There are many more variants that this, but you get the picture. Additionally, due to the scarcity of IPv4 address space, it is very common to use *private* IPv4 address ranges (RFC1918) inside a carrier or enterprise network and translate them to publicly routable IPv4 addresses at the border in a process called NAT44.

As an example of an IoT-support system that is making widespread use of IPv6 to IPv4 translations, look no further that broadband wireless 4G system. Many of these systems assign IPv6 number to mobile devices and then translate, or map, those IPv6 addresses to IPv4 address at the border gateway between the dedicated 4G network and the Internet. Even for carriers that persists with IPv4 for mobile devices, they almost always send the data through a NAT44 gateway because they have nowhere near what IoT system designers should expect: that at a very minimum NAT44 could be applied without prior knowledge to any IoT end point device or even gateway. Similarly, IPv6 is be the defacto addressing scheme for newer networks like the emerging 5G wireless broadband services.

The following two broad requirements will have a large effect on the assurance and especially the availability of IoT services.

- IoT applications and devices should support *dual stack* IP where possible. They should be prepared to operate on either IPv4 or IPv6 networks.
- IoT applications and devices should undergo testing to be certain of the effect of NATing—how do the different forms of address translation and tunneling impact the system? Address translation is known to have consequences for some applications like video, voice service, and other real time services.

WHAT ARE THE NEW NETWORK REQUIREMENTS? WHAT IS CHANGING?

Besides the fact that there will be more interdependent requirements and overall sensitivity associated with network services in the IoT, the directionality of data flows is changed; it is reversing. We discussed this in Chapter 2, The Anatomy of the Internet of Things, but it is worth reviewing to expose better the requirements for which risk managers and engineers need to possess awareness as they design IoT systems and services.

Let's run through a brief evolution of data in the Internet to understand better what is happening (see Fig. 11.2).

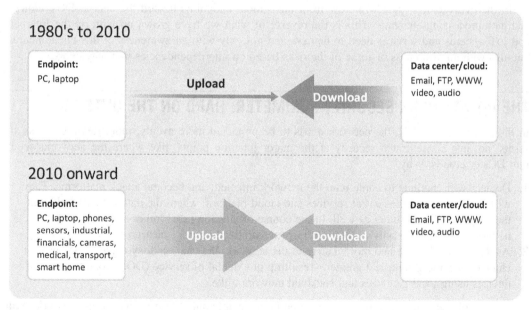

FIGURE 11.2

Data flows in the IoT.

From 1980s to ~2010: the Internet starts as an academic network with two major forms of information sharing: email and file transfer protocol (FTP). Users at the remote ends of the network access central DCs and eventually virtualized DCs (clouds) to get data. In the 1990s, the World Wide Web (WWW) comes along but still users access content from centralized sources, which grow massively: email, files, video files, streaming media, all of it coming from the central points in the network, moving out to endpoints.

Network technology is specifically developed to accommodate this balance of power. In most network access systems (3G, 4G, DSL, DOCSIS), downloading (consuming) data is typically twice as fast as uploading (providing) data.

From 2010 onward: the endpoints start generating more data, not just consuming data. Additionally, we now see endpoints that really don't consume much data at all because they are largely creators of data. These are the things of the Internet: point-of-sale machines, sensors, and monitoring and surveillance devices. At the very least, the new endpoints on the network are equally consumers and producers of data. Going away are the days when the average endpoint device consumed 20 MB of data for every 1 MB generated.

In the coming age of the IoT, the directionality of data flows will reverse, which will have an impact on security requirements.

> It is not that IoT devices will be generating vast amounts of data individually, it will be that a vast number of IoT devices will be generating more data than they consume.

In the evolved IoT, data will flow from the remote endpoints toward the central DCs, clouds, and data processing elements. This is the reverse of what we have grown up with on the Internet, and IoT systems and services need to be designed not only with an awareness of this phenomenon, but also with an awareness of some of the risks based on interdependencies that may evolve.

THE IoT NETWORK SECURITY PERIMETER: HARD ON THE OUTSIDE

In the context of the IoT, the network needs to be protected more evenly, more flexibly across all assets, not just concentrated security at the major junction points, like where the networks feeds into DCs or clouds. Why?

1. Devices will continue to come onto the network infected, and become attack platforms. They will not only attack the central services and cloud platform where the data is being held, but they will attack each other as well. In the course of attacking each other at the edge of the network, they might easily circumvent large, centralized security measures.
2. As devices push more and more data onto the network, the chances they congest the "upload" channel become greater and greater—resulting in a denial of service (DOS) condition for all devices using local gateways and backhaul network alike.

As a result, security capabilities need to be both flexible and interoperable in the network, with the ability to apply security monitoring, detection, prevention, coordination, and mitigation at multiple locations—not just at the big aggregation points.

For IoT engineers and risk managers, the requirement is to seek network services and service providers that are able to offer security capabilities in various locations. For instance:

Endpoints should be assessed to see whether *turning on* security functions is viable and worthwhile in the context of risk management. For instance, can communication be encrypted (possibly with Secure Socket Layer (SSL)) rather than left in plain text?[9] Such features are already becoming available generic IoT service platforms and will soon be ubiquitous.

Security capabilities at the IoT gateway, whether that is a custom, single-purpose gateway or a multipurpose platform like a home broadband modem or enterprise border router. These platforms need to be security enabled.

Security will typically be available at major network junction points, such as the borders between the wireless cellular network and the fixed broadband network that make up the Internet backbone.

Finally, in the DC and cloud, security will also be a matter of not only control on the ingress traffic from the Internet (also known as *north-south* traffic), but also the intra−DC traffic among the service components (also known as *east-west* traffic).

With security options and controls at the four major asset classes of the IoT, a lot of options are potentially available *if* there is flexibility in the network to gain some form of visibility or configuration controls at each of these points.

Historically, neither visibility nor configuration control has been available any of these points. Typically, networks have not been flexible.

By past convention, networks (and gateways) have been built on dedicated, specialized hardware platforms that did only a few things, but did them well. In the IoT, the network will require the ability to respond to security requirements on demand, deploying new services rapidly, at multiple points. This is a process known as "service-chaining" that will be discussed in Chapter 13, RIoT Control, along with game-changing network technologies that are moving into networks and gateways now, in 2016: network function virtualization (NFV) and software defined networking (SDN), discussed in "Control the "Net Within the 'Net'": Network Segmentation" section.

IoT designers and risk managers need to start addressing this situation as an operational requirement for RIoT control.

CONTROL THE "NET WITHIN THE 'NET'": NETWORK SEGMENTATION

One of the hallmarks of enterprise IT management is to make different logical networks for different logical assets, which share the same physical network. For instance, a branch office IT might have its own logical network in the form of a dedicated range of network addresses or *virtual LANs* (VLAN); voice over Internet Protocol (VOIP) services may share the same Ethernet but also have a distinct set of addresses ranges or VLANs; meanwhile, other assets like in-building public address

---

[9]In 2015, a variety of automobile security breaches were published that took advantage of network-based vulnerabilities. Specifically, the network connections between key fobs and the cars were unencrypted for no reason other than manufacturer convenience, apparently. Patches that were released simply applied network session encryption in the form of SSL.

(PA) systems, building controls, and physical access control systems may also share the common Ethernet platform but be logically separated.

The benefit of this approach (frequently referred to as *network segmentation* or just *segmentation*) is that different quality-of-service levels might be applied to different networks and the IoT assets they support. (Recall that the IoT is everything on the IP network, not just industrial controls.) And logical segmentation can partially mitigate attacks in one network from spilling over to another network—even though they share the same physical network platform.

The downside of segmentation associated with each IoT service is that, as more and more IoT systems come online, system complexity increases.

While network and security managers might be tempted to continue the approach of logical segmentation, it will not come without costs in the form of resources to manage increased complexity and the attendant risks of increased complexity.

The requirement logically to segregate IoT systems from one another as a matter of best practice and convention may not survive the emergence of the IoT.

IoT system designers and risk managers should consider the operational requirement for logical segmentation not only from the perspective of known benefits of this approach, but also from the perspective of the lesser known risks around complexity.

How many IoT networks within the aggregated, shared network are you willing to support and troubleshoot, especially considering the complexity increase and the resulting difficulty in assessing and analyzing faults and degradations in services?

Too many networks and network segments in the IoT will encourage network feudalism in the form of rigid management systems to maintain control and visibility. These systems in turn are known to breed inefficiencies, inflexibility, and parochial approaches to using a shared resource such as the network.

The basic requirement for networks in the IoT is to recognize that, really, most IoT networks will rely on shared infrastructure from the gateway all the way to and including the DC or cloud infrastructure. The *tragedy of the commons* must be avoided.

USER PREFERENCES

User preferences and interface design requirements address the fact that people don't know what data the IoT is collecting about them if they are not told or cannot see it somehow.

Previously we mentioned that personal information is literally personally *identifiable* information. Personal information—for the purposes of regulatory compliance—is not all information related to any activity that any individual participates in on the IoT.

In order to reduce risks associated with perceived and actual regulatory breaches, establishing clear, adaptable, and flexible requirements for user management and configuration of interfaces can do a lot.

Applications sometimes offer trade-offs between data collection on the one hand and features and functions on the other. For instance, most mobile map applications can be installed without allowing GPS location information to be collected and sent back to the central servers; however, the cost is a substantial reduction in functionality (you might see maps but not your position on the maps).

The ability to toggle a feature on and off goes a long way to managing the requirement for *consent* under many regulatory regimes.

Similarly, administrators who offer the ability to enable or disable privacy-impacting features in the IoT can provide much more flexibility for a wider scope of privacy enhancements and a wider final market for the application under discussion.

The requirement in this case is not to make every IoT feature user-definable, but to make the right set of IoT preferences configurable. The point is that user preferences can impact adoption and compliance at the same time.

VIRTUALIZATION: BOTH NETWORK AND APPLICATION

Flexibility, security, and risk management in the IoT will be heavily affected by the advent of *network function virtualization (NFV)*, above all other technologies. The requirements associated with NFV will impact both the gateways and the core, backhaul networks and the DCs/clouds in the IoT reference model we established in Chapter 2, The Anatomy of the Internet of Things. In other words, most of the asset classes in the IoT will involve the presence or absence of NFV, substantially affecting how risks will be managed at those points.

Bold statement: Every risk manager needs to understand NFV as a prerequisite to working in the IoT. Every IoT system designer and engineer needs to understand NFV as a prerequisite to working in the IoT. Maybe not in 2016 or 2017, but by 2020 NFV will be a technology of choice for all but the largest security workloads, from gateways to DCs and clouds.

NETWORK FUNCTION VIRTUALIZATION AND THE WHITE BOX

NFV is about the ability of multipurpose hardware computing platforms (also known as *white* boxes) to perform tasks associated with most network elements (routers, switches, firewalls, wide area network (WAN) acceleration, domain name service (DNS), and so on) comparably to customized, single-purpose hardware platforms. In the case of networking, this means that single-purpose network elements (which are essentially dedicated computing platforms) are supplanted by generic, white box platforms running *soft* network elements rather than hardware-based, dedicated network elements, meaning that the server platforms and the *cloud revolution* that transformed datacenters in the last 10 years is now set to transform the network, in a process sometimes referred to as *distributed NFV*.

WHY NFV?

The cost of multipurpose white box computing is dropping faster than the cost of dedicated network-computing technologies—this drives white box computing not only into the network, but also out to the very edges of the network.

Virtualization in the network means that network elements can be installed, provisioned, expanded, or collapsed using a single hardware platform running different types of software.

Contrast this with the legacy model of every function having its own physical box, and adding or subtracting boxes according to demand; basically—adding boxes.

NFV is about the cloud expanding from the DC into the network and extending all the way out to the remote endpoints eventually (see Fig. 11.3).

Fig. 11.4 illustrates the device-level concept of NFV. Take a multipurpose computing processor and install hypervisor software that allows for the management of virtualized machines (the bedrock of cloud infrastructure). Then install software-based versions of the desired

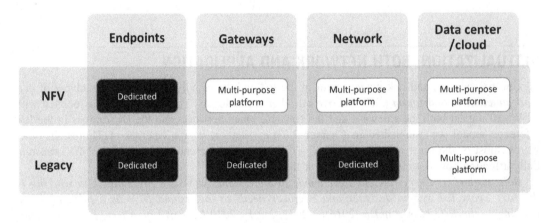

FIGURE 11.3

Multipurpose white box platform.

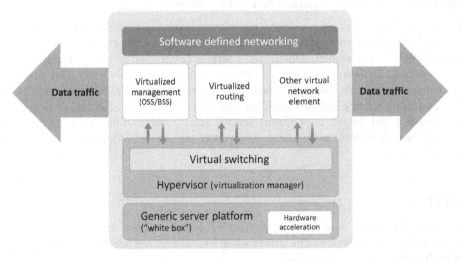

FIGURE 11.4

Network function virtualization (NFV).

network element: router, switch, firewall, intrusion prevention, proxy, virtual private network (VPN) aggregation, or the like.

In addition, NFV allows for the installation of what would typically be standalone servers or devices, and a platform shared with other network elements: for instance, a DNS server, a log collection or event management service, a directory, and just about anything else.

NFV will be a critical control element and an important asset for managing risk in the IoT. While it will not be available everywhere, or appropriate in all use cases and environments, its availability and application for any given IoT service should be assessed and at the very least indicated in roadmaps, if not the initial designs.

SOFTWARE-DEFINED NETWORKING AND NETWORK FUNCTION VIRTUALIZATION

SDN is a term frequently used alongside NFV, or sometimes even as a mistaken synonym for NFV. Sometimes it is the other way around: the term NFV is used in a way to include or encompass SDN. It is worth understanding the difference.

NFV is about replacing dedicated hardware appliances with virtualized versions and using processes known as *orchestration* to start and stop the virtual images on demand. But this does not necessarily change the fundamental network routing and switching.

SDN is about a whole new means of managing network elements, and how traffic flows through the network, regardless of NFV. SDN is divisible from NFV.

SDN makes it possible to propagate changes widely (we hope) in a vendor-independent manner, in a *layer* distinct from the traffic being routed and switched. This means that traffic can be directed according to requirements like service levels or cost, without having the controlling messages between the network elements jumbled up in this traffic redirection.

SDN is very relevant to NFV because as new virtualized network functions (VNF) are started and stopped, SDN can be used to direct traffic to and through these elements, ideally, in an automated manner, in a process called *service chaining*.

For instance, if the loads on a firewall become too great, NFV might be used to start a second firewall and a load balancer. SDN would then be used to redirect network traffic from the original firewall to the load balancer, which then spreads it across the two firewalls and improves service level as a result.

Therefore SDN and NFV work in tandem, but the resulting complexity can be numbing, and the attack surface and risk is dramatically larger with all this multipurpose software managing the network.

HOW DO NFV AND SDN CONTRIBUTE TO THE ASSURANCE OF THE IoT?

What requirements should be sought from the network, assuming or expecting NFV and SDN? Many. There are many enhancements and advantages to risk management in the IoT that can be accomplished with the advent of flexibility associated NFV and SDN. Here are a few:

- *Loadsharing, not shedding.* Sharing of processing and network power among the same sort of devices and network elements when adjacent assets have very different loads. If intelligence or advanced processing is required at the edge of the network, for instance, and the system is nearing exhaustion, traffic might be redirected to the nearest network element with spare capacity.

- *Better data segregation.* If network elements are smarter and can perform more advanced compute functions, then data from different IoT systems might be segmented through multiple different layers, rather than managed according to basic instructions at one layer in the network. For instance, rather than using layer 2 VLANs or layer 3 subnets, input/output (I/O) traffic might arrive at a gateway or router, and then be processed into upper layer, encrypted tunnels by a value-added service running on the network elements.
- *Time to market.* With NFV, an IoT security gateway can be deployed as software rather than hardware, dramatically changing the time and cost of getting products to market. The business models for the IoT will depend on rapid deployment with virtualized systems to get the return on investment (ROI) from the business processes.
- *Automated network resource allocation by smart infrastructure.* IoT service requirements call for specific levels of quality of service (QoS), but cost models do not allow for the over-provisioning that would be necessary under legacy network models. Smart(er) gateways and network elements can expand or contract QoS on logical network pipes or segments according to the established requirements on demand.
- *Collaborative information processing.* In some IoT applications, the endpoints may collaborate with intelligence, virtualized gateways, or network elements to solve complex sensing problems that require processing beyond the abilities and cost-imposed constraints of the endpoint device alone. For instance, correlation, classification, triangulation, and tracking of objects in the physical world. The data from an endpoint may be processed and refined at the gateway with a (secure!) NFV-based application that is deployed just-in-time, possibly correlating with the data from a related on-net endpoint.[10]

THE OTHER SIDE OF THE NFV-AND-SDN COIN

Flexibility = complexity = risk.

While flexibility of the gateway and network through NFV and SDN may be a requirement for many IoT systems, the management of such a system is not trivial. Unlike the dedicated gateways and networks from the legacy networks, NFV allows much more latitude for errors, omissions, and malicious activity. Any NFV-based IoT service will require that controls such as audit and assurance certification are more prevalent than might be the case in legacy, appliance-based networks.

TRANSPORTABILITY OF SUBSCRIPTIONS AND SERVICE: SUPPORTING COMPETITIVE SERVICE PROVISION

Transportability usually refers to the ability to migrate from one service provider to another service provider—versus from one product vendor to another, which is a matter of interoperability. While interoperability is an important operational and technical requirement, it tends to be a point-in-time

---

[10]ISO/IEC 29182-1.

decision. You choose a vendor and go forward with that product, allowing for occasional patches and upgrades that may or may not be applied.

Transportability of service is different from interoperability of products because the IoT system is a constantly changing the array of services that may even vary from day to day due to the myriad of externalities that vary: weather, staffing, holidays, environmental conditions, the cost of power, the cost of coffee in the cafeteria, traffic that day, and so on. As much as service providers strive incredibly hard to make services such as device management, networks, clouds, and DCs stable and predictable, they are prone to small fluctuations all the time and wholesale outages are worryingly common.

Transportability of services is very much an important operational requirement, but remains largely elusive in the IoT at its current stage of development (2016). For instance, cloud services for infrastructure-as-a service (IaaS), platform-as-a-service (PaaS), and software-as-a-service (SaaS) have continued to develop and generate new and amazing features, functions, and capabilities, yet transportability among service providers is a problem.

> While cloud technologies might appear commoditized on the outside, on the inside, the biggest service providers and their systems tend to employ highly customized operation and orchestration systems that do not allow for easy migration from one vendor to another. And that is merely a taste of things to come in the IoT, because transportability is frequently seen by service providers as against their interests.

Transportability in the IoT should be sought across the asset domains we discussed in Chapter 2, The Anatomy of the Internet of Things: endpoint, gateways, networks, and DCs/clouds. All these domains will eventually be virtualized (as previously discussed), meaning that physically or logically adjacent, competing asset and service providers are candidates for transportability or transference of service: the VNF moves to a new gateway provider to service the same cluster of endpoints in a manner transparent to the endpoints. This might occur for any number of reasons, such as better prices or better services.

The ability to avoid vendor and service provider *lock-in* and move from one supplier to another is in the interest of the IoT system owner, but not in the interests of the many vendors who may be involved in the ecosystem as a whole.

Transportability will reduce both business risks and operational risks by allowing for more diversity of services and basically *options* in the event that new risks emerges associated with a particular provider. For instance, is a given service provider headed toward being procured by a competitor or financial collapse with unknown impact? Has the incidence of service level breach slowly elevated to the point where penalties are meaningless? You just need the uptime! These are examples of events where the requirement for transportability will become a hot topic around the boardroom table.

Here are examples of risk management requirements associated with transportability of IoT services. These requirements may be useful under such conditions such as negotiations with various types of service providers: infrastructure, platforms, software, networks, and so forth:

- Device administration; monitoring of device status, management of the logs, patching, provisioning, and decommissioning

- Resource brokerage and reselling excess capacity
- Identity and access credentials
- Access networks and backhaul networks
- Legal and regulatory reporting services
- Security testing, evaluation, and monitoring
- Hardware platforms/infrastructure (IaaS/PaaS)
- Software platforms (SaaS)
- Big data repositories and analytics providers
- Threat intelligence suppliers

DIVERSITY AND UTILITY OF APPLICATION INTERFACES

Let us hope to avoid the early mistakes of the IT industry in the area of client-server architectures and design: large investments in proprietary communications languages and interfaces, eventually leading to *winners* and *losers* where entire technology platforms have to be abandoned at some point in time, with a *cutover*. Recall network technologies like Banyan and Novel that disappeared (painfully) in the face of IP networks.

Client-server IT systems predated the IoT, but the models will persist in the IoT: remote endpoints speaking to centralized resources. One of the earliest mistakes that had to be overcome was the creation of specialized and proprietary languages and interfaces between the clients and the servers. Each vendor would build its own endpoints and its own servers, and the networking protocols used to communicate were unique to that vendor, and possibly to that product!

Original client-server IT systems had no interoperability—often within vendor product families or even across versions. Soon the weakness of this approach became evident: higher costs, less utility and scalability, vendor lock-in, and inability to expand or upgrade systems.

Soon, software vendors like Microsoft, IBM, Novel, and Banyan introduced LAN systems that allowed any vendor to create client-server applications for a common set of networking protocols, which made life a lot better. Eventually, IP came to be ubiquitous and ride transparently on top of any and all local networking technologies—joining all systems together and creating the global Internet we have today, starting in the late 1980s and early 1990s. But many of the actual application interfaces remained idiosyncratic: unique to the applications.

Then software vendors like IBM, Microsoft, Sun, and Oracle started creating standardized application and database interfaces in the form of *languages* like Distributed Component Object Model (DCOM), Structured Query Language (SQL), Open Database Connectivity (ODBC), and others that allowed for standardized APIs to be used if the developers had the right software development kits and the necessary coding skills. But these toolkits had set limits on the range of the commands they could support and also came with bugs and security issues. They did not scale and they were not secure.

Most recently many client-server systems on the Internet are moving rapidly away from the API-based interface to the most standardized, flexible and easy to implement without the requirement for any special APIs or toolkits. These are called RESTful interfaces.

REST stands for *Representation State Transfer* and is essentially a regular worldwide web communication protocol, using standardized extensible markup language (XML) to encode data, requests, commands, and responses. The beauty of RESTful-like interfaces between devices is that they can be created using a minimum of communications and processing resources, and they leverage existing, well-understood, and available technologies like Hypertext Transport Protocol (HTTP), Hypertext Transport Protocol Secure (HTTPS), and SSL.

In the IoT, RESTful-like interfaces that are maximally flexible are a major requirement in order to support services and new requirements that have not been envisioned but can be supported with an extensible interface.

Dropping down just a little further in detail: flexible interfaces will allow different service providers to provider different services based on the same devices and platforms. Basically, they are able ask different questions to get the answers needed by their constituencies.

Ultimately, well understood and standardized application interfaces are easier to secure than proprietary APIs.

SUMMARY

If you speak to product vendors in the IoT, they might tell you that this chapter on interoperability requirements should have come first—or that it should have been a book in itself.

That is because vendors tend to think about getting the product to market fast, cheaply, and with the largest addressable market. Under these conditions, interoperability is the largest concern. Poor interoperability will slow growth, fragment markets, and limit services and options.

If you are a consumer of an IoT services, you are more interested in quality: you want something good for your money. You don't care much about interoperability other than to expect it! For this reason security and privacy risk management will be a higher profile requirement that interoperability for end users.

But, as this chapter discussed, interoperability, flexibility, and industrial design will themselves have a significant bearing on the security and privacy capabilities of an IoT system.

The emergence of the next generation network, specifically 5G, the fifth generation of cellular networks, will rely heavily on interoperability, flexibility, and industrial design. The primary requirements for 5G, a critical technology for the IoT, will center around capacity, speed, latency, efficiency, reliability, and agility.

This is key for IoT service providers, engineers, executives, and risk managers: interoperability decisions will have an effect on security, privacy, and risk!

Yes, interoperability is a big deal from a business or organizational risk perspective, but it will also affect operational risk management as we have highlighted in the course of this chapter.

THREATS AND IMPACTS TO THE IoT

In this chapter, the reader should gain an understanding of the range of threats that may face the Internet of Things (IoT)—they are probably broader than is supposed. The reader should acquire a decent understanding of how threats are assessed and differentiated.

THREATS TO THE IoT

A *threat* can be a person, group, or thing that undertakes an *action* against a vulnerability, which in turn drives a potential impact and therefore risk.

The *action* element is important for the purposes of this book, because vulnerabilities and threats are distinguished for our purposes based on whether an action has occurred. For instance, for a threat to be a threat, it has to be actioned by a person, group, or thing, whereas a vulnerability exists as a flaw in a system that does not require anyone to do anything—it is just there.

UNDERSTANDING THREAT IN THE IoT

Plenty of work has been previously published about understanding threat for the purposes of risk assessment, and we believe that repeating that fine work will add limited value for the reader interested specifically in what is different about managing risk in the IoT (risk and the Internet of Things (RIoT) control).

The following sections will seek to discuss what might be different about threat in the IoT from conventional enterprise or consumer information technology (IT), and distinguish what threats may be changing as the IoT evolves and spreads.

Typically, a threat will be considered to have more or less potential based on several characteristics, such as:

- Threat skills
- Threat motivation
- Threat resources
- Access

Let's discuss each of these areas one at a time in the context of the IoT and what might be different.

RIoT Control. DOI: http://dx.doi.org/10.1016/B978-0-12-419971-2.00012-1

THREAT SKILLS IN THE IoT

How much skill will be needed to attack the IoT, and will these skills be different from the IT-centric Internet and corporate networks?

Our position is that in all likelihood, *less* still will be needed to attack the IoT. This means that the population of potential threat agents increases, because the barrier to entry falls lower.

Less skill will be needed because the balance of security properties is shifting with the IoT, from a primacy of confidentiality to a primacy of availability. Successfully attacking IoT systems and services will not require captured credentials, escalated privileges, or stolen identities; it merely requires that traffic is disrupted or stopped. This can be a much easier thing to do. Therefore, the degree of skill required successfully to undertake such an attack may be significantly lower than an attack that must expose information or subvert access control systems. This is not to say that sophisticated attacks will not exist in the IoT against the confidentiality to integrity of data; it is just that the overall barrier to entry will frequently be lower through availability.

For instance, the probability is that much of the network connectivity between endpoint devices and gateway devices will be wireless in nature. Wireless communications is unfortunately not difficult to disrupt through simple, brute-force techniques such as jamming: filling the radio spectrum with *noise* that prevents signals from IoT devices being perceptible at gateways, and vice versa. Additionally, wireless signals can be jammed from great distances with simple and inexpensive equipment, meaning that threat agents can attack with minimal risk using methods that are very difficult to track and trace. The actual risk to the threat agent of being caught might also be very low, so people who might normally refrain from attacking for fear of being caught will take advantage of reduced risk and become active threat agents.

THREAT MOTIVATION

What drives a threat agent? There are many motivations and often they are aligned with the nature of the threat agents themselves. Criminals are usually after money. Terrorists seek political objectives. Hackers might be seeking the status and admiration of peers? Spies want information, and the list could go on.

The strength of motivation is also a factor. How badly do the threat agents want to achieve their objective? This will affect how much time and resources they will direct toward the attack.

Does motivation to attack change in the IoT? Again, the answer is probably yes. Motivation changes for at least two reasons:

1. *Force Multiplier*—The cyber-physical/logical-kinetic interface is vastly expanded by the IoT. This means that the potential either to cause damage, or hold an entity to ransom under threat of massive property damage or physical injury, is greater. The opportunity to do more with less from a resource perspective means that the IoT can offer a threat agent a force multiplier effect: threat agents will proportionately receive a much greater payoff for the resource they expend over a similar effort in the Internet of the 2000s. They might potentially cause more sensational damage or extort more money with the IoT.
2. *Lucky Strikes and Chaotic Outcomes*—Another motivating factor for threat agents in the IoT is the complexity of the IoT. This complexity will mean that attacks can have highly

unpredictable outcomes. Attacks that might be benign in the IT world may have profound impacts in the IoT and surprise everyone including the owners of the IoT systems themselves. In this way, threat agents may be induced to just *try stuff* to see what happens, knowing that in chaotic, complex, and sometimes fragile systems, very small inputs can have dramatic outputs. This is an ideal condition from the perspective of anyone interested more in disruption of services and political or status-based objectives, versus trying to steal money—essentially, render a series or extended series of low-risk, random pot-shots against IoT infrastructure and watch to see what happens.

In a nutshell, the IoT possesses characteristics that favor the threat agents, compared to an IT environment. The IoT gives a moderately motivated threat agent additional motivation because that is where there are more wildcards that might pay off!

THREAT RESOURCES

The "resources" available to a threat agent can be assessed in the form of time, money, and knowledge:

- *Time* is about both patience as well as how long you can afford to keep working at something. This of course plays into the *money* factor and has a relationship to motivation. The more time available to the threat agent, the more severe the threat. Another form of time is the exploit window afforded to a threat agent. How long can they attempt to exploit the system before they are detected or before some form of automated control (like cryptographic key rotation) sets the clock back to zero?
- *Money* is about what a threat agent can afford to buy to facilitate the attack. Can he buy good tools (like exploits or experts to discover exploits)? Can he hire more people to probe for weaknesses? Does he have funds to bribe insiders to create weaknesses deliberately, or even identify through investigation those insiders with personal situations that enable blackmail or forms of social engineering?
- *Knowledge* in the case of a threat agents is strongly related to the intellectual skills as well as the information at the disposal of the agent. Knowledge will vary with factors like skills, time, motivation, and money; for instance, a highly motivated threat agent, like a hacker or terrorist, often has little knowledge at first but acquires knowledge through individual efforts and open source resources. This requires time. Conversely, a state-sponsored threat agent like a spy or cyber-military unit may get extensive training and mentoring from senior individuals, all on the payroll of a large organization. Another dimension of knowledge is whether or not the necessary information to compromise a system is available at all. For many years industrial systems benefited from arcane networking and operating systems about which few people had knowledge, and specifications were not widely available; the immigration of industrial systems to Internet Protocol (IP) changed all that entirely.

In the IoT, threat agents will likely require more time and more knowledge to effect attacks, because the systems are different from conventional IT. Learning to compromise these systems may not always be a matter of reapplying a well-documented and rehearsed attack that someone else developed. The IoT will probably require more original work, from more attackers; however, once an attack is successful we can expect it to propagate out as rapidly as they do today on the Internet. What might not be required is more money, because IoT devices are frequently designed to be cheap and mass produced—meaning that they will be accessible and easy to afford.

ACCESS

The *access* a threat agent enjoys to an IoT system or information about the system is important to highlight because it underlines the difference between insiders and outsiders.

It is very important to highlight access and the difference among insiders and outsiders to an organization because there is generally nothing more dangerous to any security system than a compromised insider.

Access means more in the context of an *insiders* because it makes them a threat agent without knowing they are a threat: for instance, a negligent, or poorly trained, underqualified, or overprovisioned insider who allows access privileges to be captured or otherwise used by a malicious entity!

Even now, as networks are becoming more and more complicated and supporting more and more devices in the IoT, threats are looming larger and larger every day associated with well-meaning insiders. They do not mean to cause harm in most cases. They did not even think they were a threat in most cases.

The complexity in the IoT makes insider errors and omissions one of the most potent forms of vulnerabilities in the IoT. And the difficulty in managing access for insiders in a manner that is consistent with their skills, knowledge, and position will be one of the largest threats in the IoT.

Access as a feature of system and processes is another form of threat, because it is typical in many DCs and networks to grant *flat* broad access to resources. The assumption is that the machine or service is intrinsically good and not going to misuse access privileges. And the broader the privileges granted to a system or application, the less debugging and troubleshooting associated with failed communications and other access-related disruptions. But what if the system or service is compromised and under the control of a malicious entity? Then its access privileges—broad access privileges—those of an *insider*—allow it to become a powerful attack platform.

THREAT AGENTS

There are a variety of threat agents that will target IoT systems. Some of the agents are well understood and present the same profile and posture are they might to any typical Internet or enterprise IT system. However, they are at least a couple of different threat agents in the IoT that are distinct from Internet and IT environments.

In quick succession, these are some of the common groups in which threat agents are placed, for the purposes of contrasting them against seemingly new varieties emerging along with the IoT. The reason you might group threat agents is to understand the risk based on the threat profile in terms of skills, motivation, resources, and access.

If you have a broad understanding of the profile of the threat agents ranged against you, it may become possible to make investment decisions related to security and risk management in a more informed manner. For instance, it is not possible to treat all vulnerabilities and risks, but it is possible to focus efforts into vulnerabilities and risks that might be more acute than others. The types of vulnerabilities and risks that require more or less treatment can vary depending on who you, as a risk manager, feel are the threat agents.

The typical threat agents in an IT system or on the contemporary Internet, described in Tables 12.1–12.6, are:

- Criminals
- Hacktivists
- Industrial spies
- Nation states
- Terrorists
- Insiders

Many threat agents will in fact be a combination of these things, not easily described as occupying just one motivation. For instances, some nation states are known to use their sovereign, cyber-offensive capabilities for the purposes of spying on other countries' industries.

Note: The descriptions given here are generalized for the purposes of discussion and description. Any one of the threats discussed will have agents that span the full spectrum of capabilities: high or low skills, motivations, resources, or access.

Additionally, threat agents are not monolithic—they blend and mix with each other. A given agent can easily show all the motivations of several different threats. In some cases, one type of

Table 12.1 Criminals	
Description	Criminals may be individuals acting alone or highly organized groups and entities with multinational capabilities and members. Criminal organizations may come and go, appear and disappear rapidly as they form and decompose. Members may be part of several criminal organizations. Criminal organizations may also be highly competitive and attack each other and their *property* in the form of botnet and malware drop sites.
Skills	High—for the most part crime on the Internet is very profitable. And the more invested in skills the higher the profit. Criminal organizations are both highly organized and highly profitable, able to afford to hire the best skills or get trained accordingly.
Motivations	Cash. Money or means to get money such as fraud and theft or goods or services. In the IoT—endpoints, gateways, networks, and data centers (DCs) used to manage money. Criminals will typically be attracted to systems that manage cash or information (like credit card numbers) that can be used for the purposes of fraud.
Resources	Medium—as with skills, criminal organizations will have access to money to buy good resources. However, as criminal organizations, they will often lack easy access to hard-to-find tools and resources because they may require licenses or permits to buy and import from legitimate manufacturers.
Access	Low—many criminal organizations would focus on cyber- and logical attacks and techniques, and are less likely to have the physical access to internal control systems and networks. While gaining access remotely is definitely possible for criminals, it will be more difficult due to the lack of insiders collaborating with the breaches. Of course, bribing and blackmailing insiders with the necessary access is well within the bounds of criminal behavior.

Table 12.2 Hacktivists	
Description	Pursues a political agenda and thrills from intrusion or destruction of property, or seeks publicity and notoriety.
Skills	Medium to high—Hacktivists traditionally exploited known weakness or use tools developed by others, for instance they might deface a web site that was poorly secured, or launch denial of service (DOS) attacks against banks or governments using tools and technique obtained on the open Internet. However, some hacktivist groups can be highly skilled, such as the Anonymous group, utilizing novel, "zero-day" exploits of their own devising.[a]
Motivations	Righting or avenging political or social injustices. Hacktivists might take an approach akin to terrorist organizations, whereby the impacted target is not directly associated with the grievance, but is a target of opportunity. This makes hacktivists a significant consideration in the security of the IoT, because system weakness may be exploited for reasons unclear to the owners of the system.
	Included in this group would be *stunt hackers*, people who seek fame or promotional advantages by hacking devices—especially IoT devices, to prove that it can be done. Many small and otherwise unknown security consultants and businesses have received worldwide attention for a short period with stunt-hacks against baby monitors and tea pots, coke machines, and pacemakers. The problem is that once stunt hacks prove a vulnerability, malicious hackers take it to the street *for real*.
Resources	Low—hacktivists are not known to be wealthy organizations, though they may have sources of revenue derived from crime, associated with the hybrid nature of threats mentioned before.
Access	Low—are less likely to have the physical access to internal control systems and networks. Unlike entities such as criminals or state-sponsored threats, hacktivists usually lack resources and wherewithal to bribe or blackmail insiders.

[a]*Several examples of bumbling hacktivists in this article http://www.theregister.co.uk/2015/01/02/bristol_bus_timetable_website_ defaced_militants/.*

Table 12.3 Industrial Spies	
Description	Actors funded by companies or possibly nation states for the purposes of spying on competitors and gaining access to intellectual property (from other countries).
Skills	Medium to high—industrial spies can be expected to be well funded and hybridized with state-sponsored agents and therefore possessing the resources of a nation-state spying agency. However, not all industrial spies will be associated with nation states and not all spying agencies belonging to nation states will necessarily share what they capture with commercial interests.
Motivations	Agents seeking to gain competitive advantages through capturing valuable intellectual property or impacting competitors through means such as sabotage—targeting production outages, slowdowns, or increased defect or error rates.
Resources	High—industrial spies will often have well-defined objectives and success criteria, and have objectives linked to resources. Typically, getting caught or having actions attributed to a specific actor is especially harmful to spies, who by definition are supposed to be covert both before and after the attack. Funding would reflect the need to cover traces and obfuscate the source of the attacks as much as possible.
Access	High—expect that industrial spies will take advantage of bribery and blackmail and also patriotism/nationalism related to a country of origin to gain access or collusion by insiders.

Table 12.4 Nation States

Description	State-sponsored attacker with significant resources to affect major disruption on a national scale. Special operations units of national armed forces, or paramilitary cyber-forces funded directly by nation states or their agencies.
Skills	Medium to high—Intuitively you may think that no other threat is as likely to have more resources to recruit and retain skills, like a nation state. While skills can be bought with money, which nations states have aplenty, skills can also be recruited and maintained for reasons completely apart from money, such as patriotism, nationalism, and simply the righteous and macho feeling of being a secret soldier in *Her Majesty's service*. All that considered, nation states are not breaking away from criminals in terms of skills and their abilities. With the exception of a handful of nation states, most governments have diminished skills relative to the criminal and hackitivist threats against them.
Motivations	As with an agency, the motivation of a nation-state actor could be various: economic competition, military competition, political competition, or all of the above. As individuals, the people who are part of a nation-state threat agent will typically be motivated—as previously mentioned—by patriotism, nationalism, and being a soldier in *Her Majesty's service*. This is hard to beat, because they are often beyond the influence of money and bribery, though blackmail remains an option.
Resources	High—industrial spies will often have well-defined objectives and success criteria, and have objectives linked to resources. Typically, getting caught or having actions attributed to a specific actor is especially harmful to spies, who by definition are supposed to be covert both before and after the attack. Funding would reflect the need to cover traces and obfuscate the source of the attacks as much as possible.
Access	High—expect that industrial spies will take advantage of bribery and blackmail and also patriotism/nationalism related to a country of origin to gain access or collusion by insiders.

Table 12.5 Terrorists

Description	A person or affiliated group of people who relies on the use of arbitrary violence to support a sociopolitical agenda. Terrorists may claim an agenda ranging from religious to class-based, nationalist, or environmental.
Skills	Low to medium—terrorists commonly exploit known weaknesses or use tools developed by others. For instance they might deface a web site that was poorly secured, or launch DOS attacks against governments using tools and techniques obtained on the open Internet.
Motivations	A social or political agenda, often an agenda held by a very limited number of people, but who have a fanatical belief in the correctness of their cause. Motivations for terrorism include but are not limited to: religion, class or social justice, territory, or environment.
Resources	Low to medium—often terrorists operate on the fringe of society and are repudiated by nation states, hackers, and criminals alike. As a consequence, they have access to few resources other than the skills of the dedicated fanatics associated with the cause. However, some terrorists have certainly had access to funding from nation states in the past, if their interests aligned. Yet it is would be highly speculative to assume that what funding that is available is being diverted to cyber-attacks versus bread-and-butter issues of food, shelter, and arms training for soldiers.
Access	Low—terrorists are less likely to have the physical access to internal control systems and networks. Unlike entities such as criminals or state-sponsored threats, terrorists usually lack resources and wherewithal to bribe or blackmail insiders.

Table 12.6 Insiders

Description	Insiders (malicious or accidental)—a disaffected current or former employee, contractor or other person with detailed, nonpublic operational information, or an employee or contactor who has the potential to inflict damage through mistakes and oversights while attempting to execute their role in good faith.
	Insiders—while not a new threat in the IoT—will represent one of the largest threats to the IoT, not necessarily because of the privileged access they have, in the case of malicious actors, but because the complexity of the IoT systems means that errors and oversights can have dramatically unpredictable impacts: chaotic impacts.
Skills	High—insiders will usually have extensive permissions to internal systems and physical access to different terminals and network interfaces with which to gain access. Additionally, insiders will have probably been given training on internal systems and access controls, including some of the security features associated with the internal systems.
Motivations	In the case of malicious insiders, the motivations can be many. From grievances against the organizations to revenge intended to embarrass or get co-workers into trouble. For instance, union members have been known to sabotage equipment prior to labor negotiations or strike actions, to place pressure on management for a rapid and favorable outcome for the union.
	Social problems such as debt and drug abuse are also known to compel otherwise honest insiders to become threats, because they need money and wish to embezzle or are being blackmailed.
	Insiders with depression or other mental issues may cease to conduct their duties with the required diligence, or neglect training or safety standards and represent major threats to IoT systems.
Resources	High—consider insiders to be highly resourced because they essentially have access to all the resources of the IoT system to turn on itself. They do not need more training, or to hire skills, or to buy special equipment—they have access to all they need by virtue of their trusted position.
Access	High—while an insider may not (and usually should not) have complete access to all systems, they usually have sufficient access to execute the malicious activity upon which they have set their intent.
	As for accidents—the issue there is that cascading impacts occur outside the system under management in ways that no one expected—in ways that were never provisioned for access in the first place.

threat may be a means to becoming a different sort of threat. For instance, a spying outfit may use crime as a means to funding their politically motivated attacks. In general it is fraught to make braid assumptions about the relative sophistication of classes of threat actors. Terrorist groups, hacktivists, and criminal enterprises have evolved and in cases surpassed the capabilities of nation states in cyberwarfare, espionage and influence. This is owing to commercialization of malware technology and supply chains.

NEW THREAT AGENTS IN THE IoT

It is not that there are completely new threats in the IoT, it is that what were formerly unusual or infrequent threats in the IT world are becoming more identifiable to risk managers in the IoT.

These new threat agents might be called *chaotic actors*—which would be something fairly new to risk management jargon, and *regulators*—which is something well known as a stakeholder in industry broadly, but not specifically identified as an actual threat agent!

CHAOTIC ACTORS AND VIGILANTES

Why are chaotic actors and vigilantes (see Table 12.7) different as far as IoT risk managers are concerned? Because they simply don't care what happens. They will press buttons and start reactions and look for outcomes with hard-to-understand benefits or motivations. In the case of vigilantes, the presumption is that they want some form of perceived justice; unfortunately, the crime is all too often unclear or their actions result in collateral damage that seems grossly disproportionate to whatever crime was being avenged.

Chaotic actors will look for near random, nondeterministic impacts (unpredictable and unexpected effects). They will look to take advantage of the complexity of IoT systems and the

Table 12.7 Chaotic Actors and Vigilantes	
Description	Chaotic actors just want chaos. Vigilantes want to get even. They might have an aim, but it is not obvious, like that of spies or terrorists; it is probably more personal than all that. Chaotic actors and vigilantes will again be composed of elements of all the other threat agents, resulting in another hybrid; but there may be one distinguishing feature: they prize anonymity. They want to create confusing and disruptive situations and conditions but don't want to be found out or associated with the conditions—like spies. Unlike spies, they don't have a mandate and probably don't have a budget. They want to throw a wrench into the machinery and sit back to watch what happens. Or they want to punish a particular constituency, regardless of who else is harmed along the way—from family to investors to governments. To the extent they have a plan, it is about targeting specific systems, assets, and entities.[a]
Skills	Medium to high—like hacktivists, chaotic actors and vigilantes will commonly exploit known weaknesses or use tools developed by others; however, like spies and nation states, they may have training and resulting skills, which comes with the caveat *don't get caught!*
Motivations	*Natural justice* and nondeterministic (pseudo-random) outcomes—enjoyment of the collateral effects wrought by deliberate and predictably damaging attacks. "What happens if we push these buttons. . .?"
Resources	Medium to high—probably. Much of the enjoyment associated with chaotic events and frontier justice will require that the events become public! This means that they need to be of sufficient magnitude that they become visible from afar: i.e., they make the press. In order to make the press, it probably requires that the attacks are well planned and executed after lengthy, careful, and costly reconnaissance. (While a random hit might generate the intended effects, it is far more likely that a really critical and damaging attack that might trigger major, random collateral damage will require more than a lucky hit.)
Access	Low—while it is certainly possible, it is less likely that an insider would willingly take part in an attack without clear objectives other than chaos. Of course, blackmail and bribery can go a long way in any circumstances. . .

[a]*Example of chaotic actor group in 2015 called "Lizard Squad": http://www.theregister.co.uk/2015/01/02/lizard_squad_ddos/.*

difficulty in understanding the interdependencies among and even within these systems. Vigilantes will look to right a wrong, no matter who gets in the way. And they simply don't care about interdependencies (political, personal, technical) with other systems as long as their narrow aims are fulfilled. In this chapter and Chapter 13, RIoT Control, we will discuss this as a critical vulnerability that must be managed in the IoT.

A few recent examples of chaotic actors and vigilantes in the IoT specifically, and the Internet generally:

- German steel mill sabotaged—for no apparent reason and without any attribution or claims made[1]
- Water purification systems sabotaged—no clear motive[2]
- Ukrainian power grids sabotaged—no clear motive or claims (though the antagonists are suspected)[3]
- Sony Pictures compromised and massive amounts of intellectual property exposed[4]
- Ashley Madison—millions of individual identities exposed for no clear motivation or benefits, other than presumed moral disapproval.[5]
- The Panama Papers—terabits of legal information disclosed, presumably to expose political corruption but also vast amounts of legitimate, personal information about legal arrangements.[6]

REGULATORS

This is not a diatribe against *big government* or regulation; nonetheless, regulators may pose a serious threat to the IoT not from a business perspective, but from operational perspectives (see Table 12.8).

The core reason regulators are new threat agents in the IoT is their lack of awareness about the complexity and potential cascading effects of their decisions. Like chaotic actors, arbitrary and even well-considered decisions will have unpredictable consequences in the IoT: much more so than in the *IT Internet* of computers, smartphones, and cyber-only transactions. Regulators will deliberately or inadvertently place burdens on IoT systems and services that degrade their business plans, flexibility, and service-delivery options. In some cases, regulation will serve a public benefit, in other cases it will stifle the development of the IoT due to ill-understood system dependencies and assumptions taken from the IT world that do not apply in the IoT.

---

[1]See BBC report, December 2014: http://www.bbc.com/news/technology-30575104.
[2]See Water Technology Report—March 2016: http://www.watertechonline.com/hackers-change-chemical-settings-at-water-treatment-plant/.
[3]See BBC report January 2016: http://www.bbc.com/news/technology-35297464.
[4]See BBC—December 2014: http://www.bbc.com/news/technology-30328510.
[5]A group in 2015 called the "Impact Team," responsible for releasing all the personal information and millions of identities of the Ashley Madison dating site, for reasons that appear to be entirely vengeful, but unspecified.
[6]See The Economist—April 9 2016—http://www.economist.com/news/leaders/21696532-more-should-be-done-make-offshore-tax-havens-less-murky-lesson-panama-papers.

Table 12.8 Regulators	
Description	Regulators come in many shapes and sizes. There are privacy regulators who develop statutes and laws to safeguard personally identifiable information from undue exploitation and lose. There are health and safety regulators who are bespoke to many industries who might require certain types of inspections, reports or audits against stipulated minimum requirements or standards. There are environmental protection regulations, labor and workforce regulations, and even international regulations and laws for sharing the commons—such as the sea or the radio spectrum. Throw into this mix cross-border regulatory differences among regulators and the regulatory environments can become as accidentally complex as the IoT system they purport to manage!
Skills	Low—regulators are part of government and not know to be on the cutting end of industrial innovations. Usually. In almost all cases, regulators are not a profit center and are not intended to make a profit and therefore retain earnings (though sometimes they make staggering sums for governments through resource auctions—such as 4 G spectrum auctions, which raised $44 billion in the United States[a]).
	Regulators would be considered low skill largely because they are intended to govern, not participate in the market, and they are not required to make a profit. They are also a monopoly in what they do. Therefore, they tend not to be lavishly funded, driven to hard deadlines, or even necessarily held accountable for the market effects of bad regulation or rewarded for good regulation. Acquiring and maintaining top talent and rare skills is not always easy for a regulator.
Motivations	In the best case: the public good, security, and prosperity are the motivations for many regulators; however, there are examples of regulators being aligned with nationalist economic policy, and/or personal greed.
	In all cases, regulators will typically be subject to more or less political pressure (as an entity of government) and subject to the occasionally arbitrary nature of political decision making and even total reversal of policy!
Resources	Low to medium—governments all around the world are under pressure to do more with less. It is not uncommon to find regulators who are sufficiently funded to meet their objectives, but not necessarily with the best available resources, skills, or training. As a result, regulators may possess less than a complete understanding of the IoT system they are regulating.
Access	High—regulators will be broadly empowered by law in many cases to request detailed and proprietary information about the system under regulation; however, they may not get access to this all information—because there will frequently be resistance from regulated entities. Similarly, regulators will have access to both people and facilities in the course of regulation, allowing them to ask specific questions and make specific observations that only a virtual insider would be able to accomplish.

[a]http://www.businessweek.com/articles/2014-12-18/u-dot-s-dot-mobile-spectrum-auction-a-44-billion-windfall-so-far.

Regulatory prohibitions or market-shaping laws will probably destroy as many IoT business opportunities as they enable or create—sometimes for difficult to establish social benefit.

There are already several examples of regulatory influence aimed directly at the IoT, as we will see in the following discussion; whether these influences will be hazardous or beneficial is impossible to determine at this point. However, the fact that there are so many guns pointed in this direction from different stakeholders that don't necessarily coordinate anything together is not a good thing!

BUSINESS (ORGANIZATIONAL) THREATS

In Chapter 4, "Business and Organizational Requirements," we discussed business and organizational requirements related to security and risk management in the IoT. To continue our discussion of threats in the IoT, we will use the same basic framework:

- Regulatory and legal threats associated with laws and industry enforced minimum standards for security and privacy protection
- Financial threats that are essentially derived from the requirement to balance the costs of security and risk management against threats and vulnerabilities
- Competitive threats that come from advantages that may be handed to others in the same field for lack of good security
- Internal policy threats associated with doing what you say

By no means will we succeed in addressing and describing all potential threats—rather, this is an attempt to outline a superset of threats that might be applicable across a range of IoT use cases. These examples are intended to be demonstrative and directional rather than conclusive.

REGULATORY AND LEGAL THREATS

The following sections give a summary of regulatory and legal threats.

Privacy threats

Above all regulatory threats, privacy will loom largest for many IoT systems and services because it is a form of regulation that cuts across many industries and IoT use cases. Additionally, privacy advocates have been known to operate *above* technology and yet seek to propose (or impose) regulation with incomplete or flawed understanding of systems and services.

Privacy is also a high priority among legislators, but it is an inconsistently defined regulatory requirement with many different privacy laws overlapping at different levels of government. Privacy regulation can be found as omnibus legislation that applies across a national economy, but also as industry-specific guidance. For instance, health systems will often have their own privacy statutes and regulations over and above the omnibus legislation.

Many of the emerging use cases in the IoT are potentially inconsistent with personal privacy: they are founded on the assumption that personal information about users is accessible and linkable. In some cases this is a valid assumption, especially if the service in question is *free* and the business model calls for selling directed advertising or user profile information to a third party. But a real threat to business and user alike will arise as expectations of privacy do not match the business designs of an IoT service provider.

The balance between personal information and what can be used for business purposes is still unclear. If a business goes too far in the direction of protecting personal privacy they may retard critical value-added functions and services—and the business ultimately fails; too far in the direction of taking liberties with personal information from users and a regulatory breach may occur, resulting in ignominy and loss of subscribers.

Privacy can also generate fines for companies—while these fines have historically been modest or even inconsequential, new variations have seen privacy regulations acquire the ability to apply punitive financial sanctions of offending business—in some cases amounting to 4 percent of gross global income![7] It is the court of public opinion that does the real harm to business.

From the perspective of a normal user in a modern society, we already implicitly accept the collection of a vast amount of information about the day-to-day minutiae of our lives: from surveillance via proliferated closed-circuit television, to spending habits via store loyalty cards, or the tracking of our movements and data on our smart phones. The IoT expands this on a grand scale. Gartner forecasts there were be nearly 5 billion connected devices by the end of 2015, and over 20 billion in 2020.[8]

The IoT massively increases the opportunity for threat agents to get access to our personally identifiable data. This prompted the chair of the US Federal Trade Commission to air her concerns about privacy in the IoT at the Consumer Electronics Show (CES) in 2015:[9] signaling an awareness among privacy regulators and putting the IoT industry on notice that the Wild Wild West will not prevail. This is new ground for regulators and they are watching carefully.

In sum, privacy threats in the IoT come in two broad forms:

- Type 1 privacy threat: threats to businesses that need to collect, use, and disclose personal data, and their ability to do so without legal or market-based sanctions for breaches.
- Type 2 privacy threat: threats to individuals and users of IoT service, who will be offered services that are either free. or subsidized, through consenting to the collection, use, and disclosure of personally identifiable information.

Data security

Data security is different than privacy in that it is larger in scope. Data security encompasses privacy and goes well beyond into other forms of sensitive data such as intellectual property, strategic plans, competitive intelligence, and operational processes and procedures. Data security is about every piece of information that an entity considers valuable.

But for the most part, data security has not been regulated like personally identifiable information is under privacy laws. Rather, most of the data that would be considered valuable by a business was left to the protections considered appropriate by the management. If a major breach occurred, management and shareholders would pay the price.

Such an approach to data security made sense and served the world of enterprise IT well. By not applying too many regulatory burdens on businesses, innovation has flourished. For the most part, this logic will hold true in the IoT, but there is certainly creeping regulation.

For instance, as of August 2015, companies have an additional incentive to pay attention to data security. At this time a US federal court gave the Federal Trade Commission (FTC) the legitimacy to sanction companies for poor cyber-security practices generally, and hold them accountable.

---

[7]See *SC Magazine* http://www.scmagazineuk.com/breaking-news-eu-agrees-4-fines-for-breaching-data-protection-regulations/article/460046/ and BBC report—http://www.bbc.com/news/technology-25825690.
[8]http://www.gartner.com/newsroom/id/2905717.
[9]http://www.theregister.co.uk/2015/01/07/ftc_chair_worries_about_iot_privacy_in_ces_speech/.

The case in question involved Wyndam Hotels, which the FTC claims left corporate data (including trade secrets as well as personal information) unprotected by basic security controls. There are additional, similar cases awaiting trial, too.[10]

Resource allocation

In countries with strong private sector ownership, most capital and human resources are allocated by the private sector—but even in these places substantial economic resources are allocated according to regulation or directly influenced in their allocation by regulation.

Regulators as allocators or economic resources have the potential to be significant threats to the IoT through misallocation.

Misallocation of Resources: Natural. Natural resources come in many forms, but the form most pertinent to the IoT is probably the radio spectrum used for wireless communications such as wireless local area networks (LAN) (Wi-Fi) and especially cellular 3 G and 4 G and soon 5 G services, which connect all our smart phones to the Internet.

Around the world, radio spectrum is regulated by governments and regulations are roughly harmonized internationally. This harmonization has arisen as a matter of compelling need: chaos would ensue otherwise. Cell phones would not work as you approached national borders or areas of independent regulation, and neither would police radios or air traffic control for that matter. Harmonization of wireless spectrum regulations has always had an obvious benefit to safety and prosperity. Regulators of spectrum provide rules about who can use which frequencies of radio spectrum where, and therefore make it possible to transmit and receive and deliver wireless services without debilitating interference.

Wireless radio spectrum, like anything else, would be subject to the *tragedy of the common* without regulation: exploitation by competing interests to the point of exhaustion. It would be good for nothing, without regulation, especially because radios and wireless communications are sensitive to interference—more so even than in other forms of commons, like waterways or fields.

Wireless communications is a critical element of the IoT. Without wireless, there really will be no IoT! Without wireless there will be no mobility, no remote access, and no services available without a copper or fiber cable physically attached. How attractive would your smart phone be if it came with a cable attached to the wall? That would, actually, be called a *telephone* c.1985.

Without wireless communications, the costs of physically connecting devices that need to communication would be prohibitive.

Without wireless communications, services would also be too fragile and subject to disruption. Cutting a thin copper line to a remote endpoint is much easier to do accidentally than jamming a radio carrier.

The need effectively and convincingly to regulate natural resources like wireless communications spectrum is essential to the IoT: we rest our case. Yet it is possible to go too far or simply too slow with regulation.

---

[10]See the Wall Street Journal: http://on.wsj.com/1hDqN2z.

A significant threat to the IoT could come from regulators who do not evolve fast enough or are in thrall to vested interests. For instance, they leave radio spectrum occupied by inefficient technologies like analog television for too long, when digital television can do a better job and free up spectrum for new wireless data services and in turn support new IoT applications.

Alternately, large swaths of radio spectrum that may be reserved for government purposes like military of emergency services might be held in place for too long—to the detriment of shared bandwidth that the private sector can use for IoT development. Not that these services should be decommissioned, but as they have move onto newer technologies themselves and do not require the same degree of bandwidth that they did previously.

Similarly, space transport companies—a burgeoning field—want regulators to consider not only existing but future innovative uses of satellite (Ka-band) spectrum before engaging in further regulation. These companies have commented in this way as part of the US Federal Communications Commissions (FCC) Notice of Inquiry (NOI) on technical and service rules for 5 G in bands above 24 GHz—for fear that poor regulation might generate massive spectrum interference and degrade service levels past the point of usability.

Alternately, regulators may simply need to see merit in asking legacy communications technology firms and consumers to move on, so spectrum and other resources can be reallocated sooner rather than later.

Misallocation of Resources: Manmade. Is there an IoT without the Internet? No. Has the Internet come about from careful planning and regulation? Not really.

The Internet and the IoT prospers on the basis of voluntary, opportunistic, spontaneous, arbitrary, and unregulated joining of networks and the development of services running over those networks.

The Internet has prospered these last 30 years in large part due to the amazing innovation unleashed by a lack of regulation. This lack of regulation is not due to an unwillingness from government to regulate, but because they did not comprehend the Internet well enough to attempt to regulate it. Regulators simply had trouble keeping up with the Internet. (No shame in that—many industries have had the same challenge.)

One of the significant, existential threats to the IoT remains to be attempts by regulators to manage the networks that underlie the Internet on account of philosophies such as *"net neutrality."*[11]

Net neutrality holds that a carrier or service provider should transport all data entering and leaving the network on an unbiased basis. No favoritism should be given to sources of data or destinations, applications or protocols, peers, or subscribers.

The underlying assumption is that in the IoT, applications, and services are equal in aggregate and that subscribers value them the same, in aggregate. As we will discuss shortly, this is an ill-informed perspective and a significant threat to the IoT.

The basic threat is that net neutrality will affect bandwidth and service levels on the core network that supports the IoT and distorts networks to the point that the IoT fails. For instance, net neutrality holds that one packet is the same value as another packet and should be carried with the same degree of priority. Yet that is to say that a packet from a smart transportation system has the same assurance requirements as a packet from a social network video of a kitten chasing its tail!

---

[11]http://www.theregister.co.uk/2015/01/20/telcos_try_to_head_off_net_neutrality_rules_with_legislation/.

Net neutrality regulations can interfere with a service provider's ability to purchase or supply enhanced network assurance for a given IoT service—even if the end users of the service want and are willing to pay a premium, and will not accept the service otherwise because of its safety implications.

Net neutrality also assumes that regulators are able effectively to assess the assurance needs of the applications using the network—better than the owners and users of these service themselves. This might be possible if there were merely dozens of services, but there are more like thousands of different IoT services already crisscrossing the networks, and more to come. Regulators are already well past the point of being able to understand the specific needs and interdependencies of these IoT services, and attempting to regulate with broad strokes will only lead to inefficiencies at best, with progressively worse outcomes highly probable.

From a security and risk management perspective, net neutrality will drive increased risks associated with safety and availability, because better service levels cannot be procured or otherwise counted up. Potentially, net neutrality could result in nondeterministic (unpredictable) routing and movement of data over the networks—increasing risks associated with interception (confidentiality) or corruption (integrity).

Networks and bandwidth are a manmade resource and the heart of the IoT—poor regulation, like poor nutrition, can threaten the heart.

Misallocation of Subsidy. It is a well-studied phenomena that government subsidies can have terrible effects on economics. Fuel subsidies intended to benefit the poor can in fact benefit the elite, the corrupt, and the smugglers. Food subsidies intended to feed the masses can make a small group of farmers rich and the masses fat from eating the wrong types of food or merely make food unduly expensive. The list of failed subsidies goes on and on.

The IoT is not spared from the threat of misallocated subsidies either. The importance to IoT system developers and risk managers is related to where and how subsidies will change in the future and how this will affect IoT business cases and development.

Here are a few examples of the introduction, continuation, or cancellation of subsidies that can impact risk in the IoT:

- Crop subsidies that guarantee a minimum prices on commodities like milk, corn or wheat can delay the introduction of new, more efficient IoT-based farming techniques. As an IoT executive, do not underestimate the ability of old-school farmers and their technologies to wring new subsidies from government that undermine business cases overnight.
- Energy subsidies that make inefficient technologies practical financially after government support is included. For instance, incentives for *smart homes* are minimized if a tax credit for home heating is introduced after a cold winter! Alternately, if fuel efficiency standards were relaxed or postponed, the incentive for smart transportation may diminish.
- Transportation subsidies that make otherwise inefficient airlines or railways or trucking profitable can delay the introduction of a myriad of smart technologies that would reduce waste and increase utilization of not only the vehicles but the underlying infrastructures such as roads and runways.
- Health care—socialized or subsidized—will in part hide the costs of medical services from those consuming the services. The result may be slower deployment of smart health systems that drive efficiencies. Additionally, such subsidies might make the quality of the services delivery—such as the security and privacy elements—less visible to the end users because of the reduced costs.

- Infrastructure subsidies that might consist of payments from one level of government to another to build road and bridges distributes the cost of inefficiencies away from the end users and might delay IoT technologies for transportation.

These are just a few ways that subsidies may distort IoT business cases and threaten the development of the technologies and systems. In the event that subsidies impact the IoT business case and new savings must be found, all too often those savings come partially from reduced investment in security, which is a *forward-looking* investment, made in expectation of something bad happening.

Overall, regulation is a significant threat to the IoT because it can be difficult to forecast due to it political nature and just as difficult to assess its long-term impact once it arrives.

The greatest threat from regulation is that it is introduced too fast based on too few lessons and learning, such as regulation based on limited, early examples of failed or poorly designed IoT that generated some negative impacts. Regulation can swing too far in one direction or another. Regulators needs to forbear and learn about the IoT before trying to regulate it. Consider that vehicle safety evolved over the last 100 years and continues to do so today: IoT regulations don't need (or deserve) 100 years of forbearance—but it deserves to have regulation based on a balance of experience and conjecture associated with many of the threats we are discussing throughout this chapter.

FINANCIAL

Financial threats to the IoT are interdependent with most of the other threats discussed in this chapter and rarely stand-alone. For the purposes of discussing financial threats, we will focus directly on how poor security and risk management might result directly in losses—rather than a general business failure.

Subscriber fraud and theft of service

Any sort of IoT system or service that results in billing to the end user will be subject to fraud and theft of service—beyond a shadow of a doubt.

In the early days of cellular technology, security was weak and the impact of fraud and theft of service was extreme, not to mention the impacts of privacy, because first generation (1 G) cell technology was totally open to eavesdropping.

Where the threat will manifest itself will depend entirely on the IoT system in question, but there is no reason to believe that threats will not target all four assets classes—merely looking for the weakest point to exploit: the endpoints, gateways, network, or DC/cloud.

Threat of IoT fraud and theft of services might well appear in multiple forms:

1. Users compromise the system for free *premium* services. Legitimate users extend their subscriptions independently, circumventing the business system support (BSS), adding additional features that would normally be chargeable.
2. Users compromise the system to reduce bills or break limits on services without incurring extra fees or possibly without having the overages noticed or recorded by the accounting systems.
3. Third parties clone or masquerade as legitimate subscribers or devices, and get full services while legitimate users get outrageous bills (that they refuse to pay). Even today people *steal cable* by illicitly tapping or splitting a line into a residence.

4. Account-sharing against service agreements. A legitimate subscriber may share a service illicitly, such that a IoT service provider is actually supporting two users for the price of one. An example would be a person who parks his/her car in a smart lot, and then hands the pass off to a friend idling outside—who then parks again with the same pass. Another example might be home monitoring, where two neighbors collude to have wireless motion sensors connect to a common access point and pay a single monthly fee—to have two homes monitored.

5. Substitution of service. Devices may be provided to a subscriber on a subsidized basis, with the expectation that all transactions and services will be managed by the service provider providing the subsidy: but the user reconfigures the (subsidized) device to use a cheaper service provider. In the cellular world, a form of this is *unlocking* cell phones that have been provided to users on a subsidized basis on the condition the phone is only used with the subsidizing carrier. By unlocking the phone, users might replace the subscriber identity module (SIM) with a cheaper carrier, before the contract term is complete.

Social engineering attacks in the IoT: the shape of things to come

Another form of fraud that will plague the IoT will be associated with social engineering:[12] tricking people rather than compromising devices. These attacks have the potential to be lucrative for the threat agents, certainly in terms of fraud, but also identity theft, espionage, and even property ransom. Social engineering is one of the main attack tools enabling cyber-crime and fraud, even in 2016.

Successful social engineering attacks through IoT systems could lead to a perception of being surrounded by hostile devices, and this could greatly retard development, making the consequences of social engineering attacks in the IoT very significant.

The IoT represents a whole new and fertile territory for social engineering attacks, which blend some of the most effective attacks from the contemporary Internet with attacks more commonly found in the industrial-control world—namely, attacks that seek to capture information with intrinsic value (passwords, account details, access to vulnerable systems) while tricking users into executing complex *sequences* of commands on the basis of misinformation.

The current generation of IoT have dubious security. There are plenty of reports of devices like baby monitors[13], TVs[14], medical devices[15], and even cars[16] that have been hacked or are demonstrably vulnerable to hacks.

Here are a couple of theoretical examples in which social engineering attacks will be launched through the IoT:

Reflected targeting and compromise. Things are often too limited in processing and memory to compromise and manipulate to large effect. What is more, they might not have information of

---

[12]*"The deliberate application of deceitful techniques designed to manipulate someone into divulging information or performing actions that may result in the release of that information." Source:* https://blogs.mcafee.com/mcafee-labs/hacking-human-os-report-social-engineering.

[13]See—http://www.huffingtonpost.com/2013/08/13/hacked-baby-monitor-houston-texas-parents_n_3750675.html.

[14]See—http://mashable.com/2013/08/02/samsung-smart-tv-hack/.

[15]See—http://www.forbes.com/sites/ericbasu/2013/08/03/hacking-insulin-pumps-and-other-medical-devices-reality-not-fiction/.

[16]See—http://money.cnn.com/2014/06/01/technology/security/car-hack/index.html.

intrinsic value to interest criminals. However, they might serve as a highly effective social engineering platform to drive the compromise of the more powerful computing platforms in the home or business—such as servers, networks, desktops computers, tablets, or smartphones.

Consider this: a threat agent learns how to use *things* to display messages, or gets control of the cloud-based services bundled with an IoT product, like patching or content management. Smart TVs are a good example, because they already use cloud-based monitoring and management platforms.

The threat agent triggers a message to all the smart TVs, which is displayed the next time the TVs are turned on:

> Your TV requires a software upgrade.
> For your security, it will stop working in 60 minutes, until upgraded.
> Please go to www.example.com/smartTVupgrade and download the patching software, and run it from any Windows computer on the same network as this TV.

Imagine variations of this theme, displayed via the device human-control panel of just about any *cloud-enhanced* Thing (which is most of them).

This amounts to *IoT-phishing*.[17] Most people (but certainly not all) know that phishing emails with these sorts of instructions are to be ignored and discarded. But what if the instructions come from your smart IoT device? Most people have no experience with a smart device as an attack platform and have no reason to be suspicious. And they love their TV: "My amateur dancing show starts in 45 minutes!!"

And an additional factor associated with this attack is that it might side-step conventional security systems like desktop email protection and antivirus, malware, and URL reputation-blocking. Why? Because the attackers are not using email as the social engineering platform—the attack involves an out-of-band delivery channel, relative to where we have invested in security.

Why is this different than social engineering today? The consequences of social engineering attacks in the IoT could be worse than the same attacks in the *IT Internet* of today.

The perception goes from one of *living with weak devices*, to being *surrounded by hostile devices!*—devices that might at any time try to deceive you into doing something against your interests, like a malevolent robot from a science fiction movie. That would bad. It is one matter if your Things are being hacked and compromised behind your back; it is another matter if your Things are tricking you into hurting yourself, or others.

Fines

Massive, punishing fines associated with mismanagement of data security and privacy are getting closer. (See the discussion previously about regulatory compliance and privacy sanctions).

In the past and even today, many of the laws associated with data security and privacy have modest or even inconsequential fines associated with breaches and noncompliance. Really, the thing that scares business more is the negative and high-profile publicity that can result, and the *mea culpa* acts that regulators can demand—like sending out a notification letter even if a breach was merely judged possible. However, the stakes are already rising, and the IoT will drive the threat of fines even further, as the stakes rise.

---

[17]https://en.wikipedia.org/wiki/Phishing.

Aside from damage to reputation, it is often less expensive and easier for a business to suffer a data breach than to try and invest in a good security platform. In the IoT, where the costs of devices and services will lean toward rapid market introduction and low prices to encourage adoption over conventional ways, there is little reason to be certain of security investments. (As we have said over and over in this book.)

But with new, increased data breach fines in places, as in privacy-conscious Europe, new levels are being set in financial threat; for instance, new EU Data Protection Regulation see fines jumping to up to €100 million (or 4% of global turnover under the new EU Data Protection Regulation).[18] While these laws are coming into force at the time of writing, there is every reason to expect that they will emerge in parallel with the IoT visions for 2020 and beyond.

Swings in legal interpretations: copyright, privacy, and digital exhaust

A major assumption associated with many of the largest Internet-based services, like Google and Facebook, is that users can give away any rights associated with the analysis of their online activities with a minimum of consent. Additionally, the perceived wisdom of most users is that such information possesses little intrinsic value, and what they get in return (the online services) is a huge bargain.

The 1998 US Digital Copyright Millennium Act (DCMA) allows individuals to assert ownership rights over digital content they create through simplified processes that do not involve hiring lawyers and costs. However, recent lawsuits[19] around intellectual property have seen the expanded application of the *fair use* defense for data that is placed on the Internet—pushing back the effective boundaries of the DCMA, essentially arguing that while intellectual property may be clearly owned by an entity, it is not entitled to control over the intellectual property in absolute terms, such as, for instance, if the intellectual property is being used in a manner that is not perverting its meaning or generating meaningful income relative to the cost of putative licensing.

In the case of the IoT, this is ambiguous territory, because so much of the *digital exhaust* generated by people and devices alike will be harvested from the IoT to be repurposed, repackaged, aggregated, correlated, and sold. It will be sold to advertisers and marketers, researchers and product manufacturers, and even government regulators and security agencies.

The limits of what belongs to an individual and what belongs to the service providers are largely untested when it comes to the IoT. Service agreements—like those found in all *free* cloud services for email, storage, photo management, and so forth—usually contain provisions that severely restrict the ability of users to claim any rights associated with their *digital exhaust*—their usage patterns, preferences, logs, and traffic patterns.

While this issue may appear simple and settled now, there is a possibility that as the IoT grows, our digital exhaust accumulates to the point that it is considered a unique and conscious *work*. If we are knowingly allowing ourselves to be logged and recorded, and we are conscious of the unique picture we are creating and possibly even deliberately shaping, will rights ever be extended to this personal picture of users?

---

[18]Ibid, *SC Magazine* http://www.scmagazineuk.com/breaking-news-eu-agrees-4-fines-for-breaching-data-protection-regulations/article/460046/ and BBC report—http://www.bbc.com/news/technology-25825690.
[19]http://www.theregister.co.uk/2015/09/17/dancing_baby_victim_shaming/.

Indeed, the IoT promises the ability to create incredibly detailed pictures of people and their preferences that might certainly be sold rather than given away: for instance, sold to advertisers or service providers who acquire the right to create, bundle, and package goods and services for you on an exclusive basis.

Perhaps you sell your digital exhaust to a travel agency in exchange for the rights to build you the ideal vacation package and present it to you. You might buy or it you might not, but you probably only sell such a right when you are ready to buy... so the service provider knows there will be a good conversion rate for the investment.

If practices such as this develop based on the richness of digital exhaust generated by the IoT, today's service providers like Google and Facebook and tomorrow's service providers like car companies and grocers might find that *fair use* interpretation might collapse in the face of privacy concerns and new business models that place high value on what was formerly considered merely *exhaust*, disrupting or even destroying business plans and service models.

Liability and insurance threat

Liability and insurance are probably best discussed as a combined form of threat in the IoT, where the threat of product or service liability derived from security failures and oversights begets the need for insurance.

Product and service liability is already evolving in the IoT, where devices being placed online and sold as new and improved prove to be far less secure and trustworthy than the older versions that were offline. TVs that listen to every word spoken in the room,[20] or baby monitors that allow creeps to watch and yell at toddlers[21] are just two examples that led to liabilities and lawsuits against manufacturers. The natural response of IoT vendors and service providers will be to seek insurance against liability.

In such a scenario, the IoT becomes like an automobile for consumers—a useful tool but also something that can hurt you regardless of who might be at fault. *No fault* IoT insurance will probably be incorporated into household insurance, but may also be sold as a standalone policy to individuals and business. Similarly, errors and omissions insurance and *cyber-risk* insurance will be explicitly expanded to include IoT goods and services. Alternately, cyber-insurance policies will be deliberately written to exclude IoT coverage, without additional riders, stipulations, conditions, and costs.

Because the IoT is so young, there are many questions and scenarios around attempts to shield liability with insurance that represent real risks to both business and consumers due to rising costs and uncertainty: here are a few potential situations that might arise in relation to IoT and insurance:

- Excessive liability awards in the courts for IoT-related accidents will raise insurance costs beyond the point at which the IoT business case makes sense, or forces IoT service providers to raise prices to the point that the service is no longer attractive to users and subscribers.
- Insurers—in an attempt to manage their risks associated with punitive awards, begin disallowing broad forms of indemnification, requiring IoT services and functions to be disabled

---

[20]See "Disable this feature to stop your Samsung Smart TV from listening to you"; http://www.cnet.com/how-to/samsung-smart-tv-spying/.
[21]See *SC Magazine*; http://www.scmagazine.com/research-shows-vulnerabilities-in-video-baby-monitors/article/436547/.

and disallowed because they cannot be insured economically, strangling the IoT features available. Maybe that smart car is uninsurable if the *intelligence* is enabled: only dumb cars are predictable enough to be worth insuring?

- The complexity of IoT systems makes it very difficult to decide what is an event that should *legitimately* have been foreseen, versus a truly nondeterministic event. In other words, does fault lie with someone else and his/her insurance coverage for errors and omissions? Consequently, insurance claims end up unresolved for years and again retard the IoT market for lack of reliable means of transferring liability risks through insurance.

These are just a sampling of the financial threats that will be visible for the organizations and need to be considered by any risk management program in the IoT.

COMPETITIVE

Competitive threats, like competitive requirements, have to do with the market and the ability of an IoT good or service to enter a market, capture market share, and compete and remain viable in the face of evolving alternatives in the market. The following are some of the top competitive threats that management will need to deal with related to the technology of security (and privacy) in the IoT.

Skill deficits

IoT is highly innovative and disruptive, where failure to acquire, foster, and retain the skills necessary to launch and compete in a given market are make-or-break.

Over and over again, we have heard the high tech industry state that there is a skills shortage, and nowhere is this shortage more acute that in the high technology security domain.

The inability to obtain and relate IoT security skills is a major threat to any product or service vendor in the IoT. Creating a business plan for the IoT without some sort of consideration around how to address security from a human resource perspective would be folly.

It is baseline practice in all well-defined security standards that someone must be trained, accountable, and be an identified leader for IT security in every organization. In the IoT, the skills shortage will certainly affect many organizations and their ability to develop and maintain sufficient security the IoT devices, systems, and services with which they come to market.

We consider this a competitive matter because security is one of the largest question marks for adopters of IoT technology, whether consumers or business. Those IoT providers of goods and services that can apply and demonstrate good security and risk management practices will have differentiation opportunities. Those that go to market with goods and services and a *bare minimum* of security capability will find themselves facing threats to both products and reputations on a regular basis, and the overt threat of being branded an *insecure product* with predictably catastrophic effects on market share and customer goodwill.

Failure to use big data effectively

Failure to use the resulting *big data* effectively for competitive advantage and value-added services[22] is a threat, whereas it is an opportunity if done correctly. Many competitive

---

[22]Joan Chen, EVP ZTE, Smart Cities Conference, Sept 11–13, 2015.

opportunities may reside in the oceans of data generated by new IoT goods and services, and missing those opportunities will certainly mean the difference between success and failure for organizations.

The IoT will yield vast amounts of information about people, places, and things. This is widely understood, and privacy professionals (in particular) fret about the impacts and invasions that may occur. But these real or imaged impacts on personal information and privacy will not always come about because the holder of the information will fail to capitalize on the information and *big data* that comes into their possession via the IoT.

This is not to say that any and all uses of IoT log and event information should be open to data mining and resale, but certainly there is a large threat that organizations will fail to use what they have at their disposal in ways both appropriate and as a competitive differentiator in the market.

Opportunities for making products services more efficient will be lost due to poor analytics and management of IoT data.

Opportunities to increase service levels and customer satisfaction will be lost because no one bothered to ask the right questions from the data. Or more likely, no one had the necessary skills to ask the right questions from the IoT.

The limits to which any system can be exploited for gain are unknown and theoretical. Like a game of chess, the arrangement of the many elements in IoT and the order in which they might be moved or applied is enormous. Trying to assess which features, combinations, and permutations of services will yield the best experience customers will often hinge upon insights derived from big data and analytics. The threat that IoT systems will not see their full value and potential is closely related to the failure to properly leverage data and analytics in the IoT.

Additionally, big data and analytics can yield incredibly useful insights into matters like fraud, technical security breaches, and vulnerabilities as well as simplify security compliance reporting. It is hard to imagine an IoT service being as good as it might be without sufficient investment in analytics.

Kamikaze competition: a "Flash in the Pan" that burns the fields

Aside from being a mixed metaphor—this is a thing!

In the late 1990s, as the effects of telecom deregulation started to really show in the marketplace, many new *competitive local exchange carriers* (CLEC) sprung up in urban and even suburban areas, looking to compete with the large, incumbent local exchange carriers (ILEC).

These small carriers were seeking to take a bite out of everything from residential phone services to long-haul business data networks. Most of these entrants were out of business within a couple of years because they overinvested and the market was fragmented by the entry of some many alternatives in telecom services. As a result, the business opportunities did not materialize for them. What they also did was create a massive glut in telecom supply that depressed prices severely for the surviving carriers for many years (1999 to 2003). This competitive situation inspired behaviors that also took down some major telecom equipment manufacturers such as the former Northern Telecom, as poor credit decisions whiplashed.

In the rush to get into the IoT market, many small IoT startups are flooding the market. Many will not make it over the *chasm*—as Gordon Moore puts it—and will fail. But in the meantime, the sheer volume of these IoT market entrants will fragment markets and could drive prices for products and services down to the point of retarding the market as a whole: if margins are too low, investment will not come.

A real danger for any IoT business is that it is faced with desperate competition that will say or do anything to get a customer. In the face of such competition, IoT business managers seek to cut corners in areas like security in order to get to market faster or cheaper than the desperate competition. This is a certainty: security is a forward-looking capability from an operational perspective. Security is about what you expect to happen, but hope will never come to pass. If hope is strong enough or managers are desperate enough, they cut security investments first because in theory, the show will still go on!

> Under such competitive situations, where many small vendors are vying to create or gain share in a crowded market—a real threat is the unseen security compromises that have been made in the development and management of an IoT good or service.
>   Source: Caveat emptor.

Unstable supplier and partners

The world of Internet security products and services today is highly competitive and fragmented, making the threat of inappropriate, ineffective, or plain bad choices related to suppliers and partners a very real threat to managers of all types. In this case, the presence of intense completion in the IoT supply chain (security providers) can represent threat!

In the world of Internet security, there are about 10 major product categories (more or less depending on where you get your information):

- Desktop and server security
- Network firewall
- Data loss prevention
- Analytics and security event management
- System hardening and whitelisting
- Threat intelligence
- Database security
- Web security
- Email security

Across these top level categorizations there are at least 50 distinct firms (minimum 5 per category, sometimes duplicated across categories) that would be counted as *leaders* in Internet security by the likes of Gartner or Forrester or Yankee. On top of those 50, there are thousands of smaller security firms, boutiques, and startups associated with both products and services, all vying to be the next generation of security. Among the firms considered leaders, there are actually few very large firms—most are less than $1 billion in annual revenue and some are far smaller than that. All are desperately competing with one another and have the massive host of boutiques and startups nipping at their heels. There is no industry comparable to the technology security industry for sheer alternatives, diversity, and snake oil.

Of all the product areas, Internet security is the most crowded and splintered. Why? Because security is a challenge that is getting worse, not better (and the IoT is not helping that situation). Security is also an area of major venture-capital investment (much like the IoT).

One of the hallmarks of even the best-managed enterprises is having too many service vendors within the infrastructure. It is not uncommon to find two product vendors incumbent in a large enterprise for every one of the 10 product categories described above. In other words, many enterprises will be trying to manage their security with 20 or more different security products!

This leads to high operational costs and low security capability. The part about costs is fairly obvious: if you are buying from many small vendors in small batches you will pay more: the security capability element may not be as obvious to some readers, but it is pernicious in effect. Trying to manage many security products means that staff probably never gets good with any of them and many of the alerts and warnings are ignored or assumed to be false positives. As a result, the investment in a wide range of vendors—perhaps assuming it is always better to buy the best in any given category—is largely lost.

Some of the biggest security breaches ever to occur came from organizations with high security investment and poor security abilities due to operational fatigue. Too much for too few people to do and to know.

As a service provider in the IoT, the same threat exists: acquiring too many security vendors and suppliers in an attempt to create an effective security program and infrastructure.

As we discussed in Chapter 3, "Requirements and Risk Management," the IoT will gain in flexibility and dynamic nature from service stratification *and* overall competition. Like the security industry, the IoT will be broken into many different forms of product and service categories—we have repeatedly spoken about the endpoint, gateways, network, and DC/cloud. But in addition to the *vertical* category, which an IoT product or service providers might occupy and where they compete, there will be a myriad of other categories and layers where suppliers and partnerships will be required (see Fig. 12.1). This is vendor/partner fatigue will represent threat!

As an IoT product or service vendor, you will be presented with a wide range of potential suppliers and partners.

	Endpoint	Gateways	Network	Data center/ cloud
Application management	Vendor A Vendor B Vendor B1	Vendor I Vendor K	Vendor Q Vendor R	Vendor AA Vendor AB Vendor AC
Software services	Vendor C Vendor D	Vendor J Vendor L Vendor L1	Vendor S Vendor T Vendor U	Vendor AD Vendor AE Vendor AE1
Platforms services	Vendor E Vendor F	Vendor M	Vendor V Vendor W	Vendor AF Vendor AF1 Vendor F2
Hardware and infrastructure services	Vendor G Vendor H	Vendor N Vendor O Vendor P	Vendor X Vendor Y Vendor Z	Vendor AG Vendor AH

FIGURE 12.1

Vendor fatigue.

All of them will claim to be the best-of-breed in their product category.

All of them will claim critical differentiating features and capabilities over their competition.

In the end, the margin (or even appreciable) benefits of one security solution vendor over another will represent a threat if this is consistently expanding the number of partners and suppliers—creating an unmanageable ecosystem, especially from a security perspective. How can a small or rapidly growing IoT business effectively manage the security of multiple suppliers and vendors, who themselves are probably operating at the margins of security and risk management or lack of resources, will, or understanding?

INTERNAL POLICY

Internal IT security policy is important to any organization because it provides management-level guidance to operational groups about security and risk management. Without a security policy as a starting point for an IT security program, it is considered difficult-to-impossible to create a repeatable, measureable, and efficient IT security program.

The first major threat in the IoT from an internal policy perspective is a simple lack of an IoT security policy.

Lack of IT security policy has never stopped anyone from getting into business, but it has certainly driven many executives out of a job, if not forced companies into bankruptcy. A company may get off to a great start in life with good products or services and a happy clientele; however, for lack of any governance and management in the form of an IT security policy, what security they actually have is ad hoc, patchy, immeasurable, and rapidly falls into a dysfunctional state, yet is also expensive! Eventually, staff get frustrated by the lack of management related to IT security, and because no one is really watching (for lack of a policy to discipline negligence), they stop actually practicing security consistently or diligently and the law of probabilities takes over: a massive security breach occurs. Many hard lessons have been learned over the years in exactly this way.

The businesses that have learned the best lessons about IT security policy are the ones that possessed digital assets that threat agents have targeted from the beginning: banks, government, and high-tech industries including entertainment.

The industries that probably have the most to learn about good internal policy as the foundation for good security and risk management are the ones charging most quickly into the IoT world: industries that work with tangible goods and services versus logical goods and services, i.e., health, transportation, energy, manufacturing, water, and public safety.

Unfortunately, it is not hard to get a company up and running without any internal security policy whatsoever, and we should expect that the IoT will be no different in this regard. In the same vein, it will be a simple matter for a company accustomed to dealing in physical goods and services to go online expecting that old IT security practices would be sufficient in the IoT world.

Overall this is a major threat to the IoT—a lack of adequate, or any, internal security policy results in dysfunctional security and risk management.

IoT security policy vacuum is a standard vacuum

The lack of established international or national standards around IoT and machine-to-machine (M2M) security makes internal policy about IoT security difficult. As a result, a large threat is simply that for lack of any good examples, internal security policies are not shaped to the unique security requirements of the IoT (the subject of six full chapters in this book). For lack of internationally recognized IoT security standards, there are no examples to draw upon that provide widely recognizable credibility for an IoT security policy and program.

Over the course of work from 2014 to 2016, work in the International Standards Organization (ISO) revealed that there were over 500 legitimate, international standards that touched on IoT. This includes everything from wireless and radio frequency identification (RFID) standards to localization standards to supply-chain standards and of course security standards. By legitimate, we mean from well-recognized, government-sanctioned standards groups like ISO or the International Telecommunications Union Telecommunication Standardization Sector (ITU-T) or top-tier industry groups like the 3rd Generation Partnership Project (3GPP) or the Institute of Electrical and Electronics Engineers (IEEE). However, none of these standards specifically addressed IoT requirements, architectures, or designs. That work is underway, with the first task being an attempt to extract what is useful and meaningful from these 500 + standards into an aggregated piece of guidance.[23]

Among the 500+ existing standards that touch on IoT in some way, there was precious little about security. Certainly, the IT security standards such as 27000 (IT Security) and others in the 18000 (crypto systems) and 20000 (testing and validation) series 29000 (privacy) contained useful guidance about information security generally. However, in all cases these standards are either generic in nature—focusing on applicability to any information systems—or industry-vertical specific without touching on IoT in a given vertical.

The well-regarded and widely used 27000 security standards, along with its main alternatives such as CoBIT or the NIST 800-53 series of standards, are about information security—enterprise IT information security and risk—not IoT security and risk.

This is where the threat comes into play: for lack of defined standards, risk managers may create their own IoT security standards that can later threaten the IoT system, services, and products they support.

Any internal standards developed to fill the standards vacuum are likely to present threats and therefore risks to any IoT provider of good or services that has launched into business. This is no one's specific fault, but the late arrival of IoT security standards will be a double-edged sword in some instances. Offering needed guidance and legitimacy on one hand, but also creating problems for the effort that came beforehand:

1. Existing IoT goods and services have security policies that are incompatible with the late-to-arrive international standards—requiring expensive retrofitting of services to bring previously developed processes and technologies into line with the official standards.
2. In the event of a legal dispute or accident, prestandard internal policies are considered by courts to be ad hoc and as good as having no security policy whatsoever; therefore internal policies may be rejected as proof of due care and indicators of operational diligence.
3. Auditors—internal or external—fail to recognize ad hoc/internal IoT security and privacy policies. When auditors do not understand a security or privacy policy because it uses a foreign (novel, unique) framework, then the costs of the audit will increase as they seek to *map* the internal standard to something they know and recognize and feel comfortable providing opinions about. These sorts of remedial auditing techniques can raise the resources consumed by audit to ruinous levels.

---

[23]See ISO/JTC1 Working Group 10—Internet of Things.

4. Internally developed IoT security and privacy policies become adored as a home grown and highly clever solution to the standards vacuum—and no one ever questions them or thinks to audit them, "because there is nothing to compare them to." There is no such thing as an ugly baby to a parent, and this approach is a real threat associated with internal policies. People fail to see the flaws in their own work.

5. Top management may simply distrust an internally developed IoT security and privacy policy for the four reasons stated above. Without management support, the IoT line of business or product line may find itself orphaned and without sufficient resources. Essentially, management may assess the risk of going into operations without operational security policies based on standards as too high!

OPERATIONAL AND PROCESS THREATS IN THE IoT

Operational threats, like operation requirements, should be derived from, and trace clearly up to, business threats and risk. This makes operational threats a subset of business threats, which is why this section comes after business threats.

Operational threats are no less important or secondary to business threats, they just might be more granular and specific in the type of impacts that may occur. However, all operational threats will have an effect at the business level. At least they should. If a threat does not affect risk at the business level…is it really a threat? Or at the very least, is it a threat of consequence worth managing? (Versus merely accepting the threat and resulting risk.[24])

> Many of the threats we will discuss in the following sections might appear under more than one heading. For the most part, our intent is to show the variety of operational IoT threats as a superset of threat in the IoT rather than try to pigeon-hole them indelibly with one form of operational requirements or another.

Additionally, in the following section, we will attempt to show that for every form of requirement in the IoT, there will always be some sort of corresponding threat that should be considered.

What is important for the risk manager is to understand *how strongly* a given operational threat traces back up to a business threat. The stronger the relationship between any operational threat and a business threat or threats, the more attention is warranted from the IoT system designers or risk managers.

Lastly, the threats listed here are not exhaustive! The range of threats against the possible range of IoT products and services is infinite. This list is a sampling of some of the more novel threats in the IoT. Understanding these threats will provide a useful platform for understanding the actual threats that specific IoT goods and services are likely to encounter.

Please consider these threats as demonstrative of the range that should be considered. It is up to the risk manager to identity the appropriate threats for the IoT product or system under consideration.

---

[24]Recall that there are always three options for managing risks: treat the risk; transfer the risk; accept the risk.

Table 12.9 Classes of Safety Threat

	Denial (Temporary)	Loss (Sustained)	Manipulation
View	DoV	LoV	MoV
Control	DoC	LoC	MoC
White	View is disrupted but not controlled. Disruption to reporting and operator awareness. Production and infrastructure risks primarily if the condition remains undetected or goes unaddressed for long periods.		
Gray	Control is disrupted. Impacts (temporary or sustained) on communication interface can result in erratic or *frozen* condition on the IP communications interface, but leaves the control interface otherwise stable and the logic intact. Risk varies widely with the process under control.		
Black	View and/or control cannot be recovered automatically or remotely. Sabotage potential through misinformation delivered to control room personnel, or through malicious instructions sent to production infrastructure. Risk is highest.		

SAFETY THREATS

Safety as a requirement is different from security because it highlights the cyber-physical /logical-kinetic interfaces in the IoT. Things can go "boom" and people can get hurt because of information and data events: soft events can have hard consequences. As discussed in Chapter 6, Safety Requirement in the Internet of Things, safety often considers issues related to the reliability and predictability of device performance, well past what a typical enterprise IT device would ever contemplate.

Safety threats are heavily intertwined with those of the other logical security (and even privacy) threats and do not typically stand alone.

The following are some examples of safety threats in the IoT.

Denial, loss, and manipulation of view and control[25]

Many IoT devices, including some industrial control devices such as programmable logic controllers (PLC)[26] and remote terminal units (RTU), are relatively simple devices. There are no *escalation of privilege* threats because there is usually only one level of privilege: administrator. This can pose a major safety threat in the case of IoT devices that monitor or manage a logical-kinetic/cyber-physical interface.

Threats might fall neatly but broadly into six alternative classes with identifiable but not absolute levels of severity: denial of view, loss of view, manipulation of view, and denial of control, loss of control, and manipulation of control. This is illustrated in Table 12.9.

Depending on the state of the IoT system or service under consideration, some or even all the six classes of threat may be present.

---

[25]Source: Tyson Macaulay and Bryan Singer; *Cyber Security for Industrial Control Systems*, 2011, http://www.amazon.ca/Cybersecurity-Industrial-Control-Systems-SCADA/dp/1439801967/ref=sr_1_2?s=books&ie=UTF8&qid=1444917519&sr=1-2.
[26]Programmable Logic Controllers (PLC) and Remote Terminal Units (RTU).

Denial of view (DoV) results from a temporary communication failure between an IoT endpoint device and its control source (cloud, mobile app, or what have you), where the interface recovers and become available once the interfering condition abates. For instance, a DOS attack directed at the endpoint rather than centralized cloud resources.

Under this condition, the control logic within the IoT device may continue to function if ever a DoV occurs. DoV can manifest operationally as a slowdown in production and generate cascading (but inappropriate) slowdowns in other parts of the production process or IoT service as a whole.

Loss of view (LoV) results from a sustained or permanent communication failure where the IoT device will require local, hands-on operator intervention; for instance, a restart.

Under this condition, the control logic within the IoT devices can continue to function if even a LoV occurs. Loss of view can appear as a slowdown or stoppage in service delivery.

Manipulation of view (MoV)—the threat of deliberately harmful commands sent to either the IoT devices or the service cloud, where misinformation (forged IoT data) is used to encourage inappropriate administrator response. In other words, IoT service owners or operators are tricked into doing something that is detrimental to the system or service.

MoV does not impact the functionality of the communications or the control interfaces. MoV can dupe operators into inappropriate control sequences that introduce defects and possibly catastrophic reactions within the production process. Enterprise reporting systems can also be provided with erroneous information providing inaccurate guidance to management.

Denial of control (DoC)—the threat of a temporary inability to control resulting from either communications or disruptions.DoC can be unintentional or intentional: unintentional DoC includes operator errors and omissions, hardware failures, or DoV conditions that have a negative, systemic impact on the IoT interface, such as network failures, gateway failures, or improper network capacity.

For instance, it is possible that an attack on an IoT device or gateway is directed specifically at flaws in the IP communications stack, causing the interface to fail or stop behaving according to its programming. Once the degradation or interference on the IP communications clears and the communications interface returns to normal, the IoT control resumes its programmed behaviors.

Intentional DoC can also result from a threat against the control interface that does not impact the communications elements or interfaces, but merely disables the input/output (I/O) control interface. Under such circumstances, it is possible that owners and service providers actually see how the IoT device may be engaging in erratic or unprogrammed behavior without any ability to control it.

Loss of control (LoC)—the threat of a sustained loss of control or a runaway condition in which operators cannot issue any commands even if the interference has receded. LoC can be unintentional or intentional: like DoC, unintentional LoC includes operator errors and omissions, hardware failures, or temporary DoV conditions that have a sustained, systemic impact on the IoT device interface or gateway.

For instance, it is possible that an attack on an IoT device is directed specifically at flaws in the IP communications software stack, causing the I/O interface permanently to fail or stop behaving according to its design. Intentional LoC can result from a threat against the control interface that does not impact the IP communications interface, but disables the I/O control interface, possibly allowing operators actually to see how the industrial control system (ICS) device engaging in erratic or unprogrammed behavior without any ability to control it. In LoC situations, control of the I/O interface can only be restored by local operator intervention such as a device or gateway restart.

Manipulation of control (MoC)—under this condition, the IoT devices can be reprogrammed by a third party and legitimate operator commands overridden. MoC does not impact the functionality of the network communications interface or the control interface.

MoC can override or intercept and change legitimate commands from device owners and service providers, and apply inappropriate command sequences that result in service degradation, defects, and possibly catastrophic reactions.

The failure modes described above are useful in analyzing previously known failures or ways in which ICS network or process failures could occur due to unknown ICS vulnerabilities. For example, by reviewing LoV or MoV opportunities in a system, safety and security analysts can assess how the potential for an inaccurate or manipulated view of the current system state could lead operators to take potentially harmful actions.

An example of such as practice are the follow-on actions associated with the 2005 BP Texas City Refinery Explosion in which there were a number of operator actions taken that exacerbated the catastrophic failure—actions that were based on LoV. A full case history is available at the US Chemical Safety Board (CSB)[27] and an excellent video from CSB is available on YouTube.[28] It is important to note that the Texas City incident was *not* an intentional event, but it has been used as a basis study by many security professionals as an example of how a targeted security attack could be launched. This basis analysis has been used in the development of a variety of threat models and attack scenarios against oil, gas, power, water, and critical manufacturing processes.

Commoditization and the race to the bottom

The IoT will be a boon to safety overall because of the ability to manage more devices, at greater distance, with greater fidelity and at lower cost. Fields such as transportation, manufacturing, and energy especially are expected to benefit. But this safety boon will also invoke a flood of *me too* competitors that will compete largely on price, and compel the most successful and popular IoT services to streamline their systems and process as quickly as possible or lose market share. Inevitability this will mean that IoT device prices will stratify: with different qualities of product and service available at different prices.

But from a safety perspective—how low do you really want to go? Consumers will frequently have modest if any abilities to assess the safety element of one IoT service provider or product from another. As we discussed, regulation and standards are not keeping up!

The rapid emergence of competition and commoditization of certain IoT devices and services will result in a threat in the IoT—a threat of performance lapses and degradation related to safety. It is mostly likely that the degradation will be gradual at first, with product and service quality being slowly whittled down to address competitive elements and probably because good *hygiene* in the early stages created good safety records.

Incremental reductions in quality may see safety compromised to the point that the risks are no longer acceptable, but at the same time they are imperceptible until a catastrophe has occurred.

---

[27]Chemical Safety Board—http://www.csb.gov.
[28]CSB Safety Video: Explosion at BP refinery—http://www.youtube.com/watch?v=c9JY3eT4cdM.

Wireless safety

The US Department of Transportation put it best in 2015: "To date, wireless communications systems tend not to support safety-critical functions; nor do safety-critical systems tend to be based upon wireless systems. As such, the approach to security of the communications data delivery system draws from industry best practices but also establishes new practices to meet the specific needs and requirements of a connected vehicle environment."[29]

Unlicensed wireless threats. Wireless communications systems like Wi-Fi in the publicly accessible radio spectrum will definitely be under siege and represent a very significant threat to the safety of IoT systems in the forms of *unreliable performance*. The reason for this is simple: anyone with any objective or motivation (including chaos as a motivation) can observe, intercept, and interfere with these radio signals with very cheap and widely available tools. Wireless as a whole will make safety-critical systems unreliable and subject to a variety of related threats around availability and confidentiality.

Wi-Fi systems are based in what is called the industry, science, and medicine (ISM) spectrum, such as 2.4 GHz and 5.2 GHz. These radio frequencies are used by many different applications, not just Wi-Fi radio systems, and incidental and accidental interference is rife. Microwave ovens operate in 2.4 GHz, and if the shielding on a microwave oven should fail over time (due to age) or due to defect, it can flood a wide area with interference that severely degrades Wi-Fi systems. Even a well-shielded microwave oven can interfere with Wi-Fi.

In the author's own house, the (modern, good quality) microwave oven in the kitchen is in between the TV room and the Wi-Fi access point—as a direct, straight-shot line. When someone uses the microwave, anyone in the TV room will see a dramatic drop the bandwidth available to their mobile device.

Other common devices that will be running in 2.4 or 5.2 GHz include senior citizen *safety brooches*, baby monitors, garage door openers, light switches, video cameras, wireless domestic phones, and just about anything else any IoT vendor decides to throw in there. The only limit is the broadcast strength, which by law (in most places) will limit the potential for interference to a one or two hundred meters' radius. But again, simple tweaks and off-the-shelf antennas system can greatly increase these capabilities to interfere with and intercept ISM signals.

Licensed wireless threats. The other form of wireless that will be widely used in the IoT is licensed wireless. This is radio to which frequencies are assigned to specific applications and licenses are provided to industrial users. Licenses will often be applied for given frequencies over a given geographic range. Examples of licensed frequencies and applications include broadcast television, public safety radio channels such as police and fire, and services like global positioning systems (GPS).

Devices that use licensed radio spectrum cannot be generally bought and activated by anyone for any reason—like ISM devices. They are only sold to entities that have licenses, and these entities will typically then resell devices that use this spectrum. Alternately, manufacturers that want to create devices that use licensed spectrum do so with a lot more oversight and control related to how the device behaves in the radio world.

Threats in the licensed radio spectrum arena are probably *reduced* from a safety perspective because there is typically better management of devices and therefore less danger of accidental or

---

[29]Ibid, VIVA report from DoT.

deliberate jamming and interference. Similarly, eavesdropping and monitoring is generally more difficult in the licensed spectrum because the equipment is less readily available—though any motivated threat agent can procure legal spectrum scanners, which have many legitimate purposes.

Many IoT systems are seeking to use 3G and 4G wireless for their endpoint devices or gateways, precisely because the connection is more reliable—reducing safety threats.

However, other threats that will occur in licensed versus unlicensed spectrum include:

- Resource exhaustion. Management of well-defined but finite licensed resources means that once they are exhausted, DOS conditions can apply.
- Inflexibility (a threat mentioned below) will be part of licensed wireless infrastructure. Because control and management is central to these system, they will frequently not have the same *demand-response capabilities* as unlicensed wireless, where new gateways might be deployed on demand.
- Allocation of resources—which would be a business threat in part—will prevent the licensed spectrum being used in the most efficient manner because it is a scarce and expensive resource. While one owner might have excess capacity and another a shortage, moving spectrum from one owner to another involves regulators and complex negotiations, which will stop licensed spectrum from meeting unexpected demands.

CONFIDENTIALITY AND INTEGRITY THREATS

Confidentiality and integrity are the granddaddies of security requirements, along with availability (to come next). What follows are some examples of threats against confidentiality and integrity that will be different or accented in the IoT, compared to what might be understood in an enterprise IT environment.

Confidentiality of clouds

The confidentiality of cloud-based (Internet-based, multitenanted) applications and data storage is a significant threat to the IoT security and risk management because so much of the IoT will be predicated upon cloud-based systems and storage technologies. Many of the financial risks we discussed earlier in this chapter could easily show themselves in their worst forms if the economies and efficiencies of cloud-based technologies were less accessible or were inappropriate to the IoT due to perceived or real confidentiality (including privacy) threats.

In late 2015, the European Court struck down the *Safe Harbor*[30] agreement between the United States and the European Union. Safe Harbor had allowed European personal information to be held in US-based data clouds, as long as the business managing the data *attested* that it was applying privacy safeguards comparable to the regulatory requirements from the countries' citizens. The fallout from the demise of Safe Harbor is still uncertain at this writing, but it essentially revolves around threats associated with privacy and by direct extension of confidentiality.[31] As of 2016, some tentative patches were applied to the Safe Harbor agreements—known as *Privacy Shield*,[32]

---

[30]http://export.gov/safeharbor/.
[31]See *Get off my Cloud*, Economist Magazine, Oct 10, 2015.
[32]https://www.commerce.gov/privacyshield.

but they are still considered to be insufficient by many parties and a temporary fix by most accounts. The discussion around Safe Harbor does not even address the IoT specifically, while the Privacy Shield agreement mentions IoT a total of twice in over 120 pages as a reference to other works from the US Federal Trade Commission.[33] This means that the novel requirements of the IoT (the basis of this book) are uncertain to be represented in the current solution to protecting personally identifiable information (PII) "in the clouds," making further disruptions and risks probably as the IoT comes into clear focus for privacy advocates.

While Safe Harbor was nominally about privacy of PII belonging to Europeans, it was widespread perceptions of confidentiality threats generally that killed it. Massive data leaks about the information operations of the US National Security Agency (NSA) brought the question of the confidentiality of *any* information based in the United States to the fore. Additionally, attempts by the US Federal Bureau of Investigation (FBI) to force the disclosure of data held by US companies in their clouds outside the United States further highlighted the threat associated with confidentiality in clouds.[34]

Confidentiality threats associated with cloud-based storage and applications is by no means limited to the United States. Countries like China, Russia, and Vietnam—to name a few—already have *native cloud* regulations in place that compel service providers of all types, including IoT service providers, to use cloud services based in-country, presumably to prevent other government agencies from compromising the confidentiality of their citizen and business data stores; but these same countries are known to be less than pure in their own respect for PII and corporate intellectual property.

The fate of cloud-based applications and services has never been more unstable, due to confidentiality concerns. Even if PII is the catalyst, confidentiality of clouds at a higher level is a major threat to the IoT.

Counterfeit goods

Counterfeiting is a form of integrity threat because the good or service is an illicit copy of the legitimate good or service; the good or service that is being provided merely appears to be legitimate, but in fact has been changed through counterfeiting and is not the same.

Counterfeiting valuable goods is a well understood and common crime, from watches to cheese to cars. But in the IoT it poses new forms of threat not only because of the cyber-physical interface but also interdependency effects associated with automation and the ability of legitimate manufacturers (counterfeiting victims) to act against counterfeiters.

Counterfeit goods can find their way into product processes, homes, and an IoT system or service even though the vendors and service providers are acting in good faith: supply change corruption—discussed next—can lead to this. For this reason, it is possible that an IoT user, or even distributor, of a counterfeit good many not be aware of the counterfeit!

First, there are automation threats associated with counterfeiting. Counterfeit goods are frequently associated with poor quality and performance, and therefore dangerous if the counterfeited good is for anything more than fashion. Counterfeit drugs, cell phones, cars, and just about

---

[33]See Privacy Shield agreement text https://www.commerce.gov/sites/commerce.gov/files/media/files/2016/eu_us_privacy_shield_full_text.pdf.pdf.
[34]See *Under my Thumb*, Economist Magazine, Oct 10, 2013.

anything else that has a trademark or brand are known to perform so badly that they not only result in lost revenue to the legitimate manufacture and damage the brand, but present physical dangers to the users. Counterfeit drugs may perform poorly, or not at all—being mere placebos. Counterfeit cars will have components that perform well below safety specifications of the original equipment manufacturer. Similarly, goods intended for the IoT are already being counterfeited and will certainly come with much poorer performance than expected by the users. Automation can see threats associated from counterfeits such as these:

- Interdependencies in the IoT can be expected to be understood poorly, and the impacts of counterfeit goods in complex IoT systems will present unlimited threats.
- Counterfeit goods with poor performance could trigger automated shutdowns or slowdowns in services. For instance, a subway control system with tight safety requirements detects an apparently faulty (counterfeited) sensor and closes a line for safety reasons pending an investigation.
- Counterfeit goods perform out of specification and corrupt information and date—resulting in inappropriate automated responses. For instance, the administration of inappropriate environmental conditions in a homes or offices, or unscheduled application of drugs to a patient.
- Counterfeit goods that simply don't work at all.

Counterfeit goods in the IoT will include IT-specific elements such as third-party software stacks, physical and logical network interfaces, various software toolkits, and even security software. Such counterfeit network and security inputs will pose clear threats to the IoT.

The double indemnity of counterfeiting in the IoT

A perhaps less-expected, second form of threat associated with counterfeit goods is the tactics that *victims* of counterfeiting take to deal with the business risks posed by counterfeit goods to their legitimate products. The actions from the victims might include blind or callous responses that threaten the IoT system or service.

A good example of victims of IoT counterfeiting striking back occurred in 2014 when a processing-chip manufacturer for industrial control systems discovered that its chips were being counterfeited.[35] The manufacturer knew that most of the systems using its chips where managed by Windows operating systems; so it contrived to ship a *security update* with a global Windows OS update through Microsoft. This update was entirely benign to the operating system and the hardware platforms (desktops, laptops, and so on); however, in the course of installation, it searched for peripherals (hardware attached to the computer) using counterfeited chips.

When the Windows OS update detected counterfeited chips, it updated the firmware in a manner that essentially destroyed the counterfeits, but left legitimate chips unharmed. The upshot was that (IoT) control systems around the world were being disabled. The control elements using the counterfeit chips would cease working and control could not be regained without replacing the part containing the counterfeit chip with a legitimate, licensed chip.

---

[35]http://arstechnica.com/information-technology/2014/10/windows-update-drivers-bricking-usb-serial-chips-beloved-of-hardware-hackers/.

The original victim of counterfeiting—the IoT product manufacturer—had become the threat to the IoT service! In an attempt to counter criminal activities against them, they essentially punished their customers, who had no clear way to know if any of the devices in their possession had counterfeit chips.[36,37]

Supply chain threats

Like counterfeiting, supply chain threats include changes in the IoT good or service resulting from illicit, illegal, or unknown activates by suppliers of inputs: parts and components (hardware and software). Detecting and avoiding infiltration of tainted or counterfeit parts is necessary to maintain the trust and integrity of the security architecture.

Illicit or deliberately tainted hardware and software will pose all sorts of threats to the logical security of the IoT and, by extension, the physical security of the system and services they control and deliver. For instance, poorly made components will be unreliable (affecting availability) but will also have the potential to allow backdoors and other forms of unauthorized access.

Supply chain threats will come from different forms of threat agent: from cheapskates (who substitute fake or suspiciously cheap components to save money) to nation states (seeking clandestine access or capabilities over the IoT goods or services). Sometimes the threat will be about a maker of an IoT good trying to cut costs and procuring from suspiciously cheap sources for a known good, and turning a blind eye to the provenance of the materials. At the other end of the spectrum will be national security entities with the power to compel local manufacturers to inject unwanted, undocumented features into goods or services.

In the World Economic Forum's (WEF) report on trade and economic development entitled *The Global Enabling Trade Report 2012*, the WEF sited four questions that must be addressed when understanding supply chain threats:

1. Does this product come from where I think it did?
2. Is it made the way I think it is?
3. Did it travel the way I think it did?
4. Is it going to do what I think it will?

Broadly, supply change threats can impact all forms of operational threat and requirement covered in this book: they can impact confidentiality when backdoors are coded into software, and they can impact availability when the IoT services become unreliable due to the poor quality of counterfeits or due to tampering with original parts. Supply chain threats can also affect environmental and contextual requirements, identity and access, and interoperability requirements—all through poor quality and unreliable or insecure performance. But in the end, this traces to a single *integrity* threat—so we are placing supply change risks in this section about integrity threats.

While security practitioners might debate where supply chain threats sit in this taxonomy, all would agree they are threats nonetheless.

---

[36]http://zeptobars.ru/en/read/FTDI-FT232RL-real-vs-fake-supereal.
[37]http://www.eevblog.com/forum/reviews/ftdi-driver-kills-fake-ftdi-ft232/375/.

Are supply chain threats really any different in the IoT than for the rest of conventional enterprise IT? We propose *yes* for a variety of the reasons and requirements previously cited, such as these:

- Many IoT devices are small and intended to be cheap, often targeting price-sensitive consumer industries. The pressure to reduce costs and look the other way will be widespread.
- IoT devices will often be un-patchable—supply chain issues related to security may be irreparable and devices must be decommissioned—unlike IT systems that might be repaired.
- The multileveled, specialized, and stratified nature of IoT service development we discussed in Chapter 2, The Anatomy of the Internet of Things, and Chapter 3, Requirements and Risk Management, will make supply chain management more complex, with more players and moving parts than before—and therefore the likelihood of a threat appearing could be significantly greater.

Data quality in the IoT

Remember the seminal lampoon about the Internet from *The New Yorker* back in the 1990s: "On the Internet, nobody knows you're a dog"? If we updated the cartoon the caption might read: "On the Internet, *nothing* knows you're a dog."

An emerging threat in the IoT is associated with the quality of data related to *things*, and how they are consumed by other things, and people.

The main threat is not that the data on or in the thing is corrupted itself. The threat is that the metadata sources on the Internet referenced by the thing are fouled in one way or another, and critical decisions are made by people or automated IoT-services based on bad data.

Barcodes have been around for 40 years and represent possibly the earliest, most successful example of creating *smart things*.[38] Barcodes lead retailers and consumers to a database of information describing much more about the product than what is necessarily on the label. Barcodes enable efficiency gains from inventory management to shipping to checkout.

A barcode is essentially a machine-readable number identifying a manufacturer and product. Barcode numbers and related metadata are managed by GS1 (www.gs1.org) on an international basis, which allocates the manufacturer prefix and registers the product ID suffix assigned by the manufacturer. GS1 then maintains the metadata associated with the barcoded number. Product metadata might include information related to ingredients, product bulletins, points of contact, and so on. GS1 also is developing a publicly accessible, online database of the metadata called GS1 source.[39]

A relative of the barcode is the trendy but unmanaged Quick Response (QR) code, which typically encodes text-based uniform resource locators (URL) for accessing more information.

There are many free, third-party barcode and QR scanning applications on the Internet, allowing people and automated systems to extend the IoT to goods through scanning barcodes and QRs. However, the methods and sources by which most of these third-party applications access product metadata are ad hoc, and therefore subject to question.

A data quality threat develops when IoT goods or services use barcodes and/or QR codes or other similar information locators, which lead to online repositories that contain erroneous or unreliable information from sources without good reputation and provenance. For instance, there is little to stop an

---

[38]See www.gs1.org.
[39]http://www.gs1.org/source.

unscrupulous device maker from redirecting users to online metadata that serves their interests versus providing reliable information to users.

Data quality threats are real the more we come to rely on the IoT to deliver useful decision-making information. Threats can involve a massive range of IoT services that require deliberate choices (what size do you need?), or the potential for negative physical reactions associated with inappropriate choices or combinations of inputs and ingredients (do you need a peanut-free, allergy-safe version of that cake?).

As a specific example, a user may make decisions about parking a car on a street, based on information provided from a car-based application. Perhaps the application was from a third party, versus the official app from the city or municipality—because the municipal parking app was dry, boring, and hard to use, versus the slick parking app from the third party (which contains advertising and generates revenue for the third party). The third party creates its own metadata from an information store that may be old or out of date or incomplete compared to the municipal application. In the end, the user's car is towed away because of bad metadata, and large fines and inconvenience (or worse) must be endured.

A more serious threat associated with bad data in the IoT will relate to physical changes triggered by the introduction of inappropriate input. For example, a parent buys a cake because a smartphone app tells him that there are no peanuts in the ingredients—but the app is from a third party, not the bakery, and allergic reactions occur.

Another example may be related to chemical or pharmacological reactions; where the proliferation of *smart* applications or tools all seek to make the life of engineers, pharmacists, and cooks easier by giving them recipes and possibly providing safety warnings at the appropriate times. But these smart apps many be linked through the Internet to sources managed by product vendors that are not authoritative.

Some of the threats in the IoT associated with product data quality and proliferating third-party applications include:

- Inappropriate summarization of product data to serve application-specific purposes—like memory consumption.
- Coding errors in *smart* things that parse product data incorrectly, and inadvertently change, truncate, or omit information.
- Applications designed to execute (complete the task) in lieu of sufficient information—rather than *fail safe*. ("Git 'er done!")
- Applications that link product codes to falsified information for competitive or fraudulent purposes.
- Vendors that use *captive portals* for their smart products as key elements of the business plan—selling advertising or for cross-selling strategies. Neither their business objective or core business competency is data quality.

Yet another threat associated with data quality in the IoT is that product metadata for *smart* things has already been shown to be a delivery vector for malware. We know QR codes are being employed to propagate malware on the Internet, and many third-party barcode-reader apps offer information that is clearly not from product manufacturers.[40]

So, who is in charge of monitoring or mitigating harm caused by third-party applications leveraging the growing wealth of barcode- and QR-supplied metadata in the IoT? No one. Buyer beware.

[40]http://helpdesk.gs1.org/ArticleDetails.aspx?GS1%20QR%20Code&id=ecd867a9-2372-e211-ad68-00155d644635.

AVAILABILITY AND RESILIENCY THREATS

User assumptions and abnormal conditions

This form of threat is unlike many of the other IoT threats discussed because it is primarily attributed to the end users and subscribers, rather than operations directly. Users will become increasingly reliant on IoT services for many things, but primarily under normal conditions. The threat and risks come when users expect the same service to function in the same way under abnormal conditions.

By example, it is an often-seen phenomenon that during emergency situations, cellular services collapse under the surge in demand. They are designed for a capacity during normal operations, not abnormal operations. Just because a service appears to be very stable on casual and short-term observation does not mean it will remain that way under all conditions, or will have the ability to recover itself after a significant impact.

Aside from certain critical infrastructures, most services that surround the average consumer are not designed for high availability and have finite service levels. The agreements that surround these services state as much. The prices charged for these services also reflect a best-effort service level that allows costs to match customer willingness to pay. IoT services will certainly be no different, at least in the early years of deployment.

The unfortunate part of this observation is that IoT service providers may in some cases knowingly (thought reluctantly) expose their customers to these threats for a variety of reasons such as:

- Keeping the operational costs of services lower by applying fewer security controls or lower service levels
- Keeping management costs low through less audit and oversight related to regulatory requirements and internal policies
- Improving profitability by selling data sets and analytics to advertisers, sponsors, partners, and whoever else sees value in the data.

Similarly, user and subscriber assumptions about the quality of all the other operational requirements like safety, confidentiality (and privacy), and integrity will present dire threats to users and subscribers to an IoT service. It's just that assumptions about availability under abnormal conditions could be the first to be exposed—because the range of what constitutes "abnormal" may actually turn out to be very broad under some IoT service definitions, and therefore result in a regular impact and experience for users.

> User assumptions about service levels under abnormal conditions are a significant threat to the IoT service provider, too, at the business level (See Competitive Risks), because dissatisfied customers leave. There is no better way to disappoint a customer than for a service to degrade or fail unexpectedly, when it is most wanted.

Interdependency

Interdependency refers to how the various independently managed and owned services in the IoT (see Chapter 3, Requirements and Risk Management) also rely on each other. IoT services are not standalone systems, they are collaborative, interdependent systems.

As the IoT becomes more and more prominent, interdependencies will have a major effect on availability and resiliency. We discuss this concept in detail in the final section of this chapter on flexibility and interoperability threats. Please keep reading!

These interdependency threats will be particularly acute in the area of IoT systems associated with critical infrastructures such as energy and transportation, where near-real-time requirements will be especially threatened.

> Perhaps the largest IoT threat around basic availability and reliability is the poverty of comprehension associated with interdependency and the scope and scale of the problem now, let alone in the future.

End of Life and vendor consolidation

Previously, in the section on IoT business threat related to *competition*, we discussed *vendor fatigue*: too many security product vendors and suppliers make choices complicated and fraught. The sheer number of suppliers of security products and services requires that many will not proposer and most will submit to being consumed by other bigger or healthier vendors either by design or for lack of sufficient success.

IoT goods and services will be developed and deployed with security from third parties, sometimes integrated deeply into services. A significant threat is that IoT goods and services outlive the integrated security, and end up as stranded or orphaned security capabilities. For instance, if an IoT device is sent to market with a deliberate dependency on cloud-based security signatures and threat intelligence from a third party, and the third party ceases operations or merges or merely upgrades an interface, then the in-field devices may no longer have access to the intelligence they need to maintain an acceptable security posture.

> Given that many IoT devices and services will not be readily upgradable, the threat of being stranded by legacy security partners and vendors is significant.

Consider even large and presumably reliable vendors such as Cisco, HP, and Intel: all have discontinued or sold off major security products in the last few years.[41] Typically, these products will be supported for up to three or sometimes even five years under the terms of End of Life (EOL) warranties to customers. But if an IoT device or service has an amortization period of 10 years or more, what happens then? Does it live the second half of its planned life with out-of-date, unsupported security?

Certainly the ability to retrofit IoT goods and services with new security is there; but the threat is that new costs blow a hole in the business plans and spawn a variety of business risks.

The more likely course of action when faced with EOL situations will be for IoT service providers to wait out the EOL support period before committing to painful updates, if they are even possible. Again, this represents a security threat because during EOL periods updates and support

---

[41]For instance, the Cisco MARS platform, HP Tipping Point, and the Intel Security Next Generation Firewall were all sold off in the course of restructuring and changing corporate strategies.

will diminish to bare-bones service levels. Patches will come slowly, if at all. In the security world, it is a cardinal sin for a vendor to delay patches for products—if the product is EOL, it has much less incentive to keep *zombie* products up to date: the vendor would rather you simply changed products.

Finally, what happens if a key security provider is acquired by a third party that itself is a threat to the IoT service? For instance, military supply chain management has strict requirements about the ownership and provenance of suppliers of goods and services. Components from some countries and vendors will be restricted or disallowed in the supply chain. Sometimes, goods and services that were formally allowed become non grata because the ownership of the business changes. A simple example of this is the sale of IBM's laptop business to Lenovo, a Chinese company. Many organizations almost immediately stopped buying the Lenovo laptops for corporate use, even though they appeared, and functioned, indistinguishably—but with a change in branding.

The availability and resiliency threat to the IoT is that components in the supply chain—while available on the same terms as before—become unusable because of the ownership. The ownership in question raises fears about threat agents such as state-sponsored or corporate espionage or sabotage.

Convergence threats

The IoT will enhance threats related to IP convergence, where a single technology (Internet technology) is the foundation for a range of critical services that are viewed as functionally distinct, and historically had standalone network platforms. For instance, telephone services based on analog plain old telephone service (POTS) are still in widespread use. The threat is that a failure of the foundation technology takes more than one, if not all, services out.

In the early 2000s *IP convergence* was a hot topic: this refers to the phenomena where three basic communication technologies were all moving toward a single service-delivery platform—IP. And the services would be delivered over the same infrastructure by the same service providers. This triple play of voice/phone, video/TV, and Internet was a potent combination that came with its own risks. But even at that time, other elements like industrial control systems were also migrating to IP-based networking, even if they were still largely air-gapped (physically separated) and most endpoints were still very much *dumb*.[42]

Basically, all the eggs were in the same basket, where before the three infrastructures were separate. A threat to one was seldom meaningful to the others. Voice was delivered over analog services on *twisted pair* copper lines. Video/TV was delivered over the air waves through public broadcasting, and over coaxial cable. And Internet was essentially an over-the-top service provided by small, mom-and-pop Internet service providers (ISPs), usually through dial-up analog modems that did not remain online for more than an hour and piggybacked on the POTS.

In the IoT, the convergence threat is that when the single IP network upon which all services rely fails, then many services fail at the same time—with unforeseen or unmanaged consequences.

Voice convergence

Many use cases and services in the IoT will utilize voice as a service interface for things like customer support and help desk. When you are in need of help, what is easier: typing or speaking?

---

[42]See Tyson Macaulay, *Managing Risks in Converged IP Networks*, 2006.

Voice services will remain a fundamental customer support and emergency management technology in the IoT.

Today voice is largely delivered over an IP-based solution known as Voice over IP (VoIP). Plenty of old, legacy infrastructure persists and will for many years—any voice features built into IoT services will invariably be VoIP, with few exceptions.

Voice telephony goes back well over 100 years and every living person has grown up with an experience of it. Conversely, every living person has certain expectations around voice telephony. Those expectations will differ but in aggregate they amount to something that *always* works (if and when you can get to a phone). In Europe and North America, the term "dial tone" is equated and comparable to terms like "heart beat" and "pulse." Many people just assume telephony service is available within steps, at most.

We should expect that many IoT devices will use VoIP as a means of supporting users, with a voice interface built directly into the car, fridge, health device, lamppost, and much more. Any place where some sort of man-machine interface is required, some sort of voice-based support interface (like an intercom) will be a consideration.

But in the context of the IoT, where devices and systems are built quickly and brought to market with cost efficiency in mind, oversights related to voice telephony are inevitable. And voice telephony in the IoT will always be about VoIP. In turn, VoIP will be delivered through a variety of network *layer 1* technologies like wireless, copper, and fiber. Already we are seeing the deployment of voice over wireless technologies such a VoIP over Long Term Evolution (LTE or 4 G), which is known as VoLTE.

The upshot it that IoT service delivery data and networking will be highly intermingled with voice technology, to the point that a threat to one is a threat to the other: when one is lost both are lost. That is a threat in and of itself, related to the availability and reliability not only of voice services, but of the entire IoT service delivery ecosystem.

IDENTITY AND ACCESS THREATS

With IoT devices pouring onto the Internet at the rate of thousands every day, poor or weak identity and access controls is a major threat to the IoT.

Identity and access (I&A) threats might apply at any service elements from end to end, but will probably be targeted largely at both ends of the IoT systems: at the more remote IoT devices, such as endpoints and gateways, which are physically remote and typically more susceptible to techniques such as man-in-the-middle and traffic manipulation, and at the clouds and DCs, which will often be the key to service delivery. Threats will need to be constantly managed around questions such as:

- Is the correct device trying to join the service?
- Does the correct device have appropriate access to the service catalog?

Why would endpoints and DCs be more targeted? Because all endpoints, no matter how constrained, will always need some I&A capability, even if the rest of their security and risk management is done elsewhere, at the gateway for instance. The ability to threaten the I&A of the endpoint devices may be the only and best way to attack them in some cases. In the case of the DCs, these are the repository and service-delivery points of the I&A systems and the attribute systems—in addition to many of the applications in the IoT.

Conversely, gateways and networks might rely on the I&A process to make decisions but could be less involved in the management and use of identity and credentials—mostly they will be responding to identities and attributes shared by endpoints. This is not to say that gateways will never be threatened with I&A attacks. Gateways may in some instances be performing some part of I&A on behalf of bootstrapping, endpoint devices. Additionally, gateways themselves will undergo I&A processes as they join networks and move about from network to network.

Scalability threats

Nonscalable I&A control management systems are a big threat to the IoT. I&A will be critical infrastructure in the IoT, and like most critical infrastructure it can be exhausted under both normal and especially under abnormal circumstances.

Scalability threats will be found in at least two different dimensions:

1. The size of the population under management by the I&A services,
2. The assurance requirements (how often will reauthentication be required?), which in turn drive the volumes of I&A requests.

Scaling to populations. If the I&A system cannot scale fast enough or far enough to satisfy a rapidly growing population, then I&A services will degrade rapidly. If I&A services degrade, then new devices will not be able to join in a timely manner, or enrolled devices may fail to operate normally.

As a given IoT system grows, it is possible that endpoint devices will be attempting to join the service thousands or more at a time. It is also possible to see how populations will grow thousands at a time, day after day, particularly in the consumer space where a *hit* IoT device might sell millions in a given day. Look no further than the Apple iPhone as an example of a hit device. But in the case of the iPhone, the devices were being managed by phone companies using tried and true, standardized I&A infrastructure. The IoT I&A infrastructure will not always be so robust.

Population scaling threats might also occur during a restart or at peak times or usage every day. Similarly, crisis events and abnormal circumstances will generate large peaks in demand will affect the assurance of the entire system, which itself might be an emergency management or safety system intended to jump into action specifically under abnormal conditions.

Scaling to assurance. If an I&A system cannot accommodate increased requests from a given device population, then assurance will degrade. For instance, devices may elect not only to authenticate to central services at system start, but perhaps for every transaction. Alternately, for communications in a local system (like a car), assurance may require that all *smart* components communicating internally authenticate each other on a bilateral basis—not just the central services.

Assurance scaling might occur during system reconfiguration and change, where trust requirements change and make more I&A operations necessary. For instance, scaling threats might be driven by regulatory (legal) or market (customer or competitive) requirements.

I&A interoperability

At this time, many IoT vendors support their own unique variations on device I&A processes. While most of these processes are based on well-known techniques and are generally sound, they often do not interoperate. I&A interoperability will present substantial threats to the IoT at an operational level that will transmit up to the business level immediately.

For instance, the strength of the IoT will lie in the ability to mix and match services and devices into new combinations. This is born from the stratified service layers in the IoT. But a lack of interoperability across and among the service layers is a major threat. Poor I&A interoperability will severely limit the ability of service providers to use the best and most appropriate solutions, because those solutions may require that new I&A processes be adopted, in addition to the legacy I&A process from other vendors supporting the service.

I&A will be multifaceted in the IoT—not delivered from a single authority. As discussed earlier, the IoT will be a stratified ecosystem of service providers: equipment makers, application providers, network providers, and so forth. At different levels, different service providers will require the same IoT devices potentially to go through different forms of I&A, according to the service they are delivering:

- There will be service providers that want to stipulate that a device is what it claims it is
- There will be service providers to identify that the device belongs to a given owner or subscriber or user
- There will be service providers to define that the device is enrolled in a given suite of services
- And other forms of stratified I&A may exist well, past these examples

Beyond this process of authentication there will be layers to the process of authorization, which may or may not be part of the authentication process—again, more interoperability issues. Thus, it is a given device (or its human users) approved or subscribed for a given feature associated with an IoT service—therefore authorized. In the cellular phone world, this is like having voice services alone, versus having voice and Internet services. The phone is the same for authentication purposes, but the authorization for service subscriptions is different.

I&A interoperability might fail across any of those relationships. Given that all of these services might be delivered by multiple service providers and vendors—the odds of a misfit or a partial fit are significant.

Possibly most dangerous to the IoT is a *near fit* related to critical support infrastructure like I&A, where interoperability is partial or made to work through ad hoc hacks and patches on the device or on the service side. Such hacks will inevitably find their way into production systems and will be threats in that their stability and reliability will be suspect in many ways—impacting the entire system because they are not properly integrated.

Multiparty authentication

In Chapter 9, Identity and Access Control Requirements in the IOT, we discussed multiparty authentication as an important requirement for the IoT. The threat associated with this requirement is that we implement it badly.

Multiparty systems allow many devices to, in essence, share secure access or authentications, but not necessarily share keys: there are a variety of known cryptographic techniques in this area that are emerging or being tweaked, having been developed decades ago. Many of these cryptographic techniques were for a long time solutions looking for problems. The IoT has arrived as the problem the cryptographic techniques were designed to solve.

There is no question that the IoT will require large groups of devices to trust each other and share keys widely, in order to secure communications and make sure that the processing overhead associated with the key management does not confound the system. (Processing might be too heavy for the endpoint device to manage efficiently or might require a degree of network traffic that consumes too much power or takes too long to accomplish.)

Poor implementation threats related to multiparty I&A will come from haphazard as well was ill-conceived notions about what is acceptable security—and will threaten the entire IoT service when the multiparty systems are breached.

How not to implement multiparty security. The following I&A implementation practices will pose major threats to the security of IoT devices, systems, and services as vendors and service providers look to *quick and dirty* ways to allow large numbers of devices to authentication quickly, and in some cases with the pretext of anonymity:

1. Shared keys (or passwords—which amount to the same thing) embedded or encoded into software and/or unprotected hardware platforms. This is a very common flaw found in all sorts of IoT devices today. Once one device is compromised in such multiparty systems all devices are compromised. These keys might be either symmetric or asymmetric, and one of a wide number of algorithms.
2. Home grown and proprietary multiparty I&A systems. It is well understood that if someone cannot or will not disclose how they are securing something, it is probably not secure at all. Similarly, it is easy to implement good cryptography badly, so *new* I&A (or security) systems for the IoT built of well-understood algorithms and cryptographic processes need due diligence.
3. Unsophisticated use of commodity I&A systems such as asymmetric (public key) systems that don't scale and eventually overwhelm the devices or the management platforms as they device population grows.
4. Heavily centralized and ephemeral (constantly changing) trust-broker models that rely on remote verification services, available through the network. For instance, two devices or elements in the IoT only need to speak occasionally or maybe just once, so they trust a third party to broker trust through the multiparty system. There are likely many critical points of failure: the gateways, the networks, and the trust-broker and services in the cloud or DC.

Bootstrapping, data quality, and I&A

I&A relies on data quality—as we previously discussed in the section on availability and integrity threats—and threats to I&A will come via the vector of poor, missing, changed, or illicit information in I&A systems.

I&A services will often be part of the most basic *bootstrapping* capabilities for many IoT devices. The ability to interfere with the I&A directory systems or metadata services that facilitate I&A and service definitions can stop services dead in their tracks.

> During bootstrapping, IoT devices and services face possibly the greatest operation threats because this is when they might be most vulnerable to hijacking, sabotage, or even accidental destruction.

Bootstrapping in the technology world refers to the ability to start up and get going using local resources: whatever is at hand, for instance, a network connection. It can also imply that a device has just enough functionality at time of manufacture to start and immediately call home, going through basic I&A and then receiving its full identity, operating system, instructions, and permissions.

If the data quality in the bootstrapping process is impacted because the central repositories change or even the bootstrapping configuration on the device is changed, then the entire initialization process can be corrupted. Corrupted bootstrapping can result in IoT devices and systems being misconfigured to the point of self-destruction.

In the case of some forms of constrained devices, they might have the ability to call home just once—at start, as the self-provision. If somehow the global directories they referred to for bootstrapping are intercepted, forced, substituted, or impacted by a man-in-the-middle (MITM) attack—they may be presently *stolen* or corrupted such that the ownership can never be recovered with physical intervention at the device level.

Alternately, in a threat related to theft of service, poor management of data quality associated with IoT I&A and bootstrapping could result in entire infrastructures suffering misconfiguration to the point that the owners lose control and illicit or criminal owners take control.

Anonymous technology failures

Anonymization technologies take vast troves of what would be personally identifiable information and cleanse it in such a way that it can be used for wide-ranging analytics without generating regulatory breaches around privacy; or, alienating subscribers and citizens. Cleansed data can then also be sold to third parties for their own idiosyncratic analytics and research.

In theory, anonymization technologies will be a core part of IoT operational processes and controls around big data, and they will enable many new forms of service delivery and yield rich insights into every field of industry from government to gambling.

However, to be clear, anonymization technologies do not have to be applied to all IoT data or big data generally. Many IoT data stores will be fully identifiable and traceable to a specific individual or device, as a necessity of service delivery. Today, major online service providers like Google and Facebook must maintain detailed logs and records identifiable to an individual or account in order for their revenue-related services to work. How else would they know how to target advertising, for instance?

Anonymization technologies come in many forms, use a variety of different processes, and also present couple of high-level operational threats to the IoT.

One threat is that the technologies don't work as they claim, either knowingly or unknowingly. The other threat is that anonymization is defeated and does not survive aggregation and correlation with other anonymized datasets.

Anonymization technology failures as threat

As we covered in Chapter 9, Identity and Access Control Requirements in the IOT, there are several if not many different ways to anonymize data sets. There is no consensus on which is best or what truly works. In most cases anonymization technologies might be dictated in part by the data set that the data scientists are trying to anonymize.

This choice will surely present a distinct threat if:

- The anonymization technology chosen proves to be intrinsically flawed. It does not really cleanse data set of PII and it is possible to reverse-engineer any associated data to specific individuals or devices.
- The wrong anonymization technique is applied to a given data set, or to the wrong portions of a data set, and PII or device-specific information remains visible.

Aggregation and correlation threats. Anonymization can sometimes be defeated by combining different data sets together, which is the second major threat to these forms of technology.

It is known among data scientists that the larger the data sets, the more difficult they can be to anonymize. There are many different ways to see patterns and link associated activities to specific devices. And once you can identify a specific device, it becomes much easier to then link that device to humans.

For risk managers in the IoT who are depending upon anonymization to preserve either regulatory compliance or perhaps to protect some form of intellectual property associated with device activities, beware of combining data sets.

While a given data set may protect identity of people and devices sufficiently through anonymization while it is standing alone, the same might not hold true when it is combined with another related data set.

For instance, government data sets might well be released into the research communities, after being anonymized. But the ability to merge to large data sets and apply powerful computing and analytics may result in specific individuals being identified by assessing distinct activities across the two data sets.

Attribute threats

Increasingly it will not be about who you are but what your attributes say about you. Unfortunately, we are not accustomed to managing attributes with the same diligence that we manage identities (of both people and devices).

Attributes are distinct from identities because they are much more dynamic and might be manipulated for many reasons by many different service providers. Attributes might also be managed across many different information sources and merely linked to identities; yet identity attributes will be critical to the provision of many IoT services.

Attributes will define many of the features of service in the IoT as they are delivered to specific individuals, devices, groups, regions, nationalities, and manufacturers, to name a few. For instance, ephemeral elements like age, health, wealth/credit, location, skills, and much more will be attributes that will enable/disable or qualify service delivery in the IoT. Are you old enough to buy that beer? Are you healthy enough to rent that scuba equipment? Are you and your credit card both in San Francisco right now? Is it normal for you to open the garage door in Toronto, while your smartphone is in Germany?

This is a threat in the IoT. Attackers always migrate to the weakest area and if it is easier and more profitable to attack attributes versus identities, then this is what will happen. For instance, rather than attack the identity databases and cryptographic systems used to protect identities, attack the separate systems that manage attributes.

Attributes associated with identities of both people and devices will be stored and managed all across the Internet. They will be managed by service providers (government, banks, retailers, health care providers, and so forth), and equipment and device vendors alike (smartphone app stores, car makers, home security firms, ISPs, industrial services, and on and on).

If a threat agent wanted to attack an individual or a device, attacking the attributes associated with that individual or device may be much easier than attacking the identity or the device itself.

Attribute threats might also come under the heading of *data quality*, which we discussed above. In fact, these types of threats are surely related to data quality.

Broadly, attributes might be attacked for at least two broad objectives:

- *To provide or enable inappropriate access to goods or services*. The provision of inappropriate access would drive things like theft of services, or perhaps enable access to goods or services for illicit activities. For instance, allowing minors to buy alcohol, or allowing an imposter to masquerade as a physician and prescribe medicines or procedures. Alternately, commands and controls to industrial systems might be allowed from locations or accounts from which they are not allowed, giving attackers the ability to attack identity directly through brute force guessing techniques that would not be possible if their attributes allowing network access for a given IP address had not been changed in the first place.
- *To deny access to goods or services*. In the case of adding, removing, or changing attributes to deny access, a whole range of threat scenarios becomes possible:
  - Engineers cannot control industrial systems because they are not allowed to connect or perhaps they can connect but not with administrate privileges.
  - Parents cannot pick up children from school because their relationship to their children has been removed from the students' attributes.
  - Unknown, cascading effects in automated systems, where a sudden and uncontrolled change will have unknowable effects as interdependent systems start to fail or react unpredictably to new or unexpected attributes associated with a given account, device, or system. (Much more discussion to come on interdependency threats and risks in Chapter 13, RIoT Control).

USAGE ENVIRONMENT AND CONTEXT THREATS

Normal versus abnormal conditions is the name of the game in managing IoT threats and risks.

In some cases, understanding the IoT environment and context in which you must operate is a regulatory requirement and therefore a business-level requirement. This section is about the broader operation issues associated with environmental and contextual threats.

For instance, at a business level, the Basel III Capital[43] accord expects that banks will provision their financial reserves for risks under abnormal banking conditions especially, not just normal conditions. The Basel III regulators calls these stress tests during audit, and look to assess the banks' resilience under financial crisis conditions. In 2008, a financial crisis brought on by the subprime mortgage crisis showed that many banks had under-provisioned for crises—even though they were perfectly stable under normal conditions. Similarly, in Europe during the Greek debt crisis of

---

[43]https://en.wikipedia.org/wiki/Basel_III.

2014[44], many of the banks that were lending to Greece appeared stable under normal conditions but failed under abnormal conditions (Greek default).

There is every reason to believe that as the rest of our economies and infrastructures become as interlinked and intertwined as the banking industry, regulation will similarly require that service providers take into account operational threats under abnormal conditions.

Partner appreciation threats

This is an oxymoron, and we know it.

As an IoT service provider, do you really, really know where you stand in the queue, under abnormal conditions, when the environment and context of your partnership is changed dramatically; when many other clients are asking for special attention, too?

The idea is that IoT service providers understand the *inbound* interdependencies from other IoT service providers and critical infrastructures and provision systems and service levels accordingly. An inbound interdependency essentially means a dependency: one way. What does the service provider need from the supplier?

The counterpart to and inbound dependency is an *outbound* dependency, which is what the supplier needs from the service provider reciprocally, when viewed from the service provider's perspective: looking outward, what do suppliers and customers expect from "me as a service provider." This might be as simple as payment for suppliers or fulfillment of service levels and the delivery of goods in the case of a customer.

Or interdependency might be a lot more complicated, such as a parochial dependency that is recognized by a different part of the organization. For instance, a medical industry might depend on municipal water to operate normally. And a water purification infrastructure might depend on a medical industry to test its sample and care for its staff. But the two might never actually understand how much they need each other until they are faced with an abnormal situation. This matter of critical infrastructure interdependency has been deeply explored in other materials.[45]

Here are a few issues associated with the threat of IoT partners not understanding interdependencies (inbound and outbound):

- Inbound threats—are you really a priority?
- Are suppliers providing the right service levels? If service levels change under abnormal conditions, are subscriber aware of this? Can they respond to changes in a meaningful manner?
- Do your customers accurately understand what they can expect from you in abnormal conditions, and how might this affect goodwill and potentially legal repercussions after the fact?

The metrics in Fig. 12.2 were generated by asking executives from over 120 North American organizations (public and private) within critical infrastructure (CI) industries to rate (from 1 to 10) the criticality of their communications and data flows[46] with other CI sectors.[47] Interviews were framed as

---

[44]See *In Depth—the Greek Crisis*, TheEconomist, http://www.economist.com/greekcrisis.

[45]See Tyson Macaulay, *Critical Infrastructure Security*, 2008.

[46]A *data-flow* was characterized as any form of communication traversing the core data networks maintained by telecommunications service providers. This would normally include just about all interindustry communications: voice calls, faxes, emails, EDI transactions, multimedia, remote command and control, and so on.

[47]Tyson Macaulay, *Critical Infrastructure: Interdependencies, Threat, Vulnerabilities and Risks*, Auherbach Publishing, 2008.

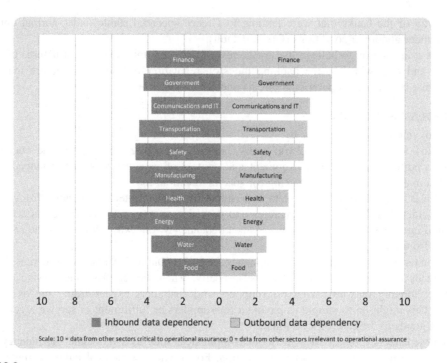

FIGURE 12.2

Data dependency score among critical infrastructure sectors.

normal operating conditions and consisted of three distinct questions about the assurance requirements related to confidentiality, integrity, and availability of information and data. These assurance requirements are averaged resulting in the *data dependency* of a given CI upon another sector. According to Standard and Poor's, qualitative executive metrics of this sort are critical to assessing operational risks[48], and provide perspectives which are not available through quantitative analysis.

Inbound refers to how the financial sector executives rate the assurance requirement of the information and data they consume from other CI players. *Outbound* refers to how other CI players rate the assurance requirements of the information and data being supplied by financial sector industries.

Fig. 12.2 shows that information and data dependencies are often out of balance between inbound and outbound requirements—generating a threat to the sectors that have such imbalances. For instance, the finance sector has the highest overall median level of outbound dependency placed upon it by other CI sector industries. Government is the next highest rated due to regulation and the delivery of social services, followed by communications and IT and transportation. Conversely, finance, government and communications and IT place significantly lower median inbound dependency requirements on the information and data they consume from other CI players.

---

[48]Standard and Poor's, *S&P Completes Initial "PIM" Risk Management Review For Selected U.S. Energy Firms,* McGraw-Hill, May 29, 2007.

Fig. 12.2 frequently represents a break from intuition for risk managers and policy makers, who may consider that energy and communications and IT and perhaps transportation are the most vital of the CIs. For the finance sector, this represents a potential risk, because government is ultimately responsible for coordinating emergency management and therefore large-scale recovery plans. To the extent that government does not understand the assurance requirements placed upon finance by the other CI sectors, they may under-resource resiliency and response to the finance sector.

Emergency condition service-floor threat

When establishing service-level guarantees, rate limits related to messages and service levels should take into account emergency conditions. One of the hallmarks of cellular service failing since the introduction of the technology is saturation and failure under emergency conditions, not usually because the infrastructure is damaged, but because demand floods the system and makes it unstable for all uses.

In the case of the IoT, network infrastructure under extreme load may cut off IoT devices from communications, even though they are using modest bandwidth. For instance, thousands of people in a cellular zone all try to make calls at the same time due to an explosion. As a result, these *personal* calls consume all available bandwidth, and infrastructure IoT (transport, water, energy) loses access to the small part of the network to which they normally require intermittent access, thus depriving infrastructure managers the ability to control them during these abnormal, emergency conditions.

A further threat under emergency or abnormal conditions is that IoT devices will exhaust their power reserves in attempts to communicate back to the home infrastructure. This may happen in the case of an energy management or traffic metering system that is running on power scavenged from the environment—like solar. It may try to report back the regular hourly logs but finds the network jammed and continues to poll until it exhausts its own battery to the point that it must enter a *limp* mode where data is lost until a charge is restored.

INTEROPERABILITY AND FLEXIBILITY THREATS

The first thing to know about interoperability threats in the IoT is that vendors of IoT goods and services consider this to be the biggest challenge and threat to the IoT. But that is a vendor perspective.

From the perspective of a user or consumer of the IoT, interoperability is merely assumed. Interoperability is someone else's problem, usually the provider of the goods or services.

What IoT users and service subscribers do *not* assume is security. They doubt the security and safety of the IoT.[49] And that is the main driver behind this book: management of the threats and risks in the IoT.

To an IoT risk manager or designer, interoperability and flexibility risks will go far beyond *simple* technical interoperability and will embody a variety of threats that might not be obvious at the outset. Here we focus on threats that are related to interoperability that—like users and subscribers in the IoT—assume the interoperability is already in place or will be in place shortly.

---

[49]There are many sources that have documented this position in detail. For a recent example see—*The CEO's Guide to Security the Internet of Things*, AT&T, March 2016.

The vendor side of things

Before jumping to a discussion of interoperability threats that assume technical interoperability, it is best to at least review the vendor-side of this concern. At least in short form.

Interoperability and flexibility are related concerns to vendors, including service vendors or service providers, because of what *poor* interoperability or a *lack* of interoperability means to them. Specifically:

- *Vendor lock-in threats*: a lack of interoperability means that service providers (or device vendors through their supply chain) must settle on a single IoT device or software provider and stick with it. For better or for worse. This brings with it several distinct threats to IoT vendors:
  - Higher unit costs: being locked into a vendor feels not unlike being subject to monopoly or a cartel. Competition to drive prices down does not effectively exist, and costs remain high or even get higher over time, rather than dropping through competition.
  - Lower innovation: being stuck with a single supplier or vendor because interoperability does not allow for substitution means that innovation will suffer for lack of different sources. A single vendor will only innovate according to its own objectives and strategies, and service providers will have to accommodate what that innovation looks like, even if it is too slow or perhaps in the wrong direction.
  - Huge migration challenges: worst of all threats related to interoperability is the pain of trying to migrate away from the incumbent. Giant cost and time overruns, data corruption and loss, and impacts to personal careers are all common outcome of attempts to leave a locked-in service platform. Migration threats exist in all classes of enterprise software and even on the *open*" Internet, where cloud service providers have made an art of lock-in.
- *Product functionality and stability threats:*
  - Multivendor solutions revert to the lowest common denominator in functions. If two vendors are selected to supply an IoT services, and each support a wide but different range of features, then only the overlapping features will be available for offer across the subscriber base. Without interoperability, a single vendor solution would probably give more options.
  - Increased errors and defects will increase as different vendors' solutions with slightly different implementation of protocols and APIs will fail to work together. Typically, such differences are undocumented and essentially unknowable until the devices are placed together in a lab and exposed to laborious testing. More usually, the services fail in operations and the interoperability issues must be resolved while customers wait and fume.
  - Inability to innovate quickly is a hallmark of multivendor solutions with limited interoperability and flexibility. Simply: it requires two competing vendors to upgrade and implement new features to get a single service upgrade for the IoT service provider and customers. Bugs and other delays in new service introduction will usually result in blame and finger pointing among vendors, rather than near-term and quick fixes.
- *Operations costs:*
  - Higher operating costs through complexity of solutions. At the best of times, multivendor solutions increase operating costs because of the need to train staff, support unique processes and procedures, track different vendors' updates and patches, and pay more for support. Noninteroperable, multivendor solutions only makes these matter worse!

- Poor security through uneven security upgrades and difficulty in monitoring announcements from different vendors. Even if patches are available in a timely manner, it is a reasonable assumption that they will occur more frequently the more vendors are in the mix, and downtime will increase.

From a vendor perspective, the ultimate risks associated with interoperability are traceable to business-level risks, especially customer satisfaction and how it might be negatively affected in so many ways as a result of interoperability threats.

Personalization and service complexity threats

Personalization involves creating an IoT service experience or profile that is tailored to an individual. This makes the service more usable and improves customer satisfaction.

In order to have personalization, IoT systems need a degree of flexibility in their design. So, a threat to IoT at an operational level is an inflexible design that limits personalization.

Conversely, too much flexibility in a design—nominally to support personalization—can raise costs and complexity (see next discussion) and introduce the threat of service failure all by itself. Therefore, personalization as a feature of the IoT will be a careful balance that will involve many different design stakeholders.

A good example of such a threat can be taken directly from the security world. As broadband wireless services became more widely available, demands to introduce controls to the content going to different types of mobile subscribers grew. For instance, parental and corporate content-controls for devices held by minors or perhaps employees using corporate devices. Mobile devices today have as much bandwidth available to them as most homes, and therefore have few if any real limits on the type of content that can be accessed.

The requirements for these parental or content controls that were sent to potential vendors through RFPs involved significant amounts of personalization. These requirements for broadband wireless content control foresaw personalization down to the device level, meaning that policies could be set for each child in a given family, or employee in a given company.

The complexity introduced by this highly granular form of personalization resulted in project failure in several cases.[50]

Aggregation of personalization threats. Several times so far in this chapter we have mentioned the potential of aggregating or combining data sources that are supposed to be anonymous or benign in the detail about individuals—but through the power of big-data analytics—resulting in detailed profile and personally identifiable data sets.

The threat in this case is that users provide incrementally more data than they should in the name of personalization. The result is that anonymity is threatened. Or, far more personal profile information is actually made available without knowing it.

For instance, perhaps an IoT adds a personalization feature that allow the user to change the color of the interface (skin). This may be a trivial thing to most people and of small importance to their experience; however, in the course of personalizing the application skin, it provide a salient

---

[50]The authors witnessed at least three RFP processes related to device security personalization and none of them reached deployment. But somewhere in the world it might have been made to work: we just don't know where!

clue to the user's preferences at large. When correlated and combined with massive data sets from other IoT services, that simple, incremental personalization feature might tip that balance that allows personally identifiable information to be captured.

Emergent behavior threats

An emergent behavior is something that is a nonobvious side effect of bringing together a new combination of capabilities—whether related to goods or services. Emergent behaviors can be either beneficial, benign, or potentially harmful, but in all cases they are very difficult to foresee until they manifest themselves. Emergent behaviors are also sometimes considered to be systems that are more complex than the sum of their parts.

An emergent behavior is essentially new, and generated by the combination of two or more different things—none of which displayed the behavior individually. An example of emergent behavior can be found in the insect world, where colonies of simple creatures like ants or termites will form together spontaneously to build very complex structures such as underground colonies or mounds that reach meters into the air, including elaborate cooling ducts and heat-dispersing fins.

Emergent behaviors are also often found in complex systems, both natural (biological) and man-made. For instance, an emergent behavior in nature might arise from the cross-breeding of a species of animal or plant. Suddenly, something new is present in the hybrid that was not present in either of the parents or genetic contributors.

In a man-made system such as software, networks, or the IoT, an emergent behavior might be related to the new creation of an interface, or perhaps the combination of traffic from different services onto a common network. The results of such combinations might be very difficult to assess, because the behavior is not predictable based on the known behaviors of the source systems.

An example of an emergent behavior could be in a home, for instance. Imagine that a number of IoT services are coexisting inside a home network and functioning normally. Then, the home-owner adds a new service from a new service provider, perhaps a new car? The car starts to use the home Wi-Fi network for customer service applications. But within minutes of the car (sitting in the garage) being configured into the home network, the car starts to show errors on the user interface. At the same time, the controls for the home security system stop working. Both failures may be related to an emergent behavior associated with the new combination of the IoT services sharing the same in-home infrastructure.

In this hypothetical example, the reason behind this might be that the home security system does routine polling of its sensors that are broadcast through the network. This polling has never *bothered* any other IoT device on the network before. But the new car in the garage is different: it sees the polls and interprets them as some sort of internal polling system for the car-management system—but on the wrong interface. The car therefore throws up an error—but also sends an error response to the home security system—which does not recognize the response and itself goes into an error state.

Because both the home security system vendor and the car vendor never attempted to test against each other, the emergent behavior was not previously known or observed.

In the IoT, with a potentially enormous range of vendors and service providers, it will be impossible to test every potential combination of IoT good and service for emergent behaviors. Many threats and vulnerabilities are bound to exist, and be largely unpredictable.

IoT systems, Chaos theory, and interdependency. Without much of any doubt, IoT interdependencies show hallmarks of being a form of *nonlinear* or *chaotic* system, making risk management in the IoT all that much more difficult.[51] In fact, further to our previous point about emergent behaviors: they are most common in systems that show a lot of entropy or disorder, which in turns drives them toward chaotic characteristics.[52]

Nonlinear or chaotic systems have a long and deep academic and mathematical pedigree going back to the early 1900s when mathematicians studying the movement of planets discovered that— very simply put—minute influences (what might be considered rounding errors) on the inputs into equations can result in dramatically different and even totally opposite outcomes. Fig. 12.3 is a graphic example of a chaotic equation, with a 10^{-5} difference in starting coordinate between blue and yellow (also known as the Lorenz attractor). Now imagine an IoT system that might change its operational profile and threats, based on apparently small changes in inputs from component suppliers of goods and services.

Chaos theory is where the famous *butterfly* effect comes from; under nonlinearity theory, a butterfly flapping its wings in Brazil can generate a tornado in Texas in two years: minute changes in inputs can have dramatic results. The relationships become so complex that they are in effect impossible to calculate and the application of quantitative attempts to measure and predict are futile.

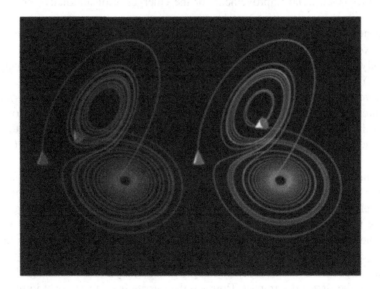

FIGURE 12.3

Chaotic equation represented as an image—the Lorenz Atractor.[53]

---

[51]Tyson Macaulay, *Critical Infrastructure: Interdependencies, Threats and Risks*, 2008.
[52]See Science 2.0, http://www.science20.com/welcome_my_moon_base/emergent_behavior_thriving_edge_chaos.
[53]"The Lorenz attractor displays chaotic behavior. These two plots demonstrate sensitive dependence on initial conditions within the region of phase space occupied by the attractor." —See https://en.wikipedia.org/wiki/Chaos_theory.

In the IoT, the equivalent might be trying comprehensively to manage risks, in systems that are frequently changing. Each change can have gigantic effects on operating conditions. Basically, the threat is that the systems are not manageable to the degree we believe.

But we still try, even though some of the greatest thinkers in the area of nonlinearity like Henri Poincaré ultimately came to the conclusion that discussions related to nonlinear systems can only be undertaken with *qualitative* measures.[54]

Weather is a nonlinear system yet we still try to forecast it; if IoT risk management reaches the level of weather forecasting accuracy obtained by weather forecasting, we might be doing well!

Interdependency in complex systems like the IoT. Interdependency may best be understood in the context of *dependency*: to be partially or entirely reliant upon another for some good or service. In the IoT with its stratified supply chain, specialized products and services and its dynamically evolving ecosystem of input substitutions, there is *lots* of interdependency.

Young children are dependent on parents, cars are (mostly still) dependent on gasoline, businesses are dependent upon customers. Interdependency is a bidirectional, two-way version of dependency with degrees of intensity: both parties are partially or entirely reliant upon each other. For instance, car manufacturers and customers are dependent on energy companies to create high quality fuels that do not foul engines, and also to have reliable distribution systems (gas stations). Energy companies in turn are highly dependent on those same cars and customer buying fuels and are affected by efficiencies and improvements or the emergence of alternative energy sources like electricity.

Interdependency is not necessarily a matter of equality, it is possible that between two interdependent parties, one is more dependent than another. (In fact, a core purpose of this book is to try toexpose not only interdependencies but the different degrees of dependency among critical infrastructure sectors.)

Cascading interdependency: first order, second order, tertiary. In the complex systems like critical infrastructures and the IoT, interdependency does not stop after one bidirectional relationship between two parties. The complexity of interdependency and the chaotic nature of the critical infrastructures and the IoT lie in the cascading relationships: A affects B, B affects C, C affects D, and so on.

First-order impacts are *direct* effects of an incident upon the entity, such as an IoT good or service. Whether this be a physical (fire, flood, earthquake, labor action) or a logical (data loss, software bugs, network failures). An impact could be a fire in a networking facility supplying physical connectivity to an IoT system, or it might be a server failure relied upon by the service in a distant cloud. The first order impact is the catalyst that sets events in motion. This brings us to the second-order impacts, driving further threat in an IoT system.

Second-order impacts are the meat of interdependency analysis; they reflect what happens as a cascading result of the first-order impact. How are the threats from the impact in the first system or device conducted outward into the user base or the supply chain? Just because a specific IoT services did not directly suffer a fire or a cloud failure does not preclude it from being indirectly impacted.

---

[54]See Nassim Nicholas Taleb, *The Black Swan: The impact of the highly improbable*, Random House 2007, 178–179 and http://en.wikipedia.org/w/index.php?title=Henri_Poincar%C3%A9&oldid=153446742.

Furthermore, second-order impacts are likely to arrive in the form of a completely distinct threat (and risk) from the original first-order impact. A first-order impact may be a fire in system A, resulting in a stoppage of services flowing to system B, which in turn requires that production of goods slow or stop in system B.

A tertiary impact is basically a third *echoing* threat resulting from the secondary impact on a given IoT system. It is the threat or impact that will be transmitted out of the second IoT system and into a third system because of the impact in the first system. Or, a tertiary impact might be reflected back to the first system, where an interdependency relationship generates a feedback loop—making the situation for the first IoT systems worse, because new threats manifest as a result of the original.

Where second-order impacts are difficult to identify and assess, tertiary threats are insidious to define and assess because there is an attenuation effect that must be accounted for.

Understanding cascading impacts is a challenge addressed by a different book from the authors.[55]

CONCLUSION

In this chapter, we have attempted to discuss threats novel or different in the IoT in their various forms: threat actors and threat incidents or events. What we have not succeeded in doing in this chapter is defining all the potential novel threats in the IoT. That would be impossible if for no other reason than the way we have finished off this chapter—with a discussion of emergent behaviors and chaotic systems.

Threat actors tend to be defined by characteristics that inform a risk manager about who might want to do what to their IoT system of service. Usually, threat actors will be represented by four key characteristics:

- Threat skills
- Threat motivation
- Threat resources
- Access

Among threat actors, there is also a useful *traditional* taxonomy that is differentiated by the four characteristics mentioned above. As a result, different actors may pose differ risk to different IoT systems; again, something for the risk manager to determine. In quick succession, the typical threat agents in an IT system or on the contemporary Internet are:

- Criminals
- Hacktivists
- Industrial spies
- Nation states
- Terrorists
- Insiders

---

[55]Tyson Macaulay, Critical Infrastructure: Interdependencies, Threats and Risks, 2008.

Additionally, we propose that the IoT is seeing the advent of new forms of threat actors, as a direct result of the complexity and fragility of IoT systems and services:

- Chaotic actors—they just want to watch things burn, for no clear reason other than they can.
- Regulators—ham-fisted laws and regulations related to both the resources and industries the IoT is expected to rely on most; such as wireless spectrum and the Internet.

The bulk of this chapter was spent consumed by discussions around high-level business threats to the IoT and lower-level operational threats to the IoT. This was not an exhaustive list, and at the same time intended to focus on IoT-specific threats or threats that have a specific flavor in the IoT. This was not an attempt to discuss enterprise IT threats and IoT threat at the same time. Enterprise IT threats at the business and operational levels have been discussed elsewhere many times, including within international standards.

RIoT CONTROL

This chapter is not about *all* risks in the IoT. Rather, it focuses on just what is different about risk management in the IoT, and what has changed in the IoT.

Vulnerability and risk are presented together in this final chapter of the book, continuing the organization from previous chapters associated with requirements. Typically, vulnerability and risk are considered separately, because a risk will be about the probability and likelihood that a vulnerability will be exploited, and the resulting severity of the impact. But because we are dealing with a superset of vulnerabilities that might be novel to the IoT, risk is very difficult to distinguish from vulnerability at a generic level. So we will discuss vulnerability and risk in the same breath and rely on the risk management professional, engineer, manager, or executive to make inferences based on this information about their own IoT system or service.

Therefore the relationship between risk and vulnerability is immutable. We can draw the following conclusions:

- A given vulnerability may face many threats from many angles. We covered threats in the last chapter.
- For each combination of vulnerability plus threat you have a likelihood that an negative effect (and impact) will occur.
    Furthermore:
- For each combination of vulnerability plus threat you have a severity associated with the effect (impact).

Risk is the single outcome of the vulnerability plus threat in terms of the likelihood times the severity.

Although this chapter may appear extensive, it is not an exhaustive list of legitimate ways of managing IoT risk. There is an almost infinite number of ways to manage IoT risks. This chapter represents a broad sample of different means and insights into some of the evolving technologies that will offer new risk management opportunities and solutions.

In a sense, this final chapter is a broad-based risk assessment for the IoT. Risk is essentially about probability and impact, assessed on the basis of vulnerabilities versus requirements, as illustrated in Fig. 13.1.

The actual risk associated with any given business or operational requirement and vulnerability will differ from IoT use case to use case, system to system, and even device to device. So we will not attempt to stipulate that one risk is larger than the others in this chapter. However, all risks in this chapter should be considered worthy of investigation in the context of whatever IoT system is under development (or in operation).

RIoT Control. DOI: http://dx.doi.org/10.1016/B978-0-12-419971-2.00013-3

High probability	4	7	9
Medium probability	2	5	8
Low probability	1	3	6
	Low impact	Medium impact	High impact

FIGURE 13.1

Risk as seen in terms of probability versus impact.

MANAGING BUSINESS AND ORGANIZATIONAL RISK IN THE IoT

Risk management in the IoT benefits substantially from coordination or even collaboration among the various service providers at the different asset classes (end points, gateways, networks, and clouds or data centers (DCs). This cannot be accomplished by a single solution provider or even a nation state, due to the scope, scale, and supply chain of the evolving IoT. Integrated security for the IoT extends outside the enterprise's domain of control. Enterprise information technology (IT) security is different because it can do security add-ons and standalone solutions because it is a single domain.

THE IoT DESIGN PROCESS

This requirement for a higher degree of collaboration means that the proper design process for the IoT must be more formal than in enterprise IT because the stakes are often higher (due to cyber-physical interfaces), and the trust models are more in depth. For instance, in enterprise IT design, many of the elements and asset classes in IT, such as the gateway and network, are simply unintelligent and not trusted. In the IoT design, elements like the gateways and networks take on a new urgency because they can become critical control points.

An essential part of managing risks in the IoT will be how designs evolve and how they are developed. One good example is the use of different layers of design that have different management objectives, as shown in Fig. 13.2.

Conceptual model[1]

The primary objective of a conceptual model is to convey the fundamental principles and basic functionality of the system it represents. This helps people know, understand, or simulate a subject the model represents. The model should provide an easily understood system interpretation for the model users.

[1] Proceedings from ISO Working Group 10, Ottawa meeting Aug 2015—submission from US expert Howard Choe.

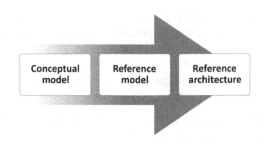

FIGURE 13.2

Layers for IoT design.

Metrics for a properly implemented conceptual model are commonly considered:

- *Comprehensibility*: How well did it help to enhance an individual's understanding of the representative system?
- *Knowledge transferability*: How well did it facilitate efficient conveyance of system details among stakeholders?
- *Common point of departure*: Did it effectively and efficiently provide a point of reference for system designers to extract system specifications?
- *Referenceability*: Did it provide an effective method to document the system for future reference and provide a means for collaboration?

So what exactly is a conceptual model? It provides a high-level, overarching perspective. It is a model made of the composition of *concepts*: a collection of abstractions, assumptions, and descriptions of physical processes representing the behavior of the reality of interest from which mathematical models or validation experiments can be constructed. It is a representation of concepts (entities) and relationships among them. It is explicitly chosen to be independent of design or implementation concerns.

How is a conceptual model used? It forms the basis for discussing the characteristics, uses, behavior, interfaces, requirements, and standards. The conceptual model serves as a tool for identifying actors and possible communications paths and for describing, discussing, and developing the architecture. It serves as a useful way for identifying potential intra- and interdomain interactions and potential applications and capabilities enabled by these interactions. It provides a context for analysis of interoperation and standards. Finally, it forms a stable basis for subsequent development of applications in the domain once the domain concepts have been modeled.

In the context of an IoT system, a conceptual model might outline the different forms of supplier and service provider that will compose the system from end to end. This will allow certain assumptions about security, privacy, and risk management to be validated early on. For instance, what degree of supply chain or networking routing risks might the system contain? Or, will geolocation of data be a regulatory issue to be accounted for?

Reference model

Below a conceptual model, the next level of detail would be a reference model for the IoT system or service under development. The purpose of a reference model is to promote the understanding of a class of problems (not specific solutions for those problems). The reference model aids the process of imagining and evaluating a variety of potential solutions in order to assist the practitioner, clarifies "things within an environment" or a problem space, clearly describes the problem that it solves and the concerns of the stakeholders who need to see the problem get solved, and provides common semantics that can be used unambiguously across and among different implementations.

Metrics of a properly implemented reference model are:

- *Standard applicability*: How effective was it to create standards for both the objects that inhabit the model and their relationships to one another?
- *Teachability*: How effective has it been to educate a wide range of population, both the technical and the nontechnical?
- *Communication*: How well did it improve communication among people compared to the case where no reference model is used?
- *Assignability*: Did it effectively help to create clear roles and responsibilities?
- *Trade-off Capability*: Did it provide effective ways to allow the comparison of different things?

In the context of an IoT system, a reference model might display the placement of security and privacy functions in an end-to-end system, without attempting to stipulate any configurations or especially vendor solutions. A reference model should start to reflect the operational requirements that have been defined through the inclusion of specific control elements or process interfaces (like a data repository). Reference models would aid in the discreet definition, placement, and specification of technical requirements, and support the selection of providers of goods and services in the IoT system.

Reference architecture

The primary purpose of a reference architecture is to guide and constrain the instantiations of solution architectures. The knowledge, patterns, and best practices gained from those implementations are incorporated into the reference architecture. The reference architecture also describes the major foundational components such as architecture building blocks for an end-to-end solution architecture.

Metrics of a properly implemented reference architecture are:

- *Evolutionary*: How easy was it continually to revise to include new insights?
- *Reusability*: How well did it help your organization in accelerating delivery of solution architectures through the reuse of an effective solution?
- *Governance*: Did it effectively promote the governance to ensure the consistency and applicability of technology use within an organization?
- *Repeatability and consistency*: Was it really effective and detailed architectural information in a common format such that solutions can be repeatedly designed and deployed in a consistent, high-quality, supportable fashion?

So what exactly is a reference architecture? It is a generalization of multiple solution architectures that have been designed and successfully deployed to address the same types of business problems or use case. It is a predefined architectural pattern, or set of patterns, possibly partially or completely instantiated, designed, and proven for use in particular business and technical contexts, together with supporting artifacts to enable their use. A reference architecture shows how to compose these patterns together into a solution. It can be a set of multiple reference architectures within a subject area where each represents a different emphasis or viewpoint of that area. It can be defined at many different levels of detail and abstraction (from specific to generalized) and for many different purposes. It consists of a list of functions and some indication of their interfaces— or application programming interfaces (API)—and interactions with each other and with functions located outside of the scope of the reference architecture.

How is a reference model used? It serves as a reference foundation for architectures and solutions, as a template solution for an architecture for a particular domain; as a framework for scope identification, gap assessment, and risk assessment to develop a roadmap to design and implement a solution; and as a source for common vocabulary with which to discuss implementations, often with the aim to stress commonality. A reference model further serves as a tool to accelerate delivery through the reuse of an effective solution and as a basis for governance to ensure the consistency and applicability of technology use within an organization.

A real-world example of an IoT conceptual model

Fig. 13.3 shows an example of an IoT security conceptual model that was developed by Verizon, as part of its IoT service platform. This model is an early example of an IoT conceptual model, from 2014, but already the notions of endpoints, gateways (labeled hubs), network (operator platforms), and then services in the cloud (partner platforms) are showing through.

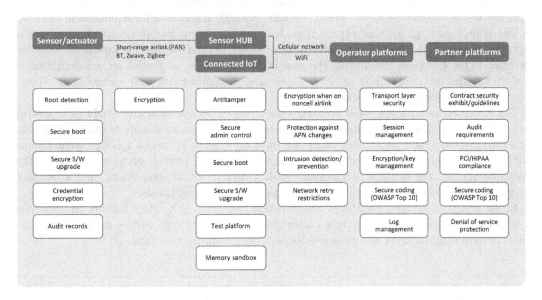

FIGURE 13.3

A real-world example of a security conceptual model.

REGULATORY VULNERABILITIES AND RISKS

Among the new threat agents in the IoT are regulators.[2] Regulation can pose a threat when it is poorly crafted, or based on bad or incomplete information about the subject of regulation—like the IoT. However, some regulation will clearly be beneficial to risk management. For instance, a bill passed by the US Senate in late 2015 related to public companies is set to require that security and risk management is not only visible at the board level, but that the board contain at least some credible skills associated with security.[3] Ironically, a lack of cybersecurity skills might become far more than a operational or technical deficiency for new and old business alike. See the section entitled "Internal Policy," later in this chapter, for a discussion on this effect on vulnerabilities and risk management in the IoT.

The development of regulatory guidelines

When it comes to discussing the laws and regulations regarding robotic devices, Isaac Asimov's first law of robotics is often cited, which states, "A robot may not injure a human being or, through inaction, allow a human being to come to harm." Asimov's three laws may be science fiction, but they are often taken to be a serious basis for robot governance. However, robotic devices raise many thorny legal, ethical, and regulatory questions. For instance, if an autonomous car is involved in an accident, who is to blame? And bionic technologies that enhance or become part of humans are trickier still. If an assistive exoskeleton is implicated in a death, who is at fault? If a brain-computer interface is used to communicate with someone in a vegetative state, are those messages legally binding?

It is to help answer these questions that a project was initiated in 2012, funded primarily by the European Union, called RoboLaw,[4] which provides meaningful guidance for regulation in the IoT.

The project gathered together experts from law, engineering, philosophy, medicine, as well as experienced regulators. They developed a report, "Guidelines on Regulating Robotics," that they presented to the European Parliament. The goal of the report was to provide recommendations on how to manage the introduction of new robotic and human-enhancement technologies without compromising principles of European law.

The RoboLaw experts suggested avoiding *excessively restrictive* laws that would stifle innovation. They recommended using a *functional perspective* rather than an attempt to create broad laws regarding robotics. Such broad laws along the lines of Asimov's laws of robotics were deemed likely to fail. Legislation should rather be developed for specific markets on an ad hoc basis. This takes into account the fact that robotics has such a diverse set of applications, and a one-size-fits-all approach could lead to needless and perhaps nonsensical regulations.

In the realm of medical prostheses and exoskeletons, limiting product liability to encourage development of new technologies was encouraged, perhaps working with a *no fault* insurance model or have manufacturers and governments pay into a compensation fund.

---

[2]See https://blogs.mcafee.com/executive-perspectives/something-old-something-new-threat-internet-things/.

[3]See Cybersecurity Disclosure Act 2015—https://www.congress.gov/bill/114th-congress/senate-bill/754/text.

[4]http://www.economist.com/news/technology-quarterly/21635318-european-policymakers-look-making-laws-automated-machines-and-come-up.

The question of the rights of machines was also brought up in the report and although the development of artificial intelligence continues, the report concluded that any autonomy granted to machines is given by humans, and they are still machines. However, it was conceded that in some limited cases it could be considered to give them certain legal authority, analogous to a corporation, so that contracts could be entered into by robotic entities and so on. As the IoT becomes more and more advanced, it will certain be the case that questions about the intelligence of a system will come up. It is not necessarily hard to image a matter where the design and security of an IoT system is brought into question because some negative event might have been avoided, if the system had "made the right decision." In an age where machines are able to beat humans at the fiendishly complex game of *Go*, there may be a basis for more RoboLaw discussions.[5]

Finally, the report states that international standards would greatly help in this area. The United States, a hotbed of IoT innovation currently, lags behind both Europe and Asia in any coordinated effort to develop guidelines for legislation in this area.

End-to-end regulatory considerations

The development of mobile edge computing (MEC) is about processing information and adding value at new places in the IoT systems, specifically the network and the gateway. This can mean that regulatory and legal requirements will be taken into account for data processing at these locations. Potential examples include:

- Privacy: restricted information should not be passed to the application if the user hasn't given consent. Does consent need to be accounted for in the development of MEC?
- Hosting an application on a network edge platform may provide certain advantages, such as low latency for IoT services with stringent availability and resiliency requirements. Such hosting offers a type of *specialized service* that ensures sufficient quality of service for such applications to function, but are they appropriate and can this be done consistently within the evolving principles of *network neutrality*? Additional technical analysis would be appropriate to determine the criteria to assess which applications and services would benefit from specialized treatment. Analysis could also examine how to configure networks to ensure sufficient capacity to accommodate demand for specialized services while maintaining suitable network conditions to support a robust user experience for nonspecialized services. Transparency and nondiscrimination within the specialized services category, and among all nonspecialized traffic, could be observed as part of a net neutrality framework that would allow end users or the owner of the content, application, or service to pay for specialized treatment subject to reasonable consumer protections important to network neutrality.
- The introduction of an MEC server in the radio access network should not reduce the provision of lawful interception. IoT systems will certainly be subject to lawful access and interception requests, and MEC will mean that *raw* data from IoT endpoints may need to be preserved as part of the chain of evidence. At the same time, lawful access will need to be done in a manner that does not (easily) reveal that interception is underway (lest the subject of surveillance change their behaviors because they know they are being observed!).

---

[5]See *Computer says Go*, http://www.economist.com/news/science-and-technology/21689501-beating-go-champion-machine-learning-computer-says-go.

- Charging requirements for access to services during roaming scenarios. For example, in the case that the same services are available in the home network and visited via access network, should different charging requirements apply? Ongoing regulatory changes to roaming charges would need to be considered.

Extraterritoriality

The US government's access to data moving over the Internet has been massive and widespread. This has put US cloud providers in jeopardy because customers may attempt to work with non-US providers to avoid this access.

This has also led to resistance on the part of the US cloud industry to comply with government demands. For example, the New York District Court ruled that the US government could use the Stored Communications Act to gain access to data that Microsoft maintained on Dublin servers.[6]

Extra territoriality in the world of the IoT could have an even more pernicious effect, where the economic models of entire systems and service rely on shared resources at a global scale and level. Especially when you consider that what one nation can do, so can another. Conflicting, extraterritorial laws from different nations could make an IoT system or service unmanageable.

IoT systems dealing with financial information and personal information may be especially subject to extraterritoriality. Where and how criminals move money through the IoT, and what the IoT knows about a given subject of surveillance, will be valuable assets to law enforcement around the world. As a result, IoT managers can expect to deal with extraterritorial regulations from the beginning, even if they are not selling goods or services offshore. Why would this be? Because almost certainly, elements in the stratified IoT supply changes for services will be located offshore.

Conflicting and overlapping standards Across borders

Many attempts are currently underway to introduce *cloud computing* standards—the European Telecommunications Standards body has identified 20 bodies creating well over a hundred documents in this area. Initiatives come from the European Union, the International Telecommunications Union (ITU), and the International Standards Organization (ISO), as well as private standards bodies such as the UK Cloud Industry Forum.

Currently, no definitive standards, contracts, or service level agreements (SLA) exist; and although cloud providers are not enthusiastic about their development, expect eventual standards, monitoring organizations, and certification schemes to emerge. As a key input service to the IoT, the fragmented standards area for cloud computing and its security is not helpful. And the situation is only getting worse as we consider IoT more broadly, as a system of services.

Standards gaps related to the IoT

Standardization for security in the IoT is still in the early stages in 2016. International bodies such as the International Electrotechnical Commission (IEC), ISO, and International Telecommunications Union Telecommuniation Standardization Sector (ITU-T) all have efforts underway related to IoT security standards, and they are moving forward in a collaborative manner. Meanwhile, however, some regional standards like Internet of Things-Architecture (IoT-A) (from Europe) and National Institute of Standards and Technology (NIST) (from the United States) are

---

[6]See "Straight Outta Dublin," http://www.theregister.co.uk/2014/09/23/microsoft_vs_the_long_arm_of_us_law/.

driving forward with their own parochial guidance. This creates vulnerability for the IoT where standards conflict and overlap.

Who is correct? What could compliance look like under these circumstances? How can you protect against negligence and show due care if the standards don't agree on what such things are to look like?

Another vulnerability is that for lack of recognized standards, investments are made that have to be overhauled or unraveled in the event they turn out to conflict with putative standards.

Alternately, for lack of standards, vendors of IoT goods and services do what appears correct. But the cost of continually justifying their approach to security with customers, auditors, regulators, and competitors can generate an operational drain.

Designers and risk managers in the IoT need to watch the gaps related to IoT and security most carefully, for this is where the conflicts, surprises, and risks are most likely to come about. Some of the more notable standards gaps related to IoT security in 2016 are summarized in Table 13.1

Table 13.1 Standards Gaps in IoT Security in 2016	
Gap 1: Gateway security	While gateways are widely recognized as critical, functional elements by IoT service providers, the standards bodies are only becoming aware that gateway security is a make-or-break issue. See the discussion on smart gateways in the section "Availability and Reliability" later in this chapter.
Gap 2: Virtualization security	Do "cloud" security standards sufficiently recognize virtualization security in transport—not just DCs? Network function virtualization (NFV) Software-defined networks (SDN) Physically insecure, virtualized devices? Routers, machine/home gateways? Remote, virtualized devices 3rd Generation Partnership Project (3GPP) evolved packet core (EPC) elements, base stations (3G, 4G, 5G) IP Multimedia Subsystems (IMS) elements Hypervisor security in DCs and transport Containers/docker security in DCs Identity and access *Least privilege* is more like a recommended practice in transport virtualization due to risk amplification
Gap 3: Management and measurement of security	*Not* for regulatory compliance For *security coverage and cost management* Old cost models based on appliances insufficient Old cost models based on security aggregation points insufficient Security in the IoT will be unaffordable and therefore left out, without informative standards and alternatives
Gap 4: Open-source assurance and security	Much of the IoT will be built on open source platforms Virtualization (DC and Transport) Embedded device platform (Linux) Do existing software assurance standards effectively support open source? Under what support models? Self-supported? Commercially supported?

(Continued)

Table 13.1 Standards Gaps in IoT Security in 2016 *Continued*

Gap 5: IoT risk assessment techniques	Do risk assessment standards sufficiently address emerging threats related to amplification due to automation? DC and Transport automation NFV/SDN automation Deployment and provisioning automation
Gap 6: "Privacy by design for IoT" and big data	Stipulations that privacy impact assessments should be conducted for IoT projects involving personally identifiable information (PII); as well has who to identify IoT PII in the first place. Guidelines on identifying personally identifiable information (PII) from the mass of IoT data. Detailed guidelines about how and when to mask or change data to protect privacy as it is collected and combined among IoT service providers. SC27/WG5 N35—Guidelines for data pseudonymization and anonymization processes as privacy enhancing techniques The amount of data flowing around in the IoT will be subject to arbitrary assumptions associated with when PII exists or does not exist. Performing privacy impact assessments will become impractical in some instances, as IoT services emerge and disappear rapidly, crossing national borders and regulatory environments almost without thought. Guidelines and high-level generalized rules about when PII exists will encourage better observance of privacy in the IoT than a complete reliance on complex methods and processes. Prior work of Working Group 5 (WG5) to be reviewed for *triage* processes suitable to IoT.
Gap 7: Guidance related to appropriate use of multiparty authentication/key splitting	To date the Internet has largely relied on just two forms of cryptography of identification/authentication and encryption: symmetric keys, and public-key (asymmetric) key sharing. Other evolved forms of these crypto-systems need to be considered, like identity-based encryption (IBE), which is evolving for IoT-specific use cases[a] Older forms of key management such as key-splitting and multiparty authentication and encryption that did not find a good fit in the *old internet* might make a lot of sense now.[b] We need recognized guidance about what type of cryptography is considered appropriate for different forms of IoT systems— because the use cases are dramatically larger than old enterprise IT use cases.
Gap 8: IoT incident response	Most incident response methodologies have been developed for IT-like devices and systems, not IoT devices. IoT devices will have different interfaces, functional requirements, and operating systems.

Table 13.1 Standards Gaps in IoT Security in 2016 *Continued*	
Gap 9: IoT secure application development techniques	Techniques exist of assessing risk (IE ISO 27002) and managing the process of assessing application security requirements formally (ISO 27034). They have not been (yet) adopted or reviewed for applicability to IoT services and systems—which probably need it above all IT systems—because IoT security is in chaos and some guidance is needed. This problem is difficult because IoT requirements, threats, vulnerabilities, and risks will vary widely by industry, and of course system to system.

[a]*https://en.wikipedia.org/wiki/ID-based_encryption.*
[b]*Key splitting/sharing (polynomial interpolation); see https://en.wikipedia.org/wiki/Secret/sharing.*

In lieu of IoT security standards in the areas, the vendors of IoT goods and services have three choices for managing this risk:

1. Do what seems right—and try to fix misalignments with the standards when they emerge or constantly justify the approach.
2. Wait for standards to emerge—and possibly miss the market opportunity.
3. Watch or participate in standards development to get some indication of the directionality of IoT security standards, and attempt to design with enough flexibility to support the broader potential outcomes.

Regulatory risk management in the IoT

Regulatory bodies are likely to subject IoT systems to substantial management and regulation. Consider that telecommunications industry: prices are often set or controlled by regulation (higher or lower than the market), unprofitable regions are required to receive subsidized service, and much capital infrastructure is required to be shared with competitors. In some cases there have been requirements for divestiture or breakup into smaller companies.

Like the large telecommunications companies, the infrastructure required for the IoT will be accomplished by large firms with substantial capital reserves and so there will be a limited number of companies involved for some forms of IoT service-provision. Monopolies are likely to develop, which, while enjoying operating efficiency, are likely to be subject to antitrust legislation and regulation. There are likely to be legal liability risks, such as for negligence associated with poor or weak administration of IoT resources.

Regulators also hold access to spectrum; more of it needs to be freed faster by regulators, such as ultra-high frequency (UHF) of old terrestrial television channels. There is a risk that the spectrum will be too expensive—government attempts to raise vast sums with auctions of spectrum weighs down the IoT industry with debt. In the previous chapter we discussed this as a threat related to resource allocation, where spectrum is a natural resource.

Emerging spectrum-related risks and fifth generation wireless networking

Radio spectrum risks associated with regulation can affect a variety of IoT systems, affecting both long-range as well as short-range network connections. However, probably the largest risks around spectrum are not related to existing technologies but new ones to come!

Will spectrum be available for new networking technologies that improve on existing technologies? Or will old technologies *squat* on the spectrum and throttle the networking technologies that will enable many IoT use cases? No other networking technology reflects this risk as much as fifth-generation (5G) cellular networking.

5G mobile networks will arrive in the market somewhere between 2018 and 2020, according to equipment manufacturers and carriers. Makers of IoT goods and services would be well served to understand what this will mean in terms of risk.

To begin, the 5G *land grab* is underway now and reflects a vulnerability and risk to the IoT: equipment vendors may rush with prestandard equipment supporting trials and limited deployments that could cause some pain down the road. Risk management will require that IoT service providers and especially telecommunications carriers ensure that the equipment vendors are able to make this equipment fully compliant to standards with software updates. More broadly, the arbitrary, corrupt, expensive, and slow pace of mismanaged spectrum licensing and allocation can be a major risk to 5G and therefore many of the use cases that will rely heavily on 5G.

5G wireless technologies will generate a variety of improvements important to the IoT and risk management. Wireless spectrum is heavily regulated around the world. What regulators do about the access to spectrum will have a major effect of the viability of 5G in a given jurisdiction and therefore the availability of 5G.

The 5G technology is important to IoT specifically because it has properties and addresses requirements that are not necessarily available in fourth-generation (4G) and early technologies, such as energy efficiency, device costs, power consumption, and battery usage. When built up on top of 4G technologies—which is the point of calling it 5G—then a picture of IoT requirements in the context of 5G starts to emerge.

This can be seen in Fig. 13.4, where the definition used in this book for IoT includes all *things*—there is no distinction between *Human 5G* (smartphones, tablets, laptops, desktops, remote access) and *Machine 5G* (everything else not nominally called Human 5G in the diagram). It is all IoT.

5G will play a major part in the enablement and development of the IoT because it will bring:

- Increased bandwidth
- Decreased latency
- Wider coverage
- More redundancy in coverage, because more than one single wireless technology is involved
    It will also rely heavily on technology to coordinate and manage how a device accesses different forms of radio technology. The degree of complexity will be remarkable and an order of magnitude beyond what we see today in 4G networks (which themselves baffle most non-telecom engineers).
    5G will use technology automatically to:
- Be aware and track distinct IoT applications and services with distinct service levels and tariffs
- Multiplex multiple channels from a single bearer technology

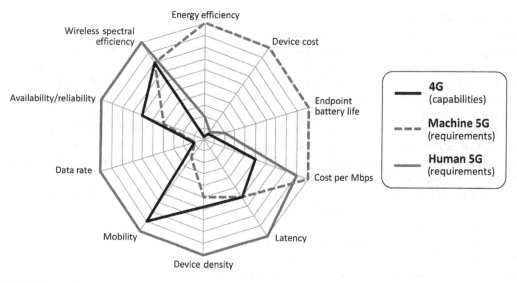

FIGURE 13.4

Properties of 5G.

Adapted from Mobile Experts *(2015).*

- Manage access controls (identification and authentication) to two or three different bearer technologies at a time, for identification and authentication purposes, to gain speed increases, to generate resiliency—all on demand
- Interface with different identification and authentication systems across bearers
     Many of the purported *killer* use cases in the IoT will rely on two main differentiators in 5G technologies: low latency and high-speed communications. The IoT use cases that revolve around these differentiators typically fall into one of two categories:
- Automated or assisted transportation:
    - inter-vehicle coordination and driving,
    - self-landing or flying planes or drones
    - self-docking and navigating boats
    - intermodal freight management
- Remote manipulation by humans of machine for fine-motor operations:
    - Health triage
    - Surgery
    - Driving, flying
    - Welding and maintenance
    - Manufacturing: sewing, product assembly
    - Bomb defusing
    - Artistic pursuits: drawing, playing instruments

These use cases will not flourish and spread to places with regulatory environments that cannot or will not support 5G requirements for access to spectrum, or impose other undue burdens on infrastructure owners and operators for reasons that might range for public welfare to corruption.

Standards development for 5G

The end-to-end network will be more complex than ever and have to work well in order to achieve drastically lower latency, shift spectrum resources around fluidly as needed, and so forth. There is not much argument that, since 3 GPP long-term evolution (LTE) became a single 4G global standard, the 3 GPP is a sure bet to be the home of the development of the 5G standard air interface.

Several standards bodies will need to be involved in 5G development because of the range of technologies applied. Standards entities include, but are not limited to, the Institute of Electrical and Electronics Engineers (IEEE), Internet Engineering Task Force (IETF), European Telecommunications Standards Institute (ETSI), and the ITU. It will not necessarily be all of these, but 5G will be a standard supported by multiple bodies dividing up the end-to-end network and working closely together. This will facilitate a 5G standard.[7]

For IoT service providers and equipment makers, monitoring these standards bodies is a costly but valuable form of risk management that will ensure that product and service plans and strategies do not conflict with emerging standards.

It is very likely that the independent pieces of 5G will form in separate bodies and appear disjointed from a distance, but then they will come together rapidly, possibly surprising some IoT providers of goods and services who have not been watching.

Later in this chapter we will continue the discussion around 5G in terms of the potential complexity and the effect on risk in the Internet of Things (RIoT) control.

HEALTH AND SAFETY REGULATION RISK

Regulators have a special role to play with regard to *safety* in the IoT, crafting legislation that compels products and service providers to be clear and honest in the publication and performance claims and their ability to meet service levels in a manner that also minimizes physical safety hazards to users. This is different from issues like net-neutrality that get involved in the business issues of how much to charge for what services, and to whom you are allowed to sell.

The risk in this instance is not only that regulators necessarily over-regulate, but that they also potentially under-regulate. In the event of over-regulation, the burden will be borne by the service providers directly in the form of excess costs and inefficiency. But in the case of under-regulation or merely mistargeted regulation, safety issues will be the most visible form of security failing in the IoT. Visible security failures will have a massive impact on customer satisfaction and adoption rates and could spur all sort of other risks such as financial and legal risks.

From the perspective of the IoT risk manager or executive, health and safety risks must be carefully considered and managed regardless of regulation because of the pernicious effects on the service overall. By definition, the IoT with its foundation in cyberphysical interfaces makes health and safety risks a top-of mind consideration at all times.

REIDENTIFICATION VULNERABILITIES AND RISK MANAGEMENT

Organizations should assess the risk of re-identification of individuals and organizations alike, based on the little understood bounty associated with the massive amount of data collected in the IoT.

---

[7]5G Core Technologies Research and Timelines, ABI Research Sept 2014.

Reidentification becomes a problem as data sets grow, and data analytics becomes more powerful under the *big data* movement. Data from one IoT source might have been theoretically scrubbed of PII to the satisfaction of the data owners. However, big data is about gathering and aggregating data from many sources and mining it for hidden correlations and meaning.

The vulnerability in this case is that big data and modern (or future) analytics will allow for reidentification and the unauthorized exposure/disclosure of PII, despite the apparently legitimate and apparently sufficient methodologies applied to the individual data sets. Beyond PII, which is increasingly regulated, re-identification vulnerabilities could lead the disclosure of commercially valuable information and intelligence about businesses and possibly lead to unforeseen liabilities.

For instance, data from a home security system and a smart vehicle might be managed and cleansed of PII separately, because they are held initially in separate repositories. But once combined, both contain enough trace information—say ZIP/postal code, average miles driven on a given day work day, time spent at home on the same days, car financing data, and so forth—to reveal a lot of about the subject in question, so much so that a single, seemingly insignificant piece of data might expose the full identity and *new or implied* information from the combined data sets.

Managing risks related to re-identification will in part fall to good practices and evolving standards around techniques for managing IoT logs and events using pseudonymization, anonymization, and randomization.

Pseudonymization

With pseudonymization, some of the identifiable attributes of a data record are replaced with a value (an alias) that can be used as a reference to access the record, but provides no identifiable information.

Anonymization

With anonymization, the precision or granularity of data values is intentionally reduced to limit exposure or identification. Anonymization is usually used in conjunction with pseudonymization.

Randomization

Randomization is an anonymization category using such techniques as noise addition, permutation, and differential privacy.

LAWFUL ACCESS IN THE IoT

IoT systems and services can face surprising and potentially ruinous risks from lawful access requests. Lawful access risks are associated with demands from law enforcement and public safety for information from a given (IoT) system, for the purposes of investigation or prosecution.

In the old days, this was about wire taps and requests to a carrier. In the Internet Age, we have seen sites like Google, Facebook, and Twitter weighed down by such requests.[8] IoT devices will inevitably be tools of law breakers, criminal enterprises and investigations associated with negligence and liability, and the law will require that substantial amounts of logging and user information be handed over, or be at least retained. These lawful demands do not come with compensation, typically.

---

[8]See Googles statistics on Lawful access requests, https://www.google.com/transparencyreport/userdatarequests/.

In the early days of voice over IP (VoIP), when long-distance calling was still expensive, many innovative companies started IP-based long distance calling over the Internet at a fraction of the cost of telephone companies. These services would become the subject of lawful access requests as an inevitable consequence of offering a consumer and business oriented communication service. Many of these small, pop-up firms simply closed their doors rather than cope with the expense of lawful access requests, often to reopen under a new name. They became known as *hell's bells* for such business practices.[9]

LABELING AND FAIR WARNING IN THE IoT

The difference in vulnerabilities and risks between a legacy offline device and an IoT device may be substantial. Consumer instruction and information will become more and more important if people are to safely and securely adopt the IoT. Product labels and warnings should provide a greater level of information about the consequences of poor in-home security for instance, in the case of a *smart home*:

- Online appliances and home heating systems may be degraded, damaged, or destroyed by online threats or even misconfiguration by users.
- Ignoring patches and updates may invalidate warranties—in ways that never occurred for *offline* systems and devices.

For IoT service and device vendors who fail to produce such labels and warnings, liability of various sorts may arise directly as a result of the *online* status of their product. Potentially, liability may even become retroactive, where judgements go back in time to the initial introduction of the good or services, which may represent years. Consumers of IoT goods and services who fail to read or comply with conditions on service may find that their IoT products receive abbreviated or lower service levels, or have service curtailed pending compliance with the terms and conditions of the product. In summary, vendors must act to protect themselves from liabilities associated with the online status of their IoT goods or services. Today, few disclaimers are applied and certain manufacturer due diligence in the area of IoT security is not a certainty.

Accountability in the land of machines

In a paper from early 2016, the Privacy Commissioner of Canada made an interesting observation about privacy in the IoT that can be extended to security as a whole:

> Accountability is a key principle in privacy law. To be accountable, an organization needs to be able to demonstrate what it is doing, and what it has done, with personal information and explain why. This may be easier said than done in the Internet of Things environment when there is a multitude of stakeholders, such as device manufacturers, social platforms, third-party applications and others.[10]

---

[9]"Hell's Bells," as they are known in the telecom world, are fly-by-night VoIP service providers that crop-up using public domain VoIP management software and offer cut-rate long-distance service over the public Internet to specific destinations (like China as an example). They are known to be frequently nonresponsive to lawful access requests and will simply fold their tents and leave rather than expend the resources to comply with LEA requests." Tyson Macaulay, *Securing Converged IP Networks*, 2005, Chapter 3.

[10]Office of the Privacy Commissioner of Canada, *The Internet of Things: An Introductution to Privacy with a Focus on the Retail and Home Environments*, February 2016.

Accountability is a great way to sum up one of the largest regulatory risks. All the complexity we have described in this book will generate issues and challenges associated with showing accountability and due care.

> Some of these players may collect, use or disclose data, and can have greater or lesser role in its protection at various points, though where to draw the line between them can be challenging at the best of times. For example, who is ultimately responsible for the data which the smart meter broadcasts? The homeowner who benefits from using the device, the manufacturers or power company which provided it, the third-party company storing the data, the data processor who crunches the numbers, all of the above, or some combination thereof? And to whom would a privacy-sensitive consumer complain? Should privacy be breached, where does the responsibility of one party end and another begin? Mapping dynamic data flows and setting out the responsibilities and relationships between various actors could help clarify how information flows among the parties and can help inform the basis of an organization's privacy management program.
>
> In the case of "machine-made" decisions, developers and owners of the underlying algorithms, systems and products may find it even more challenging to demonstrate accountability In addition to this vexing issue, the legal and ethical responsibilities in the case of errors or accidents are far from clear. The scope of privacy management programs, and the level of accountability organizations are expected to demonstrate, will be complex in the Internet of Things environment.

The fact that a regulator (the Privacy Commissioner of Canada, in this case) is calling out accountability in these early stages of the IoT emergence is telling for IoT providers of good and services: complexity of service design will not be an excuse for failings in security and privacy. You have to take end-to-end responsibility for the goods and service you bring to market.

Accordingly, to our earlier discussion about risk and *treatment* versus *acceptance* versus *transference*: the worse risks will be the ones you unknowingly accept—but may be held accountable for later.

FINANCIAL VULNERABILITIES AND RISKS

Aside from the many and usual financial risks associated with any new form of business, the main financial risk in the IoT is going to be fraud in new and many diverse forms. This fraud is possible not only because of the poor security designs going into so many IoT devices and systems, but because users themselves can be deceived more easily via IoT devices than through conventional computing resources like desktop and smartphones—for the time being.

IoT STORED-VALUE RISKS

There are many stored-value systems in the world already, and the prevalence of these systems is growing to the point that they are even considered forms of *shadow banking*; mobile phone companies such as SafariCom, and product vendors like Apple and Starbucks who accept and man-age prepaid cash deposits to facilitate later purchases without the hassle of entering (or clearing) credit card data or dealing with banks. The same business benefits will be adopted by makers of things, who will move to create ecosystems and stored-value accounts to lock in customers and their money.[11]

For example: your (future) smart espresso machine. It comes with a small touch screen for not only controlling the way it makes espresso, but also for allowing you to buy more of the coffee, which comes in special pods. This system will certainly be linked to a cloud-based portal over the Internet. The portal may or may not have good security, and the espresso device may or may not have any security at all. Assume that either the cloud service or the smart espresso machine is com-promised. The device might be compromised by a local attack, originating from a desktop or laptop or mobile app inside the home network that has been specially developed to identify and then attack the (very popular) machine.

Once compromised, the espresso Thing displays a message that says "50% off coffee pods. One Day Sale. Please enter your espresso account PIN to make your purchase." You enter your PIN into the machine like you normally do to order, which opens the trusted local storage and releases account data. Unfortunately, at this point the account data is captured, or possibly the order is chan-ged in the cloud-portal from a purchase to a gift. The bad guy then transfers the account's stored-value out to a "friend" account using the portal's send-a-gift feature! Or it merely accepts the gift you have sent as a result of the compromised device interface. All the stored value is now gone from your account. If you have some sort of auto-recharge feature enabled, maybe the process gets repeated dozens of times before someone notices!

Meanwhile, the new "friend" has been receiving the gifts and converting them into goods (expensive new espresso machines, other merchandise) at many different storefronts or has the goods sent to shipping *relays* who forward the stolen goods onwards. (This is a well-known tech-nique on the Internet.) Remember that stealing $25 at a time, 100,000 times is a $2.5 million in retail value, probably $500,000 or more once fenced? Not bad.

Managing the perceived risks from other risk categories is the best way to manage the financial risks. Good risk management will increase both operational efficiency and customer satisfaction. Robust identity and access controls at the operational level are one means of addressing stored value risks.

Social engineering and fraud prevention

The above example equates to a social engineering vulnerability in the IoT. Like social engineering on the Internet today, there is no single remedy. Layers of security, technology, education, and awareness will need to be applied.

---

[11]The Bank of England published a Research paper February 3, 2015 that discussed the possible adoption of crypto cur-rencies (like Bitcoin) for use by central banks to support national currencies. This was covered in what they called "Theme Five: Central Bank Response to Fundamental Technological, Institutional, Societal, and Environmental Change." Source: http://www.bankofengland.co.uk/research/Documents/onebank/discussion.pdf.

But we propose that there are at least two specific areas that need to be a focus: one is a *management control* and one is a *technical control*:

- *Management standards.* We need standards related not only for the security technology of the IoT, but also the security management of the IoT. Both NIST and the Industrial Internet Consortium are set to release reference designs including security for the IoT. We will have to see if these designs are sufficient to address the vulnerabilities to social engineering in the IoT.
- *Technical solutions around identity, authentication, and encryption that low-resource Things can support.* The harder it is to send and display fraudulent messages via Things, the harder social engineering with Things will become. Things need lightly, faster, more efficient authentication and encryption technology than is typical today with symmetric and asymmetric crypto. Additionally, it is likely that the multiparty cryptography systems discussed in the requirements chapters on identity and access will play an important role in defeating social engineering, essentially because more than one person or system has to be duped![12]

The demand for cheaper, not more expensive, Things will ensure that opportunities for social engineering and hacking the IoT in general will not be in short supply.

Blockchains and the IoT

Blockchains are the basis for a popular phenomenon of crypto-currencies, the most famous of which is Bitcoin. But they can have far larger applications in the IoT, and present importunities to manage risk.

Blockchains are highly distributed and publically viewable systems of sequentially linked cryptographically signed pieces of information which allow entities to validate not only systems of stored value—like cryptocurrencies—but also information and properties of things that would reduce risk in IoT systems and services. Blockchains can be applied in the IoT for:

- Automated service-level information distribution and management
- Automated warranty and maintenance information and management
- Ownership attribution and transfer
- Loyalty programs and awards
- Open and automated trading of goods like commodities or perishable resources (like electricity)
- Rapidly publication of authenticated information about product or service hazards, defects, reactions, and remediations
- Trusted publication of ingredients, side effects, warnings or revisions to products

Blockchain technology is available from several sources, including open-source software tools and vendor-support distributions.[13]

Rather than relying on banks and other trusted intermediaries like courts to mediate and validate agreements and transactions, blockchains offer a potential alternative to managing financial risks in the IoT associated with stored value systems. Blockchains also offer an opportunity to manage risks associated with poor or incomplete information about IoT devices, goods and services, in a highly trusted and automated manner. Blockchains will also support rapid assessment and settlement of discputes associated with terms and conditions through the evolving notion of

[12]https://blogs.mcafee.com/business/multi-party-authentication-cryptography-iot.
[13]See Hyperledger—https://www.hyperledger.org/ or Etherum project—https://www.ethereum.org/.

"smart contracts", and especially updates to terms and conditions associated with services levels: the chains will be visible to all devices in an authenticated manner via the block chain.

One of the beauties of blockchain technology is that it manages the *double spending* problem of digital currencies: how do you stop someone from using the same *virtual dollar* over and over. A similar problem in the IoT will be ownership transfer on short-term basis (renting) or perpetual basis (a final sale). Managing the ownership transfer of potentially thousands of devices at once is analogous to buying something for thousands of units of digital currency at once—yet publicly disclosed and easily verifiable.

Fig. 13.5 is a high-level overview of how blockchains work, in the case of cryptocurrencies. In the context of the IoT, the blockchain may be a *closed* system used by an IoT vendor of a good or a service, exclusively for that good or service, much like coffee shops will allow for real money to be deposited into a stored value system that then uses their own form of in-store debit (versus credit) for purchases. As discussed above, unsophisticated forms of stored value might be compromised and defrauded, because such systems are typically founded on very basic security such as username and password.

In the case of a blockchain-based system of stored value, data, contract or ownership management, IoT systems themselves would have embedded blockchain *addresses* (public keys) that become part of the transaction process, in addition to usernames and password which might be used to initiate a blockchain transaction by a system manager or owner. Furthermore, all transactions are vetted by multiple entities in the network, by design. These entities might also be

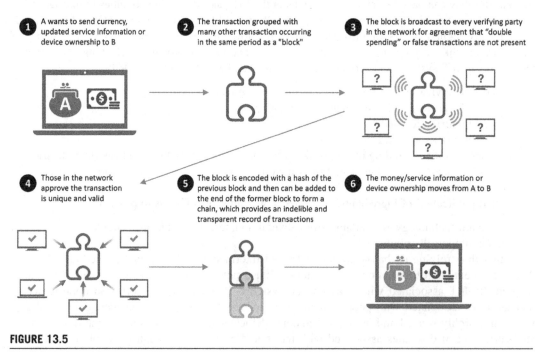

FIGURE 13.5

Blockchains at work.

Adapted from Cloud Security Alliance—IoT Working Group/Seeking Alpha—Kurt Dew.

configured as independent fraud-detection systems. Finally, an irrefutable record or *ledger* of transactions is stored and available for review, meaning that all transactions can be easily audited in the event of disputes later on (which may or may not be related to fraud).

We will touch on blockchain technologies again in this chapter, because their application and utility as a RIoT control tool are manifest and many.

LIABILITY AND INSURANCE RISKS

This could also be thought of as the risk of transferring cyber risks. As we keep repeating, you can manage risk in three ways: you can treat it, transfer it, or accept it. *Transferring* typically involves contracts like service level agreements or insurance.

In a recent case, a firm was defrauded of almost $500,000 due to an email scam, which involved a compromised email account from a CEO.[14] The insurance company refused the claim, stating *financial instruments* where not part of the coverage purchased. In this case they were apparently defining email as a financial instrument. The case is before the court. This is merely one of many pending disputes between insurers and claimants when it comes to cyber insurance.

Executives and risk managers have good reason to be cautious of transferring risk via insurance, as the market is still maturing. There is misalignment between what companies believe is covered by a cyber insurance policy and the position of the insurer.

Purchasing any sort of cyber insurance to try and transfer risks associated with IoT privacy, security, or safety lapses will likely be an unreliable tool until more precedents and jurisprudence have been established. Risk managers should practice caution when dealing with a market as immature as cyber insurance, particularly if the IoT is within scope of this insurance.

COMPETITIVE AND MARKET RISKS

It goes without saying that some of the primary risks in an emerging technology have to do with competitive and market risks. Major shifts and unpredictable or unanticipated consumer or competitor behavior must be factored in. I've briefly listed some of the key competitive and market vulnerabilities for the IoT.

USER ACCEPTABILITY

Fear of being hurt or attacked by a soulless, robot menace, or being caught up in a bloody *rise of the machines* might be an only-in-Hollywood plot, but it will not lie far below the surface for many users in the IoT. It will only take a few high profile incidents of injury or fatality directly attributed to IoT, to create major user acceptance problems for IoT services across the board. Ultimately, many of the risk management controls discussed in this book will go toward managing these sorts of archetypal user acceptance issues.

---

[14]http://krebsonsecurity.com/2016/01/firm-sues-cyber-insurer-over-480k-loss/.

User acceptance is clearly part of the overall customer satisfaction requirement that will face the IoT as much as any other form of business. But the IoT is also more complicated than a typical *offline* system, for many of the reasons already discussed, plus some quirks around user acceptance.

User acceptability is critical for new technologies. For instance, in an example provided by the US Department of Transportation,[15] the connected vehicle environment will rely on a variety of technologies that will be largely transparent and unseen by users: short-range communications vehicle-to-vehicle (V2V), longer range vehicle-to-infrastructure (V2I), and intra-vehicle-to-mobile device (V2D). In such a situation, safety applications would have the highest priority, but to gain user acceptance, privacy, cost, and safety must all be given an appropriate balance. A lapse in any one area could seriously affect acceptance.

A potential answer to user acceptance risks lies in a combination of product and service transparency (what do you make versus buy in the service design, including assumptions), user education, and, of course, what security and privacy controls are applied.

RACE TO THE BOTTOM

In a competitive environment, new entrants race to cut costs and the first thing that suffers is security.

Why is security so often the area to have investment frozen and removed from product designs? Because security is largely a forward-looking capability. Security is about stopping what has not yet happened, and success means that literally nothing happens. This can be hard to measure in terms of return on investment (ROI). True, you can use various industry-related figures learned from other people's lessons, but usually that is ineffective as an influencer, especially when it's a matter of a sexy IoT feature to drive sales, or plain old overhead like security.

Managers will seek to cut costs across the board to remain competitive and security will be affected like all other areas. But security is not something like a smaller serving of soda pop, or long waiting periods on customer calling centers: security does not fail slowly—it fails all at once. Cutting costs as IoT services race to the bottom due to desperate competition will incline many businesses to push closer and closer to the point of no return with their security.

An opportunity to manage this risk of racing to the bottom in costing may lie in a few different places, especially product differentiation. Differentiate based on demonstrable security. Add value to the product or service with security. However, the trick to doing this is to make security observable. It cannot be merely a claim. Security can be made observable with analytics and reporting about the security profile of the IoT service, the industry, and larger, and the Internet generally. But it is not easy.

SUPPLY CHAIN RISKS

Policy in the supply chain

While partnerships with technology suppliers are vital, the dependency upon these partnerships brings risk in the IoT service. Are the service providers applying the security and privacy terms

---

[15]RITA V2V paper from DOT.

and conditions in the service agreements? How do you know? Can you provide that you have an *actual reason* to be confident in policy compliance in the supply chain?

Working within a technology ecosystem itself brings risk: dependencies on such things as supplier regulatory compliance, internal security policy compliance, and even downstream management of suppliers' own supply chain risk. This means that it becomes necessary to push security policy into the supply chain and seek more than boilerplate assurances to manage risk transference. Often the answers lie in stipulating the *right to audit* suppliers in service agreements, and/or seeking to review internal audit reports. The best-run service providers will have prepared audit statements about security available for customers, performed against a recognized internal standard.

PRIVACY ARBITRAGE: VARYING COSTS TO MAINTAIN PRIVACY COMPLIANCE

This could easily be a regulatory risk, but we place it under market and completion because privacy laws vary widely across jurisdictions and IoT service providers will need to create and manage privacy controls to address all the jurisdictions in their chosen market—a difficult and fraught task.

There is no silver bullet for managing the costs of privacy requirements in the IoT or elsewhere. The largest risk is that a form of privacy arbitrage develops where regulatory requirements in one geographic domain exceed the requirements of another domain. As a result, competitors from the domain with less prescriptive privacy requirements gain a competitive advantage over those based in the *heavier* regulatory environment.

To give just one example, connected cars will receive broadcast data packets requiring verification. The industry group and US Department of Transportation recommend renewing Short Lived Certificates (SLC) every 5 minutes to "accurately identify the movement of neighboring vehicles without revealing the identity of the car owner/driver. This rapid change of SLC is required to provide an acceptable level of privacy. This proposed scheme is also designed to prevent misuse by *rogue* users and to remove bad users."[16] This would eventually amount to 2.2 trillion SLCs that would need to be produced annually just in the United States.

This is an example of a hugely expensive approach to security with difficult-to-quantify benefits to the services, especially in terms of security or safety at large.

Privacy is an incredibility important matter in the IoT and can make the difference between a success and failed service in many instances. However, privacy requirements unique among security requirements, if applied incautiously by regulators or overbuilt at the behest of legal counsel, can easily inflate costs without improving services proportionally—affecting competitiveness. The nature of the IoT and service stratification as described in this book will make privacy arbitrage a significant competitive matter to track without and across regulatory domains.

INSUFFICIENT SKILLS

There are currently not enough skills available to build and run IoT products, systems, and services at maximum efficiency—or even get good ideas to market at all. Multiple attempts have gone through the US government[17] to try to fund or mandate the type of advanced networking skills

---

[16]RITA paper DOT.
[17]See US CyberChallenge—http://www.uscyberchallenge.org/.

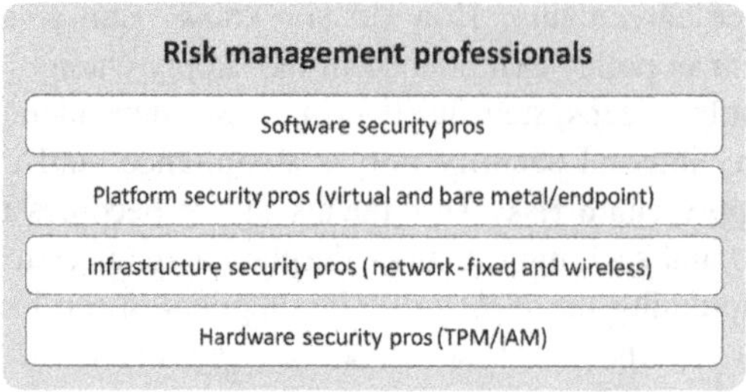

FIGURE 13.6

Core functional domains for IoT security skills.

needed to support not only the IoT today but the Internet generally. These attempts have generally died on the vine, unable to get to the top of priorities that lawmakers decide even to vote on, let alone enact.

This skill deficit results in failure to use the resulting big data effectively for competitive advantage and value-added services. Failure to acquire and foster the skills necessary for the IoT hinders the ability:

- to differentiate products and service based on security
- to demonstrate security through good reporting and audit results and by applying standards
- to manage supply change effectively through contract management and security assessment for partners within the ecosystem, minimizing assumptions to demonstrate due care for the client.

Approaching this skills deficit is a long-term problem and represents systemic risk to all IoT business. One way to manage this risk is through a simple framework to assess the problem. Fig. 13.6 is such a framework, which might be used to express what types of security skills an IoT service provider will require, or if they do not require such skills, to understand specifically why they feel that they are not required.

Starting from the bottom:

- Hardware security will be a major element of IoT systems and indispensable in some use cases, where software-based security is too expensive. Skills related to accessing the security features available in both x86 (Intel) and Advanced RISC Machine (ARM) based architectures are the rarest of the security skills. This is clearly a shortcoming in the education system, where practically no attention is given to this foundation element in IoT security. Perhaps this is the case because hardware security was considered the hard way to do things in the age of laptops, servers, and smartphones with plenty of power and processing resources.
- Infrastructure security is really about networking and virtualization skills, and the two together in the form of NFV (previously discussed and more to come on this topic). In the age of enterprise IT and conventional Internet security, much of the network is *dumb* and just passes packets around. Much of the network is also composed of simple elements that do one thing well, but never anything more. In the IoT, networks will become smart and flexible and security will become pervasive from end to end. Virtualizations (NFV) will make this possible in gateways, transport networks, clouds, and DCs. The tools and products that make this possible

are emerging now—this is new technology. A significant risk is that colleges and universities take years to integrate these technologies into curricula, and engineering professions take ages to integrate them into common practice and bodies of knowledge. This is what happened with the Internet, where even today in 2016 it is difficult to find an engineering school with more than a handful of courses on the most important communications technology in the world—the Internet!—let alone a degree program.

- Platforms refers to the clouds that increasingly serve as the only basis for IoT services—the *born in the cloud* companies that more and more underpin IoT services. Cloud technology is definitely related to the virtualization being used in the infrastructure of networking in the IoT, but is tuned for data management, processing, and storage the way a network element is not. It includes a massive focus on heterogeneous operating systems capable of running just about any application. Automation and expansion is a hallmark of cloud technology and the security applied inside clouds has even evolved its own security standards.[18] Furthermore, modern cloud infrastructures for enterprise and IoT service providers alike will not be based on one cloud platform, but many. They will be a patchwork of services from different public cloud providers combined with some private cloud infrastructure. The cloud workloads will need to be coordinated and secured using skills that did not exist even a few years ago. As a result, IoT risk managers should expect that colleges and universities will not be graduating adequately trained workers for a while. This means that other sources will be resources (poaching from across the industry) or taught to new hires from scratch.

- Software security refers to the skill of developing and managing software and applications in a secure manner. Bugs that lead to security vulnerabilities are fewer and less catastrophic if developers have tools and training to support security application development. Similarly, systems administrators will be different from platform and infrastructure administration skills, and will have a different view on security requirements and responsibilities. Software security is in slightly better shape than platform, network, infrastructure, and hardware security in the sense that it has been around longer as a defined domain. There are tools and methodologies to support secure code development and industries around this practice have grown up (though they are not large). This means that risk managers in the IoT should have no reason other than ignorance or risk acceptance for implementing application code with serious security flaws. Good security practice in systems administration is another area that is fairly well understood from conventional Internet and enterprise practices and should translate well to the IoT. The main risk around software security is that previous good work is not applied by IoT service providers in the rush to get to market.

- Risk management is the last skill domain that IoT executives should be aware of as a distinct skill that should be accessible during the development and operational phases of any IoT system. Risk management skills can be composed of *soft skills* and *hard skills*. The soft skills side of risk management especially cannot necessarily be taught, because they involve a lot of judgment and take into account cross-disciplinary considerations—like this book—such as risks associated with regulations as well as financial, competitive, and internal policy issues. Risk management is typically not taught in technical engineering or computer science courses, though it is found in business schools and as a theme in degrees such as Masters in Business

---

[18]See ISO 27017—Cloud security practices.

Administration (MBA). But not always. Perhaps the risk management skill resides directly in management? There are established methodologies for managing risk and established libraries of security and privacy controls that serve as a guide for what might be expected from a well-managed system. For instance, there are a variety of excellent, formal processes for conduction Threat-Risk Assessments (TRAs). This book itself is a superset of requirements and controls for IoT security.

> Why do we graduate doctors with specializations in ailments that afflict less than 1% of humanity, but not engineers with specializations in the technology that touches 100% of the population and is the platform for personal prosperity and their way of life?

On the *hard side* of risk management professionalism is the security evaluation and testing practitioners; Those who will look at the very granular technical elements of an IoT device: code reviewers, component testing, performance analysis, and testing. Like softer risk management, security evaluation is done according to well-defined methodologies can can often result in certifications against specific assurance criteria. The Common Criteria[19] scheme is a good example of a form of professional risk management provided by security assessment and evaluation. Common Criteria as an IT assurance scheme is recognized by over a dozen Organization for Economic Cooperation and Development (OECD) and other countries, including the United States, United Kingdom, Canada, Australia, and New Zealand (aka "the five eyes").

As before, it is okay to accept risks as long as you know what you are accepting. In this case, the risk is adequately understanding what types of skills are required to create a secure IoT service or application and comparing that to the skills that are actually available in-house or within the service provider ecosystems (transferring the skills-risks to providers).

INCREASED USER SUPPORT COSTS

The insights and granularity of view that the IoT will bring to many everyday consumer services and functions can drive spikes in user-support costs, as people suddenly wonder about what all this new information really means. Am I in danger? Am I overpaying? Am I consuming too much water or power or lawn fertilizer or engine oil or toothpaste or aspirin or diapers?

The vulnerability in this instance might be associated with the estimates associated with ongoing customer support costs and requirements and sufficiently planning to address this demand in a way that is efficient but also avoids eroding customer satisfaction—or worse—creating a poor customer experience and eroding adoption rates.

For instance, the huge growth in health devices and apps has caused some to have a concern over what has been referred to as *iPochondria*:

> Insurers may have cause to worry that, instead of reducing doctors' workloads, the spread of m-health devices and apps may only encourage hypochondria: surgeries may be flooded with the

---

[19]http://www.commoncriteriaportal.org/.

"worried well," fussing over every slightly anomalous reading. That may keep the medical profession nicely busy, but will not curb the ever-rising cost of health care."[20]

The ramification for the IoT is that the health apps have conclusively raised help desk and support costs in a very measurable manner, but the benefits themselves are slow to emerge or to be quantified.

Any IoT service needs to take into account and manage the risk of unforeseen demands for help desk and other expensive forms of support service that are enabled by the IoT, especially if the *value-added* is more of a marketing gimmick than something that definitively improves the service.

INTERNAL POLICY

Internal policy is about the management-level guidance especially given to product management and engineering about the security and privacy controls appropriate for the IoT good or service, and how it is derived. Is it based on international standards or industry best practice? Is it about regulation or self-regulation?

The importance of internal policy lies in the fact that complexity is manageable, but not necessarily managed. That is, the complexity of the IoT system can get beyond management abilities, and the risk is that many vulnerabilities and threats are not addressed, or are ignored or unknown.

Internal skills and understanding must be developed to establish an appropriate internal security policy. Weak policy at the top equals weak security throughout. This might also become a major risk for IoT goods and service providers related to liability.

This notion of the importance of internal policy and internal governance is demonstrated as countries like the United States seek to enforce a degree of internal competence, at least for publicly listed companies.

Recent bills before the US government show the merit of this type of approach, for instance the Cybersecurity Information Sharing Act of 2015/2016,[21] which seeks to compel an awareness of the importance of internal security, policy, and governance.

This might make a difference: forced disclosure of board-level awareness and abilities related to cyber security. It is not expensive or time consuming like audit. And fakery should be easy to detect and challenged as a shareholder (read the Board members' CVs and decide for yourself if there is anyone on the board who knows enough about security). However, this can generate some ridiculous outcomes, too: boards members claiming to be cybersecurity experts because they once installed desktop AV on their home computer, in 1998, for instance.

While a board-level executive with a bono fide understanding of cyber security will go a long way toward managing risks associated with internal policy, his/her judgement will only be as good as the information have available; for instance, about security posture of the organization and about the supply chain. But, at least at the board level, there will now be a capability to ask questions and get diligently composed answers about security and risk management, due to regulation.

---

[20]http://www.economist.com/news/business/21595461-those-pouring-money-health-related-mobile-gadgets-and-apps-believe-they-can-work.

[21]https://www.congress.gov/bill/114th-congress/senate-bill/754/text.

Table 13.2 Board Member IoT Security Due Diligence Question Matrix				
Board member question: what security controls do we have in place or are we planning in each of the cells of this table?				
	Endpoint	Gateway	Network	Cloud/DC
Safety Confidentiality and integrity Availability and resilience Identity and access control Context and the environment Interoperability and flexibility				

What questions should a board-level representative be asking to manage IoT risks associated with internal policy? As a starting point, a board might ask for information about the four main IoT security control points: endpoint, gateway, network, and DC/clouds.

These questions might be posed in a matrix format, looking for summary information about the main operational requirements we have identified, as shown in the example in Table 13.2.

Additionally, the following questions might be posed:

- What security controls are transferred or outsourced to suppliers along with certain services? What are the SLAs associated with this risk transference?
- What risks are being accepted? For legitimate (or not) reasons such as cost?
  Other areas that will make internal policy an area of risk and complexity will be whether internal policy can be flexible enough to deal with, and how does it address:
- Administrative errors and omissions
- Cascading failures from one system to another or one part of the supply chain to another. These are very difficult to assess because they are frequently *unimagined* until an event comes to pass.[22]
- Unintended and unforeseen user behaviors associated with:
  - Defective or emergent behaviors (see out discussion in Chapter 12, Threats and Impacts to the IoT, on emergent behavior).
  - The human-machine interface and unforeseen loads and conditions resulting from conditions of panic, frustration, impatience, sloth, negligence, and all the other deadly sins.
  Internal policy cannot just be something merely mandated with the wave of an executive hand. It requires a strategic alignment between the business requirements and operational requirements. Management or board-level executives need to understand IoT security beyond just how to spell it. This also means that IoT security has to be meaningful to the business in fundamentally two ways, as we have been repeating through this book:
- Internal policies about IoT security add value to goods and services and ultimately make more satisfied customers
- Internal policies about IoT security generate efficiencies and save money compared to insecure systems; for instance, through less downtime, faster recovery, fewer defects

---

[22]See my book, *Critical Infrastructure: Understanding Its Component Parts, Vulnerabilities, Operating Risks, and Interdependencies*, CRC Press, 2008.

OPERATIONAL AND PROCESS RISK IN THE IoT

When we were discussing business and organizational vulnerabilities and risk at the beginning of this chapter, we were talking about executive-level concerns and issues. At the operational and process level we have to move down in the hierarchy to those managing business units and *horizontal* functions within an organization like IT, finance, sales, marketing, and human resources.

Operational and process vulnerabilities and risks may be more granular and specific than management-level vulnerabilities and risks. Therefore, the following vulnerabilities and risk should be considered a superset that may apply to many different IoT goods and services, but not all will be meaningful to every IoT good or service.

To repeat—this is important to making this information most useful—not all vulnerabilities and risks will apply to all systems.

The following is an aggregation of vulnerabilities and risks that are sufficiently different in the IoT to warrant awareness, and perhaps consideration, by executives and managers alike.

SAFETY

Safety is about physical-device (vs software-system) resilience, and predictability of performance and failure (logically and physically).

Safety in the IoT might be seen more prosaically as something that is a guarantee of an expected physical outcome, resulting from of a logical or "cyber" event. The following sorts of events might be considered examples a safety impact:

- Explosions, implosions, heat, freezing, crush and pressure, vibrations, and other kinetic or physical forces
- Allergic reactions, for instance to compounds released into the environment or wearable things or to environmental conditions that change as a result of things like climate control systems
- Sensory impacts (degrade or harm hearing, or sight especially); for instance, augmented reality systems and services that temporarily or even permanently degrade senses because they are too intense or close
- Infections and tumors, related to toxic environment or wearable or implantable devices in the IoT

Typical safety vulnerabilities will be directly associated from the performance requirements we identified in Chapter 6, Safety Requirements in the Internet of Things, such as repeatability and consistency: activities and operations will be performed the same way, at the same rate with the same latency, loss, defect rate, and so on over long periods of time.

Good enough for enterprise IT is not necessarily good enough for the IoT

Enterprise IT software is not designed to support safety, which is a vulnerability when IoT software and systems are procured just like enterprise software and systems. Enterprise IT hardware is not procured to support safety either—where there may be many different generations of hardware used concurrently with the same software—and the slight performance differences are immaterial to *enterprise requirements*.

Such assumptions will not play out well in the IoT. The overall vulnerability is that performance of enterprise-grade products and services do not meet specifications or assumptions about performance metrics, so IoT systems are deployed and performance metrics are off by a margin that is meaningless in enterprise IT, but catastrophic in the IoT. In the enterprise IT world, large deviation in performance claims versus reality are typical and therefore manageable. The IoT system may prove far less forgiving.

When it comes to safety and risks, the toxicity and disposability of IoT devices, especially endpoint devices, is a potential vulnerability because the inappropriate or uncontrolled release or destruction of certain IoT devices using enterprise IT processes or assumptions could be highly dangerous. The full degree of safety vulnerabilities may not be understood if it is not part of the IoT risk assessment process.

Safety, availability, speed, and responsiveness

The speed and responsiveness of IoT systems and devices to start/stop and shutdown instructions, both from the endpoints and from the centralized control elements in the gateway or the cloud, would be a safety vulnerability. The ability to start quickly will be important for IoT devices involved in kinetic motion and movement control, where they may not be active until a person or object comes into range for the purposes of saving power, for example. These will typically be *constrained* devices, such as those with more limited storage, small batteries, or devices that scavenge power from the environment, those with low processor or memory, low network speeds, ranges, or ability to sustain transmit and receiving functions (due to power).

Once the device is called into action it must be available very quickly—potentially meaning that it must move from a dormant state to an active state in milliseconds. Under these design requirements, an IoT device might be required to forgo security controls that would otherwise make a lot of sense. Encryption technology on the device is a good example. If the time and energy it takes to decrypt an instruction set on a small, constrained IoT device will take the startup time from 2 to 500 ms, is it possible that safety will degrade or fail because of security overhead?

> In the name of managing risk and of safety in the IoT, other security requirements may be temporarily diminished under certain (abnormal?) conditions. (A message in clear text is better sent than no message at all.) This in turn may introduce a whole range of other vulnerabilities that must be treated, transferred, or accepted under certain defined conditions.

Change management as a safety risk in the IoT

The frequent weakness of update and change management capabilities for IoT devices is a safety vulnerability.

IoT devices will sometimes be deployed in the field on a permanent basis: for the duration of their useful life without any ability to upgrade software to accommodate new found vulnerabilities or attack techniques. IoT devices may be part of a critical infrastructure (CI) such as a transport infrastructure that cannot be shut down except at the very controller and distant intervals, meaning that they may be required to function for long periods in technically vulnerable states.

IoT devices may have different requirements from enterprise-grade IT devices, and change management processing for acceptance testing and regression testing may be insufficiently designed (that is, not rigorous enough) when applied to IoT systems, thus creating the risk that IoT systems are placed into service without adequate tests and fail during cut-over or operations.

Failing however *versus failing safe*

Failing safe, as previously discussed, means that an IoT device will stop working in a manner that is intentional and designed. It will stop working in a way that is predictable and will leave security and safety manageable, by virtue of the failure state being understood. This is the opposite of most IT systems, both for enterprise and consumers. In such systems, the failure state of a device, system, or service is usually unknown, random, ad hoc, or variable.

Lack of fail-safe attributes is an additional vulnerability associated with safety in the IoT. Enterprise IT devices and software are not often designed with any failure state in mind—they typically *just fail*. The exception might be certain inline intrusion prevention solutions, which are specifically designed to *fail open* rather than shut down the network when they do fail.

IoT devices, because of cyberphysical interfaces and controls, will have rigorous requirements around failing open or failing closed: which state will depend on the nature of the IoT system or service. Often the decision to fail open or closed will be a matter of software design as much as hardware configuration.

Similarly, software updates or configuration changes might affect the failure state of an IoT device in a way that is overlooked—until a failure occurs—and the failure is not the intended state—with potentially terrible consequences.

Risk management in the IoT will benefit from an awareness of failure state among vendors especially, almost like a checklist item during any software upgrade: Has the failure state changed? And if the failure state has been changed for any reason whatsoever, clear and loud notifications should be broadcast to customer and the industry at large to ensure that the operational risk profile is not suddenly and dramatically altered by what might appear to be a small thing to the product managers behind the change in failure state.

PANIC BUTTONS

Providing users information and indications about when a thing is on or off is important, as previously noted. This is a requirement useful in addressing both safety and privacy (confidentiality) in the IoT. A related vulnerability and risk is the common lack of things like an obvious physical, mechanical off switch, The lack of mechanical on/off switches can present risk in the IoT and will be important.[23] Physical shutdown procedures are often not taken into account adequately, and it is assumed that such things can be either overlooked or developed as a purely logical control. In other words, the only way to turn off a device or a feature in an IoT device will be via a software interface.

Hard lessons have been previously learned about the need simply to have an option to turn things off. Swiss Air 111 crashed in 1998 killing 229 people because an in-flight entertainment

---

[23]Economist leader about IA—May 9, 2015 issue.

system started to overheat and had no off switch: the entertainment system eventually starting a wiring fire that resulted in a catastrophic crash.[24]

In the IoT, a lack of an off switch will cause people to do things like unplug or power down devices because they want an assurance to be undisturbed or want privacy for a period of time. And then they forget to turn them on again, with critical safety of security effects. The same can happen with an off switch, but devices might also be programmed to turn on again after a dormant period, which is not necessarily possible if the power source (or the network access) is cut off.

Sometimes users will just want to know that they can disrupt or stop a device quickly, for any reason, like a panic button on an escalator.

A panic button or off switch will also address regulatory risks related to privacy, even if the risk is more imagined than real. Some people just want to be able to turn off certain features manually. Having clear and well identified *off* functions will make both safety and compliance easier to prove in some cases.

NETWORK SEGMENTATION AND SAFETY

Network segmentation separates different types of traffic logically and prevents characteristics (normal or abnormal) in one segmented network from affecting another network. Network segmentation has many beneficial applications in the world of enterprise IT and the Internet today, but will be a safety-critical function first and foremost in the IoT.

Segmentation also prevents an infected, defective, or malicious device or entity from attacking other devices and entities in adjacent systems over the network. This applies to both the IoT data traffic and the IoT applications and systems making use of that data traffic. This is sometimes referred to as *network slicing*. There will be two different forms of segmentation, at least. We can call them *north-south* isolation and segmentation and *east-west* microsegmentation.

North-south isolation and segmentation

This form of segmentation is becoming well understood at the DC, but it needs to be extended to processing done in the network and especially the gateways. Fig. 13.7 is a DC model, where traffic from the Internet or from a large transport network is bringing data and traffic flows to the applications in the DC or cloud. As traffic enters the DC, it not only passes through a firewall but is shuttled into a specific domain of control in the DC—a segment. If something in the given segment goes wrong and a threat agent compromises a platform in the segment, they cannot access other resources outside the given segment. However, within a given segment, there may be many existing services and a rich target base: no need to get outside the segment for good hunting! This leads to the east-west discussion to follow.

Fig. 13.8 is what that might look like in a large, multi-tenanted network element or gateway processing scenario, where the element is inline. In this case, data or traffic flows from the endpoint will enter the element and undergo security (or other forms of) processing. Perhaps a firewall is located on an edge gateway, protecting constrained devices at the last hop in the network? Perhaps an intrusion detection solution is located deep in the carrier network, performing value-added security functions on large populations of en point traffic flows before they converge on the DC or

---

[24]https://en.wikipedia.org/wiki/Swissair_Flight_111.

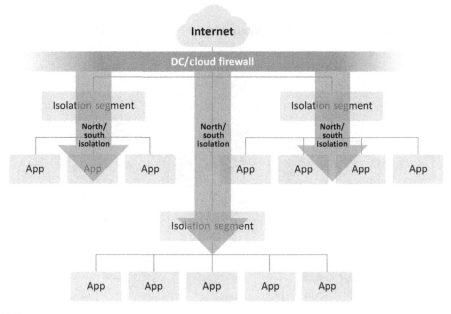

FIGURE 13.7

North-south isolation in a DC or cloud.

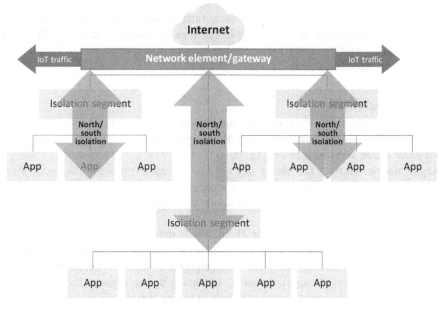

FIGURE 13.8

North-south isolation in network elements or edge gateways.

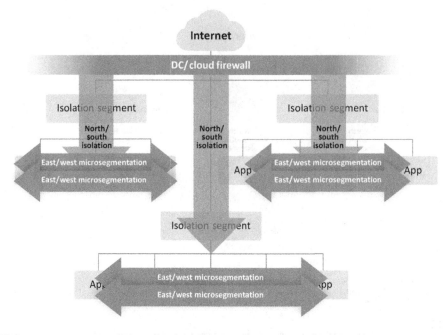

FIGURE 13.9

East-west microsegmentation.

cloud. Alternately, network elements might also normalize and security-aggregated traffic flows before it transitions to more expensive bandwidth—such as international backhaul. Recall that NFV will be a key to this capability in the IoT, allowing various applications to run directly in the network or gateway, on shared platforms.

East-west micro segmentation

Microsegmentation is about applying rules to the east-west traffic within an isolated north-south segmentation in a DC or cloud, but also potentially within network or gateway elements doing processing and value-added services (see Fig. 13.9).

Microsegmentation refers to the ability not only to segregate different classes of service onto logically distinct network segments, but also to manage and enforce rules on end-to-end connections for just a group of components in a given network segment that has already undergone north-south isolation in a DC.

An example of this would be in a service chain, where data or instructions from a device might involve services from three or four different components with requests flying back and forth among these components east-west through the north-south segment of the DC. (Or, potentially, a powerful network of gateway element. If segmentation is occurring at the edge of the IoT network, then north-south isolation might be moot because there is only one tenant to begin with!)

Microsegmentation allows the creation of private or dedicated segments within segments for applications or device classes or even distinct use cases, especially at the edges of the network.

In a conventional IT environment, microsegmentation is difficult to apply because of *humans in the loop* and the mobile and sometimes random nature of their behavior. Microsegmentation is a technology that relies on SDN because the granularity of the control needs highly automated configuration and management capacity, based on broader rulesets.

For instance, an IoT system or service is configured in advance to apply microsegmentation to new devices or new gateways, allowing the network to get higher assurance in all requirement areas. SDN is currently a technology that is widely deployed in DCs but is driving out into the networks and gateways of carriers and large enterprises.

IoT risk management will act as a catalyst for SDN technologies, specifically but not exclusively for the safety, security, and risk management benefits. For IoT, with more predictable patterns of communication, microsegmentation becomes viable and appropriate because the traffic profiles within a given segment are largely known. Why are they known? Because IoT networks will allow for a form of security management we call *white networking*, cover a little later in this chapter.

Risks need to be assessed and balanced end to end. In the conventional IT environment, the centralized resources in the DC or cloud are considered the most important, but in the IoT much important data processing and management will be done outside the cloud or DC. Data processing will be done on virtualized network platforms and gateways, especially to compensate for constrained devices. Increasingly gateways will be safety-critical systems—more so even than the central application running in the cloud or DC.

Ultimately, microsegmentation will be a powerful risk management technique in the IoT control catalogue, allowing applications and system to be tightly controlled and minimizing the attack surface. Threats and vulnerabilities in adjacent but unrelated systems using the shared infrastructure and technologies are literally firewalled in a way they are not today—and could not be using conventional, appliance-based networking and security controls.

CONFIDENTIALITY AND INTEGRITY

It is important to understand that the confidentiality, integrity, and availability balance is not the same in the IoT as in the IT world. In the IoT there is elevated focus on the integrity and availability, where confidentiality appears to dominate many IT security discussions.

Risk managers need to be aware of this in the design of systems and the application of scarce resources. Confidentiality is not always the most important security property or focus for the IoT system designer. Ironically, this is a potential vulnerability in the IoT, because insufficient confidentiality controls (such as encryption) may be designed into IoT systems as the focus shift to integrity and availability.

TO ENCRYPT OR NOT ENCRYPT?

Increasingly, the guidance is to encrypt everything, in the light of eavesdropping, espionage, and theft exposed during recent data-loss debacles.[25,26] The IETF has even started issuing guidance to this effect as a basic design requirement for any Internet protocol (IP)—based system. This creates a new and reciprocal but converse vulnerability for law enforcement and lawful intercept: how do they get through easily applied civilian cryptography, which is very nearly military grade at this point?

At the same time that the perception of a need-to-encrypt everything grows, national governments are moving toward requiring access to communications, forcing telecom carriers to do the heavy lifting. Ultimately, it may come down to the fact that communications will be blocked if it is encrypted in such a manner that law enforcement cannot see it. For the IoT, a choice to encrypt traffic among devices may carry long-term consequences depending on how it is done. For instance, in-field devices (consumer or industrial) could potentially become noncompliant with national laws. We noted this this in our discussion of regulatory risks in the IoT; this is the operational corollary: to encrypt or not encrypt?

DELEGATION OF FUNCTIONS: DETECTION VERSUS PREVENTION

For constrained IoT devices that cannot support a lot of security (because they must have efficient performance), compensating controls must be sought. Compensating controls might be found in gateway, network, or cloud-based services. For instance, a gateway may act to encrypt traffic for endpoint devices, or to normalize and compress command and control instructions from the cloud services, to reduce loads on the endpoints. Anti-fraud, abuse, and anomaly detection logic might be built into the cloud applications in order to detect endpoints that have been compromised or become defective, rather than burdening these constrained devices with security features acting in the same way.

This strategy reflects the move from *protection* toward *detection*. Increasingly, security technologies are moving toward detection because protection technologies like firewalls, antivirus, and a wide range of other established, prophylactic security solutions are proving to be too expensive in terms of resources for endpoints of all description. These same controls are proving less and less effective at staying ahead of the attacks and threat agents, especially in an age of industrialized malware development, where custom-built malware is cheap and easy to deploy against specific and small targets. It has become a better investment to rapidly detect an affected system rather than layer more protection into the system.

MULTIPARTY AUTHENTICATION AND CRYPTOGRAPHY IN THE IoT

In the IoT there will be far more multiparty transactions occurring than in the Internet of old, where most transactions were intrinsically peer to peer. By *multiparty,* we mean that more than just two sides need to agree that the transaction is legitimate because of implications such as safety, or multiple parties stand to be affected at the same time as a result of other security failings.

---

[25]See *The Panama Papers*, April 2016.
[26]*Ericsson Technology Review*, December 2015—http://www.ericsson.com/sectionspage/151222-cryptography-encrypted-world_940234653_c.

Today many transactions involve a client and a server, where the client authenticates to a server for an application or a service is being provided by the server. This might be a banking service, or a retail purchase, or a government service like filing a tax form.

But what happens when the application is a new generation of IoT service involving more than two supplying parties? It is a multiparty transaction or activity. How do you, as a risk and security manager, design such things? Do the current identity and security technologies scale?

The traditional way of dealing with nominally multiparty transactions is to look to the service provider (the server) to aggregate most or all of the suppliers and counterparties into a single relationship for the client and charge a fee for that as part of the overall price of the service. This is what a retailer or a travel agent might do: they have relationships with many suppliers and pull together a package of goods and services for the one client. Or sometimes they merely procure the good or service in bulk (wholesale) and distribute to clients. They then charge a markup or margin for this service; this is a proven and time-tested model going back to the emergence of the very first merchants thousands of years ago. This is what Amazon (online) or Sears (bricks and mortar) does today.

But the IoT and the technology underlying it allows for many new functions and value-added services to be created in thousands (if not eventually billions) of combinations among all the various sources of supply. Aggregating service providers and merchants is either not necessary or fully automated or both!

Alternately, an IoT service involves the participation of literally thousands of different devices: aggregation is not viable. For instance, location-based capabilities around detection and tracking will create many opportunities for services in the IoT. But the services and devices used to establish location will be constantly changing as a person or a device moves around. (This is related to the operational requirement in the IoT referred to as *context.*) While it might be possible, it would be expensive and complicated for a third-party aggregator or merchant to try and broker all these location-services for a given client. Possibly, it is not viable. Additionally, such aggregation creates an information base of highly personal data that you may wish to avoid creating in the first place!

An IoT service or a good might be created or procured from different suppliers and vendors, for differing prices, at differing qualities, at differing times. These providers might wish to rearrange their IoT supply chain regularly or even automatically to take advantages of small differences in service profiles, resulting in more efficiency. This is a significant element of the evolving IoT anatomy: stratification of the supply chain into greater specialization and efficiency, with competition at many different *layers* of a service stack: physical device, physical network, network as a service, SaaS, service management, and so on.

To maximize the potential of these IoT opportunities, new forms of multiparty authentication are needed to create and also un-make consortiums of service providers rapidly, with a high degree of trust and a much lower overhead than one-to-one, point-to-point, conventional authentication and authorization supports.

WEAK OR EXPENSIVE: THE OLD CRYPTOSYSTEM AND TECHNIQUES DON'T SCALE TO THE IoT

There are basically two conventional models for authentication of Internet relationships: one is weak (shared key), one is expensive (public key), and neither will address the full range of identity and access requirements in the IoT.

Secure Sockets Layer[27] (SSL) and Transport Layer Security (TLS) are the most widely used security systems on the Internet today. Both systems use public key infrastructure (PKI) and shared-key models to create a secure channel between a web browser and a website.

Shared keys are essentially shared secrets known to two or more parties. Parties authenticate themselves to another party by proving their knowledge of the shared secret to the other party (or parties) by encrypting a token, and the other party (or parties) verify the first party's knowledge of the shared secret by decrypting the token. Shared secrets can be based on passwords, biometric samples, personal identification numbers (PINs), images, gestures, and are fundamentally mutually known symmetric cryptographic keys. In simple terms, this authentication model asks the question, "Do you know the secret?"

In the shared key model, only trusted peers have the key or can get the key. If the device can show it has access to the shared key by encrypting or decrypting a token, then it is trusted. Shared key is weak because if the key is exposed, then all the devices and all the services relying on that key are vulnerable and considered compromised. In the IoT, with billions of device pouring onto the network, the ability physically to access a device and extract the key increases substantially. Also, with more and more devices potentially sharing the same key, the impact of a single key being compromised is big. Shared key is weak not because of the cryptographic algorithms, but because of the vulnerabilities introduced by the management of the shared keys in the IoT.

The other widely used identity and authentication mechanism is known as public key and is too expensive for most of the IoT. Public key involves, in fact, two keys: one for encryption (the public key) and one for decryption and signing (the secret key). Every device employing this scheme needs its own, unique key pair. Most public-key systems involve a challenge-response protocol typically restricted to two parties only. One of the two parties possesses the public key (not secret, publicly disclosed) and the other party possesses the private key (not disclosed, held very secret). One of the parties goes first and encrypts a random message with its secret key-half and sends it to the other party, the other party uses the sender's public key-half to decrypt it and sends the decrypted message back (possibly re-encrypted with the receiver public half). The sender authenticates the receiver if and when the received message matches the original message. In simple terms, this authentication model asks the question, "Can you decrypt this?"

Public key pairs, because of their utility, take much longer than symmetric keys—typically 10 times longer. This means that a device that attempts to manipulate public keys must perform significantly more resource-intensive cryptographic operations for every secure transaction, plus be able to generate, regenerate, and store its own private keys. This is very expensive from a device capability perspective: power, processor, memory, tamper-resistance. The expense of public key manipulation and management may make an IoT device itself nonviable economically in many instances.

Public key is too expensive for some of the IoT because it requires unique, point-to-point authentications for each device with its own unique key pair. This is a massive burden on the network (especially constrained, industrial, or sensor networks) and an even bigger burden on any cloud-based system and services that must maintain secure, authenticated sessions with thousands or millions of devices at once. Also, in the event of peer-to-peer secure communication that rapidly changes, public key will also take too long and/or too many resources or too much network.

---

[27]As of 2015, the IETF recommended that SSL be deprecated as a security transport because it has become fallible to a variety of well-known attacks, though it still remains in use.

For instance, as a smart car travels down the road passing road beacons used for speed and distance safety every few milliseconds, public key authentication of those beacons would probably not happen fast enough without a mini-server at each beacon! *Too expensive*.

MULTIPARTY AUTHENTICATION AND DATA PROTECTION

Multiparty authentication and data protection can be expressed simply as $2 + N$, meaning that more than two entities are involved in a shared cryptosystem. Additionally, this multiparty system can be *horizontal* and *cascading*. Mathematics to support such authentication and cryptosystems have long been known; see Euler's work from 1779 on polynomial theorems, also known as *key splitting*.[28]

The crux of these multiparty systems is that each participant *recreates* the keys common to the cryptosystem versus sharing keys under either symmetric or public key systems.

Multiparty authentication is not necessarily a novel requirement, even if its implementation has not been forced by circumstances; there are many use cases where several entities need access to a common secure resource in a timely and lightweight manner. For instance, dozens of public safety personnel need access to the secure, encrypted radio channel. This use case would typically involve a shared symmetric key. But what if the same channel was used for IoT devices controlling firefighting robots or even remote sentries? Would you trust those devices to shared-key systems—forever? In the case of symmetric (shared-key) systems, the more copies of the keys that are distributed, the greater the potential a copy *leaks* or is disclosed in an unauthorized manner and compromises the entire system. In the case of public key systems, encrypting the infobase means managing many unique keys, one for every participant!

In the IoT, with all its wealth of safety-critical, commercially valuable, and personally identifiable data flowing around, there will be a vulnerability associated around what information is available to whom. For instance, you may grant access to your health information to your doctor working from a hospital system, but not your doctor working from her home systems. In practice, the combination of your permission plus the doctor's consent, plus the hospital system's approval may be required to unlock your information in the data store. In this case, three parties are required to collaborate in a cryptosystem *agreement* to unlock your health record: the patient, the doctor, and a device located within the hospital.

Another example of a multiparty operational requirement might be IoT nodes operating as an interdependent, safety-critical sensor network. In this example, it may be that fail-safe configurations in these devices demand that they shut down the entire service as soon as one of the devices fails, stops sending data, or stops responding to a heartbeat or beacon. Masquerade attacks against these systems would be a major vulnerability, so authenticating each node related to their response to a heartbeat or beacon may be required. A multiparty authentication system based on a single key that can be *recreated* based on unique properties from each participants would be far better than a system based on a common key *shared* among all participants, or worse, a massively expensive public key system.

A consumer-oriented operational use case could relate to something like photo sharing among friends. Rather than trying to encrypt the same photos for multiple public keys, encrypt it once

---

[28]See https://en.wikipedia.org/wiki/Leonhard_Euler#Applied_mathematics and Key-splitting—https://en.wikipedia.org/wiki/Secret_sharing.

using a key that can be created strictly by the $2 + N$ coowners model of authentication. In this model of multiparty authentication and data protection, the best elements of shared key and public key are retained, while the weak or expensive characteristics are left out. No storage of keys is required on the endpoints—just enough memory initially to derive a common key, split it, and distribute the pieces among multiple parties. To do so requires only a small amount of memory and processor: enough to generate and split a common key. The only requirement is an awareness of how many parties are actually included in the *multi* part of multiparty: how many peers or participants are needed to recreate the key?

MULTIPARTY HORIZONTAL AUTHENTICATION AND DATA PROTECTION

A first form of multiparty authentication to address the vulnerabilities associated with shared key and public key encryption is *horizontal* in nature: that is, the system can scale to an unlimited number of equally privileged participants. *Horizontal* refers to the ability of an unlimited number of peers to derive a common shared key, but from unique credential properties: none of the participants, or peers, need share their credentials to derive the same key. This is like shared key, but the key is derived versus embedded or stored. Attempting to replicate such functionality under a public key system would require that a shared key be uniquely encrypted by each horizontal peer.

MULTIPARTY CASCADING AUTHENTICATION AND DATA PROTECTION

Related to horizontal authentication and data protection is multiparty cascading authentication and protection. The distinction in this case is the ability to split credentials properties (credentials) assigned to a given party potentially an infinite number of times. Splitting credentials means that an IoT element (person, device, service, whatever) can take the peer-to-peer, horizontal credential and split it in *n*, for the purposes of further controlling usage from a group of hierarchically lower peers.

Using health information as an example again: a hospital encrypts medical records with a key derived from merely two credentials: one from the patient and one from the hospital. To decrypt and access this record, the infobase needs the patient credential and a credential from the hospital. The hospital then splits its own credential into two or three or four different horizontal, stakeholder credentials (for instance: hospital systems, insurance systems, privacy ombudsman, and an assigned doctor). For the patient records to be accessed, at least one of the four medical stakeholders must supply its unique credential to generate the hospital credential, which is then combined with the patients' own credential to create the key and decrypt the patient records. In an alternate scenario, the cryptosystem designer may require that two out of four, three out of four, or all four out of four stakeholders in this cascading hierarchy must provide credentials in order to generate the higher level key-half (see Fig. 13.10).

HARDWARE-BASED VERSUS SOFTWARE-BASED PROCESSING

Many of the designed capabilities related to cryptography in the IoT are reverse engineered according to available processing, memory, and power resources—this is a significant vulnerability,

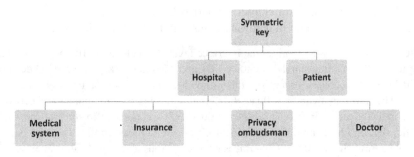

FIGURE 13.10

Multiparty cascading authentication and credentials based on key-splitting.

because often it defaults to *no security* when there are essentially no resources left to support security!

Network processing involves reading packet headers and determining how to route, switch, or process them. Application processing can involve processing layer 7 applications, starting with merely understanding what the application within the packet-stream happens to be, and going all the way to how threats may reside within the application-level traffic. Cryptography is becoming more and more common in application-level services of all types to defeat eavesdropping by criminal and state-sponsored entities. These requirements are being directly driven by several threats at once: spying nation-states, invasive policing, and criminals. A significantly underused risk management technique is to leverage hardware-based encryption acceleration. Most cryptography right now appears to be integrated by IoT vendors in software, consuming 10 or more times the memory and power that might be the case with hardware-based cryptography.

Cryptography can involve either encryption of network packets at the transport or network layer (typically) or digital signature technology (asymmetric cryptography). End-to-end cryptography is becoming a perceived necessary risk management tool, in which all data moves through encrypted tunnels, whether SSL, Layer 2 Tunneling Protocol (L2TP), IP security (IPSec), or other forms.

Cryptography acceleration has been around for a long time, but commonly in the form of *hardware security modules* (HSM). These are good for servers with lots of power and the ability to have a peripheral device to speed up processing. HSMs are likely not viable for IoT, especially for constrained things that must be cheaply manufactured or running on batteries.

The alternative is to take advantage of cryptographic acceleration capabilities available in some chipsets and systems on a chip (SOC) from vendors like Intel, using Intel Xeon with Intel Quick-assist[29] and advanced encryption standard-new instructions (AES-NI), and gateway chipsets such as

---

[29]http://www.intel.com/content/dam/www/public/us/en/documents/solution-briefs/integrated-cryptographic-compression-accelerators-brief.pdf.

Intel Core and Intel Atom. Endpoint chipset support will vary by manufacturers. Another example of network processing acceleration in hardware is through Fortinet and their FortiASIC processors:

> FortiASIC network processors work at the interface level to accelerate traffic by offloading traffic from the main CPU. Current models contain NP4 and NP6 network processors. Older FortiGate models include NP1 network processors (also known as FortiAccel, or FA2) and NP2 network processors. The traffic that can be offloaded, maximum throughput, and number of network interfaces supported by each varies by processor model: NP6 supports offloading of most IPv4 and IPv6 traffic, IPsec VPN encryption, CAPWAP traffic, and multicast traffic. The NP6 has a capacity of 40 Gbps through 4×10 Gbps interfaces or 3×10 Gbps and 16×1 Gbps interfaces.[30]

Hardware-accelerated content processing (including cryptographic processing) can also be applied for security benefits, providing added threat-inspection sophistication at lower costs to IoT security. Content processing for security application is less well understood and less widely applied than cryptographic processing. In the IoT, the ability to perform these functions in hardware might make content processing appropriate at remote, constrained points in the IoT end-to-end design. The following are some features of content processing that might be found in hardware:[31]

- IPS signature matching acceleration
- High performance virtual private network (VPN) bulk data engine
- IPsec and SSL/TLS protocol processor
- Key exchange processor supporting high performance Internet key exchange (IKE) and RSA computation
- Handshake accelerator with automatic key material generation
- Random number generator
- Message authentication module for high performance calculation of hashes such as SHA256/SHA1/MD5

Fig. 13.11 shows an example of performance differences from purely software-based cryptography to hardware. Such performance will make all the difference in what type of security can be built into IoT systems. The cost of such hardware-based systems will be determined in part by economies of scale, where the chips become cheaper the more they are produced for inclusion in IoT devices and systems. This means that the more awareness of this advantage the better, driving further economies of scale.

IoT system designers, engineers, and executives need to be especially conscious of the capabilities of hardware-based network and application processing, and what it can mean overall to the security of the IoT system they are developing.

For instance, the following opportunities present themselves to IoT security by using hardware acceleration for network and gateway applications:

- Advanced security processing at the edges of the IoT system on devices that could not support such controls if they were software-based:

---

[30]FortiOS Handbook— http://docs.fortinet.com/uploaded/files/1607/fortigate-hardware-accel-50.pdf.
[31]FortiNet Content Process v8—http://docs.fortinet.com/uploaded/files/1607/fortigate-hardware-accel-50.pdf.

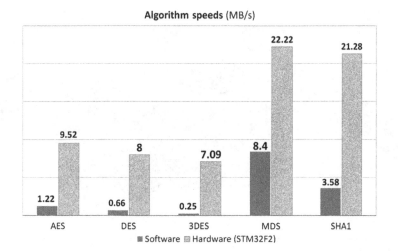

FIGURE 13.11

Hardware versus software encryption performance.[32]

- • Gateway-based firewalls and local area network (LAN)−side intrusion prevention system (IPS) on customer premises to monitor device-to-device communication (or attacks!)
- • Virtualized security elements that leverage hardware accelerations through the hypervisor, such as IPS or firewalls inside 4G and 5G base stations.
- Support for complete end-to-end encryption may be viable with hardware versus software
- Less hardware (memory and processor) is needed (lower cost) for the same amount of security
- Less power or battery is needed for the same amount of security processing
- More options for security become available for the same device or infrastructure, potentially expanding the addressable market for the device or system

MICROSEGMENTATION

As mentioned earlier in this chapter, this is a form of security management technique that has started in the DC and cloud but is moving out into the network and gateway. Evolving microsegmentation is about addressing IoT vulnerabilities related to both confidentiality and integrity, where constrained or poorly built endpoint devices cannot reliability exist in environments with a lot of unrestrained connectivity.

Whereas *microsegmentation* is all about managing traffic *within* a domain of control, such that only approved sources, destinations, and services are able to communicate with each other inside that single domain of control, with *segmentation* traffic is unmanaged, once inside the domain.

With microsegmentation, a domain of control may be a wide area network (WAN), a local area network (LAN), a network subnet, a virtual local area network (VLAN), or possibly even a mesh

[32]https://www.wolfssl.com/wolfSSL/Blog/Entries/2012/12/27_STM32_and_CyaSSL_-_Hardware_Crypto_and_RNG_Support.html.

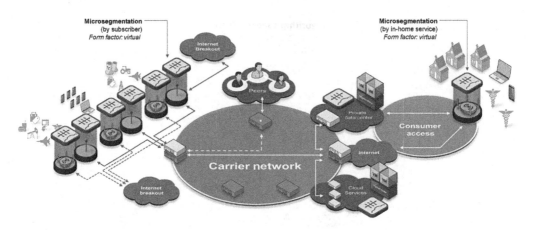

FIGURE 13.12

Microsegmentation at the gateway.

or *ad hoc* network among trusted devices. Microsegmentation is typically discussed and architected with *east-west* traffic in mind in a DC or in the cloud. For example: a customer portal server is allowed to speak to the local Lightweight Directory Access Protocol (LDAP) server and the local Domain Name Service (DNS), but the LDAP server and the domain name server (DNS) server have no need to communicate with each other. We'd place each server in a microsegment within the domain of control, effectively creating a segment inside a segment. Microsegmentation addresses the growing risk of a compromised server or device within a domain of control being able to communicate and perhaps subvert all the other devices within that domain, assuming conventional perimeter security is all that is available to the network. The ultimate risk is that somewhere in just about all domain of control will be servers that *cross* boundaries to other services. If they become compromised, they become potential attack portals to other domains.

End-to-end microsegmentation in the IoT will require moving operational techniques and capabilities that are now applied in the DC outward into the network and especially the gateway. See Fig. 13.12 for an illustration of microsegmentation applied out to the gateway, most likely on the basis of NFV technologies.

A succeeding layer of firewalls will need to be coordinated and automated to make end-to-end microsegmentation possible. This means firewalls in the DC need to speak to firewalls in the network, and the gateway at the edges of the system—the last "hop" before the endpoint IoT devices themselves. See the section entitled "Smart Gateways for the IoT," later in this chapter, for more on this important option for RIoT control.

In the end, IoT traffic will need to be highly controlled, but also flexibly routed to retain resiliency. The opportunity for unauthorized devices and networks to access IoT traffic will need to be much reduced over what it is today, and a matter of effective risk management must be developed.

WHITE NETWORKING

In some cases, vulnerabilities associated with IoT devices will be extreme in that nothing except legitimate communications from legitimate sources can be allowed to reach them. These devices will require that most if not all security controls be delegated to other parts of the system—specifically the gateways and transport networks.

White networks are a form of RIoT control that can scale and deliver the assurance required; *white* is used here as a term to imply *clean and pure*. The IoT will contain all the devices on the current Internet, plus many new devices used for machine-to-machine (M2M) and industrial applications and services. In contrast to a white network, I would assess the regular Internet as *black*—filthy, full of attacks and threats and no place for a wave of small, simple, cheap devices that were never engineered for the open ocean of the Internet; most home and small business networks are probably dark gray: unhygienic at best and usually poorly protected; enterprise networks are *ash gray*—not clean but a respectable balance of risk and cost, and perhaps the best military-grade networks as merely off-white: because there really is no such thing as pure networks. This illustrates the conditions of today's heterogeneous network environments: even with good resources it is difficult to remain clean, and with little or no resources it is pretty much wishful thinking.

IoT services will be a vast range and combination of new business-to-business and business-to-consumer applications like home energy management, healthcare services, smart transportation, augmented reality in entertainment, and on and on.

It is a hallmark of many IoT/industrial/machine networks and devices that they are fragile: they do not respond well to *Internet-like* conditions such as regular or occasional network probes and scans by adjacent devices, or seemingly random increases or decreased in traffic volumes, latency, and packet loss. Many IoT services will see merely degraded network services as a service failure—a very different situation from what most users and applications expect from the current Internet.

Many industrial services will fail or become unpredictable in performance if subjected to even mild forms of reconnaissance or attack over the network. Similarly, a large population of devices coming onto the IoT will mean that some of them will be defective or possess manufacturing defects (hardware or software) that result in them generating excess or malformed network traffic, sometimes to the point of making the network unusable.

Another effect of large numbers of devices coming onto the network will be that some will not be properly secured physically and will become platforms for unauthorized access to the IoT. They will become back doors and side doors into the IoT. In other cases, administrative errors in network management will see logically differentiated and segregated networks accidentally combined, or linked, with traffic from one *polluting* the other, with uncertain impacts on these fragile networks. Administrative errors such as this are already unfortunately common in both carriers and enterprises alike. The complexity of the IoT and the growth of the many interconnected networks supporting the IoT can only increase this operational challenge.

Industrial/machine networks in the IoT will increasingly support critically sensitive, cyberphysical, logical-kinetic interfaces: the IT world controls the real world. In these instances, the potential for an IT security issue to manifest as physical harm and damage becomes very real. Already we are seeing instances of the potential criticality of the logical-kinetic interface and the harm that can result from insecure and fragile networks and devices.[33]

White networks will be beneficial as a simplified form of security for the simplified forms of networking required by industrial and machine applications. White networks will be a matter of

---

[33]See these stories about failed in-home, IP-based security systems (http://www.fiercecable.com/story/comcast-home-invasion-lawsuit-exposes-risks-home-automation-security-servic/2014-10-02) and IP-based utilities (http://www.telegraph.co.uk/news/worldnews/asia/china/5126584/China-and-Russia-hack-into-US-power-grid.html).

allowing only very prescribed machine traffic, and then deny = * (all). In other words, a white network is like application whitelisting (where only allowed software may start and stop on desktops, devices, and servers); but for networking, only explicitly allowed ports, protocols, sources, destinations, frequencies, volumes, and possibly even application payloads and time of day, are allowed. (This list could even be extended to empirical criteria like environmental conditions, for instance, rain vs sun.) Everything else is denied and sets off alarms.

White networks are highly antiseptic, and a value-added service that might be offered by carriers or IoT service providers. They will need to be configured for the IoT services in question, so they will not be a commodity. And they will need to be established and managed carefully. But, once established they should run and provide substantial assurance in an automated manner.

Finally, another way to think about white network is to consider it "business logic segmentation" or "business logic enforcement". In this case, the service-to-service communications flows and order-of-operations are used at the filter. Only flows between services in the correct/expected order and volumes are allowed. Many enterprises—and especially industrial processes—will have their workflows specifically and carefully documented and stipulated in modeling languages like Unified Modeling Language (UML). One means of potentially applying business logic enforcement as a means to white networking would be to convert directly from UML-type process specifications into firewall filters and rules.

Picosegmentation

Picosegmentation may be the next evolution of security segmentation, and the practical operational application of white networks. Picosegmentation takes the idea of microsegmentation one step further: it's not only about building microsegments within a single domain, but further limits things such as ports used, protocols allowed, time of day, traffic volume, and packet sizes and other heuristics that distinguish legitimate traffic from unauthorized connections and attacks. We should keep in mind that the definitions of *segmentation* and *microsegmentation* have not been formalized or agreed to by a standards body. Parts of what I call *picosegmentation* are already out there and useable, but not typically combined methodically with other forms of layered segmentation.

For example, you may have some east-west, microsegmented traffic that is strictly limited to clients and servers that have a demonstrable need to communicate. But if we were to apply some additional rules to this, such as some measure of application control, upper and lower boundaries on traffic volume, what time of day this traffic should be allowed, and so on, we may be able further to limit the ability of a compromised, malicious, or defective IoT device to attack neighbors and improve our ability to spot abnormal communications. Fig. 13.13 shows how picosegmentation rules might be applied by conventional but fine-grained firewalls and IPS elements, to protect IoT systems from a wide range of business as well as operational risks.

The methodical consideration of segmentation + microsegmentation + picosegmentation is an opportunity for security architects and risk managers to model and apply a more fine-grained control into their infrastructures; or at the very least, be able to provide better guidance and more accurate assurance and risk calculations around specific information assets.

NETWORK FUNCTION VIRTUALIZATION AND ROOT OF TRUST

A *root of trust* is essentially a security process that starts with an immutable (unchangeable) hardware identity ingrained into the computing processor, which is then successively leveraged to verify

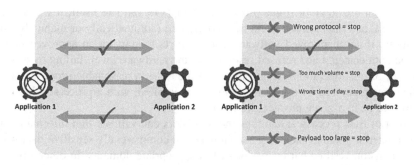

FIGURE 13.13

Picosegmentation.

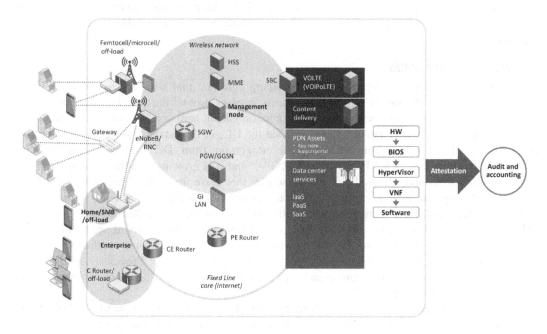

FIGURE 13.14

Root of trust in Intel architecture-based virtualized network.

the software running on the compute platform as a whole. For instance, a uniquely identifiable hardware processor (chip) starts, and its identity is validated: it is recognized and known by the system owner and appears to be located in the expected logical and physical location.

In a virtualized infrastructure, a trusted processor may spawn succeeding layers of BIOS, hypervisor operating systems, and virtual machines and services such as routers or firewalls, or even additional layers in the form of containers. Each has its integrity validated at start-up: it is the expected version and no tampering has occurred (see Fig. 13.14).

Alternately, if an unknown or rogue processor attempts to validate itself, it would fail authentication, be detected, and the network could be reconfigured (automatically or manually) to avoid the device. Similarly, if an unapproved software load attempts to start on an approved hardware platform, it can be both detected and refused resources at the hardware level, failing to start.

Through root of trust operations, it becomes possible to get a reasonable proof that a given piece of information was processed by a given system that is verified, with a processor that is itself verified and known to be in a given physical location.

Through root of trust processes, auditors and regulators can validate that information processing requirements related to matters such as personal data and commercially sensitive data was managed by verified systems on verified hardware, located in appropriate domains. In other words, the information was not handled by unknown or ambiguous (insecure) systems, in places with incompatible or inappropriate legal systems.

In the world of appliance-based networking, root of trust did not have a place. These devices where typically single-purpose, single-sourced (everything made by one vendor) proprietary, and hardened. This is changing as rapidly as the Internet itself is changing on the surface and in the plumbing.

Emigration of virtualization

In the DC, root of trust is very useful for providing evidence that data and services are being securely managed by the highly automated systems in place around the world today; and importantly from a compliance perspective, the data is kept on known hardware/software platforms.

DC technology is rapidly being adopted outside the DC, in the carrier transport and enterprise networks (see Fig. 13.15). This technological emigration from DC to network is NFV to Distributed Network Function Virtualization (D-NFV), and it is growing rapidly: in some cases, in excess of 60% compounded annually.[34] The reason for this move from DC to network is that NFV greatly reduces operational and capital costs, much as virtualization has been doing in the DC for well over a decade. D-NFV increases the potential to host and manage applications on the shared platforms from end to end in the IoT ecosystem, on demand. For instance, if you need a firewall on a particular customer router: "spin it up in software." Need more DNS capacity in this part of your network? Spin it up. Need load-balancing on that gateway? Spin it up. Previously, each one of these demands for more infrastructure meant a physical appliance had to be acquired, shipped, and configured on site by a technician.

Concurrent with the advent and growth of NFV/D-NFV (henceforth just NFV) is SDN. While NFV and SDN are not inextricably linked, and they can grow and operate independently, they have a certain amount of affinity to one another. As a result, they are often discussed in the same breath by many network stakeholders. SDN, like NFV, is expected to drive large efficiencies through the automation and granular control capabilities it brings to network management. Like NFV, SDN is expected to generate savings and bring a wide variety of new value-added, network-based services to the market.

Together NFV and SDN offer amazing potential to automate and chain network-based services together in practically unlimited combinations, for users of all types. But the advantages of NFV and SDN come with new or elevated risks.

---

[34]SNS Research on *NfV + SDN*. CAGR is 2014 to 2019.

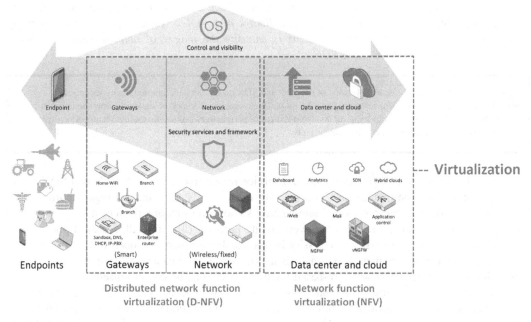

FIGURE 13.15

Virtualization emigration.

Changes to plumbing equals a change to risk

One of the benefits of legacy network and gateway infrastructure is that it was simple: single-purpose boxes, with customized software and hardware. This situation does *not* prevail in the world of NFV and SDN.

Here are a few risks that will change as networking infrastructure moves from appliances (dedicated, customized hardware and software) to NFV and SDN products based on utility computing platforms:

Risk 1: Expanded attack surface. NFV systems are based on multiple control "layers"—each of which is a potential target of attack: an infrastructure layer that may be remotely managed by incumbent local exchange carriers (ILEC) or competitive local exchange carriers (CLEC); a hypervisor layer (trending to kenel-based virtual machines (KVM) in the network, but potentially VMware, Zen, and so on) that abstracts the hardware to the virtualized functions; a virtualized network function (VNF) layer (routers, firewalls, IPS, DNS, dynamic host configuration protocol (DHCP), and so on); and potentially a fourth *container* or workload layer dealing with application-specific functions, such as caching and replication, quality of service or application-security. Of course, it is also possible that not only network services exist in the network, but cloud-based services start to distribute themselves to process data closer to its source (endpoint). *With expanded service opportunities come expanded attack surfaces.*

Risk 2: Complexity and lack of Standards. NFV and SDN infrastructure is more complex than legacy systems, meaning that small administrative (or malicious) changes (due to error or sabotage) can have chaotic impacts. An unauthorized change may have unforeseen, amplified effects through the network, without known limits. *This is a hallmark of complex systems such as pharmacology (medicine) and weather. Telecommunications is entering the league of nondeterministic, chaotic impacts with the advent of NFV and SDN.*

> Additionally, unlike many conventional forms of IT, NFV and SDN do not yet have internationally recognized operational security standards (for instance, from the ISO). This means that for lack of standards, operational security around NFV and SDN will be technically *ad hoc* from a security perspective, making issues like claims of negligence or lack of due care more difficult to manage conclusively.

Risk 3: Physical accessibility. Business and service imperatives will push NFV and SDN out to the edges of the telecommunications network—in other words, into the ceilings of offices and hotels and subway cars, into homes and remote base stations, into mobile devices managed by third parties (like delivery vans), and possibly even private property (like a small, reserved portion of a smartphone). These systems will by necessity be accessible and therefore open to tampering, cloning, and all manner of communication analysis and interception. Academics have basically proven that with physical access, any software-based security system can be compromised.[35]

Other operational vulnerabilities and risks that might arise from NFV and SDN technologies can include issues associated with policy consistency and old-fashioned software compatibility.[36] If SDN controllers (the brains of the SDN) lack sufficient administrative controls to manage and audit the SDN policies, a malicious user or piece of software may inject network policies (such as, for example, address translation rules or port mappings) that transform malicious flows such as malware command and control (C&C) into *preapproved* traffic that might be placed on fast-path processing (reduced security scanning). For instance, C&C traffic is routed through voice over internet protocol/session initiation protocol (VoIP/SIP) network segments, which might be assumed to be *clean* but can become secret passages through the networks like nefarious passages in a medieval castle!

On the side of software compatibility sit issues associated with NFV and hypervisor interoperability: porting a physical appliance to an NFV involves at least a couple of interesting issues from a security perspective: first, firewalls and IPS elements typically rely on custom drivers and UNIX kernels. When deployed on the general hypervisors, performance can be in question. Second, with a growing array of NFV management and network operations (MANO) solutions, and SDN controller solutions and vendors alike, a given virtualized security element may need to support a wide range of MANO + SDN combinations. All combinations available in the market may not be supported, and those that are supported may not be supported with equal assurance! This imposes yet more operational caution on the IoT service provider and their supply chain.

The risk associated with the Internet (of Things) is changing, and regulatory compliance associated with new technology such as NFV and SDN will bring new burdens. Root-of-trust technology offers part of the solution to managing these risks.

---

[35]See https://en.wikipedia.org/wiki/Van_Eck_phreaking.
[36]See *Cloud Security Alliance, Security Position Paper, Network Function Virtualization*, 2016.

Root-of-trust technology offers platform assurance, through multiple layers of hardware and software, potentially across multiple service providers sharing the platforms and systems of virtualized network infrastructure. This type of platform assurance may create the efficiencies and automation associated with compliance that will allow the IoT to flourish to a greater extent than under the current regime of *compliance consultancy*, which is an albatross around the neck of any chief information officer (CIO).

Managing NFV and SDN for RIoT control

There are options available to manage these emerging risks in NFV, and especially D-NFV, to satisfy regulators and help the business at the same time. These options offer not only cost savings, but might generate new revenues at the same time.

As mentioned earlier, regulatory compliance in IT can be a burden that is undertaken as grudgingly as any business overhead. With the new risks associated with virtualized networking, new regulatory burdens will follow.

Root of trust is not a regulated requirement for either DCs or virtualized network devices and may never be because there are other ways to show compliance with loosely written regulatory requirements: but few are as cost effective and elegant as root of trust.

As data is processed by more and more virtualized network infrastructure, new regulatory questions around virtualization, and eventually requirements, will emerge for the same reasons as it has evolved in the DC: sensitive information will not only be transported through the network but also processed in the network.

For instance, the IoT will see normalization of sensitive data at the edge of the network to improve efficiency and reduce the daily cost of transporting terabytes of potentially superfluous information. Normalization will include functions like compression, authentication, authorization, error checking, and format validation prior to transmission to the processing and storage systems in the (distant) DC.

Network-based normalization functions will be performed on the widest array of information types imaginable: private health information, proprietary trade secrets, and information associated with national security. Quite reasonably, the owners of this information will want to have assurances about the information processing waypoints from end to end.

Eventually, beyond information management compliance will come regulatory discussions centered on the critical infrastructure protection (CIP) aspects of NFV and SDN. These technologies will underpin the infrastructure that makes everything from ambulance dispatch to buying groceries to controlling trains and bridges. Much like the legacy infrastructures of telecommunications carriers were regulated in the name of public safety and prosperity, the new infrastructures being fundamentally different will require a significant reexamination.

The new risks associated with NFV and SDN generally as discussed above, coupled with further risks associated with data processing in the network, will require some novel solutions that go beyond practices of old. Above all, the viability of the IoT will flourish or die based in large part on the security of technologies like NFV and SDN. But do the benefits of better security cease at *compliance*? Nope.

Operational savings from root-of-trust technology

Financial benefits, not just compliance, can be derived from high assurance, virtualized networks. One of the basic functions of the root-of-trust technology is that the trust is verified by centralized systems, which perform *authorization* functions versus *authentication and validation* functions. They agree that a device can do something, versus deciding that it is actually a device in the first place.

The key to the above paragraph is in the word *centralized*. Requests and approvals for hardware devices to enter the network and software workloads to start (and stop) on the approved devices are pushed through a centralized C&C system. Such systems also tend to log such events.

In the root-of-trust technology described above, which is available and evolving within Intel products, events related to hardware and software startup and shutdown in the DC and network can be centrally recorded *and* exported (via integration services) into Enterprise Resource Management (ERM) systems, enabling metered billing for VNFs.

Metered billing for VNFs amounts to paying for what you use as it is consumed, versus paying for excess capacity to accommodate what you might possibly use under heavy load, which is the way most network services are sold today.

Metered billing is a derived benefit for root of trust, making it a dual-purpose technology. With the right integration into ERM systems, it has compliance benefits and also pays dividends.

Hardware-based root of trust is arcane, geeky, and hard to understand. Yet it addresses a dilemma solved by the transport industry about 500 years ago: are there opportunities to pay a cabbie, versus feed and stable a horse for every outing?

COUNTERFEIT GOODS PREVENTION IN THE IoT

Maintaining confidence in the supply chain is critical; so critical that supply chain concerns can lead to exclusion and blacklisting from entire countries and regions: Ask the Chinese about selling in the United States, or the Israelis about selling in the Middle East. Yet, there are some known best practices in counterfeit goods prevention that can and should be applied to the IoT above all.[37] These include:

- Maintaining authorized and verifiable distribution channels of trusted and audited suppliers, who used inputs with known provenance. This includes procurement of all hardware and software used to build and maintain the product.
- Track and trace critical components and parts involved with security and safety systems, such as, for instance, to mitigate risk associated with undocumented code potentially contained with embedded systems and components in IoT devices.
- Continuity of supply plans for spares and maintenance parts. This includes a long-term parts availability policy[38]
- Techniques to ensure that Trojans and malware are not entered into the supply chain. More assurance is associated with software development for the IoT supply chain. Hardware integrity checking is necessary to combat counterfeiting in critical IoT systems (which is basically most of them due to complex interdependencies we don't fully understand). Current research from the United States Intelligence Advanced Research Projects Activity (IARPA) has led to the Trusted Integrated Chips program, which aims to thwart the threat of hardware Trojans by

[37]Supply Chain Security—ISO 20243.
[38]http://www.mcafee.com/us/resources/white-papers/wp-automotive-security.pdf.

splitting chip manufacturing between foundries such that no one foundry would have sufficient information about the chip's functionality to insert a hardware Trojan.[39]

> Managing supply chain risk is no simple feat in the IoT, and not unique to the IoT. Yet it is important clearly to identify it as a risk that is elevated in the IoT, which is emerging as a manufacturing process based on *fast and cheap*, versus *good*.

Because much of the supply chain in the IoT will actually be services and not merely piece parts and hardware, there will be opportunities to apply management-level controls such as supplier audit in lieu of operational controls such as penetration testing or vigilant (and expensive) network monitoring.

Another potential risk for IoT system managers is that they are attacked by their own supply chain over the use of counterfeit goods! Believe it or not, this has happened!

In an incident starting in 2014, a chip manufacturer[40] of industrial control systems conspired to have an official Microsoft Windows update *brick* industrial control devices using counterfeited versions of its chips (chips with the company name printed on them). The devices in question were controlled by software developed for Windows. Once the version of Windows was patched, the controllers ceased to work. Following this incident, supervisory control and data acquisition (SCADA) lists are full of furious operators whose systems have been disabled, because they bought equipment—in good faith—that contained counterfeit chips.[41] Possibly the manufacturers of the devices themselves bought the chips in good faith... Who knows? This almost is a like a doctor administering poison to a patient for taking generic drugs. *Reckless* and *negligent* are some of the words being used to describe this event.

Beyond specific risks to IoT endpoint devices from counterfeit goods in the supply, gateways, and networks will also be subject to substantial risks associated with underperforming, buggy, or even backdoored (compromised) elements in the supply chain. This is not something that is novel to the IoT and has been around for years: knock-off vendors brand cheap, second-rate goods with name brands and sell them for top dollar. This problem is so widespread that even the US military is reporting thousands of counterfeit network elements within its networks, despite stringent efforts to keep them out! Imagine how difficult this might be for an IoT service provider without any core capability in security?[42]

DATA QUALITY RISKS

In Chapter 7, Confidentiality and Integrity and Privacy Requirements in the IoT, we spoke about data quality requirements in the IoT, where the automated use of online databases of product and

---

[39] http://spectrum.ieee.org/semiconductors/design/stopping-hardware-trojans-in-their-tracks/?utm_source=techalert&utm_medium=email&utm_campaign=012215.

[40] See - http://arstechnica.com/information-technology/2014/10/windows-update-drivers-bricking-usb-serial-chips-beloved-of-hardware-hackers/.

[41] See http://www.eevblog.com/forum/reviews/ftdi-driver-kills-fake-ftdi-ft232/375/ and http://zeptobars.com/en/read/FTDI-FT232RL-real-vs-fake-supereal.

[42] See http://www.theregister.co.uk/2008/05/09/fbi_counterfeit_kit_probe/.

service metadata (characteristics, specifications, or ingredients) to make semi- and fully automated decisions can create vulnerabilities, which might be exploited for a wide range of purposes including fraud, sabotage, or mischief. Examples of such exploitations include:

- Wrong or corrupted data that is ingested into the IoT for processing purposes from third part sources
- Malicious entities that impersonate third-party information sources to pass along illegitimate data

Much of the IoT today is relying on metadata feeds that come over the Internet, from sources they trust more due to convention than proof of trustworthiness. Until the day the Internet is governed by unified international laws and regulations, the reputation of data sources in the IoT will become a larger and larger issue.

Data quality is arguably about source reputation, and reputation is a tough thing to judge without the perspective of massive intelligence and sampling, on a scale that may itself been seen as a threat in this post-Snowden era of suspicion of monitoring. Managing risk associated with data quality will require more effort to understand the following elements:

- where the information is coming from and how to authenticate communications with that source
- the use of encryption techniques to secure and obscure the content of communications
- which elements in the IoT system being managed might be referring to outside data sources, and for what activities
- the service levels associated with the source and how to apply mitigation controls in the event that service levels do not meet the product requirements of the IoT system

Blockchains as a source of metadata assurance

In this chapter we introduced the concept of *blockchains* in the IoT as a means to reduce financial risks such as fraud associated with various forms of stored value that we can expect to appear in the IoT. Blockchains are also a mechanism to ensure data quality in the IoT.

For instance, as Things are manufactured, their serial numbers or identifiers are cryptographically linked to product ingredients, terms and conditions of use, and warranty information through the public ledgering systems underpinning blockchains. In this manner, a user of an IoT good or service can check the manufacturer's blockchain to validate goods and possibly service terms. In the same manner, counterfeit goods or defective goods might be detected because they do not have entries in the blockchain *or* the blockchain reveals that that same good or service has already been assigned to another customer—indicated that forgeries are in play; or perhaps, a good that is assumed to be new is in fact used, because the blockchain ledger shows all previous owners.

AVAILABILITY AND RELIABILITY

At the very beginning of this book we stated that availability is probably one of the most serious risks in the IoT, so much so that it should stand alone in discussion from confidentiality and integrity—the traditional *trinity*. This is the case because of the safety-critical functions associated with availability and its shared pedigree with industrial control systems, more so than conventional enterprise IT.

> Many of the risks cited before and after this section will have availability impacts, but we have categorized them otherwise to re-enforce that RIoT control is about balancing treatments and controls across requirements, rather than adapting a narrow focus on one set of requirements (namely availability).

PUBLIC CLOUD SERVICES FOR IoT

Cloud and cloud-based services will be core to IoT service delivery. They already are, in fact!

Many of the IoT goods and related services emerging on the market have never, and will never, own or run a DC. They are *born in the cloud* and will live and die there. They will assemble their service based on rented or leased cloud resources, and buy critical service components (such as transaction processing) from other companies that are doing exactly the same thing.

To review, there are three basic classes of cloud (shared DC) services: Infrastructure as a Service (IaaS), Platform as a Service (PaaS), and SaaS. These services offer some of the cheapest possible capital and operating cost options to all businesses and are attractive to IoT service providers as well. However, they also tend to offer service levels with limited guarantees and tend to be aggregated to a lowest common denominator, unless perhaps you elect to pay for different, premium services.

The service levels offered by typical cloud service providers (CSPs) is a vulnerability in the IoT and must be carefully managed.

The risk is that the CSP may breech the SLA—for any number of reasons—and offer little or no recompense or liability-support terms, relative to risks assumed by the IoT service provider and their customers, especially in the case of IoT system that may be safety-critical, such as health and infrastructure systems.

For instance, a developer at a health monitoring company posted to an Amazon Web Services (AWS) support forum claiming that the "life of our patients is at stake" on account of an outage in the CSP services. This health IoT service provider said it is tracking hundreds of patients in real time at home and could not see their electrocardiogram signals for the last 24 hours.[43] Similarly, the insurance industry is wondering aloud whether it is truly liable to pay claims that involve complete IoT service chains, and claims might not be denied based on insufficient due care in the creation of IoT services, such as the selection and management of CSP services![44]

In the end, IoT risk managers will need to understand explicitly what sort of SLAs and liability they can reasonably expect from their supply chain CSPs. Beyond that, transferring risk through insurance will certainly remain an option, but only if the IoT service provider understands the details of the terms and conditions of the policy and can balance their supplier SLAs with the insurer exclusions and limits. This is not a cut-and-dried exercise and will require significant skill and attention. Alternately, IoT service providers will need to accept risk in the area of CSP services, but at least do so knowingly.

---

[43]https://forums.aws.amazon.com/thread.jspa?threadID=65649.
[44]Insurance insight reference to smart cars.

VOICE COMMUNICATIONS VULNERABILITIES AND RISK IN THE IoT

VoIP will be widely deployed in the IoT, particularly for injecting customer support directly into products—think of a support intercom in your car, health device, thermostat, or washing machine.

For the purposes of efficiency and resiliency, VoIP will probably take advantage of existing carrier deployments like voice over LTE (VoLTE) or voice over 5G (we don't have an acronym of this yet).

Yet, vulnerabilities associated with SIP and real-time transfer protocol (RTP) are not commonly seen in enterprise environments, which are often highly segregated networks that shield the VoIP infrastructure from Internet-based attacks. The VoIP infrastructure is logically separated even from corporate IT.

In wireless broadband VoIP such as VoLTE, there are no security controls between the handset and the infrastructure. LTE and probably 5G will be flat to guarantee throughput/speed. In the older forms of voice services, the voice processing is done in a dedicated communication processor in a phone that is a proprietary and closed system. With VoLTE devices, the general processor is performing the voice processing with all the other apps, which means that the voice processing is now vulnerable to attack.[45] Similarly, the data plane of the LTE infrastructure is used both for Internet services as well as voice services.

Already, many IoT services incorporate VoLTE or voice over WiFi (VoWiFi) into things like intercoms, baby monitors, and home security systems, where things can transmit speech from user to user or provide support and product help functions through voice. In the near future, there is every reason to believe that voice functions will be embedded in an even wider range of things, such as cars or healthcare devices, meaning that the linkage between a voice technology and the critical cyberphysical interface will be made.

The ultimate vulnerability is that by building voice services into IoT services, an entirely new and poorly understood interface is introduced. This interface can be used to both as an attack surface and as a data exfiltration opportunity. For instance, the VoIP channel becomes an unguarded exit for data, and by compromising the VoIP capabilities on an IoT device, a malicious entity can get around security controls that are focused on the enterprise data channel and not the voice channels. Studies and research have shown that tunneling non-voice traffic through VoIP carriers are a highly effective means of obfuscating and evading security, which has been focused on the conventional IoT or IT communications networks and channels.[46]

Also, if VoIP is a core part of the IoT service-provision, like some sort of health device worn by seniors, or a panic button of sorts, then the service itself can involve user assumptions that exceed conventional *dial 911* assumptions.

Managing this risk will require a variety of controls:

- VoIP services must be implemented with an extended degree of care. An awareness that this is a distinct infrastructure, not something to the tacked onto a service with minimal regard.
- (VoIP) SIP- and RTP-aware firewalls and IPS are at this time unconventional and rarely seen in front of VoIP infrastructure. They may be required to support the assurance expectations of customer and regulatory alike.

---

[45]*Breaking and Fixing VoLTE: Exploiting Hidden Data Channels and Mis-implementations*, Georgia Tech, 2015.
[46]VoIP Shield, *Network Traffic Analytics Detection of Malicious VoIP Behavior in VoLTE Networks.*, December 2015.

SMART GATEWAYS FOR THE Iot

Throughout this book we have been proposing that *gateways* will play a critical role in the management of risk in the IoT. Gateways are typically the last hop before the endpoint device, or act as the interface between an IP network and a localized network connecting *things* with either IP or non-IP networking technology. Gateways will become smart and security enabled where they are often dumb today—especially home gateways, but also 4G base stations, also known as eNobeB, another form of gateway.

The primary vulnerability is that gateways will often—or will soon—allow localized switching among local IoT devices sharing the gateway. The gateway will let local devices talk to each other unmonitored and uncontrolled. Therefore, any infected, malicious, or defective devices will have free rein to attack or otherwise degrade the service levels and reliability of other IoT devices once it is on the same side of the gateway as the other IoT devices. (See the discussion on 5G technology to follow related why localized switching will become so important to critical use-cases in the IoT).

Since many of the IoT devices seen to date are fragile and ill-prepared for life in the Internet, it is very likely that they will become very unreliable in the face of attack. Health devices are known to be the worst in this area, for instance. But insecurity is more the rule of most IoT devices rather than the exception. The US Food and Drug Administration (FDA) has even started to issue its own product warning about connected health devices.[47]

Poor reliability will result from vulnerabilities associated with IoT devices themselves, as well as the vulnerability associated with the lack of gateway-based controls. Gateway security will present a range of business risks in turn related to regulatory compliance, market risks, and liabilities. While the gateway itself might not possess technical vulnerabilities, they are being deployed in a *vulnerable manner* vis-à-vis the devices they support.

The way to address the vulnerabilities of the IoT network beyond the gateway is to make gateways smarter and security-enable them, as shown in Fig. 13.16, and as shown previously in the discussion related to Fig. 13.12.

Gateways will necessarily take on a range of security functions in the IoT to manage risks that endpoint IoT devices cannot manage for reasons such as resource constraints or the economics of the manufacturing (they need to be cheap!)

Firewalling must be implemented at the application level rather than just port and protocol. Internal LAN segmentation and IPS must be utilized to monitor communications on the *LAN-side* of the network, looking for malicious devices that might have been *carried* over the gateway by people, or might have roamed into the network, or malfunctioning devices.

Data encryption or session encryption on behalf on the device will need to be utilized when it is headed towards the cloud or DC. It may also be the case that Identification and Authentication must be performed on behalf of constrained devices, for instance. Smart gateways can further be used to:

- Cleanse and normalize data (compress it, remove extraneous or superfluous information)
- Apply security policies for applications running on the gateway platform (virtualized)

---

[47]See LinkedIn post for reference.

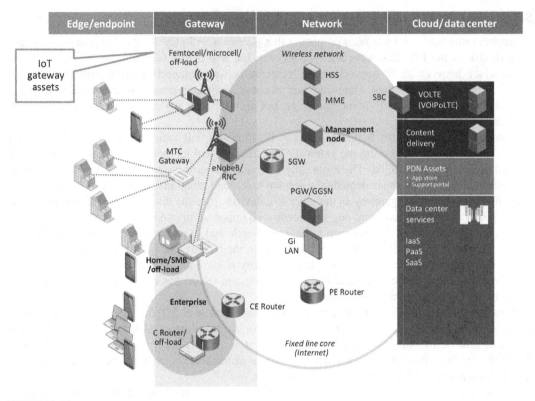

FIGURE 13.16

Gateways in the IoT.

- Apply security policies on applications running adjacent to the gateway; for instance, as application services running on a server next to the gateway
- Apply security on local-breakout connections (such as Internet traffic offloads to a different local connection from other traffic like voice)

IDENTITY AND ACCESS CONTROLS

In this section we will discuss vulnerabilities and risks associated with identity and access controls (I&As), including re-identification, granularity and scaling, and data provenance.

I&A is a *hot spot* in the area of RIoT control. Not as in a wireless access point but as in an area of intense activity and need. In previous chapters we discussed why I&A has been elevated to a unique and top-priority security and risk management requirement in the IoT. Basically:

- IoT ecosystems will frequently involve thousands or even millions of devices that must be enrolled and given access to service—with some degree of assurance. Scaling is a requirement unlike anything seen in conventional IT.

- IoT devices may have multiple levels of I&A to perform, depending on how many service providers are involved in the service's ecosystem.
- IoT devices will frequently be constrained in resources such as memory, processor, or power, and I&A will need to be cleverly managed to account for these weakness and the risk they might introduce into the service.

As before, the following discussion considers challenges associated with IoT I&A that may be novel or different from what might be seen in conventional enterprise IT. Therefore, risk managers and IoT system designers and managers/owners may benefit from specific awareness of these risks.

REIDENTIFICATION AND REIDENTIFICATION RISK[48]

In the section "Regulatory Vulnerabilities and Risk," earlier in this chapter, we had a substantial discussion related to anonymization techniques, and a means to managing risks associated with the management of PII in the IoT.

Re-identification is the process of linking the information from a de-identified data set to a particular data subject or subjects. This may be PII or it may be about identifying devices in the IoT, which then means that if the device can be associated with a user, PII may be exposed.

However, there is far more sensitive data generally that might be exposed if vulnerabilities such as re-identification emerge en masse. As we covered in Chapter 2, The Anatony of the Internet of Things, and Chapter 3, Requirements and Risk Management, the vast majority of data in the IoT is not PII or related to PII, but it has major value and sensitivities:

- Intellectual property
- Completive intelligence
- Financial information that can be used for fraud
- National and military secrets
- Safety-critical information and data (data controlling dams or traffic lights)
- Service-critical information and data (if corruption or delay can ruin voice services)

Re-identification might be applied to much more than PII. It might lead to the unauthorized disclosure of any of the above sensitive information classes related to commercial entities, governments, or other organizations such as law enforcement activities or military operations.

Re-identification, if successful, could create a new data set containing some or all of the subject records represented in the original data set. Reidentification can be achieved by:

- Singling out: isolating events and data flows until patterns emerge that represent recognizable behaviors
- Linkability: cleansed data, if it contains any field that allows it to be linked to a different data set, allowing them to be combined and entirely reassessed for patterns and information
- Inference: gaps in data generated by cleansing and anonymization may appear to one set of eyes to be incomprehensible, yet another examiner may test many inferences about the gaps until the right inference leads to re-identification

---

[48]See SC27 WG5 N35—DRAFT: Guidelines for Data Pseudonymization and Anonymization Processes as Privacy-Enhancing Techniques.

The forms of RIoT control associated with I&A vulnerabilities for re-identification will vary by the services and use cases. But certainly encryption and cryptographic functions appropriate to the IoT specifically will be useful ingredients in many instances.

In several places in this chapter we have discussed the fact that there are cryptographic tools available for IoT systems designers that are available but not commonly seen in conventional IT. Often the reason they have been seldom seen is that conventional IT has the resources available to use the same crypto-systems over and over—even if there were more efficient systems available. The difficulty with some of these alternative systems is that, being less common, they become more expensive in terms of development and operations (vs device resources) to use. In the IoT, with the emphasis on device resources, these less commonly seen crypto-systems are worth considering again.

Identity-based encryption

IBE systems originated with Adi Shamir in 1984, and were improved at the turn of the century by world-renowned cryptographers at Stanford University under US Department of Defense (DoD) funded research.[49] IBE utilizes some of the properties conventional public-key systems, but also reduces significantly the dependence on key distribution and management associated with such systems. This is a major benefit in the IoT, where a device might be in a position to present an identity of some sort, but not necessarily have the resources to manage keys or key-exchanges—costly processes both in terms of device resources and network resources.

Voltage Security[50] was formed in the late 1990s to commercialize some of these technological breakthroughs. Voltage is still around and claims to protect over 100M email accounts and is also involved in the payment space. In February of this year, HP acquired Voltage. It is worth noting that Voltage cannot be judged as a success in the Internet to date. Its solution, while full of merit, was an improvement that was not considered necessary by many; the apparent savings in resources and *lightweight* I&A it offered was not really that important when it came to powerful desktop devices linked with broadband networks.

IBE allows an endpoint to derive the public key of another endpoint from a given identity. For example, by using an e-mail address (name.surname@company.com) as a public key identifier, anyone can send encrypted data to the owner of the e-mail address. In the IoT, the identity of a thing might be a device ID or serial number that is encoded at manufacturer or assigned at provisioning time. It might be something that changes over the lifecycle of the devices or entity, but if it is unique and functions as a unique identity within a domain of control, it might potentially be used for IBE.

Another way to take advantage of IBE is through the Physically Unclonable Function (PUF) technology used on many microchips from firms like Intel.[51] PUF generates a unique identifier by exploiting random physical factors introduced in the semiconductor manufacturing process, achieving what the technology was designed to do, making it impossible to clone.

---

[49]https://en.wikipedia.org/wiki/ID-based_encryption.
[50]https://www.voltage.com/technology/data-encryption/identity-based-encryption.
[51]PUF reference from Wikipedia and Intel.

And while not originally designed to play a role in IoT, PUF technology may be positioned to become a critical IBE component in the effort to identify and authenticate things, and encrypt data to and from them, with a minimum of resources.[52]

The ability to decrypt the content lies with the entity in possession of the corresponding secret/private key—the owner of the e-mail address—as long as the name space is properly managed.

CLAE[53]

IBE's merit is the ability to encrypt for specific recipients/endpoints with reduced burden associated with key management. However, IBE is not an authentication technology. Certificateless authentication and encryption (CLAE) adds authentication capabilities into IBE. IBE can be implemented in a lightweight manner appropriate to IoT. CIP has therefore created an IoT appropriate authentication system that does not rely on *heavy* key management.

CLAE is purported to use significantly less power than elliptic curve cryptography (ECC) (per enhanced privacy identification (EPID)) or Rivest, Shamir, & Adleman (RSA). Trust and authentication systems can scale up and down through hierarchies (leaves/branches). IBE and CLAE both possess an affinity with Intel-based chips and functions that are either already widely deployed or available for widespread and cost-effective adoption within the IoT.

Repurposing cellular I&A

Firms are also developing I&A capabilities based in the lightweight, tried, and tested algorithms and key management system from cellular systems based on 3GPP standards. Such systems, too, will have benefits in the IoT unique to conventional IT where they have manifestly failed to take hold, even though they are used every day by billions of people through cellular technology!

There are more options for IoT I&A than have been discussed here—many more! The main point, however, is that RIoT control will require that we expand our ideas about I&A beyond the technologies that have served the Internet for the last 20 years. In some cases, these technologies have served us well, and in other cases they have not—such as user-name and password combinations and other forms of single factor authentication.

ATTRIBUTE-BASED ACCESS CONTROL AND ENCRYPTION

The IoT will be about possessing as many tools as possible to secure devices and the identification and authentication associated with the devices, because legacy systems and processing based on PKI, SSL/TLS, Kerberos, and above all, passwords, will not scale up or meet the performance requirements of constrained devices. We need alternative solutions to identification and authentication in the IoT, probably to mix and match them according to the usage context of IoT systems, devices, and applications under consideration.

Attributes are another tool we might call on in managing threats and risks in the IoT associated with poor, weak, or no device identification and authentication (where there should in fact be strong identification and authentication).

---

[52]https://www.linkedin.com/pulse/puf-magic-iot-dragon-bill-montgomery.

[53]http://www.google.com/patents/WO2013116928A1?cl=en.

Attributes might be a wide range of descriptors about a given device or entity in the IoT. Attributes might be assigned by the owners, service provider, manufacturer, or any other entity that has an awareness or even opinion about a device. Some examples of attributes are:

- Location of the device (see discussion of context for more on this)
- Time of day
- Season
- Temperature outside
- Make and model
- Owner of the devices
- Permissions assigned to the device by the service
- Behavior: Past and present as an attribute—what it is merely trying to do
- Reputation of the device (*this is critical*):
  - Has the device been seen to behave badly or unpredictably (frequently defective)?
  - Is the device coming from a network locations know to be a location of criminals or malware (guilt by association)?
  - Is the device made by a manufacturer known to put back doors into its devices, or simply a poor quality manufacturer injecting defects and poor data quality?

Though traditionally based on PKI crypto-systems, *Attribute-Based Encryption*[54] (ABE) takes this idea of IBE and CLAE further by encoding attributes; such as roles or access policies, into a user's secret/private keys. IBE and ABE may allow endpoints without external network connections to set up secure and authenticated device-to-device communication channels. As such, it is a good match for public safety applications and used in the 3GPP standard for proximity-based services for LTE. See the later discussion for more about attribute-based identification and authentication for the IoT.

Benefits of ABAC

Attribute-based access control (ABAC) can provide fine-grained and contextual access control, which allows for a higher number of discrete inputs into an access control decision, providing a bigger set of possible combinations of those variables to reflect a larger and more definitive set of possible rules, policies, or restrictions on access.

ABAC enables administrators to apply access control policy without complete prior knowledge of the specific subject, using other data points that might be strong indicator identity. When combined with other attributes, indicators can form the basis for sufficient trust in the device's identity and ownership to authorization access to service and transactions. The access control policies that can be implemented in ABAC are limited only by the computational language and the richness of the available attributes.

ABAC can also provide more dynamic access control capability and limit long-term maintenance requirements of object protections because access decisions can change between requests when attribute values change.

---

[54]See https://en.wikipedia.org/wiki/Attribute-based_encryption.

GRANULAR IDENTIFICATION AND AUTHENTICATION AND SCALING RISKS

Many vulnerabilities will be in part addressed by having better or more frequent identification and authentication operations. For instance, devices are asked to identify themselves for every transaction to stop unauthorized devices from masquerading as legitimate devices using simple techniques such as address spoofing or replay attacks. In the event that the IoT device cannot support session encryption and send information in clear text, regular and granular I&A can help balance risks.

Granular I&A might also be used rapidly to detect defective or infected devices that are starting to communicate in erratic ways, indicated by a failure to follow proper I&A at the start of a data exchange.

Architectural conventions like microsegmentation might even be accompanied by granular I&A operations to elevate assurance for highly sensitive systems managing safety-critical systems.

Alternately, where microsegmentation is not possible, the highly granular forms of I&A might be applied as a mitigating control: every device in the local area must first go through formal I&A with the counterparty device before communication is possible.

Granular I&A could be like introducing yourself with a handshake every time you spoke to someone at a house party—even though you have been there all night and done this dozens of times before. The analogy appears absurd and would be in the human world, where we have evolved over millions of years to recognize each other on sight, with very high degrees of accuracy using visual and aural identification and authentication. But machines don't have such senses.

The point of the house party analogy is the amount of *load* this would place of the communications at such an event. This is the risk associated with granular I&A—that constrained devices will be loaded beyond practical limits, including cost limits, if we try to increase I&A substantially.

One specific risk is that the network slows down to the point of not supporting the necessary service levels or safety levels due to identification and authentication loads.

Another risk is that devices consume too much power or processor and performance—including useful life—suffers; the batteries deplete too fast and the device must be replaced, or the device scavenges power from the environment (wind, solar) and depletes its reserves performing additional I&A before the batteries can recharge. For instance, I&A during the night drives the device into a dormant mode, 2 hours before the sun rises.

Granular I&A in the real world

A real-world use case for granular I&A might be an in-car network or car operating system where every part of the car is required to go through I&A before it is allowed access to the communications bus in the car. And every flow of data from one in-car sensor (say stability sensors) must undergo validation and possibly decryption before it is accepted by another part of the car, such as a traction control system managing torque to the wheels.

A major part of scaling risks is directly associated with the application of legacy I&A and cryptographic systems to IoT risk management. The legacy systems requiring public keys based on an old algorithm such as RSA key pairs will aggravate the scaling problems because they are so resource intensive and not designed for the IoT.

Aside from trying to use microsegmentation as an alternative to forcing I&A and encryption around local communications in the IoT, there are the novel and newer forms of encryption we discussed earlier, such as IBE and polynomial encryption schemes (key splitting), which allow for very rapid, combined operations associated with encryption/decryption and I&A.

These much lighter forms of I&A and encryption will be more suitable to the IoT and allow more scalability around the application of I&A for device-to-device communications on a local level, possibly like the human ability to recognize and distinguish each other based on our senses without need for specific, formal, or repeated introductions.

DATA PROVENANCE

Data provenance is related to the vulnerabilities and risks associated with sources of data in the IoT, which we covered earlier in this chapter. But data provenance might go further in the context of the IoT. For instance, it could be about not only where the data came from originally, but were it has been since that time. Who handled it previously and how would you identify that system or user?

We also discussed supply chain integrity and the provenance of hardware and software elements in the IoT earlier. Provenance might be applied to data also, such that we understand where it has been before it arrived for processing, either from an endpoint IoT device into a cloud or from a cloud, gateway, or user as an instruction to an endpoint device. A data provenance capability may reflect another potential layer of security control that would be appropriate under certain use cases.

North Korea as an IoT innovator (not really)

An interesting example of data provenance is to be found (ironically) in an operating system called Red Star, developed by the North Korean government.[55] Developed as the official and authorized operating system for computing in North Korea, intended to monitor anyone in North Korea with access to computers, it is based on the Fedora Linux OS.

Red Star as an operating system has been specifically enhanced to append digital fingerprints based on the hardware specific to the end of all data files that are opened by the system. (See the discussion on PUFs earlier in this chapter.) If the file is moved around, then the receiving system can see the thread of previous systems that opened the file. In the case of North Korea, this is to track who might be leaking files or creating subversive content via data provenance.

In the IoT, similar techniques might be applied for purposes such as:

- An additional form of authentication on instructions to IoT devices
- An additional form of authentication of events and logs

By itself, this is not a strong security measure because fingerprints could potentially be stripped off, but the North Koreans get integrity into the system by limiting the operating system available to all users. An IoT service might use various security controls like encryption and segmentation to limit which systems can open such file, too.

---

[55]Lifting the Fog on Red Start OS, Chaos Computer Club, December 2015, https://www.youtube.com/watch?v=8LGDM9exlZw.

USAGE CONTEXT AND OPERATING ENVIRONMENT

In this section we explore aspects of usage context and the operating environment, specifically: location and reputation (also known as threat intelligence).

In the IoT, the location of a device can have a huge bearing on its security context and operating environment. This is different from most conventional IT systems, which typically assume that everything is in the same place, or in the case of mobile devices, it just does not matter!

Another unique vulnerability and risk in the IoT may turn out to be reputation. On the Internet today, there are many sources of reputation information about IP addresses, domains, files, and web URLs. Yet generally this information is barely available because the latency associated with distributing means that much of the value of threat intelligence decays before it reaches a place where it can be applied. For the most part, IT systems continue to operate as before, seeing reputation as a *nice to have* feature of varying quality. In the IoT, where constrained devices struggle to maintain a secure posture with limited resources and gateways are trying to compensate for weak security for potentially thousands of shifting and moving endpoints, reputation and threat intelligence could become an urgently needed control.

LOCATION, LOCATION, LOCATION

There are many ways for a device to determine location, as we discussed throughout this book. The location might be determined by a GPS coordinate, it might be derived in relation to another entity or object—like location in a building, it might be about speed and direction broadly—down to tens of meters, or location might be about a position of a static device with accuracy down to less than a square meter. The vulnerability or problem is that you might want to provide a location without your identity or that location might accidentally be spoofed, or forged, or falsified, resulting in the wrong services delivered to the device at the wrong time, or perhaps services being denied outright.

For safety reasons, most in-car navigation systems will not let you program them while the car is in motion. What if the in-car location system were compromised, and emergency services sent to the wrong place?

Alternately, centralized device management systems will frequently keep updated entries of device locations that change. If these repositories can be compromised or tricked into accepting false updates about device locations, terrible things could happen.

Another scenario would be that you might want to only provide a certain degree of granularity about the location, limiting the privacy affecting effects if some sort of oversight is involved, like an employer that can trace the location of mobile phones on the company account. Is it enough they know you are in a shopping mall? Do they further need to know you are in the shoe store? Or you might want to make sure that your location information is only available to the entities that are specifically approved to see the device location.

One potential risk management solution is the use of geographic location/privacy (GEOPRIV)[56] or similar techniques to security geo-location data transmitted from an endpoint to relying part or system. (GEOPRIV is nominally focused on protecting privacy associated with location

---

[56]See https://datatracker.ietf.org/wg/geopriv/documents/.

technologies, but inherently provides useful security features too). GEOPRIV from the IETF goes back well over 10 years at this point but provides a very instructive concept about how context and location might be managed in a way to manage risks.

Because this is the IETF, GEOPRIV is founded on an Internet protocol network infrastructure and provides novel information within the application header of already established protocols like hypertext transport protocol (HTTP) (the basis of the Web). GEOPRIV might not be the ultimate solution but it is an established reference architecture that provides privacy controls for devices, protocols security, and a centralized location *portal* that could be used by many different types of IoT devices. It also acts as a centralized location that can be hardened and secured versus the more likely outcome, where all IoT vendors create their own location management system, integrated into their service platforms. Invariably these platforms will be inefficient; but more than that, some will be highly insecure due to lack of awareness, skills, or resources on the side of the IoT service provider.

Whether GEOPRIV is an appropriate design solution for all IoT services is not the intended guidance here. The point is that location information has substantial security implications that range from safety to privacy. The need to have distinct risk management systems or technologies for location information may have broad merit across many use cases. The converse would be to assume that location information is simply another piece of metadata, to be secured and managed just like the remainder of the data inside a given IoT system; such as assumptions and should be carefully examined.

REPUTATION, REPUTATION, REPUTATION (THREAT INTELLIGENCE)

Internet-based threats in the form of both malicious software and the agents that control this software (organized crime, spies, hacktivists) have surpassed the abilities of signature-based security systems; whether they be on the enterprise perimeter, within the corporate network, on the endpoint point, or in the cloud (Internet-based service). Additionally, the sensitivity of IP networks continues to grow as a new generation of *smart* IoT devices is appearing on the networks in the form of broadband mobile devices, legacy industrial control devices, and very low-power sensors.

In response to the accelerating threats, the security vendor community has integrated its products with proprietary forms of security reputation and *cyber threat intelligence*, which amounts to a reputation classification for IP addresses, URLs, network domains, and files on the Internet. Reputation is basically some form of cardinal scoring system that will range from *poison—reject all traffic* to *assumed good under all circumstances—accept all traffic*.

This intelligence and reputation is about IP addresses and domains that have been observed engaged in attack behaviors such as inappropriate messaging and traffic volumes, domain management, botnet C&C channel exchanges, and other indicators of either compromise or malicious intent. IP addresses may also end up on a security reputation list if they are identified as compromised through vendor-specific signature-based processes.

Security reputation intelligence from vendors is typically made available to perimeter and endpoint products through proprietary, Internet-based queries to vendor information bases.

Threat intelligence vulnerabilities

While offering significant potential and an important tool in fighting threats on the Internet, threat intelligence has some weaknesses that undermine its effectiveness both in the world of conventional enterprise IT and the IoT.

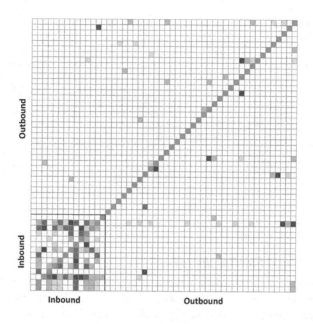

FIGURE 13.17

Comparison of overlap of indicator feeds.

Verizon Threat Report 2015.

First, threat intelligence has a short half-life. It *spoils* or decays quickly. Therefore the older it is the less value it has for the user.

Second, utilizing threat intelligence can require resource-expensive software solutions that most IoT endpoints and even gateways could not afford, capabilities that are akin to firewalls and IPS solutions which must very quickly assess the reputation on inbound or outbound connections, files, URLs and domain names and decide whether to block or allow the flows into or out of the network. This is resource intensive not only for the device, but for the network to which the device is connected.

Third, threat intelligence is usually parochial. It will contain information that is biased toward the entities and organizations that compiled it in the first place. It will be about the region or the language in which they operate. It will be about the networks that they most commonly connect to and through. For instance, in 2015 Verizon published a threat report that spent some time assessing the overlap among different commercial sources of threat intelligence (see Fig. 13.17). What it found was little overlap. In other words, they all reported different things, so to get a high resolution picture, you would need to subscribe to many different sources of threat intelligence. (It is also possible that vendors of threat intelligence deliberately filter their reports to remove information that competitors possess, in order to appear entirely unique in their services.)

To get a comprehensive picture of threat intelligence, multiple different sources will need to be procured or subscribed. This is a costly undertaking that very few organizations are able to manage successfully. Certainly, it is likely to be beyond the abilities of a smaller IoT startup, or even a large IoT service provider without a core competency in security.

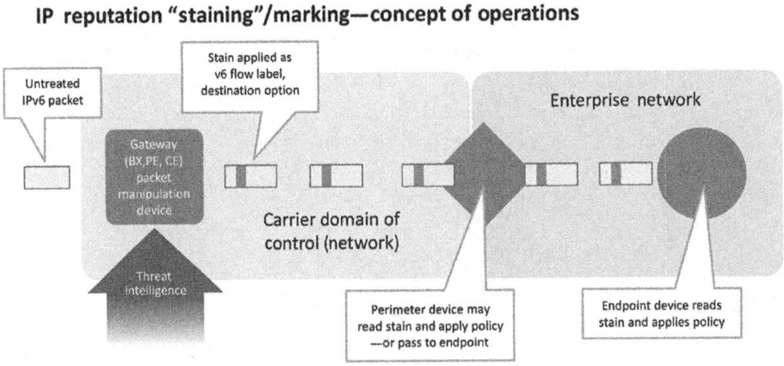

IP reputation "staining"/marking—concept of operations

FIGURE 13.18

Packet staining in IPv6—concept of operations.

Threat intelligence in real time for the IoT

Because IoT devices will often be safety critical, and constrained, the decay rate associated with threat intelligence and the resource overheads associated with intelligence-processing schemes (like firewalls) have limited appeal. One possible approach is to enrich the network itself with reputation and threat intelligence.

The usage of security reputational intelligence associated with the IP header fields enables a flow-by-flow or even packet-by-packet security classification, where the IPv6 header extensions in the form of Destination Options may be used to *stain* each packet with security reputation information such that the network routing is unaffected, but intermediate security devices and endpoint devices can apply policy decisions about incoming information flows without the requirement to assemble and treat payloads at higher levels of the stack (see Fig. 13.18). This process might be called *packet staining* or reputation marking, and was more fully described in work done through the IETF.[57]

IPv6 packet staining support consists of labeling datagrams with security reputation information through the addition of a Destination Option in the packet header by packet manipulation devices (PMD) in the carrier or enterprise network (see Fig. 13.19). Destination Options with reputation stains may be read by in-line security nodes such as network or gateway-based security functions, as well as by the destination IoT endpoints themselves for modest resource cost. For instance, an IoT endpoint device might have a simple application-specific integrated circuit (ASIC)-based function for packet processing that looks for stains in the header and applied simplistic policies. While this would certainly not be a complete security solution under any circumstances, this functionality could have merit when combined with other forms of RIoT control.

This system of using proactive, security reputation intelligence has many benefits (which we will get to shortly), but also several weaknesses and scaling challenges. Specifically, existing intelligence systems are:

- Subject to direct attack from the Internet on distribution points
- Proprietary to vendor devices

---

[57]See https://datatracker.ietf.org/doc/draft-macaulay-6man-packet-stain/.

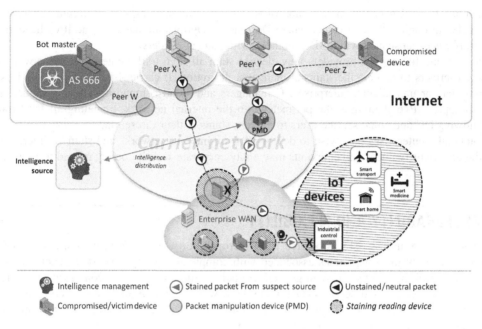

FIGURE 13.19

IPv6 reputation staining design.

- Require fat clients consuming both bandwidth and CPU
- Introduces latency while queries are sent, received, and processed

Packet staining benefits

In contrast to the challenges of current security reputation intelligence systems, packet staining has the following strengths:

- Packet staining can occur transparently in the network, presenting no attack surface
- Packet staining uses standardized, public domain IPv6 capabilities
- Security rules can be easily applied in hardware or firmware
- Reading packet stains introduces little to no latency

Implementation and support models[58]

Packet staining may be accomplished by different entities, including carriers, enterprises, and third-party value-added service providers. Carriers or even IoT service providers may elect to implement *staining centers* at strategic locations in the network to provide value-added services on a

---

[58]For further information about packet staining, see: IA Newsletter, US DOD Summer 2010, Fall 2010, Winter 2011; IETF Draft RFC Aug 2012, "Packet Staining" (https://tools.ietf.org/html/draft-macaulay-6man-packet-stain-01; WIPO Patent 2012, Distribution and Processing of Cyberthreat Intelligence Data in a Communications Network Patent # WO/2012/164336.

subscription basis. Under this model, subscribers to a security staining service would see their traffic directed through a staining center where Destination Options are added to the IPv6 headers and IPv4 traffic is encapsulated within IPv6 tunnels, with stained headers.

Carriers and IoT service providers may elect to stain all IPv6 traffic entering their network, and allow subscribers to process the stains at their own discretion. If carrier-based staining services are inappropriate or unavailable, enterprise DC managers and cloud computing service providers may elect to deploy IPv6 staining at the perimeter into the internal network, tunneling all IPv4 traffic, and allowing DC and cloud service users to process stains at their discretion.

Potentially, enterprises may wish to deploy IPv6 on internal networks and stain all internal traffic whereby security nodes and endpoints may apply corporate security policy related to reputation.

INTEROPERABILITY AND FLEXIBILITY

In this section we discuss risks associated with interoperability and flexibility, with a special focus on how potentially to manage risks associated with complexity. Complexity is the enemy of interoperability, flexibility, and security in general. As before, there is plenty of complexity to be found in existing IT systems and services. Our focus here will be to look at forms of complexity that might be especially pernicious in the IoT, or achieve higher degrees of profile as a result of the advent of the IoT on an omnipresent part of society.

5G, COMPLEXITY, AND CONVENTIONAL IT

Continuing our discussion from earlier in this chapter: 5G figures prominently in the future of IoT and therefore for RIoT control. This is not to say there will be no IoT without 5G, but the arrival of 5G will offer network capabilities that IoT service providers will seek to harness. In some cases, IoT services will be enabled by the technical capabilities of 5G.

Many of the gains associated with 5G will be accomplished by a new overlay of management technology performing as the coordinating and automating functions that drive the major performance gains of 5G. In addition, 5G will likely be characterized by more radio infrastructure and better forms of antenna technology. All this new infrastructure will be controlled and managed by IT. Fig. 13.20 is an illustration of the dimensions of 5G that allow for the performance gains over 4G, while Fig. 13.21 attempts to convey how IT underlies much of the gains in performance that are expected from 5G.

Although 5G is a revolutionary technology and a major improvement in managing and combining 4G and other wireless technologies, it is at the cost of substantial additional complexity.

The main risk with 5G is that the complexity required to make it a reality also makes it unreliable and prone to unpredictability and difficult to diagnosis service degradations. So much new IT will be introduced into the network by 5G that the attack surface for network infrastructure will expand dramatically. This means that we can expect more vulnerabilities in the network management and control systems, where today there are (relative to enterprise IT) few and they are arcane.

The 5G systems could also be very chaotic: small changes in configuration or even environmental conditions might resonate through the system and amplify to the point that failures cascade

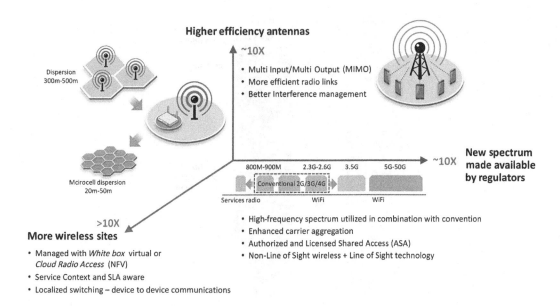

FIGURE 13.20

5G operational complexity as risk areas.[59]

unexpectedly. There will be many unexpected security failures initially, and lessons that must learned the hard way.

A 5G identification and authentication system for devices will be based on the established subscriber identity module (SIM), which has been in place for over 25 years and was the basis of second generation (2G) technology. This system is well understood, field tested, and has large economies of scale behind it now. However, the IoT will very likely require that devices will bring their identities to the network, not receive their identities from the network. Non-SIM-based identification and authentication capabilities will need to be accommodated by 5G, and it is unclear how this will be done. It is also unclear if and how this will be standardized. Will carriers and equipment manufacturers even want to allow *bring your own identity*? This could be both a significant business and operational vulnerability to the IoT if 5G is to play a major role.

As Ericsson pointed out in one of the first whitepapers about 5G security in 2015:

> The 4G LTE standard requires USIM on physical Universal Integrated Circuit Cards to gain network access. This way of handling identity will continue to be an essential part of 5G for reasons such as the high level of security and user friendliness. Embedded SIM has also significantly lowered the bar for deployment issues related to machine-to-machine communication. Still, there is a general trend of bring-your-own-identity, and the 5G ecosystem would generally benefit from a more open identity management architecture that allows for alternatives. One example would be to allow an enterprise with an existing, secure ID management solution to reuse it for 5G access.

---

[59]ZTE, *Driving the Convergence of Physical and Digital Worlds*, 2015.

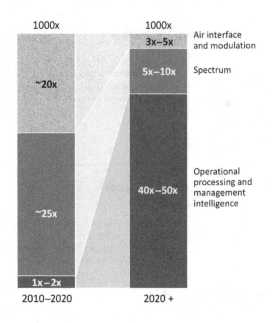

FIGURE 13.21

5G gains associated with IT in the network.

From Intel.

Examining new ways to handle device/subscriber identities is therefore a key consideration that should enter the investigation of the new trust models for 5G. Concepts such as network slicing can provide an enabler for securely allowing different ID management solutions side-by-side by confining usage to virtual, isolated slices of the network. The threat of IMSI catching, where rogue radio network equipment requests mobile devices to reveal their identity, was discussed during the 3G and 4G standardization process. However, no protection mechanism was introduced at that time, as the predictable threats did not seem to justify the cost or complexity involved. It is not clear whether this risk analysis is still valid, and enhanced IMSI protection deserves consideration for 5G.[60]

RIoT control and 5G

Making recommendations about how to manage a vulnerability that has not fully formed is fraught. But here we go regardless!

Some options for managing risk associated with 5G would be:

- Stay with 4G! Don't migrate to 5G. Stay with what is known to be manageable as long as possible. After all, 4G is going to be around for a long time to come. If the IoT use cases do not

---

[60]Ericsson white paper (Uen 284 23-3269), 5G Security, June 2015.

pivot around 5G performance, then be cautious of optimistic sales pitches from 5G service providers.

- Test extensively with 5G, especially for some of the vulnerabilities and risk we have already discussed in the chapter such as device-to-device attacks associated with localized switching.
- Have clear and well-tested fallback capabilities to 4G or even 3G.

Managing the risks associated with 5G will also be about transferring them through SLAs and service terms to the carriers:

- Ask for clear SLAs and reflect these directly in the IoT service SLA as the lowest common denominator.
- Ask for security audit results on 5G control infrastructure.
- Ask for clear coverage maps that detail the mix of wireless technologies in given areas. For instance: 5G service that relies in part on domestic Wi-Fi as an offload option might not be as reliable as offload to commercial Wi-Fi deployments.

BRITTLE AND UNPATCHABLE SYSTEMS

Brittle is the opposite of flexible, and we should expect that many IoT systems, like their forebears industrial control systems, will be brittle. By *brittle* we mean prone to breaking and or being broken by simple maintenance or basic changes. Consequently, a hallmark of a brittle IoT system is that it is not maintained.

It is a longstanding issue that industrial control systems and their new generation, the IoT, cannot be easily patched, upgraded, or migrated to new operating systems. The software written for both endpoints as well as centralized services in DCs and clouds solely for a single version of a single platform, and were never intended to take into account updates to that platform: such as security updates. This problem is especially pernicious in the case of industrial control systems (ICS) and IoT services built on earlier Windows platforms, which were (are?) notorious for their huge list of vulnerabilities.

The fact that Windows XP still persists and is even being found in *new* IoT systems and services is more sad than astonishing, but it is certainly very dangerous and a persistent vulnerability in the IoT.

How widespread is this issue, as of 2016? Well, at the end of 2015, it appeared that most news about Windows XP's end of life (EOL) was about how it would continue to be used in IoT applications and services—even sensitive IoT applications and services.

In fact, as recently as December 2015, three out of six headlines associated with the continued use of Windows XP were related to IoT systems being managed by Windows XP platforms. These included ship management (for the military), banking machines, and nuclear energy. Amazing, isn't it? This is what risk managers in the IoT must be prepared to encounter.[61]

Managing risks associated with brittle and unpatchable operating systems is very difficult because these are essentially hand grenades rolling around! It will require placing a wide range of protection and detection technologies as compensating controls all around such systems. Managing the risks associated with brittle operating systems in the IoT begins with an awareness that device

---

[61]See *The Register*.

vendors and service providers may still actually use them, despite what common sense would dictate! Here are some suggestions of how to cope with this situation:

- Ask close and careful questions during procurement processes to avoid having brittle systems in the supply chain, or part of the IoT system infrastructure. This includes stipulating what a *brittle* operating system consists of, being as descriptive as possible.
- Negotiate service levels and support that requires support for security patching, if brittle systems must be used.
- Inject language into contracts that requires updates and patches on all operating platforms, even if they are not currently considered brittle: think 10 years from now.
- Inject language related to remedial obligations if, despite claims to the contrary during contract negotiations, brittle operating systems and platforms are indeed part of the IoT service platform.
- Make staff and operators aware of the presence of such systems and implement policy, operations, and technical controls to compensate. (An auditor will insist on this in any case.)

FRACTAL SECURITY

Wikipedia defines a *fractal* as "a natural phenomenon or a mathematical set that exhibits a repeating pattern that displays at every scale." Fractal security is about repeating security structures at different scales and repeating the same structures at different points in the infrastructure. The main benefits from applying operational security designs that repeat and scale up and down will be:

- *Strength.* Fractal patterns once established are known to create strong physical forms by repeating stable properties uniformly through a physical structure. We make an assumption that the same will hold true logically (in networks and virtualized structures).
- *Operationally efficient security.* Operational tools and techniques can be developed that are uniform but scale according to the system under management.
- *Repeatability.* Fractal security is repeatable and therefore scalable and economical security.

A fractal security would mean that a carrier-level security system should be recognizable at the enterprise level, server message block (SMB), and consumer/home level. This will be important in the IoT, where communications will be constant and both north-south in nature (data traveling to and from public networks) *and* east-west in nature (locally switching to allow devices to communicate with each other).

In the IoT, many devices will be utilizing the same shared infrastructure in the DC, cloud, network, and gateways, while endpoint devices will be unique. Therefore, if security is not consistent (fractal-like) *across* assets like DC, cloud, network, and gateways (north-south), and also *within* those assets (east-west, intra-system communications in the DC or localized switching in a LAN, office branch, or home environment), then threat agents will attack the weakest links like a flaw. Network segmentation and microsegmentation implemented across different assets like the DC, cloud, network, and home gateways might be a form of fractal security (see Figs. 13.22 and 13.23).

A fractal-like security system will present a flat attack surface without handholds. The weakness in this model is that a flaw will affect all fractals. One way to address such an issue is to use the reoccuring *geometry* but use different *elements*. For instance, the same reference designs could be applied with different mixtures of vendor products; not too many vendors to make operational costs too high (which is typical), just enough to avoid a monoculture, for instance two to three.

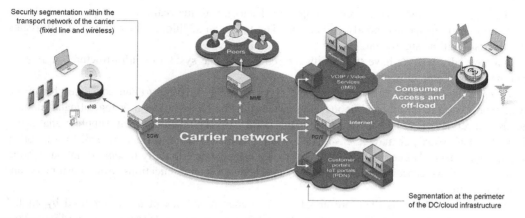

FIGURE 13.22

Segmentation and fractal-like security.

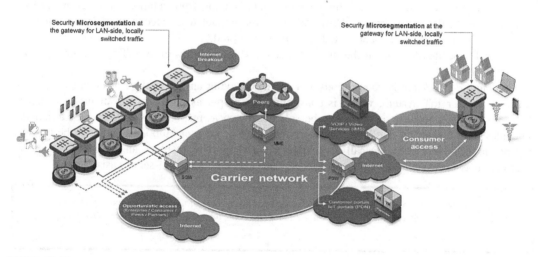

FIGURE 13.23

Microsegmentation and fractal-like security.

UNMANAGED INTERDEPENDENCY RISKS

Throughout this book we have emphasized that the IoT will be characterized by multiple layers of service providers, operating in different asset classes in the end-to-end IoT architecture. There will be product vendors, infrastructure, platform, and software service vendors, device owners, users, regulators, and other forms of stakeholders. They will create new and unimagined services through ingenious combinations of devices and services, held together with delicate web of software and service agreements. The interdependencies among these players will be largely unknown and barely understood.

Interdependency risks have been a subject of discussion in the realm of CIP for over a decade now, but remain arcane and poorly understood. The IoT is an additional layer on top of CIP issues, and the risks will be significant.

Interdependency risks have to do with the reliance of one system or infrastructure on another, and these risks come in two basic forms:

Inbound dependency[62] is about goods and services being delivered to and consumed by an IoT system or organization. Inbound goods and services may be either physical or logical/data. Inbound goods and services may be solicited (like requests for delivery schedules from suppliers that arrive through email or fax); or may be unsolicited or unscheduled (such as a customer call for support or to place an order). Call centers and web portals are established explicitly to support inbound information and data—especially unsolicited or unscheduled communications from customers and potential customers.

Inbound dependency is therefore about the assurance properties of assets required by an IoT system or organizations in order to continue the delivery of goods and/or services according to contracted or regulated specifications. For instance, how long can a water treatment plant continue to operate safety without information from testing laboratories (health sector)? How long will a bank elect to operate if confidentiality of the customer data arriving from retailers, transactions processors, or other banks is threatened? How serious is the impact to a telecommunications carrier if routing information from inter-connected carriers is corrupted?

Inbound dependency is about the interdependency vulnerabilities of an IoT system or organization in general.

Outbound dependency is about goods and services leaving an IoT system or organization, destined for another IoT system, which is consuming the output as its own form of *inbound* dependency. Outbound goods or services may be solicited (such as response to a request for a delivery schedules from customers that is sent out through email or fax); or outbound data may be unsolicited or unscheduled (such as a call to a supplier for support or to place an order). Websites are information assets established in part to address outbound data on a self-serve basis.

> Outbound dependency is therefore about the assurance properties that other, consuming IoT systems or services place upon a given service provider; *however, these assurance properties may or may not be known to the source/supplying IoT system.*

In other words, outbound dependency is substantially different from inbound dependency because the source of an IoT good or service may not necessarily be aware of how it is consumed at the destination, and therefore be aware of the assurance placed upon it by the consuming CI sector. For instance, how long can the health sector operate safely without information from the water treatment plant? Does the health sector place a reciprocal importance on information and communications from the water treatment plant as the water treatment plant does on information and communications from the health sector?

---

[62]This concept is extended from previous work by the author on Critical Infrastructure risks and interdependencies. See Tyson Macaulay, *Critical Infrastructure: Understanding Its Component Parts, Vulnerabilities, Operating Risks, and Interdependencies,* 2008.

Outbound dependency is about the interdependency threat that an IoT system can pose to other IoT systems. As a vulnerability, outbound dependency is about assumptions made by consuming IoT systems where they have not effectively understood, and, especially, communicated their dependencies to their suppliers!

In Fig. 13.24, inbound *data* dependency[63] results for the 10 critical infrastructure (CI) sectors are displayed from the highest score (most inbound data dependency) to the lowest score (least inbound data dependency).

The aggregation indicates that the food sector has the lowest overall inbound dependency vulnerabilities on information and data from other CI sectors. Food executives perceive their business as being least dependent upon outside information and communications. Food executives consider that the delivery of their sector's goods (both processed and unprocessed foods) to be substantially autonomous in their means of production relative to the other CI sectors. This is not to claim that food can continue operations if all information and data flows cease (including flows among the food sector organizations themselves) because the sector still rates itself substantially above 1. Food executives considered that coordination of activities and the exchange of information with other critical infrastructure sectors was not a critical part of *preserving the assurance* of their operations. See the following sector-by-sector analysis for a more detailed discussion of the food sector metrics. The indication is that food faces the lowest overall interdependency vulnerability when using data dependency as a proxy metric for critical infrastructure interdependency.

On the opposite end of the aggregation is the energy sector, which places the highest importance of the inbound flow of information and data from the other critical infrastructure sectors. In interviews, energy executives considered that coordination of activities and the exchange of information was a critical part of *preserving the assurance* of their operations; however, this is distinct from the ability to continue operations in the absence of outside information and data. See the following sector-by-sector analysis for a more detailed discussion of the energy sector metrics. The indication is that energy faces the highest overall interdependency vulnerability when using data dependency as a proxy metric for critical infrastructure interdependency.

Conversely, Fig. 13.25 shows outbound dependency results for the 10 CI sectors, displayed from the highest score (most outbound data dependency) to the lowest score (least outbound data dependency). These scores represent the highest-level of aggregation available without obscuring sector-to-sector differences.

Recall that outbound dependency for any given CI sector is a measure of how the other CI sectors rate the importance of data coming from the given sector. The outbound aggregation shows that the food sector indicates the lowest overall outbound dependency on information and data from other CI sectors. As a whole, executives from all the other CI sectors perceived their business as facing the lowest dependency threat due to information and data from the food sector. Executives consider that the delivery of their sector's goods and services to be most autonomous from the food sector. This is not to claim that all sectors can continue unaffected operations if all information and data flows from the food sector cease, because the outbound sector rating for food is still above *1* (but not by much). Executives considered that coordination of activities and the exchange of information with the food

---

[63]This example was based on previous work focused on "data" dependency, which is about the consumption of information as a service element, versus goods, too. From Tyson Macaulay, *Critical Infrastructure: Understanding Its Component Parts, Vulnerabilities, Operating Risks, andInterdependencies*, 2008.

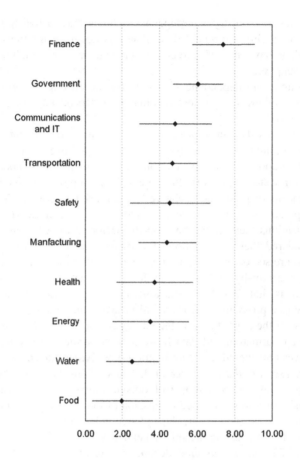

FIGURE 13.24

Inbound data dependency.

Legend:

♦ = MEDIAN (same number of responses above as below this point)

— = Standard deviation (average range in all scores from the median)

A score of *10* indicates all data and information from all sectors is critical to operations and the delivery of goods and services.

A score of *1* indicates that no data is consumed, or all data and information is derived from public domain sources and is almost immaterial to continuity of operations.

Zero is indicated in order fully to display standard deviations.

sector not a critical part of *preserving the assurance* of their sector's operations. The indication is that food poses the lowest overall interdependency threat to other CI sectors when using data dependency as a proxy indicator for critical infrastructure interdependency.

On the opposite end of the aggregation is the finance sector, which possesses the highest outbound dependency assessment score for the information and data it sends to the other nine CI

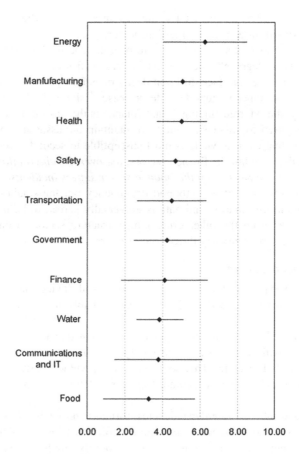

FIGURE 13.25

Outbound data dependency.

Legend:

♦ = MEDIAN (same number of responses above as below this point)

— = Standard deviation (average difference in all scores from the median)

A score of *10* indicates all data and information from all sectors is critical to operations and the delivery of goods and services.

A score of *1* indicates that no data is consumed, or all data and information is derived from public domain sources and is almost immaterial to continuity of operations.

Zero is indicated in order to display standard deviations.

sectors. In interviews, executives from the CI sectors considered that coordination of transactions and the exchange of information with finance was the most critical dependency relationship in terms of *preserving the assurance* of their business; however, this is distinct from the ability to continue operations in the absence of information and data. For executives, interdependency is as much about remaining profitable as operational. The indication is that finance possesses the highest overall interdependency threat to all other CI sectors as an aggregate when using data dependency as a proxy metric for critical infrastructure interdependency.

To what extent can or should a sector continue to operate, and for how long, once the assurance of their operations starts to degrade? The clearest indication from the outbound data dependency aggregations is that different sectors face different decay rates for operational assurance when information and data flows from other sectors degrade or cease. Using data dependency as a proxy for overall interdependency, the inferred finding is that finance is the most critical provider of information and data inputs required by other CI sectors to maintain the assurance of their business. The follow-on implication is that CI as a whole is most susceptible to second-order impacts and service interruption due to incidents within the finance sectors: *the overall vulnerability of all critical infrastructure sectors increases the most when the finance sector suffers incidents.*

Government has the second highest outbound dependency but the smallest standard deviation, indicating that government information and data is universally agreed to be important to the delivery of goods and services from the other critical infrastructure sectors. Conversely, government poses the second largest interdependency threat to CI sectors.

Unknown IoT interdependencies

There is every reason to expect that IoT service providers and device makers will have moderate understanding of their own inbound dependencies and probably less understanding of their outbound dependencies.

The first step for an IoT risk manager to get this situation under control will be to track and assess interdependencies with other systems, especially for IoT systems that might not be aware of their importance to other IoT systems. This could be a major vulnerability because it might trigger SLA breaches and penalties and/or lost income, trigger regulatory breaches and fines, and destroy customer goodwill.

In order to understand inbound interdependencies, formal methods like business continuity planning (BCP) will go a long way to documenting and consolidating inbound dependencies. BCP is a well-understood discipline; unfortunately it is often a poorly implemented practice despite the availability of know-how and well-tested methodologies and professional associations.

Once interoperability is understood, it might be managed in a variety of ways. Examples of inbound dependencies that become unacceptable must be treated or transferred are:

- By diversification of suppliers (for instance, cloud service providers, network providers)
- By clearly contracting for more appropriate service levels
- By implementing network based controls to compensate for IoT device weakness
- By implementing security and monitoring on data feeds and network links from key suppliers
- By stipulating security practices or audits in contracts and audit things like security postures, profiles, and policies from suppliers (inbound goods and services)

If inbound IoT risks cannot be effectively measured or managed, then they should be reporting the risk to customers, partners, regulators, board members, and other IoT stakeholders for guidance.

Outbound dependency risks are often left to legal departments, in the form of contracted limits on liability and service level obligations. Unfortunately, these things will not protect an IoT system from loss of goodwill (future business lost due to customer dissatisfaction—a major theme in the earlier chapters).

The best form of outbound dependency risk management is to know your customers! SLAs aside, how do they use your services? How do your services link into their own means of production or lifestyle? Are the SLAs what they need, or what you can afford? What sort of outbound dependencies might the IoT service users or customer have of their own.

It is important to understand the *cascading impacts* of an outage or impact. For instance, as an Internet service provider, if a DOS attack is allowed to pass through your network and knock out a home gateway, which in turn knocks out a medical device, and someone is harmed as a result, how much sympathy will you get by waving around an SLA that says that you don't protect customers from DOS attacks?

RISK MODELING[64]

Part of the benefit of understanding and mapping interdependencies inside and outside a complex system, IoT or otherwise, is that risk modeling then becomes possible.

Risk modeling is the process of proposing a threat and vulnerability pairing, and assessing the range of resulting impacts and risks, in order to be prepared to mitigate or manage them. Risk modeling can be a highly complex and difficult undertaking especially due to the poorly understood nature of interdependencies. Risk modeling is also something that needs to be efficient and repeatable so that numerous pairings of threat and vulnerability might be tested and re-tested to see how risk changes as managers make changes to designs and security controls within those designs. Historically, modeling was a very manual process, but there are not more and more tools and methodologies available to make risk modeling more practical at the enterprise level. However, many of these tools are not at the stage in development where they might be effectively applied against medium and small-sized systems and services. Cost versus benefit will still be a careful consideration for many IoT system designers and risk managers.

As we have asserted throughout this book: the IoT will be more complex in nature than previous generations of *conventional* IT. The IoT will have more service stratification and specialization. The IoT will have more control points as virtualization extends from DCs and clouds into networks and gateways. The IoT will have a wide range of suppliers, potentially from many different places in the work, with services provided from around the world in remote manners. The IoT will come to involve a lot of risk transference in the form of service agreements and product warranties: in other words, for the purposes of risk modeling, many assumptions will be made about the risk that has been transferred. Basically, suppliers will perform as they promise under normal and abnormal conditions. This also means that for modeling, a lot of qualitative versus quantitative data will need to be applied—making the overall output of a risk model potentially less accurate and repeatable.

---

[64]For the purposes of this book, we are not including *financial risk modeling* in this discussion. Risk modeling is a term widely used in banking, insurance, and regulation to assess specific financial risks and controls like capital set-asides, interest rates, and the true market value of certain equities. Our version of risk modeling is very much about operational risks outside the world of finance, which apply a very parochial definition to *risk modeling*.

AGING OUT: SECURITY THAT LASTS THE TEST OF TIME

Engineers, designers, and risk managers in the IoT cannot reasonably be expected to build in security and controls that can always last the planned life of the IoT device. Why? Because technology simply changes too quickly to project what will happen 10 and especially 20 years from now. Expect that security controls that are apparently appropriate and have longevity today could be useless well before the planned end-of-life for any IoT good or service.

There are too many unknowns and the emergence of new and currently unimagined techniques and technologies will bring unimagined vulnerabilities and risks. This is a very difficult problem to address and this is the bane of many legacy IT products, not just future IoT goods and services.

Given this situation, IoT risk managers, engineers, and system designers should consider *over-provisioning* resources within the IoT system (including the device) that can be applied for unspecified security purposes at a later date, such as unfilled memory or processing power. Granted, this is a very tall order given cost pressures in the IoT and will represent a major challenge to the foresight and long term strategic fidelity in the face of short-term tactical demands.

At the very least, a good risk assessment should involve examination and assessment of the costs associated with some extra provisioning and report of these risks to top management for a final decision, or inclusion of the necessary interface (logical or physical) that would allow for more resources to be appended or inserted into the system at a later date.

Ultimately, an IoT system that is intended for more than a couple years of services should assume that it will need security extensions at some point, and plan needs to be in place as to whether to treat, transfer, or accept this risk when the vulnerabilities (inevitably) emerge.

SOFTWARE-DEFINED NETWORKING AND NETWORK FUNCTION VIRTUALIZATION

Throughout this book and this chapter, we have discussed the coming virtualization of not only the DC, but importantly the networks and gateways, too. The DC started virtualizing 15 years ago, to the point that we now just speak of "clouds." Carrier networks are virtualizing now. Enterprise networks (based on long-haul capacity bought from carriers) are next, as well as 3G and 4G wireless networks and base stations, while 5G wireless networks will be "born virtual." To this can be added small office, home office (SOHO) and SMB routers as well as home gateways for consumer broadband.

While this technology will bring many advantages and in fact provide the types of security efficiencies and automation needed by the IoT, it comes with vulnerabilities. The first to consider is complexity. Software-defined networking is hard to understand and explain, and therefore manage. It is easy to make mistakes and easy to overlook mistakes in the short term.

Another aspect of vulnerability is the interconnectedness and interdependencies: cascading effects through automated systems can be very unpredictable. Small mistakes can balloon into unexpected crises. It is very difficult to assess how far and fast an impact might spread through multiple service providers using SDN and NFV for automated service delivery.

Another risk factor is the use of nonstandard solutions: SDN and NFV are evolving as fast as the IoT, and different vendors have different approaches that are not compatible. This is already a known problem in the DC world, where vendor lock-in is a hard problem.

Transportability of data is also a vulnerability in clouds now, and this must be avoided in the IoT, as discussed in Chapter 11, Interoperability, Flexibility, and Industrial Design Requirements in the IoT. There is a larger attack surface in SDN and NFV than in dedicated, hardware appliances. Common *white box* (Intel-based processing) plus open source operating system (Linux) plus open source hypervisor (KVM) plus whatever vendor solution has been virtualized to run as a *guest image*.

Open source software will dominate the network, KVM and Linux-based solutions. Flaws tend to be immediately and widely announced with little warning or opportunity to address the vulnerabilities, beyond the plans of many IoT vendors and service providers to plan, test, and patch vulnerable systems in a matter of days, let alone hours.

Common *white box* hardware means hardware-based vulnerabilities in firmware or management ports might also get released with little warning or time to patch.

Network SDN/NFV will involve physically remote and accessible devices playing intelligence versus dumb roles in the network. Because many will be in closets and ceilings and other places far more accessible than a DC rack, they will be physically tampered with from time to time. Physical ports for Ethernet and USB will be accessible.

Risk management for SDN and NFV solutions in the IoT and generally will be to:

- Be aware of standards and best-known methods available from organizations like ETSI and work underway in ISO
- Seek to extend security audit capabilities—again, using what has been done in the DC and extending it to the virtualized network and gateways
- Extend DC and cloud best practices to virtualized networking
- Lock down physical access as far as possible by establishing policies and procedures for locking out unused ports and auditing such precautions
- Due to the complexity of SDN and the power of NFV, operational procedures and control to enforcement will be more critical than ever before. This will require enhanced guidance from the developers of IT operational standards like ISO and information technology infrastructure library (ITIL). It will also require more advanced procedural monitoring and enforcement tools. Above all, NFV and SDN will require more skilled people with the right training and awareness of the issues, specifically engineers! (See the next and final piece of guidance in this book!)
- Finally, as this book was being concluded there appeared to be a trend developing toward a *middleware* solution that would act as brokers between NFV/SDN solutions (including open source solutions) and the VNF vendors. The idea with these middleware solutions is that the VNF vendors write control interfaces for the middleware *once*. Similarly, the middleware vendors write control interfaces to the various NFV and SDN vendors *once*. Thus, as an IoT system designer or service provider, you look for vendors that support common middleware and therefore reduce the complexity risks in your infrastructure. As before, this middleware drive seems to be supported by Intel.[65] But proprietary vendors have also emerged and have been acquired, such as Cisco's move into NFV/SDN middleware via a firm it bought called Tail-F in 2014.[66]

---

[65]See - https://www.youtube.com/watch?v=LJf4bmF6xiU.
[66]See http://finance.yahoo.com/news/cisco-completes-acquisition-tail-f-120000822.html.

SKILLS AND IoT RISK MANAGEMENT

Earlier in this chapter we discussed skill shortages and how to approach the matter of this risk from a management perspective. Because this is such a critical gap in security in general and IoT security specifically, let's take a few more minutes before the end of this book to discuss skills from a more granular, operational perspective—an engineer's perspective.

Engineering regulators (in countries where such a thing exists) need to define an engineering practice that is specifically intended to support the secure end-to-end network design, including implementation, and operations of DCs, clouds, networks, and gateways used in the IoT (recall that our definition of the IoT is *everything* on the network, the Internet of today and tomorrow).

An example of such an early attempt is the Professional Engineers of Ontario, Canada (PEO) who have developed a body of knowledge and a certification process for professional Communications Infrastructure Engineering (CIE).[67]

What is a professional engineer? The *practice of professional engineering* means any act of planning, designing, composing, evaluating, advising, reporting, directing, or supervising that requires the application of engineering principles and concerns the safeguarding of life, health, property, economic interests, the public welfare or the environment, or the managing of any such act (Professional Engineers Act, Ontario section 1).

What is a CIE, and how will it support risk management in the IoT? There is an emerging field of engineering for critical infrastructure in the public and private sectors, involving:

- Planning, design, and implementation of trusted communication networks
- Operational oversight of trusted communication networks
- Auditing, risk analysis, and contingency planning for network infrastructure
- Risk analysis and mitigation of other critical infrastructure that is dependent on network infrastructure

An example of who might satisfy these requirements for scarce skills in the IoT security world by becoming an CIE:

- A "full" license to practice professional engineering within the scope of one's self-declared competencies
- Academic requirement: four-year engineering degree
- Experience requirement: 48 months of relevant engineering work, including 12 months in Canada under the supervision of a P.Eng.
   or a *limited license* to reflect people who have been doing this work for years (Internet network security, for instance) but don't meet the new, academic qualifications:
- A license to practice professional engineering within a specified scope of practice proposed by the applicant
- Academic requirement: Three-year degree in engineering technology, science, or equivalent relevant to intended scope of practice
- Experience requirement: 13 years of supervised, relevant engineering work within that scope (includes up to three years of academic time credit)
- Issued an LL seal with category and limitations to be used to stamp engineering drawings, reports, and so on.

---

[67]See http://peo.on.ca and http://www.peo.on.ca/index.php/ci_id/22496/la_id/1.htm.

COMMUNICATIONS INFRASTRUCTURE ENGINEERING SCOPE OF PRACTICE

A CIE scope of practice or similar sort of engineering discipline established by universities and/or regulators should have the following in scope to security design the coming IoT—at least for the infrastructure joining all the endpoints together.

The following is extracted from a draft frequently asked questions (FAQ) from PEO. Readers are referred to the PEO website for up-to-date information:

Planning and design of assured communication networks

Any communications infrastructure whose failure, compromise, or unavailability can adversely affect society's well-being is critical, and must be secured against a broad spectrum of threats and failures.

The CIE is not intended to encompass the configuration of network devices and interfaces (which is the purview of the network technician or technologist), nor is it intended to encompass the design of secure applications (which is the purview of the software analyst and/or designer). However, the CIE practitioner is expected to understand these works and take overall system responsibility for the work done.

CIE practitioners apply their engineering discipline—which includes comprehensive risk assessment and mitigation strategies—to develop and document requirements for network assurance and security, along with specifications and designs that will meet those requirements.

Implementation of assured communication networks

As in most other engineering disciplines, there is a requirement for a licensed CIE practitioner to monitor, inspect/review, and provide oversight to the implementation of an assured network to ensure that it is implemented in accordance with its designs. In some cases, issues will arise during implementation that may require the design to be revisited and possibly revised. Any such reviews and revisions cannot be left to persons less skilled than the designer without risking compromise of the network security. Thus, CIEs are expected to be involved in implementation of their designs, just as other engineers are. A CIE should *sign off* on the *as-built* implementation of an assured network as verification that it may be trusted.

Operational oversight of assured communication networks

Just as a certified aircraft must be operated in accordance with its Pilot Operating Handbook to be flown safely, so a secure network that has been properly designed and risk assessed must be operated in accordance with documented operating procedures to avoid failure or compromise.

The role of the CIE practitioner in operation of critical communications infrastructure is to provide the oversight necessary to ensure that its operation is in accordance with design limitations and secure practices, and to ensure that those practices are updated as and when required to reflect any changes in the design or configuration of the network.

This role includes ensuring that monitoring facilities are in place to detect any compromises of the network, and that appropriate corrective action is taken to address any threats detected.

It is not intended to encompass routine day-to-day operation and control of networks (which is the purview of network operators), or repair and configuration of network devices (which is the purview of network technicians and technologists).

Again, however, the CIE practitioner must understand the fundamental technologies and be able to run tests to assure that all implementation and maintenance work does not compromise the reliability and security of the network as originally designed.

Auditing and risk analysis of network infrastructure

With networks, network technology, and cybersecurity threats evolving rapidly, it will be necessary to evaluate existing network infrastructure on a regular basis to ensure that risks are properly identified and mitigated. Many existing networks were designed when technology was simpler and threats were fewer, without the end-to-end design undergoing formal risk analysis.

This scope of CIE practice emphasizes the critical engineering aspect of risk analysis in secure network design and operation. It also encompasses oversight of remedial analysis and contingency planning for corrective actions that may become necessary following a network failure or security breach.

Risk analysis and mitigation of other critical infrastructure that is dependent on network infrastructure

Because so much of society's critical infrastructure depends on network infrastructure, risk analysis and mitigation for infrastructures such as energy, finance, health care, public safety, and transportation will require knowledge of network infrastructure and its vulnerabilities. Communications infrastructure engineers will therefore be called upon to bring their specialized knowledge and skill to bear on designing, operating, and protecting other critical infrastructures.

CIE body of knowledge

Beyond the scope of practice, a CIE will need to possess a body of knowledge that will enable him or her not only to design end-to-end networks for the IoT, but to do so securely! The following table lists the extracted body of knowledge (BOK) from the PEO. The reader may recognize some of the elements from the IoT security requirements chapters in the table that follows. This is not entirely deliberate, but is a reflection of a common perception around requirements; while the author was a member of the PEO task force that generated CIE BOK, he was by no means the only contributor, or even the major contributor.

We direct the reader to the later, main sections of the CIE BOK, the ones on risk management and governance. This is an indication of how a new field of engineering skills and training should position security and risk management, to support RIoT control.

Core Knowledge	Definition
Signals and systems	An understanding of the systems and their types, functions, and applications based on their input/output signals, input dependencies, the nature of their processing signals, and their certain characteristics such as leaner or non-linear systems.
Transfer theory	Because transfer theory is the main tool of classical control engineering, it is necessary for the CIE engineers to understand this function, which is the mathematical representation of the relationship between input and output of a system to be able to analyze the system's end-to-end behaviors

Continued	
Core Knowledge	**Definition**
Digital signal processing (DSP)	An understanding of the DSPs that are the key elements of the major industry CIE applications such as audio signal processing, audio compression, digital image processing, video compression, speech processing, speech recognition, digital communications, RADAR, SONAR, sensor array processing, spectral estimation, statistical signal processing. seismology, and biomedicine.
Real-time systems	As real time systems are considered the major parts of the mission critical applications that are normally priority driven (quality of service (QoS)), a detail understanding of the real time systems, their dependencies to time, and their types of hard-real time and soft-real time systems are mandatory for CIE engineers.
Reliability	An understanding of the system reliability and differentiating it from other system characteristics, such as high-performance or fast response time, and being able to address the major reliability issues as follows: The system cannot safely be shut down for repair, or it is too inaccessible to repair. The system must be kept running for safety reasons. The system will lose large amounts of money when shut down.
Fault tolerance	A general knowledge of fault tolerance that is the ability of a system to respond gracefully to an unexpected hardware or software failure. There are many levels of fault tolerance, the lowest being the ability to continue operation in the event of a power failure. Many fault-tolerant systems mirror all operations—that is, every operation is performed on two or more duplicate systems, so if one fails the other(s) can take over.
Communication	An understanding of the core elements of modern networking, including the knowledge of both legacy and evolving networking systems. Insight into the characteristics of networking that are not necessarily observable or obvious but are essential to CIE.
Communication/information theory—stochastic, emergent, and non-deterministic systems	As networks grow and are interconnected, they become extremely complex. This complexity has been compared to that of living biological organisms. This knowledge is required to appreciate the caution with which networks must be designed or changed, and to fully appreciate the risks inherent in CIE.
Digital communication	An understanding of legacy, layer 2 analogue systems versus digital communications. And understanding of the recent evolution of layer 2 digital communications from older, point-to-point, time division multiplexing (TDM) technology to services such as Ethernet/ multiprotocol label switching (MPLS) and IP-based networking.
Telecommunication protocols	Layer 3 and above protocols, with an emphasis of the IETF protocols including lower levels IP and higher level TCP, user datagram protocol (UDP) and internet control message protocol (ICMP) communications. Understanding of the distinction between unicast and multicast services. Understanding of basic elements of integrity and error correction, quality of service, flags, payloads and other variables and services which may be managed by protocols (as opposed to applications).

(Continued)

Continued	
Core Knowledge	**Definition**
Wireless communication	Layer 2 wireless protocols differ from layer 2 fixed line (fiber, copper) and affect speed and range in ways not seen with fixed line systems where these features are typically a function of the network element rather than the layer 2 protocol. Similarly, wireless networks possess specific requirement associated with signal to noise, elevation and azimuth of antennae, Fresnel zones, attenuation and signal reflection, and refraction.
Networks	An understanding of the relationships among networks, information assets, and end-point devices; how to they relate to and affect one another in a logical manner and what are the intellectual tools and methods used to understand and define networks for the purposes of CIE.
Convergence	Convergence is the phenomena of information assets that were formally isolated on standalone networks moving to a common networking medium, most typically Internet protocols. Convergence is also the phenomena of fixed-line and wireless networking becoming transparent if not irrelevant to the application and user, whatever medium is most appropriate and available will be automatically used.
Computer communications and network architecture	The logical design of networks to support the assurance properties of the assets they are intended to support. This includes but is not limited to techniques such as network zoning and requirements analysis such as capacity assessment and planning, redundancy planning and security architecture.
Distributed Computing	An understanding of who distributed and virtualized computing platform functions and how hardware and software services can be dispersed around the world in a manner completely transparent to application owners, administrators, and users. Distributed computing imports heightened assurance requirements on networks, which in effect become part of the operating system—not just a means to move data from independent system to independent system.
Internet Protocols Communication	Internet protocols form the dense center of networking technology, with (transparent) physical mediums and associated datalink protocols on one end, and application-specific protocols on the other. From layer 3 to layer 5 internet protocols dominate the moderate network totally and are fundamental elements of CIE.
Testing and Diagnostics	The centricity of networking to modern IT means that faults can appear to be network-related but in reality be application and device related; conversely, applications and device faults can have their roots in the network. In order to support high assurance and probably highly converged network, the tracing, tracking, determination, or mooting of network faults is a functional imperative for a CIE engineer.
Risk management	An understanding of the practice of identifying possible threats to networks and network elements and the endpoints they support, judging the likelihood and potential severity of these threats and determining appropriate safeguards.

Continued	
Core Knowledge	**Definition**
CIA of data in transit	Comprehending and assessing the requirements for confidentiality, integrity, and availability of data on the network and as it passes through the network elements, including the borders between networks.
Threat Assessment and Mitigation	The ability to identify possible threats to networks whether they are natural or man-made, deliberate or accidental. The ability to judge the likelihood that a given threat will occur using quantitative and qualitative assessment techniques. The ability to judge the severity of impact associated with a given threat using quantitative and qualitative assessment techniques. Understanding how given controls and safeguards may be applied individually or as layers to mitigate threats, and the performance and financial costs associated with the controls and safeguards and potential new risks they may introduce themselves.
Governance	An understanding that CI engineering must be conducted in accordance with the laws of the jurisdiction in which it is practiced, and that data is subject to the laws of the jurisdictions it not only resides within, but also subject to the laws of jurisdictions it travels through at the time of transit.
CIE Regulatory Environment	Telecommunications is highly regulated in all modern economies. Depending on the jurisdiction, prices and services may be determined more or less by the regulator. Some services will be entirely defined in regulations while others entirely forborne. CIE regulations have a significant impact on the feasibility of any large-scale CIE undertaking, where networks connect outside a single, physical premise. A foundation understanding of CIE regulation avoids erroneous and costly designs assumptions or oversights.
Privacy	Privacy is about the appropriate management of personally identifiable information. In the case of CI engineering, this means the management of personally identifiable information as it moves through the network. Privacy is a potent form of regulatory requirement in any western economy, usually associated with substantial sanctions for breech. Additionally, privacy requirements are often a business-language expression of security properties: confidentiality, integrity, and availability. An understanding of privacy aids the prioritization and specification of a variety of design features such as zoning, monitoring, routing, encryption, and network element management practices.
Sovereignty	Modern networks frequently route information in manners that can be transparent to users and even the original CIE designers. As data enters and traverses new networks, they can become subject to shifting legal regimes, which can affect not only the assurance of the data but of the network path itself. Sovereignty issues are also fundamental considerations in the design of computing clouds, which in turn are entirely dependent on networks.

SUMMARY

In this final chapter, we have taken a broad view of the many risks and vulnerabilities associated with the IoT and RIoT control. Rather than discussing each possible risk or vulnerability, we have focused on those areas where the risks or vulnerabilities are either especially unique to the IoT, critical to the IoT, or different for the IoT. When appropriate, we've also cited real-world examples of risk, as well as some proposed or existing techniques for addressing vulnerabilities or managing risk, sometimes taken from existing best-known practices of enterprise IT, the DC, or other industries, and sometimes from the nascent standards bodies of the IoT itself.

We discussed how managing business and organizational risk in the IoT is different from enterprise IT, the unique financial vulnerabilities and risks, and some unique competitive and market risks of the IoT, as well as some that are common to all emerging technology markets. We covered internal policy, operational and process risk, and unique aspects of those risks in the IoT.

We covered some inherently critical points that will be particular challenges (sometimes due to resource constraints, sometimes due to scale, sometimes due to lack of standards), involving confidentiality and integrity, integrity and supply chain risk management, availability and reliability, and identity and access controls.

We also covered some vulnerabilities technically specific to the IoT and related technologies, such as usage context and operating environment, and the operating complexity in 5G, which was followed by a more general discussion of the risks of trying to achieve interoperability and flexibility.

Finally, we touched on the urgent need for highly skilled engineers to accomplish these tasks, providing some suggested standardized qualifications as outlined by the example of the CIE program from the PEO.

It is our hope that having read this book, risk managers, designers, and executives will have a foundational understanding and set of resources to ensure the successful fulfilment of the truly transformational technology that is the Internet of Things.

Index

Note: Page numbers followed by "*f*" and "*t*" refer to figures and tables, respectively.